ALLEN COUNTY PUBLIC LIBRARY

FORT WAYNE, INDIANA 46802

You may return this book to any agency, branch,
or bookmobile of the Allen County Public Library.

THE MARKET ECONOMY

BY THE SAME AUTHOR

Beyond Capitalist Planning *(ed.)*
Capital versus the Regions
The Global Economy (volume 2 of
    Towards a New Political Economy)
Out of Crisis *(ed.)*
The Regional Problem
The Socialist Challenge
The State as Entrepreneur *(ed.)*
Uncommon Market

THE MARKET ECONOMY

From Micro to Mesoeconomics

Stuart Holland

St. Martin's Press
New York

To Katina and Dimitri

© Stuart Holland, 1987

All rights reserved. For information, write:
Scholarly & Reference Division,
St. Martin's Press, Inc., 175 Fifth Avenue, New York, NY 10010

First published in the United States of America in 1987

Printed in Great Britain

ISBN 0–312–01324–8

Library of Congress Cataloging-in-Publication Data

CIP data applied for

Contents

7155962

Acknowledgements

I am grateful to several people who have helped in the commissioning, writing, processing and publishing of the trilogy of which this is the first volume.

They include Robert Baldock, formerly an editor with Weidenfeld and Nicolson and now with Yale University Press, who first commissioned the work; Ben Buchan, still with Weidenfeld, who helped see it through several drafts with understandably varying degrees of patience and desperation; and Heather Sherrat, who drew the diagrams, often from fragmentary sketches.

I am deeply indebted to Bill Bourne, who word-processed the text with sustained and enthusiastic interest, and to Gareth Locksley, who not only read successive drafts but also made a major contribution to both the empirical evidence and the analysis. I am also grateful to Michael Barratt Brown and Roger Opie. They read the final draft with a critical eye which contributed much to the form and substance of the final published version.

Throughout this text I have been able to draw on the excellent work of former students such as Henry Ergas, Richard Luedde-Neurath, Dan Jones and Edmond Sciberras, all of whom have established reputations for their own analysis of multinational big business. Christopher Barclay and members of the statistical division of the House of Commons have also been helpful in providing information which has been both useful in debate and relevant to specific parts of the argument.

My thanks to Jenny Holland are very much due for encouraging me to complete the work on as wide a canvas as originally envisaged, and to keep on with the job. Not least, both we and our children are grateful to our extended family in Greece – Katina and Dimitri Voyazides. Without their remarkable hospitality this work might still be a mote in its author's eye.

Introduction

Trilogies are more familiar in fiction than economics, although there have been some notable exceptions in their time. The three volumes of this trilogy are part of a single work with the overall title *Towards a New Political Economy*. This volume, *The Market Economy*, is the first of the three. It covers issues normally described as price theory and the theory of the firm and industry, or plain microeconomics. The second volume, *The Global Economy*, considers what is normally described as macroeconomics and the theory of international trade. Volume three, *The Political Economy*, will deal with issues which in much conventional economics teaching are barely covered at all, yet are precisely those in which many students are most interested.

It might well be asked why a practising politician should bother with theoretical issues in such detail. There are two main reasons.

Subjectively, on starting the study of economics as a graduate student I was struck by the divorce of conventional theory and reality, and encouraged to highlight this by Paul Streeten, Teddy Jackson and John Hicks. As a government adviser, in my twenties, I was further impressed by the divorce between theory and practice, and encouraged by Thomas Balogh to counter it. Thereafter, in several publications and other initiatives, I have tried to contribute to redressing the balance.

Objectively, such a divorce of economic theory from reality has recently resulted in the temporary demise of Keynes and the apotheosis of Milton Friedman and his works. But Friedman's alleged economic rigour has proved to be *rigor mortis* for creative political economy. In the name of monetarism and market theory, millions of people in recent years have become unemployed. Hundreds of millions in Third World countries have seen low hope turn to no hope for a minimal survival, far less a better future.

There is no golden mean which can transform depression and deprivation overnight. But there are some principles on which the basis of a better future could be constructed. Not all of them are bedside reading. Pursuit of some of the arguments in this trilogy will be an exacting task. But there is a need for new theory to relate to a changed reality. Because theory both implies and affects economic policies, we need new ways in which both theory and policy can be taught.

Teachers and professional economists will probably have little trouble in recognising why this volume tackles issues on the theory of the firm which in some cases may be unfamiliar to today's students. For instance, in their recent *Economics*, Begg, Fischer and Dornbusch (1984) simply assert that long-run average costs for firms rise because of managerial and locational dis-economies. The latter has been disproved in practice through this century by the multiregional location of multinational companies in the global economy. The former case on managerial diseconomies is not a fact but a claim contested by the evidence that some two hundred companies now dominate a third of the world's gross domestic product, and that the main constraint on the export market penetration of leading Japanese firms has been the threat of protection by other countries rather than any internal limits to their growth.

One of the claims of this text is that it is historical in its treatment of fact and theory, rather than suggesting that there is a unique and scientific paradigm by which economics can claim to represent reality irrespective of time or space. This is one reason why so much attention is paid in Chapter 3 to the theoretical paradigms put forward by authors such as Samuelson and Lipsey, or in Chapter 4 to the theories of the firm elaborated since the war by Penrose, Downie or Marris. It is in part by rediscovering the scope and limits of such debates that we shall be able to help students move beyond the simplisms of texts like those of Begg, Fischer and Dornbusch which give such a misleading impression of the real market economy.

If *Towards a New Political Economy* helps counter unreal teaching of the real world, it will have been worth writing. If it reinforces the case for new national and international policies, that will be a bonus. Some of its arguments have already registered in economics teaching. Others have been adopted by trades unions, political parties and some governments. In the meantime, I trust that the reader will at least feel the effort of following the argument to be worthwhile.

Stuart Holland
House of Commons
April 1987

1 Meaning and Method

1.1 The Economic Agenda

All economics implies policy and all economics is political. Some economists will not admit as much. But not so long ago, many were proud to be known as political economists. The founding fathers of political economy – such as Smith, Hume, Ricardo and the Mills – tackled the big issues of politics, economics and society. They analysed the social basis of value, exchange and trade, and pressed for policies which would change the distribution of income, wealth and power. In the eighteenth and nineteenth centuries, Marx was not alone in wanting both to describe the world and change it.

The Polymaths

Such classical political economists combined a range of skill and experience. Many of them were polymaths – masters of many arts and sciences. Adam Smith, David Hume and John Locke regarded themselves more as moral philosophers than economists. The Utilitarians, including Bentham and James Mill, consciously related their philosophy and political theory to political economy. Marx came to economics through philosophy and politics. Pareto was both an economist and a founding father of modern sociology. John Stuart Mill was a philosopher, a political theorist, a political economist and – like Ricardo – a politician and member of parliament.

Nor were the founding fathers alone in combining politics and political economy. Notable Marxists such as Rosa Luxemburg and Rudolf Hilferding were also active parliamentarians. Rosa Luxemburg was a member of the Independent Social Democratic Party in the German Reichstag. Hilferding became Finance Minister of Germany. Joseph Schumpeter, best known in the anglo-saxon world for his economic theory after he emigrated to the United States, had formerly been the Finance Minister of Austria.

Whether or not they ran for elected office, the great political economists were passionately committed to political issues and campaigns. Adam Smith saw himself as breaking the bonds of feudal society and describing the principles on which a new social and political order could be based. Ricardo analysed the role of the state in determining the framework in which the economy could flourish, especially revenue raising and resource allocation through taxation. The Utilitarians not only campaigned vigorously for free trade but also developed a general philosophy of society.

Plain Economics

It was Alfred Marshall, in his *Principles* (Marshall, 1890), who began the trend which changed political economy into plain 'economics'. This was less because he thought economics had little to do with ethics, than because he was convinced that its ethical ends of increasing welfare would be best served by giving it scientific status (Skidelsky, 1983, pp. 40–44). It is only since the 1950s that the distinction between macro and micro economics has become established in common parlance and methodology. Mainstream mathematical economics and econometrics are just out of adolescence – not much more than a quarter of a century old. It may not simply be ironic that, as their claims have become more pronounced, economics has fallen into increasing disrepute.

For if classical political economy confronted the big issues, plain economics has a narrower agenda. Its initial scope, however, may be large. In response to the demand of beginners for a short definition of economics, Samuelson observed that there is no shortage of supply. As a few sample definitions, he includes (1976, p. 3):

(1) the study of exchange transactions among people;
(2) how people choose to use scarce or limited resources;
(3) the study of people in their ordinary business of life, earning and enjoying a living;
(4) how human beings go about the business of organising consumption and production activities;
(5) the study of wealth, and
(6) the study of how to improve society.

Samuelson himself judged the list as a good one. He added that a scholar could extend it many times over. Yet he claimed (ibid., p. 3) that economists today agree on a general definition something like the following:

> Economics is the study of how people and society end up *choosing*, with or without the use of money, to employ *scarce* productive resources that could have alternative uses, to produce various commodities and distribute them for consumption, now or in the future, among various persons and groups in society. It analyzes the costs and benefits of improving patterns of resource allocation.

Questions for Students

Thus Samuelson's agenda has shrunk. Such a reduced agenda may confine rather than refine the thinking of those who start economics in the hope that it will better equip them to answer the big questions about the economy and society as a whole. Most students expect at least a thread to knowledge, if not the tools to tackle major problems. Yet, like Alice, many rapidly find themselves in a Wonderland or Looking-Glass world. They are given 'as if' and 'but suppose' assumptions which mystify rather than clarify reality. Required to give limited answers to contrived questions, they may well find themselves failed in assessment – the equivalent for economics (as 'queen of the social sciences') of 'off with their heads'.

Some students drop out of economics courses because they prove so different from their expectations. Others, having briefly studied the theory of perfect and imperfect markets, can spend the rest of their lives amazed at the contrast between the harmony of conventional textbook principles and the chronic economic problems of the real world. Members of the public, or those in the professions or trades unions who lack the time or facilities for formal study, may simply find conventional economics as relevant to their needs as metaphysics or astrology.

Problems for Teachers

One of the problems is that many introductory texts in mainstream economics have risen to such a theoretical stratosphere that such issues as the balance between public and private economic power, or monopoly and multinational corporations, have been scarcely visible. Milton Friedman's efforts to dismiss the significance of the rise of big business and deride public intervention – as analysed in Chapter 2 – are examples of a market theory which in practice amounts to myth rather than reality.

In recent years there has been a growing discontent among many professional economists with such a divorce between theory and practice. Obliged by conventional texts to reason extensively in terms of perfect and imperfect competition, or harmony of interests and balance through market forces, many teachers who wish to address themselves to the economic problems of the real world find not only that there is too little in conventional texts to which they can refer, but that the models and methodology of mainstream theory obstruct their own teaching of reality to students.

The trilogy of which this is the first volume draws on elements of both conventional and radical economics. It seeks to synthesise aspects of theories which have otherwise been unhelpfully opposed or claimed to be mutually exclusive.

Towards Political Economy

So what is the essence of the following argument? How is it different from either classical political economy or modern 'plain economics'?

(1) It is polarised neither on the Marxist nor Keynesian revolutions.

(2) It is neither marginalist nor monetarist in its analysis of markets.

(3) It is historical in its treatment of fact and theory, rather than suggesting that economic theory is unchanging, uncontroversial or universal.

(4) It allows for imbalance and disproportion, rather than assuming harmony and balance through market forces.

(5) It reasons in a world of public spending, public enterprise and planning, rather than in a world only of prices, profits and private markets.

(6) It is neither 'positive' nor 'normative' *per se* but both describes market mechanisms and prescribes public policies.

(7) It seeks to clarify the social implications of policy, rather than abstracting policy from social realities.

(8) It allows for explicit models of government and state power, rather than for an implicit theory of institutions and pressure groups.

(9) It recognises social groups and classes – and sexual and racial discrimination – rather than analysing capital and labour only as market factors of production.

(10) It considers the structural, social and spatial distribution of resources, rather than treating distribution only in terms of the share of income allocated to capital and labour.

(11) It stresses the different roles of national and multinational capital in national and international trade.

(12) It analyses both micro and macro economics, and the new *meso-economics* between the micro and macro sectors of the economy (Greek: *micros* – small, *macros* – large, *mesos* – between).

1.2 Economic Philosophy

Market theory often claims to be norm or value free. For its admirers this is part of its attraction. Thus, its protagonists claim, market theory only describes rather than prescribes policies. In their jargon, it is *positive* rather than *normative*.

Yet in key cases, to express their preference for market over non-market forces, the same theorists argue that public intervention *should be* reduced or eliminated. This is itself a value judgement concerning normal or abnormal behaviour (in markets or by governments). Even the vocabulary of the argument on positive markets versus negative state 'interference' rapidly becomes value-loaded.

What are the real issues and what do they mean in practice? Clearly they are not simply economic. They imply the philosophy of meaning, the psychology of perception and the politics which are always implicit or explicit in policies concerning the market mechanism.

According to Richard Lipsey (1975, pp. 4–5):

Positive statements concern what *is, was* or *will be*. Positive statements, assertions or theories may be simple or they may be very complex but they are basically about what *is* the case. *Thus disagreements over positive statements are appropriately handled by an appeal to the facts*. Normative statements concern what ought to be. They depend upon our judgements about what is good and what is bad; they are thus inextricably bound up with our philosophical, cultural and religious positions. We may say that normative statements depend upon our *value judgements*. Disagreements may arise over normative statements because different individuals have different ideas of what is good and bad and thus of what constitutes the good life. *Disagreements over normative statements cannot be settled merely by an appeal to facts*.

Lipsey adds (ibid., p. 6) that 'the separation of the positive from the normative is one of the foundation stones of science' and that, 'very roughly speaking, the scientific approach consists in relating questions to evidence' (ibid., p. 7). His claims for positive economics are in line with the reasoning on scientific method of some of the so-called 'logical positivists' in philosophy such as A. J. Ayer (1936).

Facts and Truths

Certainly facts and figures have given some support to the pretension of economics to be 'the queen of the social sciences' (Samuelson, 1976, p. 6). In his introduction to basic economic concepts and methodology, Samuelson (ibid., p. 7) has stated that:

It is the first task of modern political economy to *describe*, to *analyze*, to *explain*, and to *correlate* the behavior of production, unemployment, prices and similar phenomena. To be significant, descriptions must be more than a series of disconnected narratives. They must be fitted into a systematic pattern – i.e., constitute true analysis.

Thus, beyond the framework of what Lipsey has stressed as positive economics, Samuelson has moved from analysis to claims for a *true* analysis. He has taken us from the realm of fact to the realm of truth. Clearly a testable hypothesis is one which by definition must be capable of being found either true or false. But the frontiers between positive and normative in economics are open rather than closed.

Lipsey (1975, p. 5) has admitted as much in writing in a footnote of his text that 'philosopher friends have persuaded me that, when pushed to its limits, the distinction between positive and normative becomes blurred, or else breaks down completely. The reason for this is that when examined carefully most apparently normative statements reveal some positive underpinning.' However, he adds that he remains convinced that 'at this stage of the development of economics, the distinction is a necessary working rule the present abandonment of which would contribute more to confusion than to clarity. The justification for this view is that although we are not sure what to make of an apparently normative statement (because it may have a positive underpinning) we usually know a purely positive statement when we see one.'

Price-Takers and Price-Makers

One of the problems for a purely 'positive economics' lies precisely in how to relate *objective* data and *subjective* evaluation. It is understandable that Richard Lipsey's philosopher friends should have sought to persuade him of this issue. It constitutes a central area of philosophical enquiry and is crucially related to the positive/normative distinction between what is and ought to be.

For instance, much reasoning in economic theory is *a priori* in character. In other words, it is true by definition. To take a classic example from elementary microeconomic theory, *if* price is determined by consumers and *if* it is also assumed that costs rise with increased production, it follows *a priori* that at a certain volume of production the marginal cost of producing a good will equal and then exceed the marginal revenue to the enterprise from sales. Such *a priori* reasoning can be tested later, or *a posteriori*, against empirical evidence. Thus it is assumed in positive economics that propositions which are true by definition can also be verified or falsified by an appeal to facts.

However, it was only some half century after the development of neoclassical marginal theory in Austria in the late nineteenth century that Hall and Hitch in the 1930s undertook one of the first empirical enquiries into the cost and pricing decisions of actual firms. In contrast with the *a priori* assumption in the theory, this *a posteriori* testing of the evidence showed that entrepreneurs tended to price their products on the basis of an estimate of average rather than marginal costs of production, i.e. 'cost plus', or an estimation of cost plus an average profit mark-up.

Virtually all subsequent enquiry confirmed Hall and Hitch's finding. But the *a priori* reasoning of neoclassical marginal analysis, for half a century to come, continued to argue as if firms actually set or determined their prices in relation to marginal costs and revenue. The reasons may have seemed complex, but in essence were simple. If firms set their prices on the basis of an estimate of cost of production plus a given 'mark-up', they could be acting as *price-makers* rather than *price-takers*.

This distinction is crucial to the theory of the market economy and its assumption of consumer sovereignty. If firms face both rising costs and a market price determined independently by consumers, there will be a limit to their economic growth and thus to their share of any given market. If, by contrast, there is no necessary limit to the growth of individual firms, then imperfections in the competitive process may be translated into oligopoly (the dominance of markets by a few sellers) or outright monopoly. Sovereign consumers get displaced by sovereign producers.

The reluctance to admit monopolistic pricing is not simply myopia among professional economists. The triumph of *a priori* neoclassical reasoning for nearly half a century after the *a posteriori* evidence from Hall and Hitch relates to the legitimation of the kind of economic and social system in which we live. Consumer sovereignty and a competitive market theory acquit capitalism with flying colours. Producer sovereignty and monopoly indict it.

In many introductory texts, oligopoly dominance by a few sellers or outright monopoly are admitted as secondary, marginal or peripheral qualifications of perfect or imperfect competition.* And the increasing share of world trade between the same multinational companies in different countries is either discounted in conventional theory or is not recognised at all.

Ought and Is

Conventional market theory embodies social, philosophical and political views of what ought to be rather than what is. It also implies value judgements on politics in the market economy.

This is illustrated by Milton Friedman in *Capitalism and Freedom* (1962b, p. 13), where he claims that 'fundamentally, there are only two ways of coordinating the economic activity of millions. One is central direction involving the use of coercion – the technique of the army in the modern totalitarian state. The other is the voluntary cooperation of individuals – the technique of the market place.'

Such claims contrast markedly with Friedman's *Price Theory*, published in the same year (Friedman, 1962a), where he wrote that: 'economics is sometimes divided into two parts: positive economics and normative economics. The former deals with how the economic problem *is* solved; the latter deals with how the economic problem *should be* solved.'

---

* Notable among recent exceptions are the texts of Scherer (1978), Shepherd (1979), Heilbronner and Lekachman in the United States, as well as the pioneering and pace-making work of Galbraith.

Yet it is clear from Friedman's *Capitalism and Freedom* that he is not talking simply about the distinction between what problems are and how they should be solved. He is making a subjective plea in favour of capitalism and the capitalist market rather than what he calls 'the alternative system'. The same subjective values about how a system ought to be rather than how it is, show in Friedman's reasoning on the role of the money supply in the market economy. Much of Friedman's academic work has the form of purely empirical or positive economic analysis. But Friedman also moves without inhibition to judgements lacking empirical foundation such as 'inflation starts in one place and one place only, national treasuries' (Friedman, 1980). He changes gear from 'positive' description to 'normative' judgement without advance notice.

Subjective factors also influence Friedman's definition of macroeconomics and microeconomics. Thus he writes that: 'professional jargon has come to designate monetary theory as *macroeconomics*, price theory as *micro-economics*.' This is hardly so. In practice, conventional usage already ranges much wider.

Samuelson is still on Friedman's side in identifying the capitalist market economy with freedom and the 'alternative system' as totalitarian. As we will see in Chapter 2, this conveniently ignores fascist regimes in interwar Europe or others in Latin America and South East Asia which have combined market economies with totalitarian and coercive military government.

But for Samuelson, unlike Friedman, macroeconomics does not mean monetary theory. Rather, it 'is defined as the study of the aggregate performance of the whole GNP and of the general price level' (Samuelson, 1976, p. 205) and as 'the modern theory of income determination . . . why and how incomes, job opportunities and levels of price fluctuate . . . how money and banking fit in with income analysis; and most significantly . . . how fiscal and monetary policy can keep the aggregate system working tolerably well' (ibid., 1976, p. 379).

In other words, by Samuelson's more careful standards, Friedman's definition of macroeconomics is less 'positive' than 'normative'. Friedman is not describing macroeconomics as it is, so much as how he judges that it ought to be. The difference with Samuelson reflects a basic division between the *monetarists* of whom Friedman has been the recent apostle, and the economics of John Maynard Keynes (1936) of whom Samuelson was one of the first disciples.

Equilibrium and Disequilibrium

The question whether the free working of the market tends to equilibrium or disequilibrium is crucial to public policy. If the market – even over the long run – balances supply and demand, prices and output, or available labour and full employment, then government intervention may be minimal or unnecessary. If by contrast, through market forces, the economy tends to depart from equilibrium, a whole range of public policies will be needed to offset such imbalance.

The argument cannot be settled by deduction alone. For instance, Figure 1.1 shows an economy fluctuating over time, at and below two employment levels. Full employment is represented by E^1 and the average level of employment by E^2. On first observation the Figure may seem self-explanatory. But what do the fluctuations mean? What turns the market economy down from its ceiling, at A^1 and A^2, or up from its floor, at B?

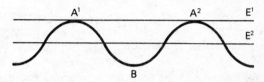

FIG. 1.1   Cycles and employment

Thus a simple diagram like Figure 1.1 may well be based on observable data. But it requires interpretation. For one thing it raises the question of the appropriate definition of 'full employment' in a market economy. For some people this will be seen in terms of the upper line E^1 in Figure 1.1. Yet many market economists argue that if we are to avoid inflation, the economy needs to be run permanently at a given level of *un*employment such as the lower line E^2 in the same Figure. (This issue is separate from how one defines full employment, in the sense of taking account of 'frictional unemployment' or those people who are unemployed in the period in which they are changing jobs.) The implicit question is whether the market economy can only avoid inflation through unemployment.

Pretension and Pretence

Therefore, despite its pretensions, positive economics frequently implies that what is also ought to be. The implication depends on how we see and on how we interpret the facts. For example, in Figure 1.2, facts alone do not tell us whether the market forces behind the fluctuation are 'implosive' and converging towards equilibrium (as represented by the arrows on the left of the diagram), or 'explosive' and working towards disequilibrium (as in the arrows on the right-hand side). 'Positive' economics will not provide the answer – or the appropriate policies – since we have no means of knowing whether the data is valid for all time, for some time, or for whom. Further, the argument does not occur in a social and political vacuum. The length of time from top to bottom of the cycle (or from peak to trough) may well be socially unacceptable, promoting at best a policy reaction by government and at worst a political or social crisis.

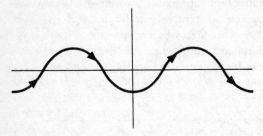

FIG. 1.2   Towards or away from equilibrium?

Possibly, if employment fell for only a few years, if social security was sustained and if temporary job losses were followed by an upswing in employment, a government policy of minimal intervention might prove acceptable. If, by contrast, mass unemployment were to last from five to fifteen years, the fabric of the political system could prove subject to grave social discontents. The argument is not merely theoretical. This is very much what happened in Italy in the 1920s and Germany in the 1930s, when mass unemployment spawned the seeds of fascism, rearmament and global war. In the 1980s in Britain, monetarist market policies have been matched by increases in arms expenditure, cuts in the urban programme and riots in inner city streets. In the United States, President Reagan has cut Medicare and the welfare state and boosted the biggest-ever arms programmes in American history. Meantime some people have lost out, some have moved out, and all of us may be threatened with armageddon.

How can economists address such problems? Should they do so? Are they competent for the task? It is often claimed that if you put two economists together, you will get three opinions. It is also evident that while policy-makers are delighted by one-handed economists, they dislike one-way no-return policies. What lies behind the conventional witticisms are fundamental differences in economic and social philosophy.

Positivism and 'Positive' Economics

One of the philosophers least concerned with economics but most relevant to analysis of the market economy is Ludwig Wittgenstein. He started doing philosophy under the influence of 'logical positivism' – a theory developed early in the twentieth century in Vienna, at the same time as Austrian marginal economists theorised about 'atomistic' markets divided between small producers, laying many of the premises for later 'positive' economics.

In his early work, the *Tractatus Logico-Philosophicus* (1922), drafted during the First World War, Wittgenstein sought to reduce propositions about the real world to their essential or 'atomistic' components. He then tried to express this in algebraic 'truth functions'. This is strikingly comparable with many of the algebraic formulae by which economists seek to reduce the real market economy to its allegedly 'true' constituent elements.

But, in contrast with many economists who quit the *terra firma* of facts for the stratosphere of algebraic theory, Wittgenstein later downplayed abstract models. His *Philosophical Investigations* (published in 1958) were completed by 1949. Thus just when the parallel Keynesian 'revolution' was gaining international acceptance by addressing key problems of the real world economy, Wittgenstein rejected the positivist approach to philosophy and tried to show a wider range of possible answers to real questions.

Wittgenstein and Sraffa

It is said that Wittgenstein's change was inspired by a conversation with the economist Piero Sraffa, who asked him to give a specific example of his symbolic truth-function. Wittgenstein allegedly repeated the *method* of his analysis. When then asked by Sraffa to give the 'real meaning' of a Neapolitan gesture, which in fact had a range of meanings from the impersonal to the impolite, Wittgenstein could not deliver.

In his later work, Wittgenstein emphasised the psychology of perception. Thus of Figure 1.3 he wrote that 'you could imagine the illustration appearing in several places in a book, a text-book for instance. In the relevant text something different is in question every time: here a glass cube, there an inverted open box, there a wire frame of that shape, there three boards forming a solid angle. Each time the text supplies the interpretation of the illustration.' But Wittgenstein stressed that we can also see the illustration now as one thing, now as another: 'So we interpret it, and *see* it as we *interpret* it.' Figure 1.4 further illustrates the point. As he puts it, 'this triangle can be seen as a triangular whole, as a solid, as a geometrical drawing; as standing on its base, as hanging from its apex; as a mountain, as a wedge, as an arrow or pointer, as an overturned object which is meant to stand on the shorter side of the right angle, as a half parallelogram, and as various other things' (Wittgenstein, 1958, p. 200).

FIG. 1.3 Wittgenstein's 'box'

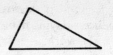

FIG. 1.4 Wittgenstein's 'triangle'

Ducks and Rabbits

In making such arguments Wittgenstein was drawing both on his own previous work and that of others. They included not only Sraffa but also an eighteenth-century German philosopher – Lichtenberg – as well as the twentieth-century psychologist Jastrow. It was from Jastrow that Wittgenstein derived his *gestalt* or 'form' figure of the duck-rabbit (Figure 1.5). As Wittgenstein says, the figure 'can be seen as a rabbit's head or as a duck's. The picture might have been shown to me, and I never have seen anything but a rabbit in it.'

FIG. 1.5 Jastrow's duck-rabbit

FIG. 1.6 Samuelson's bird-antelope

In later editions of his *Economics*, Samuelson is sensitive to such issues of form and perception. Thus he includes a figure (our Figure 1.6) of which he asks 'is this a picture of a leftward-looking bird? Or is it a rightward-looking antelope (or rabbit)?' The moral is that 'facts may tell a different story to scientific observers who wear different theoretical spectacles'.

Samuelson versus Galbraith

But Samuelson does not follow this issue through in his own analysis. In fact, his normative judgement on what an economist ought to be shows in his own approval of sympathetic analysts of the market economy and his disapproval of its critics. Take, for instance, the differing treatment which he assigns to John Kenneth Galbraith and two less well-known Nobel prizewinners – Professors Ragnar Frisch of Norway and Jan Tinbergen of the Netherlands.

To Frisch and Tinbergen, Samuelson pays the following tribute (1976, p. 6): 'Both men have been pioneers in the statistical, theoretical and mathematical advances of the modern generation. Yet each has also been passionately concerned with economic policy, within his own country and for the world at large. In honouring these men of genius, the Swedish Academy of Science could not have more fittingly summarised the nature of economic scholarship. May their successors live up to their example!'

Of Galbraith, by contrast, Samuelson (ibid., pp. 848–9) writes that he 'began as an agricultural economist. After achieving early fame as an impudent price controller at the wartime OPA [Office of Price Administration], he became editor, philosopher, political speech writer, politician, brains truster, novelist, art connoisseur, ambassador (to India for John F. Kennedy), memoirist, jet-setter and skier. . . . Galbraith in a sense has no disciples. There are few testable, researchable, propositions in his writing that could serve for the purposes of Ph.D. theses or articles in learned journals. How can a jury prove his attitudes and insights right or wrong?'

Normative Judgements

The contrast is suggestive. Frisch and Tinbergen merit accolades because they offer no threat to Samuelson's basic assumptions. Galbraith, by contrast, is on trial because he challenges Samuelson's perception of the real world.

Samuelson does not try to disprove that big business of the kind which Galbraith characterises as the 'planning system' can have significant influence on macroeconomic price levels. Yet an admission of such influence by big business on the macroeconomic performance of the economy would amount to a recognition that the micro foundations of Samuelson's macroeconomics had been undermined. In this respect Samuelson has hardly followed through his own use of the figure of the antelope/bird derived indirectly from the psychology of *gestalt* or form/perception. To do so would have revealed his own view of the role of the market economy as incomplete and one-sided.

The limits of Samuelson's objectivity are reflected in his criticism both of Galbraith and of radical Marxist political economy. He claims that Galbraith's criticism 'cannot itself kill. But it acts like a virus, softening the way for the more deadly critiques of the New Left and its professional radical economists' (Samuelson, 1976, p. 849).

Deadly viruses may be part of the framwork of positive analysis in medical biology. But in economics such a term is plainly normative. In reality, Samuelson is concerned to defend a particular version of the macro-micro synthesis which Galbraith sedulously undermines. Indeed, for the popular student market, it was Samuelson's own synthesis of elements of Keynes' macroeconomic theory and the conventional microeconomic theory of competitive markets which Galbraith was undermining. Therefore Samuelson had a vested interest in preventing their divorce by Galbraith's arguments on the role of big business.

1.3 Challenge to Conventions

Multinational big business has transformed both the demand and supply sides of the world economy, and with them the relevance of the conventional macro-micro synthesis (whether Keynesian or monetarist). Yet economists use different names for such global big business. Are the differences meaningful, or – as Wittgenstein stressed – does meaning depend on its use?

From National to Multinational

There are three main terms or labels for global big business: *international*, *transnational* and *multinational* companies. Throughout this work the term multinational has been used, for the following reasons.

International tends to confuse separate roles, since different companies in different countries clearly enter into international trade but without necessarily undertaking direct operations through investment, production or services in different economies typical of multinationals.

Transnational is favoured by some economists who stress that the companies concerned operate across national boundaries and owe no special allegiance to a particular nation state. But international trade is more strictly transnational than international investment and production.

Multinational designates activities undertaken by the same companies in different countries. For one thing, all multinational companies are incorporated in some form under the national law of different states and in that sense formally acquire different nationalities. Besides which, most multinationals are very clearly based in one home state or nation. For instance, as we will see in more detail in Chapter 7, of the world's top 200 corporations, with sales equivalent to a third of global GDP, more than half have their headquarters in just five countries (the US, the UK, Japan, West Germany and France). Rare exceptions such as Royal Dutch Shell, with headquarters in both Britain and the Netherlands, tend to prove the rule.

The New Dual Economy

A conventional view of the market – represented in Figure 1.7 – implies that the centre or core of the economy is typically composed of small competitive firms. Some allowance may be made for *oligopoly* (competition between a few producers), *duopoly* (market sharing by two producers), *monopoly* (domination by a single enterprise) or *multinationals* (firms operating in more than one country). But such qualifications are viewed as marginal rather than central to the market mechanism.

FIG. 1.7   The conventional view of the market

FIG. 1.8   The dual market economy

In reality, the twentieth-century economy has been transformed by the rise of big business. As in Figure 1.8, oligopoly, duopoly, monopoly and multinationals have moved from the periphery to the centre of the market. Their place is centre stage, irrespective of our judgements on the role they play. To deny as much would be either Hamlet without the prince or Macbeth without the king. The result is a dual market economy.* The small national firm of the microeconomic market model still exists, but it is secondary rather than primary and peripheral rather than central. Mesoeconomic oligopoly, duopoly, monopoly (in some cases) and multinationals (in most cases) now dominate the heartland of the modern capitalist economy.

The failure of conventional theory to analyse such dualism can be represented in a horizontal rather than circular form. Thus box (A) in Figure 1.9 illustrates the sequence of conventional market theory from left to right. This starts with perfect and imperfect competition and leads to analysis of oligopoly, duopoly and monopoly. Sometimes – though very rarely – it may admit the existence of multinational or transnational companies. Similarly, as illustrated in box (C) of Figure 1.9, macroeconomic theory can be

---

* Such a use of dualism to distinguish the role of big and small business has already been made by Averitt (1968). It complements the more traditional use of dualism to distinguish urban and rural sectors of the economy. See further this text and Holland (1976a), ch. 5.

represented on a horizontal plane as including the consideration of savings, investment, employment, prices and trade. Clearly other elements could be introduced to the representation of both micro and macroeconomic theory, including specific assumptions about cost structures, the role of the rate of interest, etc.

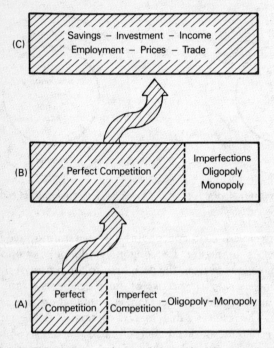

FIG. 1.9   From micro to macro: the apotheosis of perfect competition

However, as represented in box (B) of Figure 1.9, the striking feature of conventional texts on economics such as those of Samuelson or Lipsey is that up to three-quarters, four-fifths or more of the exposition of their microeconomic theory is within the framework of perfect competition. This perfect competition model then is translated by apotheosis to the sphere of macroeconomics without any intermediary imperfections. The results are misleading, for students and theoreticians alike. Elaborate macroeconomic theories are built on unreal foundations: beautiful to some beholders, and redoubts of the competitive system, they are theoretical castles in the air.

Samuelson and Lipsey not only are unwilling to follow through the logic of imperfect or monopolistic competition. Even in analysis of the domestic economy, as elaborated later, both authors return time and again to examples drawn from agriculture rather than modern industry or services. They also hesitate to analyse its implications abroad. As already indicated, neither include multinational or transnational companies in their main text at all.

Rules and Techniques

Wittgenstein knew the issue from his own inability to escape from the limits of 'positive' philosophy of the logical atomist variety. He described it as the problem of showing a fly the way out of a fly-bottle. With considerable relevance for the scope and limits of market theory, he said elsewhere (1958, p. 50) that: 'We lay down rules, a technique, for a game, and then when we follow the rules, things do not turn out as we had assumed . . . we are therefore as it were entangled in our own rules.'

One of the ways in which rules may first explain but later constrain analysis can be shown by the orthodox economist's illustration of costs. During an historical period in which it was assumed that profits were normalised or equalised by the competitive process, it was further assumed that cost curves could therefore include a normal profit. But this not only denies the basic meaning of cost versus profit (i.e. the fact that firms account for profit as the difference between cost and price). It also inhibits analysis of the degree to which unequal costs and unequal price-making power are the outcome of different efficiencies and different commercial success. Thus inclusion of normal profit in a standard cost curve became at best an analytic cul-de-sac and at worst a theoretical trap of the kind against which Wittgenstein, in philosophy, had warned. Economists thus laid down rules and techniques for analysis of the competitive process which hindered rather than helped explain a changing reality.

Much of the analysis of this volume and also of *The Global Economy* (Holland, 1987) seeks to demonstrate the consequences of 'changing the rules' in the analysis of the modern market economy. This includes not only (i) revision of the conventional assumption that costs should be represented as including profits, but also (ii) analysis of the implications of falling long-run costs for the process of unequal competition between the micro and mesoeconomic sectors, and (iii) extension of this analysis to the arena of the international and multinational economy.

Paradigms and Presumptions

Disentangling redundant rules may be entertaining for the professional analyst, but perplexing for both students and general readers. Alexander the Great taught us that one of the most effective ways of coping with a tangle is to cut it, as he did with the Gordian knot. But when the tangle is one of theory, and when there are several knots, cutting alone may only do part of the job. It can certainly expose the premises of a conventional economics or 'meta-economics' such as monetarism which, like metaphysics, offers at best a tenuous relation to the real world. But to displace the presumption and at times the plain prejudice often imposed by conventional theory on reality, it is also necessary to offer an alternative view of the real world economy.

Kuhn has put the case well by claiming that when we follow rules implied by our assumptions and techniques we generate a 'paradigm' (Kuhn, 1962). The paradigm dominates a particular intellectual discipline. It affects both our overall view or vision as well as the way problems are approached or perceived.

Developed in the framework of the natural sciences, there is a parallel between Kuhn's paradigm and Wittgenstein's emphasis on perception/deception and question-posing/problem-solving. In line with Wittgenstein, Kuhn also stresses that during periods of 'normal science' the paradigm may be sufficient for scientists both to achieve results and feel professionally secure. The paradigm amounts to a 'plateau' along which the discipline and its professional hierarchy can proceed. Kuhn argues that on these plateaux there is less questioning of the basic assumptions and presuppositions of the discipline and less call by scientists upon themselves to prove basic assumptions. Accepted theories are taught and standard questions answered.

However, when the puzzles or problems generated by the paradigm become more difficult to solve or insoluble within its own framework, it may increasingly be challenged or displaced by a new one. In the scientific field this amounts to a revolution such as the displacement of Newton's physics by those of Einstein. In economics, it may mean the arrival of a Marx, a Keynes or a Sraffa. Or it may simply mean cumulative challenge by a series of analysts and scholars which finally breaks up the prevailing paradigm and establishes the conditions for an alternative.

Baroque Methodology

Often the seeds of destruction of one paradigm and the creation of another are sown early in the period of its own dominance. Some of the main features of challenge to the Keynesian paradigm were planted by Milton Friedman in the 1950s, but needed twenty years to achieve widespread acceptance (Holland, 1987, ch. 2). Moreover, some of the main elements of post-Keynesian economics had reached adolescence, if not adulthood, before the monetarist counter-revolution for a while displaced Keynesian orthodoxies in the treasuries and finance ministries of most of the world's leading economies. Not least, the development of an alternative paradigm is likely to incorporate many elements of those which it supersedes, while rejecting others.

However, it is notable that during the period in which a particular paradigm gains dominance, much of the work undertaken by professionals becomes arcane, decorative or baroque in character. Put differently, while the apostates responsible for positing a new view may challenge the whole architecture of an established paradigm, its apostles tend to elaborate its details. In economics, this is illustrated by the testing and retesting by Keynesians for years of an assumed trade-off between inflation and unemployment (or by monetarists of correlations between inflation and money supply), rather than questioning whether successful economic performance (as in the fast growth of postwar European and Japanese economies) was related in any significant manner to such findings.

This is not to say that what Samuelson calls mainstream economics consciously misrepresents change in the structure and performance of the economy. But in many cases it resists questions posed by new information because they cannot be answered within its prevailing paradigm. Often this amounts to what Wittgenstein calls asking 'the wrong question' in the first place.

The Role of *Gestalt*

Throughout this work extensive use has been made of graphic representation. It will be clear that several figures and diagrams bear a relation to the previous argument on *gestalt* or form, and perception. In other words the argument seeks to encourage the reader to view the issue in a different way, whether this be on the relations between micro and macroeconomics, meso and macro-economic concepts, or multinational versus national capital.

But just as there are different ways of viewing facts, so there are also different ways of making sense of them. The issue is not simply whether the creature as perceived from the same data is either a duck or a rabbit, despite the fact that it helps to conclude that if it has four legs, two ears and a tail it cannot fly and may not easily swim. Rather, it is important to be able to develop *divergent* analysis, away from the conventional paradigm, when the evidence strongly contradicts it. Thus a psychologist who gives a patient a pattern of ink blots or shapes and asks what they mean is not expecting to gain an intrinsic meaning 'in itself' but rather to learn and understand what the patient sees in them or takes them to mean.

The analogy between a scatter of ink blots and a scatter diagram in economics is relevant. The issue is not just what we see in the diagram but what this implies for actual understanding. The significance of the role of factors X and Y (such as unemployment and inflation, or devaluation and competitiveness) may not be fully explained simply by their correlation. We may need to incorporate extraneous factors A and B (such as foreign investment or falling commodity prices) in order to be able to grasp what is happening to factors X and Y in the first place.

This does not mean to say that we cannot *seek* to be objective in economic analysis. Nor does it mean that new hypotheses or theories cannot be tested in the sense emphasised by so-called 'positive' economics. Theory can and should be subject to verification or falsification against available evidence.

Statistical Choice

However, such economic evidence – published by statisticians and governments today in terms of yesterday's paradigm – may not be readily available for comprehensive testing of a new theory. Such categories as gross national or domestic product, savings, consumption, prices, balance of payments, etc., are readily available in aggregate form through the publications of national statistical offices, the Organisation for Economic Cooperation and Development, the United Nations and other international agencies.

But whereas we have quarterly and even monthly figures available for such Keynesian *demand* macroeconomic aggregates, most of the developed countries still publish only a ten-yearly census of the *supply* structure of the market economy, with an interim five-yearly sample census. Such censuses for the most part gain low priority in government statistical departments or academic research institutes. It can frequently take three, four or even five years from the gathering of data on the structure of enterprise in a general census to its publication and analysis. The scope and share of multinational enterprise is still not regularly represented in national accounts, despite the fact that it dominates the modern market economy, typically representing up to two-thirds or four-fifths of production or export trade. Numeracy and economic statistics as used by governments are thus confounded by the difficulty of gaining up-to-date information in detail on the structure of the supply side of the market economy. This is one of the most familiar problems associated with inter-industry analysis, where there may be a three, four or five-year delay between the availability of data and its incorporation into an input-output table. Add to this a similar period of time over which the analysis may be forecast into the future, and one can easily find that there is a whole decade during which major changes in the coefficients of production through technical progress and innovation have transformed and outdated the original 'picture' of the structure of the economy.

Attraction or Distraction?

If number and numeracy are crucial for understanding the real world economy, what of the role of mathematical models? Do such models contribute to our understanding of the real world, or distract us from it? Are they useful techniques aiding analysis, or private language games which entangle professional economists in their own rules? Do they aid or abet policy-making in the real world?

Some of the mathematics used in conventional economic theory restricts perception rather than generates new insights. This is partly because of the difference between *convergent* and *divergent* thinking. In other words, most mathematics is convergent or linear in character. Its questions imply a single correct answer, such as the solution of simultaneous or difference equations. But, by the same token, mathematical techniques imply answers in a way which are valid in mathematics but may be irrelevant in economics. As Pennant-Rea, Cook and Begg (1985, p. 5) have observed: 'The winner of the 1983 Nobel Prize for economics, Professor Gerard Debreu, made his name by establishing the theoretical circumstances in which a set of competitive markets could achieve simultaneous equilibrium; but many sceptics wonder whether the Debreu approach makes economics any more relevant or fruitful a subject.'

Moreover, some of the most common mathematical techniques, when applied in economics, may produce a misleading or false image of the real world economy. For instance, in economic theory the technique of differential calculus is crucially related to marginal changes in market data. Since calculus cannot cope with 'leaps and bounds', discontinuity or asymmetry, the expression of supply and demand in marginal terms tends to imply not only that the mathematics works in a logical and symmetric way but also that markets do so.

Algebra and statistics, despite appearances, are no more value-free in their *application* than the economic assumptions to which they are applied. Edward Chamberlin, shortly after the war, was much concerned about the matter and wrote about 'the danger, so widespread today in economics, that the mathematics of the problem may literally replace the economics of it' (Chamberlin, 1952).

Maths and Graphs

Clearly mathematics has a *key* part to play in any economics of the real world. Without statistics and econometrics (the testing of economic data), little real knowledge would be possible of actual economies. The case is not that economics should be unmathematical or eschew algebra and geometry. Their combination – with empirical testing – give it claims to rigour. But the techniques should not constrain analysis in such a way as to imply that reality is an abstraction from theory.

Nobel Prize winner Wassily Leontief, recognised as one of the greatest twentieth-century economists for his application of mathematical techniques to the empirical testing of evidence, recently analysed the kind of economics published by *The American Economic Review*. As illustrated in Table 1.1, this analysis showed that over half the articles published were mathematical models without any empirical data and less than one per cent were based on data researched by the author. As Leontief commented: 'Page after page of professional economic journals are filled with mathematical formulae leading the reader from sets of more or less plausible, but entirely arbitrary, assumptions to precisely stated but irrelevant conclusions.' Or, as D. H. Robertson (1950) has lamented: 'geometry ascended the throne left vacant by philosophy and common sense' and 'ingenious youths and maidens, beguiled into the belief that here at last was a true picture of the real world, spend the best moments of their young lives in memorising generally wrong and fantastic pictures of tangencies and intersections'.

Besides Leontief or Robertson, it may be useful to bear in mind the warning by Keynes – himself an accomplished mathematician – about the use and

TABLE 1.1 Mathematics versus Empirical Economics: Content Analysis of Articles Published in the *American Economic Review* 1972–81

	1972–76 %	1977–81 %
Mathematical models without any data	50.1	54.0
Analysis without any mathematical formulation and data	21.2	11.6
Statistical methodology	0.6	0.5
Empirical analysis based on data researched by author	0.8	1.4
Empirical analysis using indirect statistical inference based on data published or researched elsewhere	21.4	22.7
Empirical analysis not using indirect statistical inference based on data researched by author	0.0	0.5
Empirical analysis not using indirect statistical inference, based on data	5.4	7.4
Empirical analysis based on artificial simulations and experiments	0.5	1.9

Source: Wassily Leontief, *Science*, cit. Pennant-Rea, Cook and Begg (1985).

abuse of mathematical techniques. Keynes stressed that social psychology was central to the working of the market economy. While abstractly expressing profit expectations as the 'marginal efficiency of capital' he also gave a central role to the 'animal spirits' of entrepreneurs and their lemming-like over-reaction to events.

Later neo-Keynesian analysis tended to underplay the uncertain and indeterminate nature of profit expectation and its impact on the real economy, with the implication that Keynes himself had overstated the problem. Monetarist analysis has recently stressed what it claims to be rational 'augmented expectations' as a key factor in economic behaviour. But as Keynes put it (1936, p. 161), with a warning worth note:

> Even apart from the instability due to speculation, there is the instability due to the characteristic of human nature that a large proportion of our positive activities depend on spontaneous optimism rather than mathematical expectation, whether moral or hedonistic or economic. We should not conclude from this that everything depends on waves of irrational psychology. On the contrary, the state of long-term expectation is often steady and, even when it is not, the other factors exert their compensating effects. We are merely reminding ourselves that human decisions affecting the future, whether personal or political or economic, cannot depend on strict mathematical expectation, since the basis for making such calculations does not exist. . . .

1.4 Micro-Meso-Macro

Any analysis claiming to give new dimensions to our understanding of the market economy is bound to be not only analytic but also synthetic. Similarly it is likely not only to draw on facts and figures, but also to imply certain prescriptions. In addition if the analysis is really likely to break new ground then it will probably lead to a qualitative change in our perceptions, rather than simply an addition to the quantitative sum of knowledge.

The Mesoeconomy

This study, with its accompanying volumes, makes extensive use of the concept of *mesoeconomics* or the *mesoeconomy*. *Mesos* in Greek means 'in between' or 'intermediate', and has been widely used in other disciplines for some time (e.g. mesolithic, mesozoic, etc). In terms of a new political economy, mesoeconomics means the structure of big business between the small firm of the microeconomic model (Greek *micros* – small) and the aggregate performance or policies for the macroeconomy (Greek *macros* – large).

Analysis of mesoeconomics or the mesoeconomy in this book is both deductive and inductive. In other words it shows the analytic consequences following from changed assumptions in micro and macroeconomic theory. But the change was first suggested by the contrast between theory and practice, in particular the evident failure of much Keynesian and monetarist theory to relate to the real-world market economy as it has evolved since the mid-twentieth century.

For instance, it has become increasingly obvious that the assumptions of perfect and imperfect competition in conventional microeconomic theory bear little relation to the reality of oligopolistic structures on the supply side of the economy. Similarly, the assumption in conventional macroeconomic treatments that international trade takes place between different companies and different countries, bears little relation to the dominance of such trade now represented by the same multinational companies in different countries.

A key to the concept of mesoeconomics thus lies in its recognition of the extent to which the rise of multinational big business has divorced the conventional micro-macro synthesis. The analysis of this process, and the conclusions to which it leads, suggest a new and different synthesis in its place. If the behaviour of big rather than small business merits a clear distinction between meso and microeconomics, then the different relation of the meso and micro sectors to the macro economy also demands a fresh analysis. In other words, the claims made for mesoeconomics go beyond analysis of the role of the large firm per se and imply a new synthetic framework for parts of economic theory which have increasingly become divorced or estranged.

Such a synthesis cannot be a simple matter of adding the mesoeconomic dimension of analysis to pre-existing micro and macro theory. It is essential to mesoeconomic analysis that the rise of big business on a global scale has negated the relevance of much conventional microeconomic theory and also much macroeconomic theory and policy of both the Keynesian and monetarist variety.

Arguments on Aggregates

One of the key problems with the macro-micro synthesis is aggregation. Some economists are very sanguine in the matter. Thus Richard Lipsey, in analysing what he calls the 'law' of large numbers, says (1975, p. 10) that 'we may now ask how it is that we can predict group behaviour while never being certain what a single individual will do.' He answers it by saying that 'successful predictions about the behaviour of large groups are made possible by the statistical "law" of large numbers', and continues by arguing that 'very roughly this "law" asserts that random movements of a large number of individual items tend to offset one another.'

Such a heroic treatment of aggregation is misleading. Its treatment of 'large groups' like 'a collective individual' in practice assumes away much of the problem of aggregation itself.

But this happens time and again in macroeconomic theory, which tends to assume that while there are differences between the behaviour and perform- ance of individual firms, these will 'average out' in aggregate in such a way that Marshall's assumption of 'the representative firm' still retains validity. Such an approach was still being stressed by one of the pioneers of the Keynesian economic growth theory, Sir Roy Harrod, when he argued in the mid-1960s that macroeconomic theory, on the demand side, could continue to assume that the supply side of the system was composed of representative or 'average' firms conforming with the main characteristics of the competitive microeconomic model.

The same was true for some time for Sir John Hicks. Nonetheless, by the later 1960s and early 1970s, Hicks was qualifying such an assumption. By then, Hicks 'believed that the aggregation [of the household sector] raised no difficult problem: our theory of individual household behaviour made the passage from the individual to the collectivity smooth and easy.' But he also admitted that 'when we passed to the income-expenditure accounts of firms we come to much more awkward territory. Here *we could not avoid* such issues as the measurement of profits and *issues related to oligopoly.*' (Hicks, in Harcourt (1977), p. 373, italics added).

A similar stress on the arbitrariness of the distinction between micro and macroeconomics has been made by Paolo Leon (1967). As he put it:

> In general, it is not possible to build models which show both a uniform profit rate and a monopolistic market structure. It seems important to stress this contradiction because it has been often ignored. Yet unless one builds a quite unrealistic model entirely composed of absolute monopolies all having equal 'power', it would be absurd to admit monopolistic structures which would then assure a structure of profit rates throughout the economy identical with that obtained by free competition.

He adds that 'Marx appears to have committed this error. He does not try to modify the assumption of uniform profit rates when he analyses monopolistic concentration in the third volume of *Das Kapital*.'

The Micro-Macro Synthesis

Paolo Leon argues not only that there are different profit rates, but also different categories or classes of firm. In his own analysis, he distinguishes between 'the free-competition entrepreneur' and the 'monopolist or oligopolist'. He stresses (1967, p. 31) that the latter, unlike the competitive entrepreneur, 'is far enough above the market to observe the economy as a whole. In addition to their ability to influence prices and costs, monopolists can calculate, more or less approximately, the effects that the adoption of more productive techniques will have on the economy, particularly because these effects will also be felt by their enterprises. Thus monopolists know that decisions regarding their enterprises influence the economy as a whole, and that changes in the economy as a whole in time affect their enterprises.'

Similarly, Alfred Eichner (1976) has described the purpose of his own main work as being 'to provide a theoretical understanding of how prices are determined in the oligopolistic sector of the American economy and how those prices, so determined, affect the growth and stability of the economy as a whole.' Eichner's work is important and considerable further reference is made to it later in this volume.

Nonetheless, other important contributors to the theory of oligopoly have not followed through their analysis of the behaviour of oligopolist companies with the development of a new concept appropriate to the power structure of dominant enterprise, and its impact on the aggregate macroeconomy. In other words, while their work qualifies micro theory, it still stays in a conceptual paradigm of microeconomics *per se*.

Keynes Perplexed

Keynes himself stressed the problem of aggregation, writing in *The General Theory* (p. 37) that the three perplexities which most impeded his writing of the book included the part played by expectations in economic analysis, the definition of income, but first and most important, 'the choice of the units of quantity appropriate to the problems of the economic system as a whole'.

It is also striking that many, if not most, of the radical analyses of the role of oligopoly and monopoly pay little or no attention to the phenomenon of multinational capital. In other words, like the analyses of Marx and Keynes before them, they have been limited by the terms of reference of the national economy. This may well be simple omission rather than errors of commission. Moreover, it is important to recognise that, at least until the 1970s, relatively comprehensive data and information on the scope and scale of multinational capital was limited. For instance, it was not until 1973 that the United Nations report on *Multinational Corporations in World Development* revealed that the volume of production by multinational companies worldwide was already greater than the total volume of world trade, and that the foreign production of British and US companies abroad amounted to more than twice and more than four times, respectively, those countries' total export trade.

Nonetheless, especially when taken in conjunction with the concentration of export trade in the hands of a very few companies (in the British case, some 75 firms account for half the visible exports and some 30 firms for two-fifths of visible export trade), it is clear that there is a significant relationship between the concentration of domestic production in the hands of a very few firms and the global expansion of those enterprises. Added to the distinction stressed by Baran and Sweezy (1966) between 'price-makers' and 'price-takers', these factors profoundly qualify the assumption of a micro-macro synthesis.

Leijonhufvud

Aggregation problems have been well illustrated by the essentially sympathetic treatment of Keynes' economics by Leijonhufvud (1968). Having stressed (p. 31) that 'Keynes envisaged a grand synthesis of the theory of value and the theory of money', Leijonhufvud emphasised that 'a major part of the value-theoretical content of a macro model will often be hidden in the aggregates from which the explicit analysis starts. . . . The immediately antecedent stage in model-construction, the selection of aggregates, is often the stage where implicit theorising enters in' (ibid., pp. 38, 39).

Leijonhufvud continues his argument with further reference to Schumpeter's discussion of the 'vision' which the theorist seeks to embody in a model. As he puts it (ibid., p. 39),

> in terms of this vision of how the world works, certain classes of events are regarded as of little or no significance to the overall picture. An example of such a class of events may be changes in the relative prices of a given group of goods. If changes in these relative prices are regarded as having no significant consequences, or no significant *predictable* consequences, e.g. for aggregate employment, there is no reason for them to clutter up a model whose principal purpose is to provide an explanation of the forces determining employment. The 'unimportant' price variables can then be removed by aggregating the corresponding group of goods.

Leijonhufvud was concerned to salvage Keynes' economics from the so-called Keynesian theory which had wedded him with neoclassical supply theory. He sought to do so mainly by arguing that Keynes had never accepted the 'harmony of forces' argument implicit in the Keynesian-neoclassical synthesis, and that Keynes' own economics stressed disequilibrium rather than equilibrium. However, if we are to relate Keynes' own economics to late-twentieth-century realities, we need to focus on not only the demand but also the supply side of the economy. In particular, in contrast with Keynes' own assumption that no group of firms could have a significant impact on macroeconomic phenomena, a meaningful distinction can be made between the pricing and employment behaviour of small-scale national capital, conforming with the microeconomic model, and large-scale multinational capital in the mesoeconomy, which does not necessarily do so.

Competition in Question

Thus a key theme of mesoeconomics is that the rise of oligopolistic enterprise on a global scale has divorced the conventional synthesis between macro-economics and the microeconomy. But mesoeconomics is not simply a matter of big business or *mega*-corporations. Nor does it claim an end to the competitive process through oligopoly or the trend to monopoly in individual sectors of activity.

The monopoly problem has been a skeleton in the cupboard of the liberal market model since the later nineteenth century. Leading anti-trust and anti-monopoly authorities in Europe and the United States realised long ago that a few large firms can easily get together and collude on price increases, thereby acting in practice like a monopolist. Not only were cartels and collusive pricing major preoccupations of governments in such countries before the turn of the century. Even Adam Smith – in a quote readily neglected by Milton Friedman and 'supply-siders' in the United States – wrote that 'people of the same trade seldom meet together even for merriment and diversion, but the conversation ends in a conspiracy against the public or in some contrivance to raise prices.'

While recognising the dynamism of the new industrial capitalism of his time, Smith was also concerned about the fragility of the competitive process. The 'invisible hand' – which appears only once in the *Wealth of Nations* – was less an economic than a metaphysical concept. In Smith's view it was not so much market forces which restrained the self-interest of the entrepreneur in the collusive process, as the force of 'sympathy' which cemented the social and economic fabric of society and stemmed from 'the sympathetic feelings of the impartial and well-informed spectator'. This was an ethical and moral force explained not in *The Wealth of Nations* (1776) but in the book which Smith himself considered more important and his greater claim to posterity – his *Theory of Moral Sentiments* (1759).

One of the problems for anti-trust or anti-monopoly legislators is the extent to which their policies contradict the internal dynamics of the competitive process in a modern capitalist system. In other words, as stressed throughout this volume, the competitive process now is neither perfect nor uniformly imperfect but a process of unequal competition between big and small, national and multinational business, a process which itself results from the rewards to efficiency and returns from scale which have been gained from the winners in the competitive process.

The Real Supply Side

While monopoly may be an explicit abuse of competition through trusts or cartels, a monopolistic structure is the logical outcome of rewards for winners and penalties for losers through competition. Thus equal competition where individual markets were initially composed of many small firms in due course gives way to unequal competition between the micro and mesoeconomic sectors in what in practice constitutes a 'dual economy'.

Such a dual economy is not in itself a recent phenomenon, despite the continuing trend to concentration and centralisation of capital in both Europe and the United States. It has been estimated that at the turn of the century less than one per cent of enterprise in Germany and the United States was responsible for between half and two-thirds of output in the industrial sector of the economy. But the so-called managerial revolution of the twentieth century, and the trend to multiproduct and multisector companies, reinforced this dominance of mesoeconomic big business over small firms in the micro sector. This was associated in many cases with the trend to multiregional and multinational enterprise (as analysed in Chapter 6).

Such a trend to dual economic structures on the supply side of the economy – ignored by the so-called supply-siders in the United States – has transformed both the structures and strategies of the modern business corporation. As we will see in Chapter 3, the postwar debate on the aims of the firm, still modelled on the 'representative firm and industry', has given way in the boardrooms of big business to corporate strategies reflecting the multisectoral and multinational priorities of enterprise now operating on a global scale rather than simply the local or national economy. Mesoeconomic power has transformed the real supply side of the economy and with it the relevance of conventional microeconomic theory.

Antecedents

This author first used the concept of mesoeconomics in the early 1970s (Holland, 1974).* Its use has gained ground elsewhere in recent years. In Germany, both Tuchtfeldt and Peters (1981) have related mesoeconomics and the intermediate economic structure of big business to 'the theory of associations and groups, and the economic theory of democracy . . .'.

In the Netherlands, Van Duijn and Lambooy (1983) have developed this author's earlier application of mesoeconomic theory to regional analysis (Holland, 1976a). Similarly, Professor Wijers (1982) has undertaken a critical

---

* For further use of the concept, see also this author's *The Socialist Challenge* (1975), *Capital Versus the Regions* (1976a), *The Regional Problem* (1976b), (ed.) *Beyond Capitalist Planning* (1978), *Uncommon Market* (1980) and (ed.) *Out of Crisis* (1983).

analysis of the application of the mesoeconomic concept in the wider context of social and political economy. This includes the use of tripartite negotiation between big business, trades unions and governments, developed by the present author in the early and mid 1970s (Holland, 1975) and reflected in the Planning Agreement or Development Agreement approach endorsed by several parties of the European Left and the Socialist International (Holland, 1983 and Brandt-Manley, 1985).

In the United States one of the most forceful advocates of the meso-economic concept has been Lee Preston of the University of Maryland. As Preston (1983) has argued: 'the lack of connection between conventional micro and macro modes of analysis is a familiar criticism of contemporary economics, and a survey of current textbooks reveals little evidence that the economy is conceived or presented to students as a dynamic system with interrelated and recognisable parts. Our major economic policy document – the *Annual Report* of the Council of Economic Advisers – rarely sugggests a systematic view, but focuses primarily on the macro aggregates and on selected problems or topical sectors.' As Preston also claims: 'a meso-economic approach would supplement, but of course not supplant, the major well-established modes of analysis: micro, macro, and institutional.'

Galbraith and After

In citing antecedents of the mesoeconomic concept, including the present author's work, Preston allows that in one sense it could be argued that the idea of mesoeconomics offers nothing new. Monopoly domination of markets, or their domination by a few firms (oligopolistic competition), has been on the agenda of economic analysis for many years. In the United States, Fellner, Bain and especially John Kenneth Galbraith put the issue of big business and its dominant role within the economy on the agenda of mainstream economics, while more recently Averitt (1968) and Eichner (1976) have also stressed the key role of big business in the foundations of the macro economy.

Galbraith's analysis is crucial to the challenge to neo-liberal orthodoxies.* In contrasting the 'planning system' of big business with the 'market system' of smaller enterprise, he showed not only the domination of big business in the real world economy, but also the way in which it had profoundly qualified the conventional macro-micro synthesis. His authoritative contribution –and explicit support for the Labour Party's Planning Agreements with big

---

* John Kenneth Galbraith, *Economics and the Public Purpose* (1974), which completes Galbraith's major trilogy of *The Affluent Society* (1958) and *The New Industrial State* (1967).

business in 1973 – played a key role in gaining widespread support for the Planning-by-Agreement approach in Europe and in the United States, where a new generation of younger economists has recommended its adoption in the American big-business sector (Shearer and Carnoy, 1980, and Bowles, Gordon and Weisskopf, 1983).

The approach is not without its critics. But as Professor Zinn of the University of Aachen has observed (1978), such critics 'might well recollect Immanuel Kant's observation that while concepts without empirical perception are empty, empirical perception without a concept is blind. The new power structures of big business need a new conceptual framework of the kind which mesoeconomics provides'.

1.5 Summary

(1) The founders of political economy were polymaths concerned to understand and formulate principles concerning the economy and society as a whole. Several of them were also author-actors in the drama of political and economic history. In the eighteenth and nineteenth centuries Marx was not alone in wanting both to describe the world and to change it.

(2) It was only from the late nineteenth century that political economy shrunk its agenda to narrow 'economics'. This shrinkage was related to the claim that 'positive' propositions could be supported with facts while 'normative' political economy could not.

(3) The positive-normative distinction is relative rather than absolute. Many of the questions posed by conventional theory are answered by reference back to the premises of the theory (e.g. the equilibrium of the firm) rather than derived from facts (e.g. competitive disequilibrium and the rise of big business).

(4) Such issues concern the psychology of perception or form (Gestalt) and the way in which the market process is perceived. They also involve methods and techniques of analysis (e.g. differential calculus and marginal analysis) which imply an answer which may prove unreal when tested against the real world economy. Thus conventional market economy gets caught up in its own rules, even to the point of giving 'wrong' answers to the 'right' questions.

(5) The is-ought dichotomy stressed by the distinction between so-called positive and normative economics therefore gives results which are at best bizarre or at worst mystify reality. Some theories of the firm deny that enterprise can grow beyond a certain size or given rate. Most fail entirely to admit the dynamics of multinational investment and growth.

Their 'paradigm' of the market therefore cannot explain the rise of global big business since the war.

(6) Such limited micro foundations compromise effective macroeconomic policies. In admitting imperfect competition and oligopoly only as exceptions to the rule of perfect competition, conventional market theory fails to recognise the extent to which the rise of multinational big business has established a mesoeconomic sector between conventional micro and macroeconomics, thereby invalidating key elements of the Keynesian or monetarist syntheses of micro and macro theory.

(7) Numeracy and statistical analysis are crucial to understanding the real world economy. But mathematical models based on irrelevant or outdated premises constrain rather than help us to explain the working of the market economy.

2 Market Facts and Fictions

For its supporters – and even some detractors – the capitalist market constitutes the most powerful engine of change in human history.

Its most influential recent apostle is Milton Friedman. For many, Friedman also is the founding father of monetarism, or the theory that stable money supply plus a market economy will realise the best of all possible economic worlds. For others, Friedman is the leading *neo*-monetarist economist, in the sense that primacy for stable money and freedom for market forces has been the hallmark of conservative economics for over two centuries. Friedman's popular works are quite explicitly political. Thus in *Capitalism and Freedom* (1962b) he wrote of '. . . the role of competitive capitalism – the organisation of the bulk of economic activity through private enterprise operating in a free market – as a system of economic freedom and a *necessary condition* for political freedom' (italics added).

2.1 Free to Choose

Capitalism and Freedom examines specific issues such as the role of government, monetary and fiscal policy, discrimination and poverty. Friedman's *Free to Choose* (1980) is, in his own words, 'a less abstract and more concrete book which treats the political system symmetrically with the economic system. Both are regarded as *markets* in which the outcome is determined by the interaction among persons pursuing their own self-interests (broadly interpreted) rather than by the social goals the participants find it advantageous to enunciate.'

Friedman and Freedoms

Stressing the links between economics and politics, Friedman also argues (ibid., p. 21) that :

> Economic freedom is an essential requisite for political freedom. By enabling people to co-operate with one another without coercion or central direction, it reduces the area over which political power is exercised. In addition, by dispersing power, the free market provides an offset to whatever concentration of political power may

arise. The combination of economic and political power in the same hands is a sure recipe for tyranny. The combination of economic and political freedom produced a golden age in both Great Britain and the United States in the 19th century.

But what is meant by freedom? Friedman claims (ibid., p. 53) that 'freedom is a tenable objective only for responsible individuals. We do not believe in freedom for madmen or children.' He admits that 'we must somehow draw a line between responsible individuals and others, yet doing so introduces a fundamental ambiguity into our ultimate objective of freedom. *We cannot categorically reject paternalism for those whom we consider as not responsible.*'

British and American Realities

But the claim that freedom is only tenable for responsible individuals – and that paternalism may be justified – has been widely used to justify the restraint of political freedoms.

In nineteenth-century Europe, the ruling landed aristocracy opposed the extension of the franchise or right to vote to those without property. Similarly, throughout the nineteenth century the franchise excluded women – in Britain they were not given the right to vote until 1924. In the United States, slaves were excluded from the political process before the Civil War and were still excluded after Emancipation by the ruling elite in many of the Southern states for another century to come. It was in this context that the Civil Rights Movement in the United States in the 1960s made its basic demands for the right to register to vote without recrimination, the right to equal access to better schools (the bussing issue) and not least – in economic terms – the right to a job.

For males, whites and entrepreneurs, Great Britain and the United States in the nineteenth century may well have approached the image of Friedman's 'golden age'. For women and blacks it did not.

The European Democracies

The logic of Friedman's argument is also open to discussion. If economic freedom is a necessary condition for political freedom, does this mean that economic freedom entails political freedom? In reality it does not, for anyone with a casual acquaintance with the rise of modern democracies. The new middle classes who established sufficient economic freedom in Europe in the seventeenth and eighteenth century to accumulate capital and hire and fire independent labour, were almost entirely excluded from the political process. In seventeenth- and eighteenth-century France, economic freedoms enabled fortunes to be made in commerce and trade and threw a feudal crown into increasing dependence on a summoned 'estates general' for raising tax and financing expenditures. But it was not until 1789, some two centuries after the rise of the French bourgeoisie, that this social and economic class gained political power.

Central and Latin America

More recent contradictions of the claim that economic freedom entails political freedom are found in those countries of the world selected by Friedman as model examples of market freedoms – in particular South East Asia and Latin America. Both areas include capitalist societies in which slavery has been abolished and in which everyone has the right to engage labour or be engaged as labour in a free market.

However, the recent political reality of market economies in South East Asia or Central and Latin America has seen the temporary or permanent suspension of political freedoms by military regimes or juntas. The United States has supported rule by a privileged elite – rather than pluralism – in Central and Latin American countries. (In El Salvador this is illustrated by the claim to rule of only fourteen families.) Such political oligarchy has been matched by economic oligopoly, i.e. control of the economy by a few firms. In agriculture, a fraction of the population in Latin America typically controls a majority of arable land. A handful of United States multinational companies have commanded the processing, manufacturing and agribusiness exports of Central America under what, until recently, has amounted to a US protectorate.

Foreign business, foreign intervention and domestic dictatorships have dominated Central and Latin America. They are the reality reflected by US General Smedley Butler, who in 1935 described his achievements as those of a high-class muscleman for big business, Wall Street, and the bankers – making Mexico safe for American oil, Haiti and Cuba a decent place for the National City Banks, purifying Nicaragua for Brown Brothers, bringing light to the Dominican Republic for American sugar interests, and helping make Honduras ripe for the United Fruit Company (Pearce, 1982, p. 20).

In Chile, a military junta overthrew a democratically elected government and allowed monetarism and market forces their head for more than ten years – without economic success, but thereby devastating the one parliamentary democracy in Latin America which had survived uninterrupted since the nineteenth century.

The Asian Quartet

Put simply, economic freedom does *not* necessarily entail political freedom.

It may well entail political fascism – and indeed has done so through many of the newly industrialised countries which alone among the countries of the Third World have managed to gain a significant – if still minor – penetration of the industrial markets of the developed countries.

The 'Asian quartet' of Singapore, South Korea, Taiwan and the Philippines under Marcos have not been models of political freedom. Nor does South Korea represent market freedom of choice in the sense that Friedman argues. As Richard Luedde-Neurath (1984) has shown, South Korea is one of the most ardently interventionist states in the world, employing a range of controls over prices, credits, subsidies, import licensing and also state enterprise. While some of these countries may enshrine the principle of the right to vote, few of them allow the freedom for labour to organise in independent trades unions, the freedom to form any political party or the freedom to impartial appeal courts in the judiciary system.

South Africa is another outstanding example of a country where market forces are combined with a ruthless repression of the (black) majority of the populace, and democracy limited to minority elites.

Freedom From or Freedom To?

Friedman also neglects one of the critical issues considered in virtually any preliminary course on philosophy, political theory or politics – the difference between freedom *from* and freedom *to*.

For instance, while an unemployed worker in Mrs Thatcher's Britain may perhaps feel free *from* government 'interference', he or she is less free *to* take a job or work overtime than in an economy whose government is committed to state intervention to achieve fuller employment. In other words, there is a crucial difference between *formal* freedom and *effective* freedom (much as there is between the formal principle of demand in elementary economic theory, and effective demand which can mobilise the supply of actual goods and services).

Economic freedom implies the right to sell goods and services. But it does not imply the freedom to sell or buy *any* good and service. For instance, few civilised societies have so far condoned trade in narcotics – so seriously damaging to health – even though most condone a trade in arms which can be seriously damaging to life.

Thus economic freedom is not unqualified even in the most democratic societies. Some individuals may feel 'free' to drive on the wrong side of the road to assert their individuality. But most individuals will support public authorities who restrain their right to do so.

2.2 Unequal Choice

Even in the area of public versus private utilities and services, opinion is divided over the appropriate balance between public and private sectors – the appropriate mix of the mixed economy. This includes not only the share of markets controlled by public enterprise, or the scale of public contracts to the private sector in the provision of services such as gas, electricity, water distribution and transport. It also includes the question of whether people in democratic economies have the *right* to housing, health, education and social services provided by the public sector rather than private markets. Such expressed differences over the appropriate size of the public sector are crucial to the functioning of any effective democracy. They are not the denial but the expression of political freedom.

Free Markets

The essentials of the freedom to sell in a market economy imply roles broadly supported by both 'supply-siders' and monetarists in the United States, the United Kingdom and elsewhere. Friedman claims that the price mechanism performs three functions in organising economic activity: first, it transmits information; second, it provides an incentive to adopt the least costly methods of production or distribution; and, third, it determines who gets how much of the product, i.e. the distribution of income. But there is a fourth and questionable principle of market theory: that, left to the forces of supply and demand, markets 'clear' – in other words, overpriced goods will be unsold and underpriced goods sold out, so that prices are adjusted to balance supply and demand. There is also a fifth principle, that prices should be competitive rather than monopolistic. If they are not, dispersed consumer sovereignty is qualified by concentrated producer power.

Market Power

The last point is critical to the defence of the market economy. It poses major problems both for Milton Friedman and for that theory stemming from Marshall and Walras which is known as *neo*classical economics. For instance, in arguing that economic freedom is a requisite for political freedom, Friedman claims that it enables people to co-operate without coercion and that 'by dispersing power, *the free market provides an offset to whatever concentration of political power may arise*' (Friedman, 1980, p. 21, italics added).

In reality it is the dispersion of political power in the developed market economies of Western Europe and North America that has been qualified in the twentieth century by the rise of the modern capitalist corporation, the trend to monopoly and multinational capital, and what President Eisenhower described – with warning – as the military-industrial complex.

The perfect or imperfect competition – assumed in liberal or conservative defences of the market mechanism – has been marginalised and reduced to secondary importance by the rise of multinational big business. For instance, the combined sales of the world's largest 200 corporations now amount to nearly a third of the world's Gross Domestic Product, and some one and a half times the Third World's GDP (Clairmonte and Cavanagh, 1984). Rather than the market offsetting concentrated political power, the scope and scale of multinational business qualifies political sovreignty.

Economics and Geography

Friedman simply ignores such concentration of economic power. He prefers to argue the case of a pencil maker whose productive resource is 'the capacity to organise an enterprise, co-ordinate the resources it uses, assume risks, and so on'. But independent pencil makers are disappearing. For instance, family firms making pencils in Tokyo survived for much of the postwar period by producing as subcontractors for major conglomerate firms such as Mitsubishi. But when the Japanese combines went multinational during the 1970s – as this author has witnessed at first hand – the Tokyo pencil makers found their contracts cancelled, their workshops closed down and their futures undermined.

On the market of the small entrepreneur, Friedman (1980, pp. 39–40) then claims that:

> *The existence of the modern corporation does not alter matters.* We speak loosely of the 'corporation's income' or of 'business' having an income. That is figurative language. The corporation is an intermediary between its owners – the stockholders – and the resources other than the stockholders' capital, the services of which it purchases. *Only people have incomes* and they derive them through the market from the resources they own, whether these be in the form of corporate stock, or of bonds, or of land, or of their personal capacity.

Such a claim that 'the existence of the modern corporation does not alter matters' is at best inaccurate and at worst arcane. An economic geographer doing a transport model for the Netherlands and Nepal who claimed that 'the existence of the Himalayas does not alter matters' would be dismissed as a fraud or a fantasist.

TABLE 2.1 Companies and Countries: Total Reserves* of Countries *v.* Assets of Companies

	$million		$million
USA	246,665	Standard Oil (Ohio)	16,016
ATT	151,969	Hitachi	15,814
Royal Dutch Shell	69,746	Occidental Petroleum	15,772
Exxon	62,288	Petrobras	15,283
W. Germany	51,108	Nippon Steel	15,069
BP	42,495	Siemens	14,544
General Motors	41,398	ITT	14,132
Mobil	36,439	Canadian Pacific	14,047
IBM	32,541	*UK*	13,856
Texaco	27,114	*Spain*	8,672
Japan	25,608	*Austria*	6,453
DuPont	24,342	*Belgium*	5,537
Standard Oil (Ind.)	24,289	*India*	4,904
Standard Oil (Calif.)	23,490	*Brazil*	4,151
Petroleos de Venezuela	22,802	*Chile*	1,985
Ford	21,962	*Portugal*	1,372
Atlantic Richfield	21,633	*Pakistan*	1,098
General Electric	21,615	*Greece*	1,066
Shell Oil (Houston)	21,376	*Sri Lanka*	374
France	20,777	*Uruguay*	239
Pemex	20,712	*Bangladesh*	194
Gulf Oil	20,436	*El Salvador*	135
Elf	19,732	*Jamaica*	115
ENI	19,623	*Zambia*	70
US Steel	19,432	*Upper Volta*	65
Tenneco	17,378	*Niger*	31
Philips	16,493	*Mali*	19
Mitsubishi Heavy	16,452	*Chad*	14

*Total Resources with gold at $35 per ounce end 1982 at Dec. 1982 exchange rates.
Sources: IMF, *Business Week*, *Fortune*.

Oligopoly and Oligarchy

In reality, the concentration of private economic power today is such that a minor fraction of one per cent of enterprise control from a half to two-thirds or more of economic activity in key sectors of the market economy.

If a similar fraction of the population controlled the same share of political power, this would constitute *oligarchy* rather than democracy. In economic terms, the massive concentration of economic power in the hands of a few firms amounts to *oligopoly* – or the dominance of a few – rather than the dispersion of economic power stressed by Friedman as the critical condition offsetting 'whatever concentration of political power may arise'.

Table 2.1 dramatically illustrates one of the central weaknesses of Friedman's analysis. It indicates comparative economic size by contrasting the reserves of both leading and less developed countries with the assets of the largest corporations in the world in 1982. On this basis of comparison, eight corporations had bigger assets than Japan, sixteen had larger assets than France and thirty-two had larger assets than the United Kingdom. Each of the companies formed when ATT was broken up in 1984 are bigger than British Telecom.

Free to Buy

In *Free to Choose* – both in book form and in the television series – Friedman uses a vegetable market stall to illustrate the principles of supply and demand. But such an example is as relevant to today's market realities as is the paper dart to the jumbo jet. Certainly John Smith or John Doe may be interested to learn that they share the common feature that 'only people have incomes' with John D. Rockefeller, and wonder how the Rockefellers are multi-millionaires, while they are not.

In reality, Friedman does not explain (1) why there are such major differences between the wealth and income of individuals; (2) why some are free to buy goods and services of a kind which simply are inaccessible to others; nor (3) why there is so persistent and similar an inequality in the distribution of personal income between different countries at different levels of development. Thousands of millions of people in the world today lack a significant disposable surplus. Hundreds of millions lamentably lack an adequate subsistence. Tens of millions die each year of disease and starvation, even without the drought disaster which gripped regions such as sub-Saharan Africa in the mid-1970s and 1980s.

Unequal Wealth

A contrast between neoclassical and classical economics is that while neoclassicals have been mainly concerned with the economics of production, the classicals were mainly concerned with the economics of distribution. As John Stuart Mill wrote, over a century ago: 'It is only in the backwward countries of the world that increased production is still an important object: in those most advanced, what is economically needed is a better distribution. . . .'

Moreover, Mill contrasted the objective nature of the economics of production with the subjective nature of social choice on distribution. As he put it:

> The laws and conditions of the production of wealth partake of the character of physical truths. There is nothing optional, or arbitrary in them. Whether [mankind] like it or not, a double quantity of labour will not raise on the same land, a double quantity of food, unless some improvement takes place in the processes of cultivation. . . .
>
> It is not so with the Distribution of Wealth. That is a matter of human institutions solely. The things once there, mankind, individually or collectively, can do with them as they like. . . . The Distribution of Wealth, therefore, depends on the laws and customs of society. The rules by which it is determined, are what the opinions and feelings of the ruling portion of the community make them, and are very different in different ages and countries; and might be still more different, if mankind so chose. [Mill, 1848, pp. 114 and 350.]

In reality, wealth in less developed countries tends to be markedly more unequal even than the distribution of income – often by a factor of two to three. This means that from one to five per cent of the population typically own and control between a third to two-thirds of land – a key source of income and subsistence. In developed countries a similar share of population typically owns and controls between a third and two-thirds of personally held assets. These are *disposable* wealth in the form of bond or share holdings, rather than *functional* assets such as owner-occupied houses or pension and insurance schemes which in due course will be sold or liquidated to provide for pensions and retirement income.

Unequal Distribution

Friedman's stress on equal freedom to buy, as if people were equally able to purchase, becomes unreal when one compares differences in personal income in either developed or less developed countries.

For instance, Table 2.2 illustrates the percentage share of household income commanded by the upper and lower fifths of the population, plus the income share of the highest ten per cent of households for a range of countries.

It is notable that in the developed industrial market economies the top 10 per cent of households represent on average between a quarter and 30 per cent of total household income. In intermediate or middle-income economies, the share of the top 10 per cent rises on average from under a third to a half (in the case of Brazil). In low-income economies the share of the top 10 per cent ranges from just under a third to over 45 per cent of total household income. However, it is notable that among the least developed countries and

TABLE 2.2   Unequal Income Distribution

	Year	Lowest 20%	Highest 20%	Highest 10%
Low-Income Countries				
Bangladesh	1976–77	6.2	46.9	32.0
Nepal	1976–77	4.6	59.2	46.5
Malawi	1967–68	10.4	50.6	40.1
Tanzania	1969	5.8	50.4	35.6
India	1975–76	7.0	49.4	33.6
Kenya	1976	2.6	60.4	45.8
Sudan	1967–68	4.0	49.8	34.6
Middle-Income Countries				
Thailand	1975–76	5.6	49.8	34.1
Turkey	1973	3.5	56.5	40.7
Brazil	1972	2.0	66.6	50.6
Korea, Rep. of	1976	5.7	45.3	27.5
Mexico	1977	2.9	57.5	40.6
Hong Kong	1980	5.4	47.0	31.3
Industrial Market Economies				
Italy	1977	6.2	43.9	28.1
United Kingdom	1979	7.0	39.7	23.4
Japan	1979	8.7	37.5	22.4
France	1975	5.3	45.8	30.5
West Germany	1978	7.9	39.5	24.0
Australia	1975–76	5.4	47.1	30.5
USA	1980	5.3	39.9	23.7

Source: IBRD, *World Development Report*, 1985, Table 28, and 1986, Table 24.

intermediate or middle-income economies the top 20 per cent of households uniformly commanded from around 45 per cent to two-thirds of household income.

By contrast, the lowest 20 per cent in both low-income and middle-income countries (with the marginal exception of Malawi) uniformly received less than 10 per cent and in Brazil only 2 per cent of total household income.

Strikingly, the picture is the same for the developed industrial market economies, where the lowest 20 per cent of households all received less than 10 per cent of household income – with less than 7 per cent or less in the United Kingdom and Italy, and less than 6 per cent in Australia, France and the United States.

Social Markets?

Table 2.3 sumarises the major overall difference in GNP per head between developed 'first world' and less developed 'third world' countries in 1983. Income levels in Northern Europe and North America averaged over $11,000 (ranging from around $5,000 for Spain to over $16,000 for Switzerland). But nearly half of the world's economies and more than half its people had an average product of less than $1,000 while a quarter of the world's economies in the low-income bracket had an annual product per person in 1983 of less than $400. Nearly 30 countries had an average personal product of $300 or less, including the subcontinent of India with a total population nearly equivalent to that of all the industrial market economies combined.

TABLE 2.3   Unequal Chance – Unequal Choice

	Population (millions)	GNP per head (dollars)	Life Expectancy (years)
Low-income			
economies	2,335.4	260	59
China and India	1,752.3	280	62
Other low-income	583.0	200	51
Sub-Saharan Africa	245.2	220	48
Middle-income			
economies	1,165.2	1,310	61
Oil exporters	542.6	1,060	57
Oil importers	622.6	1,530	64
Upper-middle-income	500.1	2,050	65
High-income			
oil exporters	19.9	12,370	59
Industrial market			
economies	728.9	11,060	76

Source: IBRD, *World Development Report*, 1985, Table 1. All figures 1983.

Message or Massage?

In effect, on a global scale, 'free to choose' is less message than massage. In the least developed countries, only a minuscule elite is free to choose to spend its income on higher education for its children or a private health system. As indicated in Table 2.3, in the least developed low-income countries of the world, life expectancy at birth is only some two-thirds of that in the industrial market economies. The cause is lack of the most basic health provision.

Nearly 20 million children die each year in the Third World countries from malnutrition or diseases such as diarrhoea, diabetes and influenza, which in welfare state economies are considered trivial because treatable by simple drugs or a basic balanced diet.

In contrast with adult literacy rates of 95 to 99 per cent in the industrial market economies, adult literacy ranges from 50 to 5 per cent in the least developed countries. Neither literacy nor life expectancy in the Third World can be improved without public education and health programmes. The success of such programmes can be illustrated in a major country, such as China, or in minor countries such as Nicaragua (Holland and Anderson, 1984). But this has been through public intervention rather than the private market economy. The ill, illiterate and impoverished peasantry in much of the Third World is no more free to choose better health, longer life or a higher education through market choice than it is free to fly.

Social Goods

Moreover, even in the most developed countries such as the United States, only some people, by exerting market choice, can choose a better quality of environment, less pollution, less urban congestion or better medical care. In the United States the two main medical insurance companies, Blue Cross and Blue Shield, will not insure against chronic ailments such as cancer. The families of many of those hit by the human tragedy of cancer (or AIDS) may be forced to sell their homes and disposable assets to pay for medical care for relatives who, while dying, are forced to face the fact that their illness has deprived and possibly bankrupted their families. Such is the reality of the free market in health and lives rather than Friedman's vegetable markets.

On urban crisis, the free market has little or nothing to offer to Calcutta or Sao Paulo. In Britain it was recognised by nineteenth-century Conservatives that the market could not ensure sewage or sanitation in the East End of London and thereby avoid the spread of typhus or cholera to the affluent West End. Disease, despite the market, knows no class barriers. It was through municipal intervention that sewage, sanitation, and public health were achieved in many of the world's major cities. Through public rather than private initiative, they created the basis for civilised urban life – not only in this or the last century, but through most of human history.

2.3 Free to Trade?

Friedman claims that ever since Adam Smith there has been virtual unanimity among economists that international free trade is in the best interests of the trading countries and of the world. He also argues (1980, pp. 74–5) that:

> The century from Waterloo to the First World War offers a striking example of the beneficial effects of free trade on the relations among nations. Britain was the leading nation of the world, and during the whole of that century it had nearly complete free trade. Other nations, particularly Western nations, including the United States, adopted a similar policy if in somewhat diluted form. . . . As a result, the century from Waterloo to the First World War was one of the most peaceful in human history among Western nations, marred only by some minor wars – the Crimean war and the Franco-Prussian wars are the most memorable – and, of course, a major civil war within the United States. . . .

The Role of Tariffs

The reality was strikingly different.

In the United States the 'somewhat diluted form' of free trade which Friedman claims was adopted in the nineteenth century is contradicted by Samuelson's franker admission of the massive scale of US tariffs (Samuelson, 1976, p. 702). In the early nineteenth century US tariffs were over 50 per cent and averaged over 45 per cent from the Civil War through to the First World War. This coincided with the heroic period of US industrialisation from 1880 to 1910.

In Italy, the economic revolution which transformed the 'golden triangle' of Milan, Turin and Genoa between 1890 and 1910 occurred behind tariffs of 45 per cent or more for key industrial products (Sylos-Labini, 1983, p. 65).

In Japan, the transition from a feudal to an industrial economy faced enormous difficulties in the thirty years which Friedman describes as the key era of Japanese free trade. Friedman claims that this free trade at the end of the nineteenth century was from market choice. He thereby ignores the 'unequal trade treaties' of 1858 with the Western powers which forbade Japan to impose any tariff higher than five per cent. He also fails to advise his readers that these treaties followed the arrival of Commodore Perry's fleet in 1854 and his demands from the United States that Japan opened up her boundaries. Such demands were accompanied in 1862 and 1863 by the bombardment of Shimoneski and Kagoshima by American and British warships.

Thus, it was due to US military pressure rather than market conviction that the Japanese tolerated a period of free trade for a quarter century until 1899.

Since those unequal treaties were repealed, Japan has been among the most proctectionist nations in the world, using tariffs and non-tariff barriers.

In Germany, following the Franco-Prussian war, Bismarck 'dished' the free-trade party, the National Liberals, and introduced protection from 1879 which deliberately aimed to exclude British goods and thereby make possible industrial modernisation. As in the United States in the same period, it was between 1880 and 1910 – behind protective barriers – that the emergence of Germany as a modern industrial economy occurred. Similarly, France industrialised behind the barriers of trade protection, combined with increased state intervention in the economy.

Infant and Adult Industries

We see a similar contradiction of the claimed empiricism of 'positive' economics in Friedman's argument on so-called 'infant industries'. This case, advanced at the time of American independence by Alexander Hamilton in his *Report on Manufactures*, amounts to the argument that there are potential industries which, if once established with assistance during their early growth, could then compete effectively on the world market. Temporary tariffs or other non-tariff barriers, according to the infant industry case, are justified in order to shelter the infant and enable it to grow through adolescence to maturity, when it can stand on its own feet.

Friedman dismisses this case by claiming simply that 'the infant industry argument is a smoke screen. *The so-called infants never grow up.* Once imposed, tariffs are seldom eliminated. Moreover, the argument is seldom used on behalf of true unborn infants that might conceivably be born and survive if given temporary protection. They have no spokesmen. It is used to justify tariffs for rather aged infants that can mount political pressure' (Friedman, ibid., pp. 71–72, italics added).

Friedman's claims that protected infant industries never grow up is contradicted by three of the most powerful of today's world economies – the United States, Japan and Germany, as well as a range of the South-East Asian countries which in other respects he applauds, including South Korea and Taiwan which have not only tariffs but import licences and direct state controls (Luedde-Neurath, 1984).

The Japanese case has been well put by Beida (1970, pp. 15–16) in the following terms:

> The remarkable fact is that in Japan, unlike in most other countries, all 'infant industries' have already become or are on the verge of becoming 'adult industries'. Many other countries seem to carry indefinitely the heavy burden of a large number of 'infants' which are not growing, but often are even slipping back. Not so in Japan.

There are various reasons. For one thing, Japan has managed to pick winners in the first place by thinking ahead from today's to tomorrow's technologies and techniques of production. For another, rather than *defensively* hanging onto a protected domestic market share, Japanese government and leading firms have invested *offensively* in mass production, covering this in the first instance by domestic sales and then achieving economies of scale and low costs when the rest of the world is wondering whether to enter the market. Further, both government and leading firms have put a high priority on *cooperation* with labour, guaranteeing lifetime employment and training programmes to extend skills, rather than the *confrontation*, de-skilling and threat of the dole adopted by some key competitors abroad. Also, rather than assume *a priori* that size necessarily implies abuse of competition, the Japanese have sought to match the efficiency gains from scale with forms of government intervention which have traded off one business group against another, to sustain a competitive market environment – what Beida calls 'the unique Japanese combination of large scale oligopolistic organisation of industry together with a high degree of competition' (Beida, ibid.).

The Role of Government

Several points of Beida's main argument are worth emphasizing. In the first case he makes the claim that (1) *all* infant industries have become or are becoming adult industries in Japan; (2) in contrast with Friedman's claim that 'the existence of the modern corporation does not alter matters' (Friedman, ibid, p. 40), Beida stresses that it is precisely the size of big business in the Japanese economy which has permitted what amounts in many cases to the promotion of satellite small firms into larger units; (3) again in contrast with Friedman's claim that post-Meiji Japan represents an example of the flourishing of free market forces, Beida stresses that '*government has always played an important role in the economic development of Japan by assisting capital formation*' (our emphasis). Admitting that in underdeveloped countries it is often suggested that the government entrepreneurship should step in to compensate weak private entrepreneurship, and claiming that concentrating enterprise in the hands of government is justified only if the private entrepreneurs are 'shy because of lack of experience', Beida stresses that in Japan all these conditions seem to have been met and that the state plays now and has played from the start an important role in the growth of industry, including outright ownership:

> The Meiji government started a large number of state-owned enterprises. Almost immediately after the Restoration the new government set out to build railways and a telegraph system. Further, in that age of free enterprise in the West, the Japanese government was eclectic and pragmatic on many points. Thus the government

started coal mines, built and operated iron foundries, shipyards and other factories to *pioneer* production of cement, paper, glass and other products. It was also the government that introduced mechanical silk reeling and spinning in the cotton industry. . . . The government responded pragmatically and flexibly to the various needs felt at the time, such as providing 'hardware' for the military, trying to increase exports, or even trying to increase government revenue. [Beida, 1970, pp. 43–4.)

Beida adds that it was *only when it became obvious that private enterprise could take over*, in 1882, that the government (motivated by its financial needs for building up the navy and the army) gave up the policy of owning enterprise and sold many of them to private businessmen. The famed Japanese Ministry of International Trade and Industry – MITI – is the former Japanese Ministry of Munitions, and a direct inheritor of this longstanding interventionist tradition.

List versus Friedman

It was from his experience in the United States in the early nineteenth century of the combination of massive protection, state intervention and a large and tariff-free domestic market that Friedrich List pioneered the infant industry argument. The issue which List addressed, which he held to be nothing less than the central problem of economics, was to discover how the less developed countries of his time could be raised to a level comparable to that of the then dominant world economy: Britain. To List the answer to the problem lay substantially in protection which, he claimed,

forms the only means of placing those nations which are far behind in civilization on equal terms with the one predominating nation (which never received at the hands of nature a perpetual right to a monopoly of manufacture, but which merely gained an advance over others in a point of time).

Moreover, rather than regarding the system of protection as damaging for international co-operation, List argued that:

The system of protection regarded from this point of view appears to be the most efficient means of furthering the final union of nations, and hence also of promoting true freedom of trade.

This was not a paradox inasmuch as List did not believe prohibitive tariffs a virtue; he thought that they should be reduced after infant industries had achieved adulthood. He also argued strongly for the establishment of regional customs unions, or areas with internal free trade with a common external tariff. This included the Zollverein in Germany in the nineteenth century, on which he had a very considerable influence, and which foreran the European Common Market and other regional common markets in the world today. Putting the point very simply, List maintained that his argument against unqualified free trade

> appears from this point of view to be that science which, correctly appreciating the existing interest in the individual circumstances of nations, teaches how *every separate nation* can be raised to that stage of industrial development which union with other nations equally well developed, and consequently freedom of trade, can become possible and useful to it. [List, 1965, p. 168]

As will be seen later in this book, although List wrote before the rise of the modern multinational corporation and its massive dominance of world international trade, his case is directly relevant to the issues facing a world economy dominated in the market countries by the United States, Western Europe and Japan, and where many less developed countries are falling behind rather than increasing their share of global investment, employment, income, trade and welfare. In this sense, the case for degrees of protection, state intervention and regional trading groups cannot easily be dismissed by Friedman or other advocates of unrestrained market forces, or by counter-factual claims such as that 'so-called infants never grow up' (Friedman, op. cit., p. 71).

Beggar-my-Neighbour

A further argument developed by Friedman in support of the unqualified free working of market forces is the beggar-my-neighbour argument. In other words, the in-itself-important argument that one country's imports are another's exports, is related to the claim that tariffs necessarily reduce total trade.

Friedman also makes the claim of tariff retaliation, i.e. that if one country raises tariffs others will follow suit, with a resulting contraction of trade. Contrasting this with the alleged benefits from wholly free trade, he states that 'few measures that we could take would do more to promote the cause of freedom at home and abroad than complete free trade'.

The simple point to be made on both free trade and protection is that neither are neutral, nor do they occur in a policy vaccum.

(1) Prohibitive tariffs or non-tariff barriers which entirely prevent imports may thereby make possible the development of indigenous modern agriculture, industry or services in the country or regions in question;
(2) Such a development may thereby raise the purchasing power of those in modern rather than traditional employment, their disposable surplus income, and their overall purchases in non-protected products and services from abroad.
(3) Tariffs and non-tariff barriers either may be prohibitive or may restrain

the growth of imports in a period of expansion of the domestic economy. If controls (whether tariff or non-tariff) restrain the *rate* of imports, then global trade still could be increased rather than decreased.

Better-my-Neighbour

(4) In such circumstances, reflation and expansion of a domestic economy, with a degree of import controls (provided these are not prohibitive for aggregate or macroeconomic trade) can promote a *better*-my-neighbour syndrome, or virtuous circle, rather than the *beggar*-my-neighbour circle of contraction and decline.
(5) Inversely, with total free trade, countries facing major balance-of-payments difficulties may not be able to pursue reflation or recovery programmes but be forced to pursue deflationary policies, restricting domestic demand and resulting in an overall contraction of imports.
(6) Less developed countries with little comparative advantage in international trade and minimal export earnings – such as Bangladesh, Chad, Niger, Mali or Upper Volta at the lowest end of the league tables of international income per head – may never be able to generate significant imports from other less developed countries or the developed world economies.

In other words, the question of beggar-my-neighbour versus better-my-neighbour depends on (a) the initial income level of the countries concerned, (b) the structure of domestic demand and (c) whether the country is deflating or reflating its overall purchases in the world economy.

2.4 Public and Private

The case of protection vividly illustrates the *gestalt* or perception argument made in Chapter 1. Viewed now from the premise of *laissez-faire*, and with the amnesia of some economists who are prepared to neglect their own country's economic history, protection may be claimed to be an unwarrantable misallocation of resources. Viewed alternatively from a historical perspective and the standpoint either of a less developed economy or a developed economy seeking to sustain a recovery programme, selective protection on an interim basis may be considered the *sine qua non* of either development or recovery.

Manichees and Monetarists

Similar arguments on perception obtain for the 'high theory' of government intervention versus market forces in areas crucial to issues of development and welfare such as public spending. In such a context, neglecting economic history in his dismissal of the case for infant industries, Milton Friedman also neglects other historical precedents in his presumption, presupposition or plain prejudice against public expenditure.

For instance, the Manichees were a group of medieval Christians who believed – like the Calvinists of the Reformation period – that the world was irreconcilably divided between the bad and the good, the vicious and the virtuous, with no open frontier between these two extremes. Friedman's strictures against the public sector and in favour of the private market amount to a Manichaean division of the world between public and private enterprise.

His case that money supply alone causes inflation is widely contested. On other key claims, his argument amounts to saying that the crisis of capitalism results from an excess in the money supply either through the printing of money, or through public expenditure, or both. His simplistic recommendations include (1) a reduction of personal taxation to improve incentive; (2) a reduction of public expenditure on welfare state type policies in line with the reduced taxation; (3) a reduction of the public sector in both industry and services; and (4) a re-privatisation of the remaining public sector. Such prescriptions have been swallowed wholesale by the Thatcher government in Britain.

In stressing greater incentives as crucial for a flourishing private market, Friedman wholly ignores the problems posed for small firms by unequal competition between large and small enterprise in modern capitalism. It is not the lack of incentive which prevents the small-scale entrepreneur in Birmingham Alabama or Birmingham in the UK from entering the stakes on equal terms with IBM, but the monopoly domination of multinational markets which IBM has already established. The failure of thrusting small-league entrepreneurs to make it into the big-league world of monopoly capital is well illustrated in the United States, where the stability of the top two hundred companies in the postwar period has been remarkable. It is also contradicted by European evidence, where the figures, as we shall see, indicate a clear trend to monopoly rather than self-balancing competition between a myriad of free-market entrepreneurs.

Public Spending – Draining or Sustaining?

Friedman also claims that public spending is inflationary and 'crowds out' private spending. But the crisis of the welfare state is not simply a matter of deficit spending or public expenditure financed by the printing of money in the manner posed by the monetarists. Nor is it a question of first producing the wealth through the private sector before one can afford public distribution in the form of welfare services or social income.

Public spending *sustains* rather than *drains* private spending in the European economies. The principle is simple and involves the circularity of income stressed by Keynes.

Thus, in arguing that the public sector crowds out the private sector, Friedman totally misunderstands the nature of public expenditure and its real 'supply side' implications in postwar capitalism. Public expenditure may hover around half of total spending, but public enterprise constitutes around a tenth or less of total supply for most of the developed economies.

As a result, up to 90 per cent or more of public expenditure actually provides demand for the private sector. The furniture for housing, the health equipment for hospitals, the drugs prescribed, and the books used come almost without exception from private enterprise. The vast bulk of the wages and salaries are spent on goods and services supplied by private enterprise because of the low share of the public enterprise in the economy.

Practical examples abound. For example, In England and Wales since 1980 some 93 per cent of public housing constructed and managed by local authorities was built by private enterprise. Therefore, every £100 cut in public spending, designed on Friedman's reasoning to release resources for the private sector, actually contracted private-sector demand by about £93. The result in Britain, with the major cuts imposed by the Conservative government, has been the collapse of tens of thousands of firms in private construction and more than a third of a million construction workers unemployed.

Lines of Defence

For such reasons, public spending is the first line of defence of the modern mixed economy against collapse of investment and income. As elaborated in *The Global Economy* (Holland, 1987, chapter 3), it is the floor below which contractions in private spending and income will not sink unless public spending itself is cut. Similarly, the rise in public spending was integral to and associated with the so-called 'miracle growth' of key European economies in the postwar period, when in key countries such expenditure rose from around a quarter to a half or two-thirds of total spending.

Friedman and the monetarists also neglect the real role of transfer payments or social spending in the form of pensions, security payments and welfare. Such transfer payments are the second line of defence of private income in the economy. Taken from taxation they nonetheless are re-injected into the economy through the spending of pensioners and the unemployed. Monetarists neglect this circularity of payments.

Public-sector wages and salaries are the third line of defence of private income in the economy. The vast proportion of salaries paid to professional public employees goes to either private consumption or private savings, and not least to private housing finance and pensions. Some wage earners, especially in Europe, may also live in public housing. But the major share of their expenditure is still on private-sector goods and services.

Privatisation and Profit

Friedman's fourth claim is that governments should sell existing public enterprise back to the private sector. This neglects the fact (1) that much public enterprise, such as Britain's Post Office Telecommunications or West Germany's railways, was never private in the first place, and (2) that public enterprises hitherto run with low profits or at a loss to service the rest of the economy will have insufficient earnings to attract buyers unless it raises prices and thereby aggravates inflation.

Friedman argues that selling off public enterprise would result in a market for their shares, pressure for greater accountability, and therefore an approach to profitable functioning. But there will only be a market for the shares if the enterprises are expected to earn a profit. In 1984–5, for instance, the Thatcher government protected the market share of British Airways – and delayed its privatisation – precisely to render it more profitable for sale on the market. In practice, since such public enterprises in Europe are mainly monopoly providers of services and basic inputs for industry, this means private monopoly or joint monopoly profits, rather than a model of market competition.

The real reason why several governments are pursuing privatisation has little to do with better value for money or consumer sovereignty. It is clear that the rate of profit achieved by big business has been declining with recession. Despite the increased share of total profits by the big business sector, the private sector can best defend and extend profits in prolonged recession by taking over already profitable public enterprise. It is for this reason that big business is buying into public industry services such as oil and telecommunications in countries like Britain. It is doing so on bargain terms allowed by governments who offer shares below real market values. In some cases, governments may also be willing to write off the debt burden of public utilities which have seriously impeded their commercial viability under public ownership.

Political Capitalism

The claim that the economic development of the United States represented the growth of unadulterated private markets is also a myth. The evidence is worth citing at this stage as a counter-balance to market mythology. It is also interesting because of the extent to which state capitalist enterprise and state intervention in the growth of the US economy has its own implications for the debate on the mixed economy in Europe and the United States today.

In contrast with Friedman's 'golden age' of the market throughout the nineteenth century, the government of the United States immediately after the War of Independence pressed and extended a policy of rigorous protection to create a sufficient home market for the development of infant firms and industries. Even in the colonial period, as Kolko has shown, the capitalist entrepreneurship of the Protestant ethic was less significant than 'a political capitalism in which economic success was determined far more by political and social connections than by any special religious motivations' (Kolko, 1962). The British government in the eighteenth century had been determined to secure a closer supervision of the administration of the colonies through the granting of government contracts, tax collection, customs regulation and bestowal of land grants, to a chosen 'inner circle'. Bailyn chronicles the accumulation of New England fortunes through such inner-circle means – very similar to the 'oligarchies' which dominate so many Latin and Central American economies today. He also points to an initial accumulation of capital which had little to do with the self-adjustment model of primitive accumulation of an agricultural surplus to be later invested in industry. (Bailyn, cited in Bruchey (1965).

State Enterprise

Further, Bruchey has shown that, in the immediate post-Independence period, 'given the strength of the American desire for economic development, the scarcity of capital funds and the sharpness of competition from foreign suppliers, manufacturing was endowed with a quasi-public and not a private character, and given numerous encouragements by the State'. The main instruments of this public intervention compare directly with the use of state shareholding in public companies in Italy and France from the 1930s onwards – incorporation of the business enterprise as a state agency to fulfil public rather than merely private ends. Bruchey points out that, during the colonial period, public incorporation had been employed only about half a dozen times for business organisations. But, in contrast, state governments created more than three hundred business corporations between the end of the War of Independence and 1801. Two-thirds of them were to establish inland navigation, toll bridges and turnpike roads. Thirty-two companies were initiated in insurance to underwrite risks which private enterprise would not take, thirty-four in banking, and thirty-six in water resource projects and dock building. (Bruchey, 1965, pp. 128–30.)

Visible Hands

This 'visible hand' of the American state was only a foretaste of greater things to come. At the turn of the century Guy Callender challenged the private-enterprise mythology of US economic development with a major analysis in the *Journal of Political Economy* of 1902 (p. 111):

> It is a commonplace observation that the last century witnessed everywhere a great extension of the activities of the State into the field of industry. Americans are not accustomed to think of their own country as taking a prominent part in this movement, far less as ever having occupied a leading position in it. To them, as to the rest of the world, America is the land of private enterprise *par excellence*; the place where 'State interference' has played the smallest part, and individual enterprise has been given the largest scope, in industrial affairs; and it is commonly assumed that this has always been so. Nevertheless it is a fact that this country was one of the first to exhibit this modern tendency to extend the activity of the State into industry.

Callender showed that government intervention in the economy was not simply a post-Independence accident, but the precondition and continuing accompaniment of the opening of the Mid West. State governments with federal blessing and participation opened up the transport links which pierced the Appalachian barrier and created the conditions under which new emigrants could export to the Mid West from the Eastern seaboard. As Callender (ibid., pp. 132–3) says:

> Up to 1815 the improvements of rivers and building of canals which alone could enable remote regions to send their produce to market, had been almost entirely neglected. Numerous efforts had been made to induce capital to take up this work, but with very little success. . . . In the settlement of the West and the development of its resources *men were even less inclined to risk their capital. I have found no evidence that any Eastern capital was invested in this way before 1815.* The settler moved into the wilderness with his own little stock of household goods, farm implements and cattle.

The State and Finance Capital

It was intervention by the states which transformed this situation. New York led the way with the Erie canal in 1817, and Pennsylvania followed in 1825 with an equally extensive system of canals. Maryland, Virginia and the federal government began the Chesapeake and Ohio canal in 1828, and Virginia pushed through a project to connect the James River with the Ohio from 1820 onwards. Railways were pioneered by the states – the Baltimore and Ohio in 1828 and the Erie in New York in the early 1830s, with subsequent developments of state-financed railways and canals in Indiana, Michigan and Illinois. It was this breakthrough in railway construction through state finance that attracted foreign capital to follow up. In the words of Callender (ibid., p. 153):

> To construct these important projects required several millions of capital – an amount far greater than had been brought together in any industry at that time. For corporations to secure so much capital it was necessary to bring together the small savings of the country and to attract the large ones of foreigners. There was no body of private individuals in the country well enough known and with sufficient influence in the business world to establish the credit of a corporation so that it could command the confidence of both these classes of investors. *The only securities that could do so were public securities, or the securities of corporations which were guaranteed or assisted by the government.*

The role of the federal government was less important in these developments than that of the states themselves. Federal expenditure anyway declined temporarily before the Civil War, as the southern states increasingly opposed federal intervention. However, according to Davis and Legler, federal expenditure approximately equalled the states' expenditure throughout the nineteenth century. Military expenditure accounted for nearly 40 per cent of the federal total from 1815 to 1902, administrative expenses for about half, and public works for the remainder. In general, they claim that federal policy was 'designed to grab whatever was at hand to pay the bills for expenditures dictated by the political process' (Davis and Legler, 1966, p. 156).

From Old Deal

The effects of this nineteenth-century federal expenditure in the US were massive by any standards, even by those of the Roosevelt New Deal. For instance, the Old South was a regular and substantial deficit region, with the income transfer in its favour increasing as federal expenditure increased. This arose partly from the fact that Baltimore was the only major international port in the region, partly from the inclusion of Washington DC, and partly because of the increased political responsibility for the South after the Civil War. But the result was a deficit (or federal transfer in the region's favour) reaching nine dollars per capita in 1900, or one dollar for every eight of the region's income. The Mountain States' benefits from federal expenditure were even more marked. With more or less free land after 1863 and a high level of expenditure on Indian and Mormon pacification (40 per cent of the federal total in 1880), they averaged a deficit of twelve dollars per capita over the last quarter of the century, reaching a peak of 45 dollars per capita, or one dollar in four of income, in 1870.

To New Deal

A federal budget proper, rather than taking what was available for what was regionally necessary, did not emerge until 1921. Also, planned federal intervention in favour of depressed and problem regions did not emerge in the United States until after 1929 and the Democratic New Deal. Two of its most important dimensions were (1) the general infrastructure expenditure programme on roads, and (2) selective infrastructure projects on water-resource power and control systems, of which the Tennessee Valley Authority and major dam projects are the most notable and best-known examples. Granted the scale and nature of government intervention in infrastructure and water-resource projects over the previous 150 years, the New Deal was less brand new and more the Old Deal resurrected. Even the cost-benefit analysis which stemmed in part from the Tennessee Valley project and was heralded as a twentieth-century 'discovery', had been employed as a justification for government regional development expenditure in congressional debates in 1818, when Henry Clay argued, in relation to water and road projects that:

> The capitalist who should invest his money in these projects might not be reimbursed 3 per cent annually, and yet society in various forms might actually reap 15 or 20 per cent. The benefit resulting from a turnpike road made by private associations is divided between the capitalist, who receives his toll, the lands through which it passes and which are augmented in their value, and the commodities whose value is enhanced by their diminished expense of transportation. [Annals of Congress 1817–18, p. 1377, cited in Callender, 1902.]

It was as a result of such a divergence between private and social benefits that Clay and others promoted direct government expenditure projects to open up inaccessible regions, promote markets and sustain growth.

One of the problems faced by twentieth-century New Dealers was the hold which market mythology and market concentration had already established by the 1930s – as again in the 1980s – in the United States. The post-1929 Depression had followed a period of unprecedented dynamism in the distribution of new products, techniques and facilities in entirely new industries and services. The concept of the federal government intervening directly in the market appeared illegitimate or unprecedented to many Americans who either had forgotten – or had not bothered to learn – their own economic history.

2.5 **Summary**

(1) Milton Friedman fantasises a 'golden age' of economic and political freedoms when unfettered entrepreneurs transformed the world unaided and unhindered by government or state through the workings of the market economy.

(2) Free trade has been the exception rather than the rule for all leading world economies, with the exception of the United Kingdom which did not need industrial protection during its own revolution since at the time it had no significant industrial competitors.

(3) Germany, Japan and the United States grew behind prohibitive tariffs designed to create a sizeable domestic internal market and also through major state intervention in the economy.

(4) In contrast to Friedman's claim, there are important differences between small and big, national and multinational businesses and their impact on both the micro and macro economy.

(5) In practice, freedom to choose depends on freedom to buy, which in turn depends on the distribution of income and wealth. The citizens of at least a quarter of the world's economies are not free to choose in the manner ascribed by Friedman, nor are those of the remaining market economies free to choose collective social or public goods through the market mechanism alone.

(6) The concentration of economic power in the form of oligopoly is matched in many cases by oligarchic political control, and there is no necessary coincidence between market freedoms and political freedoms.

(7) Public spending sustains rather than drains the private sector of the economy, most vividly through the military-industrial complex in the United States, and through civilian and social spending in Europe.

(8) Privatisation of public utilities, as pursued on Friedmanite lines by the Thatcher governments in Britain, transforms public monopolies into private monopolies rather than promoting increased competion.

(9) State credits, public works and public enterprise played a critical role in the economic growth of the United States and of Japan, as well as other economies in Europe.

3 From Perfect to Imperfect Competition

The conventional theory of the firm depends crucially on assumptions concerning the structure of supply and price competition. The microeconomics of supply – wedded by Keynesians and monetarists alike with the macroeconomics of demand – assumes a paradigm of competition between equals, subject to minor imperfections in product demand and consumer sovereignty.

The main principles of such conventional microeconomics are as relevant today to a global economy dominated by multinational big business as are those of physics before Galileo to the world since Einstein. Yet such conventional theory not only is produced and reproduced in teaching economics in many courses worldwide. It also survives in a form which exerts a profound influence over policy-makers who are attracted to its social and welfare implications. For example, the theory of perfect and imperfect competition underlies the exaltation of market myths as produced and propagandised by theorists such as Milton Friedman, and with them what has become known as Thatchernomics and Reaganomics. With less pretension it still dominates teaching texts such as those of Lipsey (1983) and Begg, Fischer and Dornbusch (1984).

3.1 The Price-Competitive Model

Conventional microeconomics was identified with the 'firm and industry'. Indeed, for some time the terms 'microeconomics', 'price theory' and 'firm and industry' were synonymous. But even conventional theory gave such terms different meanings at different times, even for the same purposes.

For Marshall (1890) the firm was founded, owned and managed by a single entrepreneur. In the 1930s Kaldor still defined it as 'a productive combination possessing a given unit of co-ordinating ability' (Kaldor, 1934). After the Second World War, however, Joan Robinson (1953) admitted the entry of the great company of the 'managerial revolution', controlled by a self-perpetuating cadre of managers and directors, and claimed that such a firm had 'a kind of personality, like a college, with which many and successive individuals identify themselves'. For Robin Marris (1964), big business under 'managerial capitalism' rather than the 'owner-entrepreneur' of Marshall's time had been transformed, and theory should recognise it. J. M. Clark (1961) recognised that the 'firm' may be 'a single self-employed odd-job man, a one-family farm or retail store, or anything up to Du Pont, General Motors or U.S. Steel'. Or as John Kenneth Galbraith (1974, p. ix) has put it, on the one hand there is 'the world of the great corporations with the decisive part of the economy. . . . There also is the world of the farmer, repairman, retailer, small manufacturer, plumber, television repairman, service station operator, medical practitioner, artist, actress, photographer and pornographer.'

Theories and Firms

But this poses key questions. If the twentieth-century modern capitalist firm is so different from the nineteenth-century model on which Marshall founded 'economics', should we continue today with the economics of the 'firm and industry' which plays so large a part in many textbooks and much conventional theory? Should we not look for a theory of *firms* – in the plural – and try to identify their different behaviour characteristics?

Many firms range beyond one product, market or sector and thus become multiproduct, multimarket or multisectoral enterprises. This gives them gains from size through spreading their risks, increasing their profit volume, raising their creditworthiness, and extending the range of their hold over both buyers and suppliers. Moreover, multinational firms can compound many of these gains with access to lower-cost labour in other economies, and a competitive advantage which they may well exploit by importing goods or components to the 'home market' at lower cost than local firms.

While such gains do not necessarily imply, at least to begin with, production on a major scale, they tend to promote it. The result is an increasingly dual economy of bigger multinational and smaller national business. These are some of the differences between what we have called micro and mesoeconomic enterprise. Yet the conventional theory of 'the firm' relies on a conceptual framework which makes recognition of such differences either difficult or impossible.

Several chapters of this volume therefore seek to develop a theory of *firms* – micro and mesoeconomic – rather than a theory of *the* firm. But to understand the hold for decades of the conventional wisdom on economic theory, it is important to consider the scope and limits of that theory 'of the firm and industry' which ranges through perfect, imperfect and monopolistic competition.

From Classical to Neoclassical

Despite some of the simpler contrasts of 'positive' and 'normative' economics, variations on the themes of competition or monopoly have as much to do with judgements on the system in which people live as with factual analysis. 'Competition' and 'monopoly' are both descriptive categories *and* value terms. By convention – for consumers – competition is a 'good thing' if it results in better quality and lower prices, while monopoly is very much a 'bad thing' if it does not.

In Britain the convention can be traced back at least as far as the attempt of seventeenth-century monarchs (especially James I) to sell monopoly rights over trades and industries. Against a background of local and state monopolies, competition was a newcomer for the classical political economists. But, for them, the competitive process was also part of a wider analysis of growth and distribution in the economy. Adam Smith's emphasis, as implied by the title of his main work, was on the question of wealth. Ricardo, like Marx and John Stuart Mill, stressed distribution between different classes in society – landowners, capitalist, and workers.

From Utilitarianism to Marginal Utility

Within the classical tradition there was the 'utilitarian' school of Bentham and James Mill (John Stuart's father). Put simply, this argued that there were various units of utility – 'utils' – which could indicate the usefulness of production and consumption within the economy. The problem with such 'utility' was that it was difficult to measure. The usefulness or 'use value' of an activity did not necessarily coincide with its value in the market or 'exchange value'. Bentham was well aware of the point in his aphorism that 'poetry is as good as push-pin' (the Space Invaders of his time). Besides, utilitarianism gave only an *ordinal* ranking of value, i.e. the order in which individuals would subjectively rank their utility preferences. *Cardinal* ranking or absolute value, for the classicals, was catered for by the labour theory of value, i.e. the assumption that the value of a 'product' or 'commodity' (terms used synonymously by the classical economists) objectively reflected the labour time embodied in it.

The new or *neo*classical theory – sometimes known as 'the marginal revolution' – was in basis very simple. Instead of reasoning in terms of ordinal utility, it argued that individuals would rank their purchases (and thus the prices they would be prepared to pay) in terms of marginal change or utility.

Essentially *marginal* means what it suggests – on or at the margin of either supply or demand, sales or purchases. In practice it has been applied to the extra or additional unit of supply or demand which a producer or consumer would be prepared to undertake, and the reasons for this. For instance, it would make little sense for a firm to produce an additional unit of output if the costs of the marginal product were greater than the marginal revenue which the firm would gain from selling it. With small products, such as a can of beans, the point seems trivial. When they are large, such as ships or oil rigs, it can affect both profits and possibly a company's survival.

Supply and Demand Curves

When products are relatively homogenous (like fruit or vegetables) and when there are few constraints on increased output (such as barriers to competition or the weather), supply and demand may conform with the standard supply and demand curves in conventional literature.

Thus in Figure 3.1(a) the demand curve slopes downwards from left to right, i.e. consumers buy more tea the lower its price. Inversely, in Figure 3.1(b) the supply curve slopes upwards from left to right, i.e. producers will put more tea on the market the higher its price.

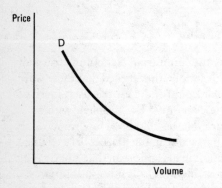
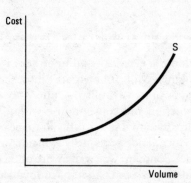

FIG. 3.1(a)   A demand curve for tea   FIG. 3.1(b)   A supply curve for tea

Putting the supply and demand curves together, as in Figure 3.2(a), shows that the willingness of consumers to buy extra units at a lower price is offset by the unwillingness of sellers to incur the costs of producing, transporting, wholesaling and retailing the goods in question below such a price. In principle this intersection of demand and supply gives rise to the prevailing or *equilibrium* market price (*e*) in what has become known as Marshall's scissors (i.e. the intersection at the crux or fulcrum of the twin 'blades' of the supply and demand curves).

Relative taste is a subjective preference by consumers with which conventional theory deals well, if sometimes at inordinate length. For

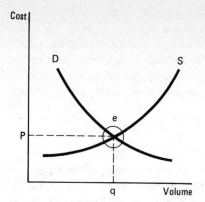

FIG. 3.2(a)   Marshall's 'scissors'

instance, if the prices of tea and coffee were the same, consumers might choose more of one or the other in terms of their real preference for tea versus coffee. If the price of tea temporarily fell by half relative to coffee, they could well buy more, and if it fell further, more still. But there would be a diminishing *marginal utility* to the consumer of buying only tea rather than coffee, whatever their relative price, for anyone who wanted to drink both.

Income Distribution

Relative income is an *objective* matter, crucially affecting demand, with which conventional theory deals badly, briefly or not at all. Thus the theory of 'diminishing marginal utility' assumes away or abstracts differences in income distribution or the ability of consumers in different social classes to buy or not to buy specific products or services. For costlier items, a fall in price still may leave the product out of the reach of those on lower incomes. Moreover, the theory has difficulties in explaining items of 'conspicuous consumption', i.e. where goods such as watches, furs, or cars may be bought because they are expensive, and to show the wealth of the owner, rather than because they reflect improved marginal utility in terms of telling the time, keeping warm, or travel.

Such issues of income distribution significantly qualify conventional theory in two senses. First, some consumers are more sovereign than others in the range of goods and services which they can command and the bargaining power they can exert on producers. This becomes especially important when we move from personal consumption to the demand for goods and services between different kinds of firm. Second, by neglecting the role of income distribution on actual demand, conventional microeconomics is of little help in any macroeconomic focus on the demand effects of income distribution. This tends to block perception of the way in which low demand, or slow demand growth, may reflect consumer saturation at prevailing levels of income inequality, which could be offset by redistribution. Put differently, one of the best ways of promoting an economic recovery may be to shift it through the pockets of those on low pay by raising their basic income and expenditure.

Stability, Instability and Advertising

Besides this, even in the short run, supply and demand may not settle conveniently at an equilibrium price in the manner of Marshall's scissors. Theorists have tried to accommodate this by the so-called 'cobweb' theorem illustrated in Figure 3.2(b). In other words, demand and supply may take time to converge towards the equilibrium price, *e*, as illustrated in Marshall's 'scissors' model. On the other hand, as in Figure 3.2(c), they may as easily diverge from *e* in a disequilibrium process. At any one time, the price trend may be difficult to determine. Certainly it may be unstable rather than stable, and engender uncertainty for buyers and sellers alike. Such price instability tends to be the case the bigger and more homogenous the markets concerned, for instance those for world commodities exported by less developed countries, for example tea, coffee, copper, zinc, etc.

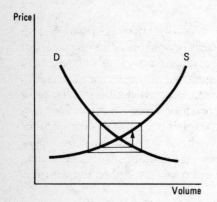

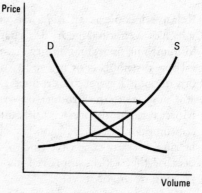

FIG. 3.2(b)   Convergent or implosive cobweb and price determination

FIG. 3.2(c)   Divergent or explosive cobweb and indeterminate price

This is one reason why bigger business seeks to secure relative stability in prices and markets rather than experiment in the short run with changes designed to prompt consumer shifts up or down a demand curve. To do so could wreak havoc with the planning of the investment necessary to match rapid changes in demand, and consequent shifts along the supply curve. Much of the product or brand attachment possible through advertising comes into this category of the search for relative stability and security of markets. It is part of the economics of 'imperfect' competition analysed later in this chapter, and is one of the reasons why firms spend so much on advertising (estimated at some £4.4 billion or 1.3 per cent of UK domestic product in 1985). Doubtless many firms are advertising product differences which are more apparent than real. Other advertisements are simply misleading, offer no significant information on the product, or suggest instead that unfulfilled social aspirations (e.g. to be an airline pilot or fashion model driving to work in a high performance sportscar) can be fulfilled by maintaining or changing preference for a minor article (such as a cigarette brand, a special after-shave lotion, or a particular eye shadow).

Subjectively, individuals may reckon advertising to be soothing, spurious or sexist, depending on their tastes and values. There may be strong grounds for claiming that there are better ways to camouflage derelict building sites, or 'break' radio and television programmes, than claiming that product 'X' gives better support or that six of 'Y' gives sex appeal. Certainly the aims of advertising might still be achieved at lesser cost to the consumer (since advertising expenditure is passed on in the price paid) by rules which provide for a ceiling to its share within any company's budget. If all companies' advertising budgets were lower, some at least might charge a lower price. But objectively, within the paradigm and values of a market economy, it has to be recognised that advertising is employed by firms not only to protect or increase market share, but also to gain a stability in demand relative to supply which a purely homogeneous product system would not ensure. In terms of Marshall's 'scissors', it may be one way of gaining equilibrium rather than ending up in a cobweb. In another sense it may simply suggest that personal consumption is good for well-being or welfare, while public services are good, bad or indifferent.

The Marshallian Framework

In practice, Marshall's contribution to modern economic theory was not limited to the 'scissors' of an equilibrium price of intersecting demand and supply. He was the foremost English-language exponent of the theory of perfect competition in the late nineteenth and early twentieth centuries. He has also thereby been the primary target for critics of the divorce between such a competitive model and the real world. By today's standards the criticism is valid. But by those of his own time, they are in part unfair. For one thing, Marshall developed his analysis when the structure of British industry was diverse and by and large competitive. For another, he was always careful to qualify his arguments. Indeed, in successive editions of his major text (Marshall, 1890) his qualifications often ranked as long or longer than the basic exposition. This gave rise to the not unfounded claim by some of his students, who included Keynes, that both the prosecution and defence of competition were 'all in Marshall'.

Moreover, Marshall himself did not employ the term 'microeconomics' (any more than Keynes in *The General Theory* wrote of 'macroeconomics'). Nor did he employ many of the graphical or algebraic simplifications which were later taught to students not adequately briefed on their restricted assumptions.

Nonetheless, the theory of perfect competition has with reason been identified with Marshall and broadly become known as 'Marshallian'. Marshall's basic model has become virtually the *sine qua non* foundation of the competitive process in elementary texts. Even if some authors such as Samuelson and Lipsey have shifted its exposition into the centre pages of their analysis, and started their exposition with macroeconomics, like the classical economists, their analytic structure is grounded on Marshallian micro-economic foundations.

The Basic Model

Despite the allowance for his own time and context, the basic Marshallian model of perfect competition depends on a number of assumptions which are hard or impossible to find in real world markets. They not only assume consumer sovereignty, but also imply specific conditions for the exercise of such sovereignty by consumers, including:

(1) *Many sellers*, i.e. a large number of independent firms in the market. This was clearly a key condition, since if the number of firms supplying goods was limited, or if their action was interdependent, there was more chance of their combining to raise price, dominate the terms and conditions of sale, and impose producer sovereignty.

(2) *Free entry* into markets by new firms. This related to the condition of a large number of firms from whose products sovereign consumers could choose. If those firms already established on the market can prevent new entrants to it, consumer sovereignty is very much in question.

(3) *Price-taking* by firms from consumers, rather than price-making by firms. In other words, consumer rationality meant that if one firm in the market raised its price over that of others for the uniform product, it would lose sales as consumers switched to other firms with lower prices.

(4) *Homogeneous products*, or in effect that the same rather than different

goods are being produced in given markets. This was one of the first aspects of the model challenged by critics in the 1930s for its unreality, since most firms offer and accent differences in their products. But it was demanded by the perfect competition model since different goods could command different prices on the market, qualifying the assumption of a uniform market price.

(5) *Perfect information* by both consumers and producers. On the consumer side this was important since information on lower prices offered by other firms was crucial to the effective exercise of consumer choice. For firms it was also important to know the prevailing market price lest by charging more the firm lost sales and revenue.

(6) *Rising costs* per unit of production at a given level of increased output. This is crucial since if costs fall indefinitely with increased output there is no reason why an early entry to a market with command of a new technology or product should not gain such a commanding lead as to end with an outright monopoly. Such rising costs are therefore a premise of three of the other conditions of the basic competitive model already cited, including (1) a plural supply side, composed of 'many sellers'; (2) 'free entry' (since the freedom is formal and unreal if an early entrant has already 'run away' with the market), and (3) 'price-taking' (since an earlier established and dominant firm could be able to impose prices if it also can block new entrants to the market).

Consumer Sovereignty

The combined six-point package of what we have called the basic model is not simply a theoretical device. It amounts to the preconditions for a paradigm of consumer sovereignty. As indicated earlier, Adam Smith was well aware of the importance of the relation between the first three conditions for the competitive process. As he put it in a phrase not often quoted by those who cite his 'invisible hand' as justification for unfettered competition: 'People of the same trade seldom meet together, even for merriment and diversion, but the conversation ends in a conspiracy against the public or in some contrivance to raise prices' (Smith, 1776, vol. 1, bk 1, p. 130).

As a result, despite the accolade sometimes paid to him by presidents of trade associations, Smith was opposed in principle to producers' organisations because in getting entrepreneurs together they helped them tie up the market and limit consumer choice. Such producer combinations and trusts to restrict competition were already becoming a major force in Germany and the United States at the end of the nineteenth century when Marshall was expounding the basic perfect competition model. They fulfilled many of Smith's fears, contradicted the perfect competition model and – in the US case – led to strong demands for anti-trust powers. Thus emergent producer power broke up the Marshallian model almost as soon as he had formulated it.

Information and Expectations

Perfect information, rather than effective information, is a rigid condition for the perfect competition model. But its assumptions ranged wider than consumers and producers knowing what was being charged elsewhere on the market. In a folklore market place, of the kind taught to children and romanticised by Milton Friedman, information can be gained on the price of mussels by 'shopping around'. But such local information may be offset by joint monopolies in small communities, or the collusion on pricing of such concern to Adam Smith, where only two or three sellers may easily agree to set mutually advantageous price levels.

Moreover, models of perfect competition stress information to producers rather than consumers. 'Disinformation' from certain forms of advertising are discounted in the model, despite the fact that in the modern economy they may involve millions of pounds or dollars spent on claiming fictitious differences between effectively identical products.

But advertising is not the only problem. As stressed by Richardson (1960, chapter 2), information becomes highly imperfect when a firm is trying to foretell future demand rather than respond to current demand in the market-place. Indeed, perfect information on markets and their response to price changes may be not only difficult but impossible. The best current information can be rendered redundant by change in consumption patterns, new products or services or new technologies by the time that investment has been committed. This weak link, which was to prove important in the so-called theory of 'rational expectations' stressed by monetarists in the 1970s and 1980s, stemmed directly from the rational information assumptions of perfect competition. It is a link which French planners since the war, with varying degrees of success, have tried to overcome through 'indicative' planning of a kind which spelled out overall trends, and set targets, based on information which no individual firm could itself collate.

Elastic Assumptions

Price-taking by firms from sovereign consumers is also crucial to perfect competition. Lipsey (1979, p. 245) made it his first assumption in setting out the theory of perfect competition. He also stressed that the individual firm in perfect competition is assumed to be faced with a perfectly elastic demand for its products – meaning that demand will be proportionately responsive to

changes in price. Thus in place of the old Latin warning of *caveat emptor* –
that the buyer should take care – the perfect competition model stresses
caveat vendor – that the seller must take care not to sell above the market or
industry price.

The concept of elasticity is widely used by economists – more so than it may
be by firms themselves. In principle it means that a given change in X will
produce a given change in Y. Thus the price elasticity of demand is the ratio of
the change in the amount purchased to the change in price; the price elasticity
of supply is its inverse, i.e. the ratio of the output response by firms to a
change in price; income elasticity of demand means the change in demand as a
ratio of the change in the level of income, while *cross-price elasticity* means
the change in demand for one commodity at a given price (or change of price)
in relation to the prices (or changed prices) of other commodities.

There is a conventional vocabulary on elasticitiy. Thus if the percentage
increase in demand is greater than the percentage increase in price (or
income), the elasticity of demand is said to be greater than unity, whereas if it
is lower it is less than unity. Conventional textbooks have elaborated such
concepts of elasticity in detail for decades. One of the most realistic
expositions is Lipsey's (1979, chapter 9).

The theoretical principles are simple enough, granted a little attention. But
principles and practice diverge. For one thing, while measurement of
elasticities *ex post*, or after the event, may be straightforward (depending on
the availability of data), forward forecasts of elasticities *ex ante* are much
harder to establish. This is not only a matter of anyone's difficulty in
foretelling the future, but is especially hard in terms of estimating overall
cross-elasticities for any institution other than government, which itself may
find the exercise unduly complex without information on anticipated
advance price changes from at least the leading firms in a given market.
Further, there is no way, short of collusion, by which firms in a given market
can predict in advance rather than assess the response to their own price
changes from leading competitors. Consequently, leading firms in an
oligopoly group watch the pricing of other leaders as closely or more closely
than they do price followers in the micro sector, or the response to price
changes of the consumer.

There are some reasons, despite textbook assumptions, why most firms in
practice do not bother to estimate demand elasticities in relation to
alternative price levels in setting prices on their products. Some may promote
market research for a new product in a particular area (such as Hampshire in
the UK or New Hampshire in the US) to test price elasticity. But even in
sample testing, such companies face the need to offset not only the cross-
elasticity of demand for competing products – sometimes sold under different
brand names by themselves, whether cars or cosmetics – but also income

elasticity – where average income in Hampshire or New Hampshire may be different from York or New York. Put simply, how much you have to spend will influence how much you are able to buy, at whatever price. Such social distribution of income therefore will influence the spatial or regional distribution of a firm's sales efforts.

3.2   The Role of Rising Costs

To preserve its key condition of many sellers, conventional theory needed to assume that an enterprise incurred higher costs with an increased volume of output. As already indicated, if total costs did not rise but fell with a larger production run, those firms first in the industry could 'run away' with the market, leaving would-be entrants behind, and possibly ending with an outright monopoly.

Marginal or Average?

The debate between the forces working for or against competition has taken both basic and esoteric forms. A basic tool of the theory was the role of marginal versus average costs. Its esoteric application was the defence of a particular shape of a cost curve assumed to be representative for firms in a given industry or market.

To assess the scope and limits of the theory we need to be clear about the concepts of average and marginal cost. The concept of marginal cost concerns the cost of an additional unit of output. Beloved by many economists, it has proved the bane of those firms which have tried to measure it (as shown later in this chapter). The concept of average costs is well known to firms themselves and means what it appears to mean – i.e. the average costs overall for a given level of output.

The difference between the marginal and average concepts may become plainer by a comparison with football scores (whether British or American). Thus if a given player, for our purposes Billy Hero, has an average score for the season so far of one goal per match, but in the tenth match of the season scores twice, this marginal score of two will raise his average score to 1.1. If, by contrast, after pulling a muscle in the first half, a row with the team manager or simply better opposition, he scores nothing in the tenth game, his marginal score of zero will reduce his average score to 0.9.

Translating this through to cost schedules in Figure 3.3(a), if marginal cost represented by mc is falling (as when Billy Hero pulls a muscle), it will in turn pull down the average cost ac. This results in a downward trend of both the marginal and average cost curves for the firm at volume x. Inversely, Figure

3.3(b) shows that when marginal cost rises (as when Billy Hero carries all before him and increases his average score), average cost also will rise,. In other words, the rise or fall in marginal costs implies a corresponding rise or fall in average costs. For conventional theory there is an additional factor of importance to the equilibrium theory of markets. In terms of Figure 3.3(b), this assumes that firms will continue producing until their rising marginal cost, *mc*, intersects the prevailing price level at output *y*. This is the so-called equilibrium price which is supposed to adjust supply and demand in a perfectly competitive economy.

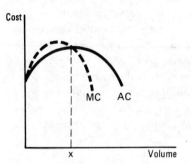

FIG. 3.3(a) Falling marginal and average cost

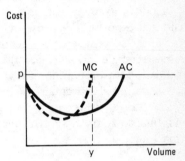

FIG. 3.3(b) Rising marginal and average cost

Constant and Variable Costs

But why should marginal costs rise in the manner assumed in conventional theory and faithfully reproduced by Samuelson (1976), Lipsey (1975) and Begg, Fischer and Dornbusch (1984)?

For instance, Begg, Fischer and Dornbusch (1984, p. 145) claim that average costs rise because of growing managerial inefficiency with an increase in the size of the firm, or through locational diseconomies (or locating the second or third plant in a less optimal location than the first). But as we will see in Chapters 4 and 6, the first claim is contentious, while the second is counter-factual (i.e. multinational big business has located its second and third plant in less costly locations, taking advantage of lower cost labour, in less developed regions or less developed countries in the world economy).

Certainly the initial fall in the average cost of the firm is not hard to understand. No production is for free. Firms incur costs in purchasing, renting or building premises, of connecting power, water or communications supply, buying or building equipment, gaining insurance cover, etc. All of these are so-called fixed costs. Added to them are the costs of hiring workers –

more with an expansion of demand, less with a contraction; using more or less energy or raw materials or components with an expansion or contraction of output etc. These are so-called variable costs.

Granted given fixed costs, the so-called *unit* costs (or costs per unit of output) will fall, and in the first instance fall very substantially. For instance, if the constant or fixed investment for a given product such as a refrigerator is £6 million, and if it assumed that in the short run variable costs are also constant (inasmuch as energy costs or wage rates do not change within a few days), then the nominal cost of the first fridge will be £6 million; that of the second fridge £3 million, that of the third £2 million, etc., until in due course a larger volume of output reaches the more reasonable cost of, say, £100.

Such a fall in average costs is described in the curve of Figure 3.4(a). Conventional exposition dispenses with the upper extreme and focuses on that part of the curve where costs get more realistic (i.e. that area within the horizontal rectangle in Figure 3.4(a)). As shown in Figure 3.4(b), for the understandable reason that no firm would wish to sell its first 'off the line' product at its initial marginal cost of £6 million when average cost may shortly fall to £100, firms tend to set price at a level reflecting average rather than marginal costs, or, as shown later in this chapter, at average cost plus a profit mark-up.

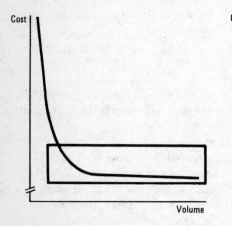
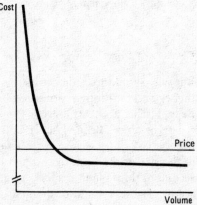

FIG. 3.4(a) Declining long-run average cost with increased output

FIG. 3.4(b) Declining long-run average cost and average/normal price

Marginal Costs and Revenues

So far so good, without loss of realism. However, perfect competition theory (and the neoclassical theory derived from it) is not notably realistic. Unlike our football hero, whose marginal score per match pulls up, pulls down or equals the average score, perfect competition assumes that at a given point the marginal costs of the firm always rise, thus causing an increase in average costs.

This implausible assumption is not accidental. It plays a crucial role in the theory of the equilibrium of the firm and of the structure of supply in the conventional model of the market economy. It also thereby legitimates the claim of consumer versus producer sovereignty.

The point can be seen clearly by taking Samuelson's own figures representing the different implications of falling or rising average costs. Thus in our Figures 3.5(a)–(c), derived from the tenth edition of *Economics* (1976, p. 486), Samuelson admits that when costs fall indefinitely, as in Figure 3.5(a), with marginal costs lower than average costs, any one firm can expand to monopolise the industry. In figure 3.5(b) it is assumed that for some reason costs eventually rise (in which case it is the rise in marginal costs which forces average costs up). But because this allows a sizeable volume of output before costs rise, the market could be supplied by only a few firms. For perfect competition to fulfil its condition of many sellers, as in Figure 3.5(c), industry demand must be *much* bigger than the maximum efficient production for any one firm. Thus whether marginal and average costs rise quickly, rise late or continue to fall will influence whether a market is competitive, dominated by a few firms, or an outright monopoly.

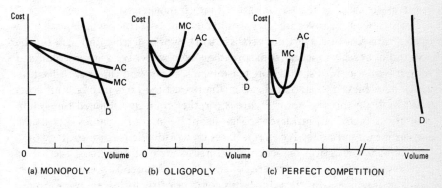

FIG. 3.5   Monopoly, oligopoly and competition: the key role of cost structures

Short-Run Shift Work

As already indicated, the initial fall in a cost curve – from left to right – is not hard to understand. Investment involves fixed costs, and increased pro-duction spreads the cost per unit of output. But it is harder to grasp why costs should later rise in a U-shaped manner – as in Figures 3.5(b) and (c) – rather than fall with increased output and economies of larger-scale production.

One of the best ways to avoid total loss of realism may be to analyse those conditions under which costs can rise in the *short run*, which is the time-period considered by the basic U-shaped exposition in perfect competition theory.

Take for instance the situation of shift work in a single-plant company, i.e. an enterprise with only one factory or establishment. As represented in Figure 3.6, the unit costs of production, or the costs per unit of output, fall during the first eight-hour shift of the day. They fall further during the second eight-hour shift, approaching their lowest point at *a*. Thus it is only during the second eight-hour shift that the plant achieves its optimal operating efficiency. But in the third shift, unit costs rise from *b* to *e* on the 'realistic' assumption that workers would be paid more for late evening and early morning production with 'anti-social' hours. Tibor Scitovsky (1952, pp. 315–16) stresses such principles of different costs with shift working and the fact that a producer faces different cost implications 'by overtime work, by introducing a night shift, or by expanding plant capacity'.

However, there is no necessary reason why even short-run costs for a single plant should rise in a symmetric U-shape. Whether unit costs rise, stay constant or fall in the third shift will depend on a variety of factors. One will be the ratio of extra pay rates for overtime in the third shift to normal wage costs. It is possible but unlikely that overtime rates alone would push the cost curve in the third shift up to *e*, rather than somewhere short of it.

Just where higher overtime pay would push the cost curve will depend both on the rate paid for overtime versus normal working time and also on the economies of scale or gains from spreading fixed costs over a larger volume of output with the third shift. Quite feasibly, if 100 per cent capacity utilisation could be achieved at standard rather than overtime rates of pay, unit costs would fall on the line *ac* in Figure 3.6 rather than *abe*. Indeed this 'plant utilisation' factor is considered so significant by some companies such as the Swedish multinational SKF that it bases its worldwide pricing strategy on a 'full capacity' criterion or benchmark, irrespective of other cost factors or even exchange rates (see further Holland, 1987, chapter 5). Certainly higher overtime payments during a third shift could be offset by lower costs through fuller capacity use, resulting in the average line *abd* in Figure 3.6.

External versus Internal

There is an alternative 'realistic' explanation of the rise of cost curves for existing plant and production. This would result from exogenous (i.e. external) cost increases in inputs to production in the longer run over which

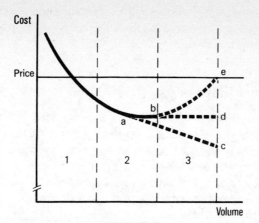

FIG. 3.6   Rising, constant or falling costs with three-shift plant utilisation

the firm had no control. Thus, under inflationary conditions such as those of the last quarter-century, and especially the last fifteen years, firms may find that an increase in the cost of energy, raw materials or components increase the cost of production per unit of output (unit costs). They also may find that wage increases in the industry or market as a whole raise their costs, since they need to meet them or face losing labour (especially skilled labour) to competitors.

In following chapters it is recognised that costs may rise for both big and small business through such exogenous or external factors. But the analysis also stresses that big-business leaders may destabilise the cost schedules of smaller enterprise by setting the pace in upwards wage settlements. They may achieve the same effect by charging higher prices for components used by smaller firms. Moreover, especially since the formation of OPEC and the oil price increases since 1973, big and small firms alike may be subject to cost increase at short notice in both direct energy costs and the higher costs of raw materials or components reflecting such cost increases in suppliers, e.g. higher cost electricity, aluminium or other metals, or manufactured components themselves.

However, such long-run external factors play no part in the assumption of rising cost curves in the basic perfect competition model, where rising marginal costs are assumed to be both short run and internal to the analysis.

For some time, stress was laid in the conventional theory of the allegedly representative firm on the claim that bigger business was more complex and more costly to manage than the smaller firm of the owner-entrepreneur. Conversely, and as elaborated in the debate on the size and growth of the firm in the following chapter, management specialisation in bigger business can bring with it the same kind of efficiency gains from division of labour and job expertise as Adam Smith observed in most forms of production including his classic example of pin-making.

Empty Economic Envelopes

Besides, the conventional model of rising costs runs into difficulty when it tries to combine short-run average costs for individual plant with long-run average costs for the enterprise as a whole. For instance, Figure 3.7(a) shows the conventional model of a long-run average cost curve or *LAC*, which 'envelopes' three *sac* or short-run average cost curves. Though nominally simple, both the shape of the envelope and what it contains – crucial to the theory of competitive markets – are very much open to question.

First, does the 'envelope' refer to different plant of the same company, or different firms in the same industry? If the long-run average cost curve is for an individual firm with three separate plants, and assuming a 'homogeneous' product, the assumption of rising short-run costs of plant utilisation is inapplicable and unrealistic. It does not explain why the LAC should rise from its minimum point for plant 2 to the higher point enveloping a raised cost for plant 3. If average costs rise with further production, why should any well-managed and profit-maximising firm decide to proceed with plant 3 at all? The higher cost curve for plant 3 is certainly inconsistent with efficiency gains from technical progress or economies of scale through lowering units costs in mass production.

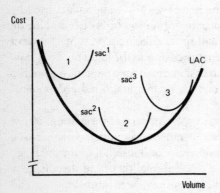
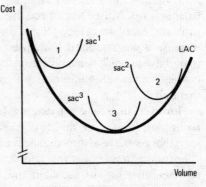

FIG. 3.7(a) The conventional short- and long-run cost 'envelope'

FIG. 3.7(b) The conventional model with reversed plant sequence

Nor can the conventional U-shaped *LAC* 'envelope' be defended on the lines of Figure 3.7(b), where its form is preserved but the positions of plant 2 and plant 3 are reversed. This conforms more with common sense. Through applied technical progress and innovation over time, the second plant (sac^2) should have lower short-run costs than the first (sac^1), and the third plant lower costs still, for the same reasons.

In principle it is easy enough to join the minimum short-run average cost or *sac* curves for the three plant and emerge with a long-run LAC 'envelope' which appears to conform with the conventional model. But the appearance is misleading. For one thing, the volume of production or scale of overall operations has to be taken off the horizontal axis of the diagram where it is traditionally placed: i.e. the envelope LAC curve no longer represents an association over time of rising costs with rising scale of production, but an abstraction picturing the second plant as occurring after the third. As a *gestalt* it may make sense. But it is not a conventional cost curve.

If the representation of short and long-run costs is to be realistic for plant with different levels of efficiency, it will be closer to the situation in Figure 3.7(c). This assumes that the individual plant achieve lower short-run average costs sac^1 to sac^3 over time, which is at least consistent with the assumption of applied technical progress and greater productivity. But the LAC is not U-shaped rather than a half-U. Nor is there any reason why long-run average costs should rise from the lowest point reached rather than fall further if additional plant with increased efficiency and lower short-run costs are added to production.

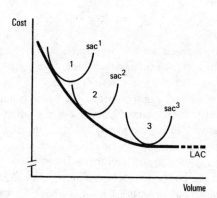

FIG. 3.7(c)   The falling long-run cost curve

Different Efficiencies

Conventional microeconomic theory is not salvaged from these difficulties if it allows differing efficiencies between either different plant or different firms in an industry. This is especially clear when we combine unequal costs with price levels implying a normal profit over and above those costs.

For instance, assume in the first instance that sac^{1-3} in Figures 3.8(a)–(c) represent short-run average cost curves for a homogeneous product *by the same firm*. It does not make sense for the firm to charge different prices p^1–p^3 for the goods produced at different short-run costs in different plant. If it charged an average price for the three plant equivalent to p^2, this would 'normalise' their respective profits, thereby enabling the firm to meet demand without closing down its least efficient establishment and thus losing market share.

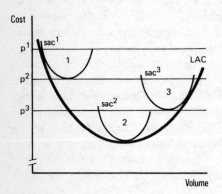

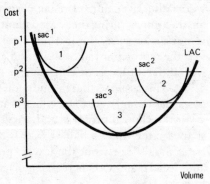

FIG. 3.8(a) The conventional cost 'envelope' with prices

FIG. 3.8(b) The reversed plant sequence with prices

But the situation is transformed if sac^{1-3} in Figures 3.8(a)–(c) represent the costs of *different firms*. In such a case, under competitive conditions, there is nothing to prevent the least-cost enterprise – firm 2 in Figure 3.8(a) and firm 3 in Figures 3.8(b) and (c) – from charging a price, p^3, which is below the least-cost point of the short-run average cost curves for the other firms in the market. If we take Adam Smith seriously, this is precisely what the competitive process is supposed to be about.

However, if we put together Smith's warning that when two or three producers are gathered together 'even for merriment or diversion' they will seek to conspire against the public interest by a contrivance to raise prices, with Samuelson's oligopoly structure in Figure 3.5(b), it is far from impossible that the few firms concerned would seek tacitly or explicitly to agree to determine price at the level of p^1.

Alternatively, the enterprise with the lowest short-run average cost could seek to adapt its capacity to meet market demand at price p^3 by investing in

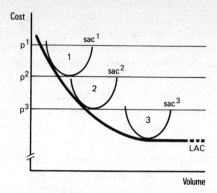

FIG. 3.8(C) The falling long-run cost curve with prices

new plant. In principle, under conditions of perfect competition, where information, capital and technology are freely available to all, there would be no barrier to the firms with the higher short-run average costs following suit by undertaking further investment themselves in new capacity on the lower cost schedule. But in fact, as elaborated in Chapter 6, there is a range of barriers to such 'follow-the-leader' investment and pricing by firms with initially higher cost schedules. Rather than following the leader, they may fall behind in investment and innovation, fall back in sales, and shortly fall out of the market.

Non-Sequitur

Even staying with the paradigm of the conventional competitive model, the assumption of U-shaped long-run average cost curves is unrealistic. For the shape of the curve itself implies that if firms are producing at the lowest point on their long-run cost curve, they must by definition have spare capacity which they have not employed because of (assumed) rising short-run costs. In other words, the conventional competitive model as applied by Samuelson, Lipsey or Begg, Fischer and Dornbusch implies excess capacity and a less than optimal use of resources not only for the individual firm but also for society as a whole.

As Lipsey himself has put it (1975, p. 259): 'if a perfectly competitive industry is in long-run equilibrium, each individual firm must be producing at the minimum point of its long-run average total cost curve – i.e. it must not have further unexploited economies of scale within its grasp.' As he adds, 'these would be shown by a downward slope of the long-run cost curve at the firm's present level of output.'

But Lipsey does not follow through the logic of the observation. The diagram he introduces relating short- and long-run cost curves – similar to our Figure 3.9(a) – is literally a *non-sequitur*. It is not without reason that in his fourth edition he advises readers in a footnote that this section of his text (on economies of scale) 'can be skipped without loss of continuity', and indeed he drops the diagram (ibid., Figure 20.5) from his fifth edition. However, the same diagram is reproduced in Samuelson, despite the fact that its U-shaped long-run average cost curve is hypothetical rather than real.

In Chapter 24 of the tenth edition of his *Economics* (1976, p. 471) Samuelson describes the conventional long-run cost curve and its envelope of shorter-run costs, claiming that this now gives us all the technical apparatus of the various costs concepts needed to tackle the problem of how any firm will find its maximum profit equilibrium. But he admits that, if the firm builds a larger plant, the new *sac* or short-run average cost curve must be drawn further to the right. Samuelson then supposes that: 'The firm is still in the planning stage, still quite uncommitted by any fixed obligations. It can write down all possible different U-shaped *sac* curves, and then choose to select for each prescribed output the *sac* that gives it the lowest costs.'

Forms and Facts

Samuelson therefore assumes that firms anticipate that their long-run marginal cost, or *LMC*, will intersect their hypothetical long-run average cost curve at point M, and that as a result of *assumed* rising long-run average cost they will not install the plant represented by the short-run average cost curves 4 and 5 to the right of M in the diagram. The assumption of a rising long-run average cost curve is preserved. But Samuelson admits that the company would not in fact invest in plant 4 and 5 since this would mean a rise in its long-run average cost. Thus it is only the left-hand, or half-U, downwards curve of the *LAC* in Samuelson's figure which is for real. The right-hand upwards shift, completing the theoretical U-shaped *LAC* curve (drawn solid in his figure but broken in ours), is simply imagined. Such unreal conclusions from unreal premises are faithfully reproduced by Begg, Fischer and Dornbusch, who derive their figure of rising long-run average costs from purely hypothetical data (1984, Fig. 7.5, p. 146 and Table 7.4, p. 142).

By the same token, it is not only the rise in the *LAC* curve on the right-hand side of Figure 3.9(a) which is hypothetical, but also the rising long-run marginal cost curve *LMC*. As already admitted in Figures 3.5(b) and (c), derived from Samuelson, if marginal costs rise at all they do so after stemming from short-run rather than long-run cost curves. So such assumed rising marginal costs have already been accounted for in the U shape of the *sac* curves themselves. Their application to a rising long-run marginal cost curve,

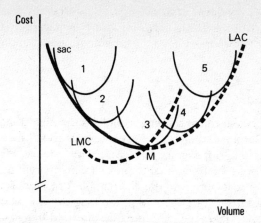

FIG. 3.9(a) Samuelson's hypothetical rising long-run average cost curve

LMC, intersecting the long-run average cost curve, *LAC*, as in Figure 3.9(a) reflects only the assumed rising long-run average cost curve after *M*. It is a (long-run) abstraction derived from a (short-run) abstraction, both which are premised on pure hypothesis in the first place.

The question whether the marginal cost curve of the plant is horizontal or falling cannot be settled at the theoretical level alone. If the principles of 'positive' economics are to be followed through by the empirical testing of *a priori* assumptions, the relative shape of the curves needs to be determined by actual experience. Yet, as already indicated, virtually no firm in practice tries to estimate marginal costs and (as shown later) some of those which have tried have given up the effort. By contrast, as stressed in the analysis of Figure 3.6, most firms are highly sensitive to the importance of full utilisation of capacity. In the real world any enterprise operating at half capacity or at the lowest point on its *LAC* curve, is likely to be making a thumping loss. Few firms, depending on market circumstances, make a profit at two-thirds of capacity. Some need to get near to four-fifths or more before breaking even.

Many firms, including the giant Japanese *keiretsu*, react to any actual increase in long-run costs by analysing its specific reasons and responding to them rather than assuming theoretical constraints. Indeed it is not entirely frivolous to suggest that one of the reasons why Japanese business succeeded in penetrating markets in the postwar global economy is that its managers never learned, or were taught to ignore, the principle of rising costs with larger output as expounded by Samuelson and Lipsey to millions of economics students in the English-speaking countries. Japanese management is prophetic, as evidenced by Soichiro Honda standing on a tangerine box in 1948 and predicting to his two dozen employees (Ohmae, 1985, p. 86) that his company would conquer world markets. By contrast, Anglo-American economic theory is prophylactic, advising future managers that there are necessary and intrinsic constraints to the growth of output, and thus of the firm.

Falling Long-Run Costs

This lapse in basic management training is doubly surprising granted that the Lipsey-Samuelson argument allows for average costs to fall for the first U-shaped half of the long-run average cost curve. For instance, Figure 3.9(b) translates the previous analysis of constant or falling marginal cost to the context of long-run cost curves. In the diagram, mc^a and mc^b represent the marginal costs for two plant lying within the long-run average cost curve envelope LAC^1. LAC^1 takes the same form (despite the different shape of the marginal cost curves which it envelopes) as the half-U-shaped LAC curve derived from Samuelson in Figure 3.9(a).

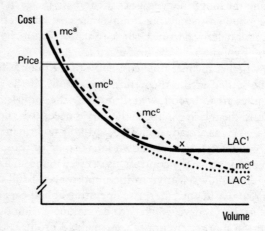

FIG. 3.9(b)   Long-run costs in practice

But with continuously falling marginal cost curves on the line mc^c to mc^d, a lower and still declining long-run average cost schedule, LAC^2, is probable. In contrast with Samuelson's assumption of rising marginal costs, it is possible that, due to failure to fully utilise the third plant through insufficient demand, there may be an output limit at x. For demand reasons of insufficient sales, rather than Samuelson's supply constraints, this gives the same kind of result for the long-run average cost curve LAC^1 as for Samuelson. However, if marginal costs continue to fall with fuller plant utilisation from mc^c through to mc^d, then both marginal and average costs would continually be falling rather than rising in the manner assumed by Samuelson and the conventional textbook model. Logically, the long-run average cost curve would lie not at LAC^1 but at a new low of LAC^2. An indirect illustration of such falling long-run average costs is given by Toyota, which trebled its vehicle output between the early 1970s and the early 1980s without increasing its labour force (Ohmae, 1985, p. 4). Such analysis anticipates the theory of the growth of micro and mesoeconomic enterprise in following chapters.

4.3   Imperfect Competition

The theory of imperfect competition is familiar in various basic forms from many elementary texts. What is less familiar to many students is the wider context in which it has been applied, and the reasons why it has continued to play a key role in the macro-micro synthesis many years after some of its main exponents – such as Joan Robinson – have themselves discarded or dismissed it.

It is important to recognise how such market theory in the interwar period influenced Keynes himself, as well as Hicks, Samuelson, Lipsey and others who have dominated the teaching of postwar macroeconomics. Keynes, for instance, assumed a framework of 'perfect and imperfect competition' on the supply side of the economy. He claimed that macroeconomic demand theory could be safely founded on such perfect or imperfect economics of supply. Depending on one's viewpoint this may or may not have been as understandable as Marshall's assumption of a competitive supply structure. Certainly concentration in British industry in the first half of the twentieth century was relatively unpronounced while in Germany and the United States from the 1880s until WWI, as well evidenced by Hilferding (1910), it was dramatic. But this *stasis* in supply structures prompted Keynes and his disciples to overestimate the significance of demand management relative to public intervention in the structure of supply.

A Demand Theory

There were other reasons for Keynes' neglect of the significance of changes in supply structures. For one thing, while the theory of imperfect competition advanced in the Cambridge of his time qualified Marshall's assumption of consumer sovereignty, it did so by stressing imperfections in *demand*. Such imperfections stemmed essentially from the 'real world' assumption of heterogeneous or differentiated products, i.e. products which are different between – or within – firms due to brand attachment, differences in specification, etc, thereby giving a margin of price discrimination to firms over and above the concept of a prevailing market price. For example, in today's terms, Ford produces many different automobiles such as the Escort, Capri, Sierra, Granada, etc. Each of these 'brand names' are further differentiated with L, GL, GLS and Ghia versions of the same model.

But imperfect competition nonetheless does have implications for the theory of the supply side of the economy. In assuming that (1) there are limits to discrimination by individual firms, it also assumes, by implication, that (2) there is a limit to the share of the overall market which firms can gain at such differentiated prices without losing customers to other firms, and (3) a move away from price as the main instrument of competitive behaviour to other non-price factors such as 'image' and 'brand attachment'.

The pioneers of imperfect or monopolistic competition theory were Joan Robinson in Britain and Edward Chamberlin in the United States. Joan Robinson's *The Economics of Imperfect Competition* appeared in Britain in 1933 and Chamberlin's *The Theory of Monopolistic Competition* in the US in the same year. But one of the most important challenges to perfect competition theory in the interwar period was an article in *The Economic Journal* of 1926 by Piero Sraffa. This stressed the implications of both differentiated products and economies of scale in modifying the competitive process.

Sraffa's Insight

Sraffa stressed something missing in perfect competition theory – the plain and clear influence on demand of non-price factors. These included habit or custom, familiarity, confidence in the quality of the product, proximity, the possibility of obtaining credit, the reputation of a trade-mark, sign or name with high traditions, or other special features. As he put it:

> When each of the firms producing a commodity is in such a position the general market for the commodity is sub-divided into a series of distinct markets; within its own market and under the protection of its own barrier each enjoys a position whereby it obtains advantages which – if not in extent at least in their nature – are equal to those enjoyed by the ordinary monopolist.

Sraffa's article is justly famous – but perhaps insufficiently so, since it is hard to find much of significance in the later and more elaborate theories of 'imperfect' and 'monopolistic' competition which it does not in briefer form contain. Joan Robinson's *Economics of Imperfect Competition* includes specific indebtedness to Sraffa and the admission of the need for a 'new approach' beyond perfect competition analysis. Much of the considerable debate about the contrast or similarity between the Robinson and

Chamberlin theses might have been avoided had the respective authors managed to light upon the other's title. For Chamberlin's work is more an analysis of what is generally known as 'imperfection' than of what is generally understood by 'monopoly', while Joan Robinson's work is as much a thesis on monopoly proper as an analysis of the problems of 'highly substitutable but not identical' commodities. Certainly both Chamberlin and Robinson had been anticipated by Sraffa in his elaboration of product differentiation and its consequences.

Structural Imperfections

When allowance has been made for both the varying terminology and variable geometry in the original debate, the essentials of the theory of imperfect competition remain important.

But to get at these essentials, and identify how different or 'imperfect' prices imply different and unequal profits, we need to cut away the assumption in conventional exposition of micro theory that average cost curves in turn imply average or normal profits. In this exposition and our later analysis of the competition process, profit is represented by the difference between cost and price, and not implied by cost curves.

For instance, even following part of conventional theory and assuming a rising U-shaped cost curve, as shown in Figure 3.10(a), differentiation and brand attachment imply that whereas the perfectly competitive company would only be able to charge price p^1 at output x, the imperfectly competitive company can charge price p^2 at output y.

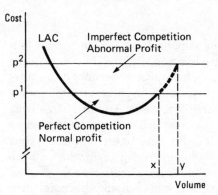

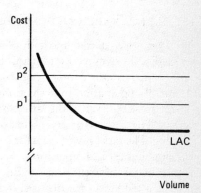

FIG. 3.10(a) Imperfect competition with rising costs

FIG. 3.10(b) Imperfect competition with constant returns to scale

But arguments have already been made against the standard assumptions of U-shaped cost curves. In the long run, declining cost schedules for individual plant through productivity-raising technical progress will result in a half U-shaped or L-shaped LAC envelope. Thus, as indicated in Figure 3.10(b), the imperfectly competitive company with an 'L-shaped' LAC curve could still increase price from p^1 to p^2 because of product differentiation and brand attachment. The difference on the supply side is that in the case of Figure 3.10(a) – with a U-shaped LAC curve – there is a limit to the growth and market share of the imperfectly competitive firm. With L-shaped cost curves, as in Figure 3.10(b), there is no such limit.

On the demand side, the case described in Figure 3.10(a) and (b) is directly relevant to real markets. For instance, the role of brand attachment is evident in the fact that supermarket chains in Britain, Europe or the United States sell instant coffee (which in essentials is no different from Maxwell House or Nescafé) under their own house name – while also selling Maxwell House and Nescafé at higher prices on the same shelves. Similar brand attachment is evident in the manner in which Wimpy and McDonalds licence the use of their name (with specified standards of presentation and service) for hamburger sales in premises which they do not own. Otherwise, individual companies may become synonymous with quality and low price, as with Marks and Spencer, where the company name is more important than the brand name St Michael. Inversely, the parent company may be almost anonymous to the individual consumer, as with the Matsushita Electric Industrial Company of Japan, better known in different world markets through its various brand names of National, Panasonic, Technics, Quasar and JVC.

Social and Spatial Dimensions

However, two of the most important imperfections in demand are not stressed in the original literature of imperfect competition. These arise not so much from structural imperfections through product differentiation, as from the social and spatial 'imperfections' of class and location. Tibor Scitovsky (1952, pp. 407–8) cited the latter soon after World War Two in the following terms: 'There is a variety of factors that may make price discrimination possible. The most obvious factor isolating different sectors of the . . . market is their geographical separation.' Scitovsky is describing a firm which can sell its product at different prices in different localities. He also cites the practice in the United States for doctors, dentists and some hospitals to charge their fees according to the patient's income. This amounts to discriminatory charging on the basis of social class. Such price discrimination is also common between domestic and industrial users of energy, off-peak and peak commuters on trains, or business and economy classes on airlines.

The second example given by Scitovsky assumes that a lower price will be charged, the lower the income of the individual or family concerned. But in fact, situations closer to the insights of the original theory of imperfect competition often combine social and spatial imperfections. For instance, local corner shops in both Europe and the United States are frequently able to charge higher prices than supermarkets or hypermarkets. One reason is sheer convenience buying. Another is necessity. The consumer with an automobile may have forgotten tea or coffee, butter or margarine on the big weekly shop, and be prepared to pay a higher price at the local corner shop when 'topping up' the weekly purchases. The consumer without an automobile may offset transport costs by buying locally, but have no option other than to pay the higher local price.

In Europe and to a lesser degree in the United States, elderly people or those on lower incomes may not be able to use or afford private transport to travel to a supermarket and load up with a week's groceries at a time. On public transport they will tend to be limited to literally what they can carry in both hands. When spending on food and drink constitutes a higher proportion of the personal expenditure of lower income groups, such a basic social 'imperfection' is not inconsiderable.

Paradox and Practice

Moreover, both the original theory of imperfect competition and its application to the market economy today share a common problem. Where does the power to raise prices through 'imperfections' confront the falling demand suggested by conventional theory and common sense and lower income?

Michal Kalecki (1954) stressed this point in his analysis of costs and prices. In other words, consumers will be less price-sensitive when income is high or if real incomes have been rising than when income is low or falling. In terms of conventional demand and price schedules as indicated in Figures 3.11(a) and (b), they may be willing to pay higher prices on the higher demand line D^1 rather than on the lower demand line D^2.

But hence a paradox. While the higher price and demand curves represented by Figures 3.11(a) and (b) imply fuller utilisation of capacity for individual firms through perfect competition and reduced price sensitivity, the conventional theory of imperfect competition for various reasons maintained that imperfections would give rise to spare capacity. The graphic form of the original debate took various arcane forms including so-called 'tangency' solutions. These amounted to saying that a firm with a 'differentiated' product would be able to gain only a limited share of an overall industry market. Focusing on such limits, it is therefore understandably claimed that such a 'differentiated' firm would not produce at any point

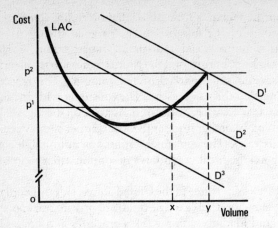

Fig. 3.11(a)   Demand, costs and imperfect competition

where demand was below (or less than tangential to) the least-cost point on its cost curve.

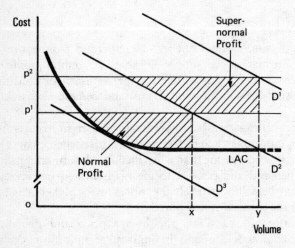

Fig. 3.11(b)   Demand imperfections and falling or constant costs

But if we change the reasoning from the industry as a whole to different firms in a given industry (or service), Figures 3.11(a) and (b) can give diametrically opposite results. Thus assuming a rising LAC curve as in Figure 3.10(a) and translating this through to Figure 3.11(a), it is true that demand at p^1 and D^2 would result in considerable under-utilisation of capacity. But the higher price p^2 and demand D^1, possible through the brand attachment and consumer loyalty of 'imperfect' competition, enables the firm concerned to achieve a fuller utilisation of its individual plant capacity (at volume y rather than volume x). The same in essence obtains with a half-U or L-shaped cost curve for the firm benefiting from scale economies in Figure 3.11(b). Thus those of us who might not be seen dead in a Ford but insist on a Volvo or BMW not only may (or may not) get a higher performance vehicle for a certainly higher price, but thereby help reduce spare capacity for relatively small Swedish and West German auto manufacturers, and enable them to achieve a higher volume output than would be possible for a homogeneous or undifferentiated motor vehicle at a uniform market price.

Qualifications

In these respects, it could be argued that the theorists of imperfect competition had come to precisely the reverse conclusions than the essentials of the theory itself would suggest. Combining brand attachment on the demand side with production economies of scale, both bigger and smaller enterprise should be able to avoid spare capacity, minimise costs and maximise profits.

Also the focus of the original theory of imperfect competition may have been misplaced. The key issue represented by the theory's assumption of 'price-making' power through differentiation may have been less limited scale economies in supply than the power of 'imperfect' business to raise prices over and above normal levels and therefore contribute to inflation. This is a theoretical issue to which the monetarists and so-called 'supply siders' in the United States have understandably paid little attention.

However, there are other respects in which the 'imperfect competition' debate should be reconsidered. They include such issues as demand elasticities, entry conditions to markets and the role of consumer goodwill.

Demand Elasticities. Joan Robinson (1954) defined competition as a market representing 'very high' elasticities of demand between producers of the same commodity. This is well and good within its own terms of reference. But such high demand elasticities could as readily penalise rather than profit a new entrant to the market. In other words, if products were really homogeneous and consumers could switch with impunity from one to another within a given market, there would be little incentive to a possible new entrant to undertake the costs necessary to penetrate a given market since on any day of the week or any quarter in the year the consumer might purchase the entire production of producer X while leaving the new entrant Y on the shelves. Thus the so-called competitive condition of 'homogeneous' products could ruin as many producers as it helped. Hence a paradox.

In some cases, at least, rather than limiting competition, product differentiation may be necessary to achieve it. There are other examples.

Entry Conditions. For instance, without equal financial resources or an established market share, the only way in which a new firm can hope to get a return on its initial investment is to establish some form of market identification which will ensure that it is not passed over in any month's or year's sales by the product of an established competitor from which it is indistinguishable. If it were required that products be homogeneous (by some governmental or trade authority), one might expect no new entry at all in markets with critical minimum economies of scale except from firms large enough to take a continued loss for some time in the market. On the other hand, as illustrated later in the case of IBM's dominance of the computer market, it can be argued that in many markets product differentiation and brand attachment operate in practice as barriers to entry.

Identification and Advertising

Therefore a key question is less whether products should be differentiated than to identify what kind of differentiation serves which purpose for whom. In turn this implies not only that there are types of differentiation which may prevent rather than promote competition (as with blocking entry), but also that some forms of differentiation are socially acceptable to consumers, while others are not.

For instance, the public may want a guarantee that the differentiation is not specious and that the consumer is not the victim of deceit. Thus they may demand descriptive advertising, with stringent penalties for unsubstantiated claims for products. To some degree legislation concerning safety standards on advertising drugs and medicines has increased the degree of consumer control over the 'imperfect' producer. On the other hand, especially when a new product is 'protected' for several years by patent or licensing legislation, its privileged brand name may give it a commanding consumer hold at monopolistic profits which other firms cannot later challenge, or will not risk challenging through fear of retaliation from an already dominant producer.

Goodwill. The term 'goodwill' has been used to describe much of the consumer attachment assumed in imperfect competition theory. The phenomenon of 'I always buy British' (or Japanese or American) comes under this category. Yet if some consumers do not know that their Rover in essence is a Honda or that their Ford Fiesta was made in Spain, not all consumers are unaware of differences in quality-price ratios, most especially those who are intermediate rather than final consumers, i.e. firms buying from other firms. Indeed inter-firm purchases tend to be 'rational' rather than the reverse. Firms cannot afford otherwise: few of them would stay in business for long if they bought from others merely because they had bought from them before, even if consumers may buy indefinitely on the basis of familiarity and past purchasing.

Overall, however, the goodwill reflected in consumer brand attachment can be crucial in modern markets. When General Motors bid to takeover the truck and car divisions of British Leyland in 1986, it did so not only in the hope of gaining plant and equipment which had been modernised under public ownership of the Leyland company. It also hoped to gain Leyland's share of the UK market which, hitherto, it had not been able to get simply by improving its Vauxhall product range. Product differentiation – however spurious in the case of the Honda car with a Rover badge – represented a barrier to GM's own expansion.

Kinks and Curves

Theorists influenced by the imperfect competition debate rapidly admitted that firms could not assume that they would be able to sell indefinitely at a raised price. They therefore claimed that there would be a 'kink' in the demand curve for the product. The theory of 'kinks', of entertainment value to students ever since it was devised, was pioneered by Hall and Hitch (1939) in their seminal study on actual costs and pricing – to which reference has already been made, and which will be developed further in the 'cost-plus' pricing argument in this chapter.

Hall and Hitch argued that the demand curve could take the form DD^1D^2 in Figure 3.12(a) rather than the path of DD^1D^3 assumed in the basic perfect competition model. A consequence of the 'kink' at D^1 is that the firm cannot count on standard elasticity of demand by lowering price.

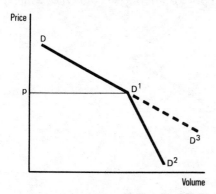

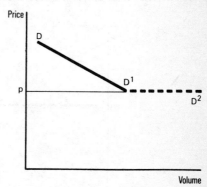

FIG. 3.12(a)   The Hall-Hitch kinked demand curve

FIG. 3.12(b)   The Wiles reverse kinked demand curve

The 'kink' does not simply limit sales and act as a disincentive to lower prices. It also has implications for the share of a given market which any one firm can command. In other words, the original kinked demand theory qualified perfect competition, but posed new conditions limiting sales which individual firms could achieve. The theory assumed markets will be composed of at least a few firms (oligopoly) rather than outright monopoly. The key point about 'kinks' is that if one of a group of oligopolies breaks loose from the pack and lowers price, the others will have to retaliate to retain their market share. It therefore pays them all to 'do as they would be done by' and keep price at its higher initial level.

However, Wiles (1961) has pointed out there is no reason why the demand curve for an individual enterprise should not be kinked in a reverse shape. In other words, as illustrated in Figure 3.12(b), the enterprise may find that whereas its imperfectly competitive sales fall for a given category of consumers on the demand line DD^1 at a given price, sales may continue for other categories of customers on the line D^1D^2.

Perverse or Practical?

None of this is quite so perverse as it may seem. In reality, reverse kinks are likely to occur either in the form assumed by Wiles and illustrated in Figure 3.12(b), or in the more accentuated reverse form of Figure 3.12(c). In Figure 3.12(b), it is assumed that sales would fall on the demand line DD^1 (similar in shape to the demand curve DD^1 in Figure 3.12(a)) but then 'flatten out' on the line D^1D^2 because consumers (whether individuals or other enterprises) are prepared to continue buying at the prevailing price.

Alternatively, as in Figure 3.12(c), a number of consumers may be served by the enterprise on preferential terms at price p^1 for the demand DD^1, while

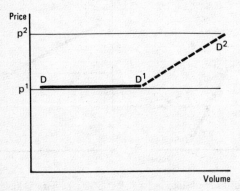

FIG. 3.12(c)   The reverse preference kinked demand curve

other consumers are prepared to pay the higher price of p^2 for the demand D^1D^2.

None of this is without foundation. Peter Holmes (1978) found that leading exporters from the UK were prepared to give preferential or lower prices to their regular customers on given product lines (comparable with the line DD^2 in Figure 3.12(c)) while charging higher prices to non-regular customers.

Similarly, some 70 per cent of the UK domestic automobile market is composed of 'fleet buyers' or car-hire firms which gain major discounts below the price charged to individual buyers. For producers, such 'reverse' kinks are less perverse than highly practical. They count on such preferential buyers (albeit at lower prices) to cover their basic fixed costs and facilitate volume production. Whether such 'kinks' are seen in the same light by any personal consumers who know of them is another matter. Certainly the 'sovereign consumers' in the UK passenger vehicles market are a handful of oligopolistic firms. The individual consumer is simply the target for 'profit creaming' at the higher price.

Gains From Scale

What already emerges from this analysis of the price implications of 'reverse' kinked curves is a pattern of unequal pricing for big and small buyers. Putting this together with an analysis of production economies of scale brings us closer to realistic analysis. For instance, Figure 3.13(a) indicates that in principle it is possible for an enterprise with a long-run average cost curve LAC^1 to achieve an equilibrium between average costs and average revenue

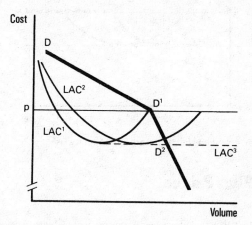

FIG.3.13(a)   Conventional kinked demand and spare capacity

at point D^1 for a prevailing price of p at the kink in the relevant demand curve. Conversely, assuming a rising U-shaped cost curve in the manner of the conventional microeconomic model, an enterprise with a long-run average cost curve LAC^2 would not achieve full capacity utilisation due to the kink in the demand curve. Therefore, at the prevailing price, the firm would not be able to equate average costs and average revenue. By contrast, a firm achieving constant economies of scale on the long-run average cost curve LAC^3 would still have spare capacity and unexploited economies of scale at point D^2.

However, in terms of Figure 3.13(b), under conditions of a reverse-kink demand curve of the kind hypothesised by Wiles, firms with long-run average cost curves rising in a U-shaped form equivalent to LAC^1 and LAC^2 would achieve an equilibrium solution at points D^1 and D^2 on the reverse-kink demand curve. Similarly, on the assumption of a level demand line after point D^1, the firm achieving long-run constant economies of scale on the line LAC^3 would not only be able to cover its costs but also achieve greater volume profits relative to the other two firms. It therefore would gain market share, and potentially market dominance. Such qualifications of the conventional model implied an alternative theory. A big step towards it came with the theory of 'cost-plus' or 'full-cost' pricing.

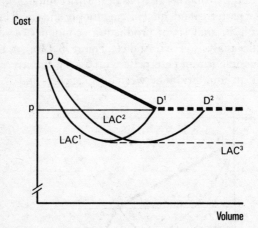

FIG. 3.13(b)   Reverse kinked demand and full capacity use

3.4   Cost-Plus Prices

In essentials 'cost-plus' or 'full-cost' pricing rejects the marginal cost analysis of perfect competition, and substitutes a theory of average costs.

Edward Chamberlin was always anxious to claim that the introduction of the 'full-cost' pricing hypothesis was a part of his theory of 'monopolistic competition' (Chamberlin, 1933, pp. 105–6). It could also be claimed that Marshall had not demanded more than that revenue should have a reasonable margin over cost.

Certainly, by the 1930s, as was already clear from the initiation of the kinked demand debate, the time had come to question the assumption that a large number of sellers could dispose of as much as they liked of a product at an established market price. As Romney Robinson (1961) has put it: 'Things simply do not come out this way. To suggest that they do is to encourage the opinion prevalent among businessmen that price is too important a thing to be left to the economists.'

Average versus Marginal

Some economists were coming to feel the same thing before the Second World War when Hall and Hitch (1939) quit the ivory tower of theory and asked some businessmen how they did it.

Hall and Hitch concluded that managers look for a price that covers average cost, regardless of marginal revenue and marginal cost – which they seldom know. This results *inter alia* from tacit or open collusion, consideration of long-run demand and costs, moral conviction of fairness, and uncertainty of the effects of price increases and decreases. Managers are afraid that, if they raised their price, rivals will take customers and markets by not following suit. Conversely by lowering price, competitors could at once do the same to avoid losing their customers – i.e. price competition could break out.

The Profit Mark-Up

Hall and Hitch claimed that price is not determined on the basis of equalising marginal revenue and cost, but by an average profit mark-up. As they put it: 'Prime (or direct) cost per unit is taken as the base, a percentage addition is made to cover overheads for indirect cost and a further conventional addition (frequently 10 per cent) is made for profit.' They believed this situation to be very common in pricing. Combined with their kinked demand theory, they called it a condition of 'imperfect competition with oligopoly'.

But how oligopolistic is the Hall-Hitch analysis? Roy Harrod (1952, Essay 8) claimed that their findings agree in general with the traditional view of the long-run results of competition, so long as there is free entry, and particularly if the firms in question are approximately 'representative' in the Marshallian sense.

Harrod's assumptions are very limited. Nonetheless, there are grounds for claiming that although nominally about monopolistic competition or oligopoly, the analysis of full or cost-plus pricing by its first-generation exponents stayed firmly within the paradigm of equal competition. In other words, however imperfect the market through product differentiation, and even in markets commanded by a few firms, the competitive process as assumed in the theory was still a competition between equals. The analysis of Chapter 5 on unequal competition between big and small firms – with the use of both price and unequal costs to prevent or force entry, or eliminate competitors – is not implied by the conventional full-cost argument.

Demand Conditions

It is not clear that firms pricing on a cost-plus basis have no sense of demand. No firm can avoid considering prices in relation to both demand and costs. In principle the firm has to solve two sets of simultaneous equations – cost as a function of turnover and sales as a function of price. If the producer is oligopolistic and influenced by comparable alternative suppliers for the product or service, this does not mean to say that no one has made any calculation concerning demand as a function of price. Indeed, it is *a priori* possible that in some full-cost calculations producers work back from prospective selling prices to possible cost-price combinations. If costs turn out *a posteriori* to be higher than an acceptable market price, the product may have to be (1) redesigned, (2) further differentiated to find its own market niche, (3) planned on a larger scale, or (4) abandoned.

Thus 'full-cost' or 'cost-plus' pricing can be indulged only if demand permits. The claim that it ignores demand is unwarranted. It is more true to say that it presupposes adequate demand to support a substantial volume of sales at cost plus price. Thus a producer will quote a price which will cover the full average cost of production including a conventional net profit margin. The main contrast with neoclassical marginal analysis is that producers do not chase demand fluctuations with changes in price. They even them out, taking averaged costs as well as expected average demand into account.

Variable Price Tactics

In practice, as already stressed by Richardson (1960), the pricing policies of firms will be influenced by macro as well as micro phenomena. It is even more vital for a firm in many circumstances that overall demand should be growing rapidly than that its competitors within the industry should be charging any particular price. If demand is sufficiently great, firms may lead prices upwards without loss. In a recession, they may be forced to cut price. Alternatively, price-setting leader firms may compensate for falling sales during a recession by raising price – less to abuse a dominant position than simply to protect cash flow.

J. M. Clark made several comments on the cost-plus principle in the light of an investigation of twenty large American companies. He found that most of them aimed at a 'target return' on investment by estimating the relation between costs and potential demand. Other pricing policies were pursued by the firms, but they were subordinate. These were (1) stabilisation of price and profit margins, (2) pricing to maintain or improve market position, (3) pricing to meet or follow competition, and (4) pricing determined by product differentiation (Clark, 1961, pp. 378ff).

Thus Clark's findings of a target profit mark-up on costs for US firms appear to corroborate the Hall–Hitch claims for pricing in the UK. But Clark found himself exasperated by the open-ended and unspecific nature of 'cost-plus' or 'full-cost' theory, commenting that: 'it appears about equally possible to construe it as a manifestation of far-sighted monopoly, limited by potential competition, oligopoly of a similarly far-sighted sort, workable competition or (finally) a minimax policy in accordance with game theory.' Hall and Hitch (1939) themselves comment that 'the nearest thing we can get to an exact statement is that the price ruling is likely to approximate to the full cost of the representative firm.'

Challenge to Convention

Both quotations indicate that cost-plus or full-cost analysis is less than a complete theory of the pricing decisions made by firms. In fact, to come closer to a more complete theory we need to be able to analyse the way in which firms of differing size and character will behave under specific conditions. Such an approach will be analysed in some detail in Chapter 5.

Nonetheless, cost-plus or full-cost pricing was a significant advance over the Marshallian model of 'normal competitive price' for 'representative' firms modified by an assortment of special cases. One chief difference is that cost-plus is conceived as being deliberately adopted as a matter of corporate policy, anticipating gained cash-flow rather than responding to demand by adjusting price as the outcome of a 'cobweb' process of trial and error. Another is the extent to which the profit added to cost may reflect monopolistic competition or market power in a sense ranging far beyond the imperfect competition framework – including inflationary pressures of a kind excluded by the conventional competitive model.

Most economists, including this one, use conventions of price lines, revenue curves and cost schedules as 'tools of the trade'. As a tool kit they are essential, enabling us to identify relationships and focus both specific and general arguments. The problems arise not so much from the tools as from how we use them. Students certainly can be forgiven for asking themselves why curves are so smooth, lines so clear and results so geometric as in conventional market models.

Much of this book challenges conventional assumptions. In doing so it in part builds on critiques of conventional theory which have been made by earlier practitioners themselves. But, before moving from the framework of the small microeconomic firm to mesoeconomic and multinational big business – using a cost-plus rather than marginal price framework – it is worth noting the criticisms of conventional analysis that have been made by leading theorists of the firm.

Are Demand Curves for Real?

For instance, there is not even unanimity on the issue whether demand curves are for real. There certainly is a difficulty in showing where the demand curve of a firm would actually lie. Joan Robinson (1953) has claimed that for most firms the demand curve is at best 'a mere smudge'.

Kaldor has made a distinction between 'the traditional "market demand curve" for a certain product' and 'the demand curve which is relevant in determining the actions of the individual producer'. As he puts it: 'The first denotes a functional relationship between the price and the amounts bought from a particular producer. The second concerns the image of this functional relationship as it exists in the mind of the entrepreneur. The second may be much more, or much less, elastic than the first; it may be discontinuous while the real demand curve is continuous' (Kaldor, 1934).

Kaldor also claimed quite simply that 'the apparatus of "curves" becomes progressively less useful as one makes the basic assumptions more realistic' (Kaldor, 1934). Clark has maintained that the limitations of existing theoretical models of the competitive process go down to the 'timeless, static demand and cost curves' with which they were built (Clark, 1961). Romney Robinson has claimed that 'even in the stablest conditions, illustration of market demand as a single line on a graph is a simplification, that the demand curve is subject to such random disturbances as to be constantly "wobbling" in position [and that] the total absence of a demand curve accounts for much of the environment of uncertainty to which businessmen so often allude' (Robinson, 1961).

Eichner later echoed this, in claiming that under administered pricing and leadership by large firms within given industries, 'a demand curve in the conventional sense cannot be said to exist' (Eichner, 1976, p. 43).

Margins in Question

Thus the demand curve, used only sparingly in this chapter, may serve some purpose as a theoretical device, but in practice may prove to be at best a smudge, probably unusable and at worst unreal for firms themselves. The same tends to be the case for the framework of marginal analysis of costs, prices and normal profits.

Many firms go in for market research and certainly estimate probable sales. But they rarely try to estimate marginal costs. For one thing they are very difficult to isolate from other costs. In 1982 ATT (then the largest company in the world) gave up a 10-year project which had aimed to measure the marginal costs of its various operations. It did so because of the difficulties of isolating the marginal costs of textbook production theory from the joint or shared costs for each subsidiary enterprise of overall research and development, advertising and marketing, finance and administration. In short, it found textbook market theory impossible to apply in practice.

D. H. Robertson (1950) has criticised marginal cost and price theory on other grounds, claiming that: 'Marshall represents his producer as being in the literal sense a quantity-adapter, i.e. as accepting or rejecting, as the case may be, orders placed at a particular price, rather than setting a price himself.' He added that, for this reason, 'the use of the word marginal in the "marginal supply price for short period" is at best redundant and at worst apt to mislead. The supply price of a given output is by definition the smallest price which will elicit that output, and needs no qualifying adjective. And the use of the word marginal tends to obscure Marshall's own doctrine that the price in question is not in all circumstances equal to the marginal cost of all or any of the firms concerned.' (Robertson, 1950).

Even Marshall himself qualified his argument on actual equilibrium pricing in specific circumstances, claiming of short-term markets that 'higgling and bargaining might probably oscillate around a mean position which only would have some sort of right to be called the equilibrium price' (Marshall, 1890).

Equilibrium and Disequilibrium

Such matters might not merit footnotes in the history of economic thought were it not for the key role which marginal analysis has played in mainstream economics since Marshall's time. From 'partial' equilibrium analysis of the point at which marginal costs equalled marginal revenue, the theory was extended from 'the firm' to 'the industry'. From such extended 'partial' equilibrium analysis, it proceeded by leaps and bounds (over premises otherwise hard to bridge) to a 'general' equilibrium analysis for the economy as a whole.

This amounted to macroeconomics as the microeconomic market writ large. It clearly contrasted with classical political economy which – without using the macro or micro labels – tended to work from the general (macro) mechanisms of the economy to the particular (micro) enterprise. The attraction of marginal theory was its superficially 'positive' measureability, backed by a plausible explanation of reality. Yet the measureability remained in large part theoretical rather than real. The foundations were less positive than unsupported; less concreted by evidence than theoretical sand.

This was to become especially important in the postwar Keynesian neoclassical synthesis of which Samuelson was the main populariser. In successive editions of his *Economics* Samuelson realigned Keynes' disequilibrium analysis of income, expenditure and demand with equilibrium neoclassical models of supply. Both Samuelson and other Keynesians of the first rank such as Gardner Ackley (1961) applied Keynes' concepts to both micro and macro equilibrium conditions.

Qualifying Keynes

In his *Concluding Notes to the General Theory* (1936) Keynes observed that if governments would intervene to manage demand on the lines he recommended, the theories of perfect and imperfect competition would by and large take care of supply. But as Leijonhufvud (1968, p. 37) has stressed, Keynes did not accept equilibrium models of adjustment of the assumption that 'if "competition" could only be restored, "automatic forces" would take care of the employment problem. Thus the modern appraisal that "Keynesianism" in effect involves tacit acceptance of the traditional Theory of Markets with the proviso that today's economy corresponds to a 'special case' of that theory, namely the case that assumes rigid wages. *Keynes, in sharp contrast, sought to attack the foundations of that theory*' (our emphasis).

It could well be argued that if Keynes had been so concerned to argue a macroeconomics of disequilibrium, he should have paid more concern to the theoretical basis of its microeconomic assumptions. As stressed earlier, Keynesians after Keynes stayed in a stratosphere of macroeconomic reasoning from whose august heights the changing behaviour of individual firms and industries was hardly visible. They therefore left the supply side of the economy open to attack from so-called 'supply-siders' or 'born-again marketeers' according to a revised gospel of Adam Smith. In such an apocryphal version, Smith's own concern about producer combines was excised and it was claimed that all would be well in the best possible market economy provided politicians rolled back the frontiers of the state and got the tax collector off the backs of business. It did not matter much to such theorists, any more than it did to Milton Friedman and many monetarists, that in the 1970s big business in many economies was paying either little tax or no tax through generous rebates from government. The theory had a simple emotive appeal, and found a ready audience among those politicians who were ready to dismiss Keynes without ever having opened his *General Theory*.

Rigour, or *Rigor Mortis*?

The theory of 'harmony of interests' and the assumption of welfare through competition have been amply served by models of equilibrium conditions. The pity is that the theory itself was founded on such shallow assumptions. The harmony implied by such 'integration' is little more than a theoretical curiosity if the demand curve itself is arbitrary, kinked, wobbling or non-existent. It also needs to assume away the process of cut-throat competition between big and small, national and multinational business. Therefore the strenuous defence made for an otherwise arcane and outdated theory of inevitably rising cost curves and necessary limits to the size of firms.

The problem is part one of *gestalt*, part paradigm, and in large part the role which such theory plays in legitimating a particular social and economic order. Put simply, if the market adjusts supply to demand in a balanced way, there is little or no case for state intervention to protect consumers, prevent abuse of dominant positions by big business, or avoid the system getting stuck in an under-employment equilibrium.

But there are more still implicit assumptions in the theory of harmoniously self-adjusting markets. The classical economists had been concerned with what they called *real value* and its unequal distribution between different social groups and classes. Neoclassical economics substituted a theory of *subjective value* in the form of marginal utility analysis. As Gunnar Myrdal (1953 p. 204) pointed out, this divorced the valuations of individuals as consumers from the social psychology of groups. Focus on individual choice in demand distracted attention from the different role of owners and workers in the production and control of wealth.

Thus pursuing Wittgenstein's argument of chapter 1, subjective or marginal theory of value invited the student to view the 'box' or 'triangle' of a social system from one viewpoint only. In turn, as Myrdal (1953, p. 30) also stresses, such theory is implicitly conservative rather than radical in its assumptions – again unlike the classical theorists who, in considering real values, opened up a Pandora's box of possible contest as to which class gains what through production, distribution and exchange in a market economy.

In this sense, the theory of perfect competition is misleading in suggesting that the world would be perfect if government got off the backs of business (Friedman's case and that of the so-called 'supply-siders' in the United States). Imperfect competition theory is misleading in suggesting that there is little wrong with the real supply side of the economy which could not be remedied by a better Trades Descriptions Act. Oligopoly theory, in turn, has constrained itself both by claiming that there are limits to the overall rate of growth of firms, and in other cases maintaining that the number of firms dominating a particular market does not matter much so long as potential competition still prevails.

Such theory consigns competition to an ideological cul-de-sac. Its technical rigour is theoretical *rigor mortis*. It is in part to rescue the partial insights of such theory from this irrelevance that the following chapter considers the main issues in the theory of the firm, as argued by its leading exponents in the postwar period.

3.5 Summary

(1) The basic model of perfect competition is derived from Marshall, but has been applied as the basis for both micro and macroeconomic models without the 'real world' qualifications which Marshall himself stressed.

(2) Marginal short-run costs do not necessarily rise in the manner assumed by conventional theory, except when full capacity is reached or under other explicit circumstances such as 24-hour three-shift plant use with overtime.

(3) Where short-run costs rise, this is frequently due to exogenous cost rises in raw materials, inputs (or wages) rather than endogenous factors intrinsic to the growth of the firm.

(4) There is no necessary limit to falling long-run average costs with successive rounds of investment in new plant and equipment.

(5) The conventional assumption of rising long-run average costs in part reflects what Wittgenstein called getting 'entangled in our own rules' and in part the concern of market theory to legitimate the norm of a plural model of competition, to which exceptions of market dominance represent collusion or abuse of the competitive process.

(6) Imperfect competition with higher-than-normal prices and profits is not only (i) *structural* in the case of consumer brand attachment, but also (ii) *social*, reflecting the unequal capacity to purchase of different groups of consumers and (iii) *spatial*, depending on unequal market access by consumers in different locations.

(7) So-called imperfection through differentiated products may be a necessary condition for market entry, and is a device widely used by both new and established firms – including multinational companies using different brand names in different markets – to establish or increase market share.

(8) Most firms use standard average costs plus a profit mark-up, or cost-plus pricing, rather than marginal costs as the basis of their pricing behaviour (although such cost-plus pricing embodies a range of competitive strategies and tactics which qualifies the assumption of a 'normal' cost-plus profit).

(9) Kinked demand curves are less an analytic curiosity than a typical feature of oligopolistic markets dominated by a few firms which prefer to compete above certain limits through non-price factors rather than by cutting price to their mutual disadvantage.

(10) Reverse kinked demand curves are common features of modern markets where firms give preferential prices to bulk buyers and established customers, and 'profit cream' from the rest (including individual consumers).

(11) The theory of perfect competition implies that all would be well in the modern economy if the state got off the back of business. Imperfect competition implies only that the state should intervene with an appropriate Trades Description Act.

(12) Both the Keynesian and monetarist paradigms of the economy are based on the assumptions of perfect and imperfect competition theory. For this reason both have been profoundly qualified by the new dominance of the national and international economy by multinational big business.

4 From Small to Big Business

4.1 The Structure of Supply

The assumption of a market composed of many firms is crucial to consumer sovereignty. But a competitive structure is also central to the political defence of a capitalist market economy. In other words it is axiomatic to the pluralist model of the modern capitalism that no single group of producers will be dominant in the economy. Milton Friedman has been well aware of this, consciously relating a competitive framework to the political freedoms of a capitalist market economy, and its main claims over alternative economic systems.

In practice, both Friedman and Keynes reckoned that the market mechanism would by and large assure a competitive supply-side structure. Thus in the last chapter of his *General Theory* Keynes argued that provided the state was able to intervene effectively at the level of demand, through a combination of fiscal and monetary policies plus incentives to enterprise, there was no special reason for it to intervene in the structure of supply, where mechanisms of perfect and imperfect competition were expected to ensure that the level of demand determined by government called forth a competitive supply of goods and services.

But a monopolistic supply structure disrupts this assumed harmony of private management of supply and public management of demand. Monopolistic structures imply that the government should intervene not only at the level of demand but also on the supply side. Such intervention may be to ensure that the means of production, distribution and exchange are aligned with a wider public and social interest. Or to fulfil commonly accepted objectives of that interest such as a fair price system.

Such political and economic considerations are important in the debate on the structure and size of the modern capitalist firm.

Marx and After

Radical political economy and its Marxist variants have little difficulty in explaining the rise of big business. One of the strongest elements in Marx's analysis is the claim that *competition itself causes monopoly*. This is not a matter of some imperfections in a competitive market, but a direct consequence of competition, since if gains go, through higher sales, to those firms able to produce either better or cheaper products for the consumer, this will tend to increase the market share of the successful competitor. For Marxists, such a trend to monopoly through the dynamics of the competitive process amounts to one of the central 'contradictions' of capitalism. It is also assumed that the emergence of monopoly from competition amounts to a qualitative rather than merely quantative change in market structures. Thus, after business gains a critical size, it will tend to become a price-maker rather than a price-taker and to substitute producer sovereignty for consumer sovereignty.

Marxism is not monolithic on this matter. Ironically, Marx himself in general assumed a price-competitive market structure. It was the 'second generation' Marxists such as Hilferding and Bukharin who (with Lenin, who derived much of his own argument from them) stressed the trend to monopoly capital in countries such as Germany and the United States in the second half of the nineteenth and early twentieth century. Much of their analysis rejected the price-competitive framework of Marx's own model.

Nor do Marxists have a monopoly on the argument. There is a considerable overlap of shared assumptions between Marxist theories of the firm, the oligopoly theory of Bain (1956) and Sylos-Labini (1962), and the theory of the 'dominant firm' developed by François Perroux (1964) and by Galbraith in his 'Planning System' (1974).

Limits to Growth

But such theory – Marxist or otherwise – has to explain how it is that leading firms have not in practice come to dominate sectors outright through increased returns from economies of scale. Not least, account also has to be taken of Galbraith's world of small manufacturers and farmers, repairmen, retailers, photographers and pornographers who together 'supply about half of all we use or consume' (Galbraith, 1974, p. ix).

Thus, while there certainly is a trend to big business in the modern capitalist economy, the small firm continues to survive and in some cases to flourish. How come?

While the product-cycle theory analysed later in this chapter clarifies why some big business lessens its rate of growth and market share, there are other reasons why the trend to monopoly has been restrained. Policy-makers like to claim credit for anti-monopoly or anti-trust action, and in some cases this is due. More significantly, as analysed in Chapter 6, big business has been constrained in its rate of growth in national markets and has gone abroad, thereby avoiding anti-trust or anti-monopoly authorities and also avoiding domestic taxation by scheduling profits through tax havens. Further, as analysed in Chapter 7, while technical progress has increased the rewards to winners in the innovation stakes, it has also increased the risks from over-concentration in individual product markets. Big business, which for many years achieved market power through vertical integration and internalising economies of scale, has in recent years been concerned to avoid high-cost and inappropriate technology and in some cases has externalised its supply to other risk-taking producers, or spread its risk by diversifying into other activities, analysed through this text, and summarised in Chapter 7.

The Structure of Costs

Nonetheless, the key arguments about the scope and limits to growth of individual firms concern the structure of costs, and the issue of increasing versus decreasing returns to scale. Some of the main issues in the debate on rising, constant or falling costs with increased output have already been raised in Chapter 3 in the context of perfect and imperfect competition.

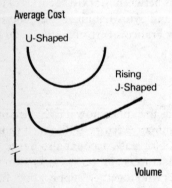
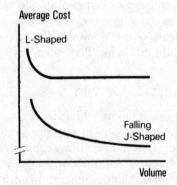

FIG. 4.1(a)   Rising average cost curves   FIG. 4.1(b)   Constant or falling average cost curves

Figure 4.1(a) shows the conventional U shape of the (envelope) long-run average cost curve. This has already been criticised and is due for more critical examination in this chapter. In reality there may well be rising costs for some firms – not least inflation – which do not produce such symmetric semi-circular shape. Also, a rising J-shaped curve as illustrated in Figure 4.1(a) may well be more realistic for some firms in some circumstances.

Figure 4.1(b) includes an L-shaped curve, indicating constant long-run average costs. Such an L-shaped curve is widely assumed and generally used in analysis of the competitive process in the contemporary capitalist economy, especially under conditions of oligopoly. But Figure 4.1(b) also illustrates a falling J-shaped long-run average cost curve, indicating decreasing rather than constant returns to scale.

One of the key factors determining the shape of long-run cost curves is the return to scale from the individual plant within the U-, J- or L-shaped 'envelopes'. But − bearing in mind not least the argument on gestalt or perception in Chapter 1 − it is important to stress that conventional graphic representation of costs in most economic texts tends to exaggerate the significance of the shape of long-run average cost curves and their implications for internal economies or diseconomies of scale.

The key convention is to break the vertical cost axis. In itself this is not devious. It simply saves space and paper, thus reducing unit costs for publishers and − hopefully − increasing unit profits for authors. This text, like others, employs the device − in the form of two diagonal lines across the cost axis − for such reasons.

But, in reality, the vertical cost axis of any enterprise is far higher than

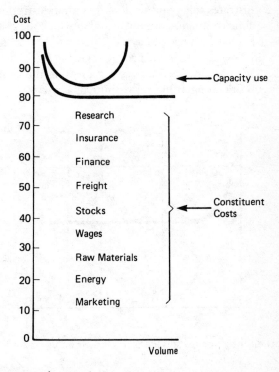

FIG. 4.2   The structure of enterprise costs

implied by convention. This is illustrated in Figure 4.2, where the cost axis is unbroken and measured from nought to 100. Even Figure 4.2 needs to be interpreted before it approaches reality. For instance, in the advanced capitalist countries the wage bill easily may amount to two-fifths or half of total costs in manufacturing, or three-quarters of total costs in services. By contrast, as illustrated in Chapter 6, in cases where the company is multinational and production is in a less developed country, the wage bill may be as little as a fifth or even a tenth of total costs.

Plant Capacity and Firm Size

Throughout our analysis of the debate on size, it is crucial to maintain the distinction between the size of *plant* and the size of *firm*. For instance, Figure 4.2 essentially concerns production costs either for a single-product firm or for the product division or plant of a multimarket enterprise. Specialists in the theory of the firm sometimes forget the distinction, thereby causing themselves problems by seeking an answer to what Wittgenstein would call 'the wrong question'.

Figure 4.3 illustrates this point. It describes an industry market in which two mesoeconomic companies dominate and in which the rest of the market is occupied by smaller microeconomic enterprise. Meso firm I controls segment *ab* of the market, meso firm II segment *bc*, and the micro firm segment *cd*, with the U-shaped curves representing the short-run costs of individual plant operating at full three-shift capacity.

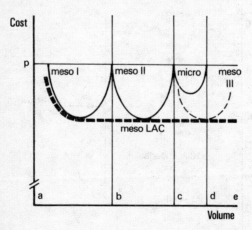

FIG. 4.3 Technical economies and limits to market share

The long-run average cost curve in Figure 4.3 reflects the technical economies available to mesoeconomic enterprise. But the edge of the actual market is at *d* rather than *c*. Therefore if either of the mesoeconomic companies were to undertake investment in an additional plant reflecting available technical scale economies, the result would be less than full capacity utilisation – in terms of Figures 4.3, only half utilisation – of meso plant III.

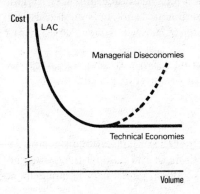 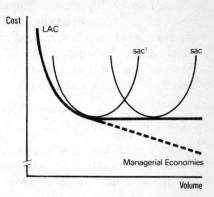

FIG. 4.4(a) Technical economies and managerial diseconomies

FIG. 4.4(b) Technical economies and managerial economies

Thus additional investment increasing the market share of either meso firm I or meso firm II is not worthwhile unless, over time, the expansion of the market would be sufficient to achieve fuller or full utilisation of additional investment. If the firm was Japanese, it would probably invest anyway in plant III and wait for demand to catch up. But technical *economies* rather than diseconomies can explain why bigger business does not take over an entire market.

We now turn to claims of inherent 'limits' to the growth of big business, as made by more conventional theories of the firm.

Managerial Diseconomies?

One such explanation is that of so-called 'managerial diseconomies'. In considering this, it is important to distinguish between the 'technical' and 'managerial' costs of production.

Figure 4.4(a) shows that technical economies of scale – in essence, gains from mass production – may be offset by managerial diseconomies, i.e. management organisation cannot match the technical efficiency of machinery and may result in rising costs (or slower expansion) for the enterprise over the long run.

The counter argument is that technical or production economies of scale can be matched or excluded by managerial economies. As illustrated in Figure 4.4(b), this implies that even if long-run average costs are L-shaped rather than J-shaped – and thus constant rather than falling – efficiency gains through the employment of specialist management could lower total costs, with a resultant J-shaped falling long-run average cost curve for the enterprise as a whole. Such management cost savings could cover the range of constituent costs illustrated in Figure 4.2, i.e. insurance, finance, freight, stock control, the purchasing of components and raw materials for production, and the use and saving of energy, as well as wage cost savings through effective labour relations.

However, there are further factors affecting the cost structure of enterprise, including the specific form of management organisation itself.

Vertical Management

Chandler, in a pioneering work, stressed that the organisational structure of an enterprise will affect the scope and limit of the competitive strategies which it can adopt. Structure will also affect gains from management

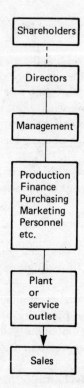

FIG. 4.5(a)   Vertical management

specialisation and declining costs with larger output (Chandler, 1962).

Figure 4.5(a) illustrates a vertically structured enterprise. This could be a classic single-product firm conforming to the textbook model of a micro-economic company. It could be a private company run by an owner-entrepreneur of the textbook model, or a public company in which the shareholders control the directors who in turn control the manager or managers. These in turn take direct responsibility for the range of products or services undertaken by the enterprise within a vertical organisation structure, such as finance, advertising, labour relations, transport etc. In the vertically structured firm, the same manager or managers also thereby take direct responsibility for the production or the service, and its distribution and sale. Such a vertical structure is typical of many firms in the microeconomic sector.

Multifunctional Management

Figure 4.5(b) shows a multifunctional management structure in which the directors are nominally responsible to the shareholders, but a management board rather than an individual manager is responsible to the directors. This management board will be responsible for the same kind of functions as in the vertically structured enterprise, but with an individual manager responsible for each of the functions concerned.

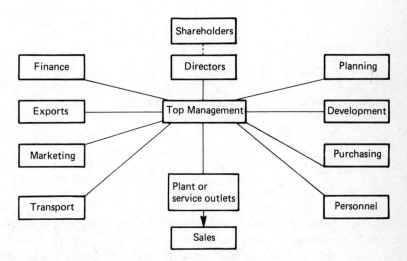

Fɪɢ. 4.5(b)   Multifunctional management

In principle this should reflect efficiency gains for management specialis-ation similar to the classic division of labour which Adam Smith applied to

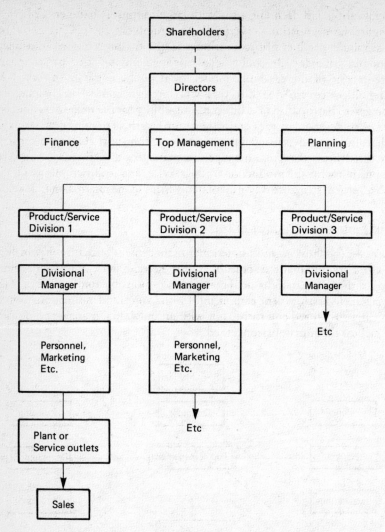

FIG. 4.5(c) Multidivisional management

pin-making, where he demonstrated that workers specialising in producing the stem, sharpening the point and applying the head of the pin should be much more efficient than one worker doing all three jobs. Thus managers who specialise in production, labour relations, finance or marketing should be more efficient and more effective than the owner–entrepreneur who tries to manage all four tasks in one 'song and dance' act. In other words, specialised or multifunctional management should be able to achieve efficiency gains greater than those of the vertically structured enterprise. However, as shown in this chapter, conventional theory has been remarkably resistant to this simple implication of economies from management specialisation.

Multifunctional enterprises can be small or large. In other words they are found in both the micro and mesoeconomic sectors. But when companies are multifunctional in structure, they are likely to be concentrated in a single market or dominant product range – whether furniture, fabrics, engineering or steel – rather than be multiproduct, multisectoral or multinational in structure.

Multidivisional Management

The bigger the firm the more likely that it will adopt the multidivisional management structure illustrated in Figure 4.5(c). Called simply the M structure by Chandler, this incorporates the management services such as finance and accounting – and possibly research and development – at a new top management level. These top managers are again responsible to directors who are nominally responsible to shareholders. But below them, in a hierarchical structure, are a range of product or service divisions which replicate the roles fulfilled by multifunctional or vertical management.

The greater the size and the wider the range of products or services, the more likely it is that the company will take a multidivisional form. This has been stressed by Chandler (1982), Kono (1984) and others with a range of supporting evidence from the United States, Europe and Japan.

Multinational Management

The structure of multinational enterprise is considered in more detail later in this book. But in general multinational enterprise is likely to combine a multidivisional structure with a geographical or area division of management responsibilities at national level. As illustrated in Figure 4.5(d), the more international or multinational the enterprise the more probable it is that it will replicate a multidivisional management structure within each multinational region or area in which it produces and sells.

Such an area structure is also evident in the organisation of many public enterprises at national level. In the British case, the National Coal Board and British Steel combine specialisation of management in a multidivisional structure with specific areas in which regional managers undertake responsibility for a range of operations which otherwise would fall simply within the divisions of multidivisional enterprise. Such structural differences, either

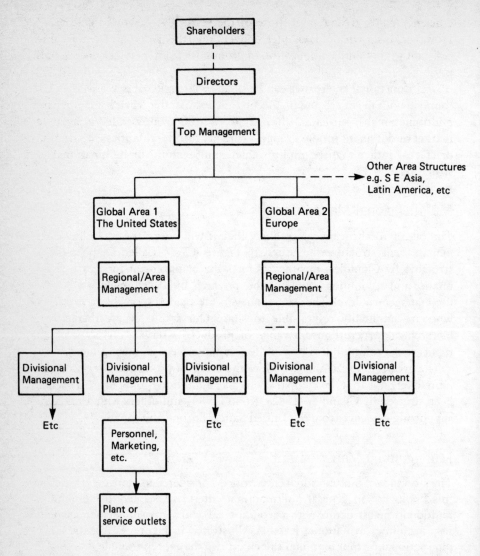

FIG. 4.5(d) Multinational management

hindering or helping the growth of different kinds of firms, have been neglected by some of the most influential texts on economic theory, not least Samuelson and Lipsey.

4.2 Fishers and Farmers

Marshall on Big Business

Marshall is often quoted on the growth of the firm. As often his key work has stayed in the library of the great unread – untouched by students, and even some teachers. Yet, contrary to received opinion, Marshall did not deny the possibility of big business dominance through gains from size. In a section of his *Principles* entitled 'Profits in Large and Small Businesses' he admits that

> there are indeed some trades in which the rate of profit on large capitals tends to be higher than on small. For if two businesses are competing in the same trade, that with the larger capital can nearly always buy at the cheaper rate, and avail itself of many economies in the specialisation of skill and machinery and in other ways which are out of the reach of the smaller business: while the only important special advantage, which the latter is likely to have, consists of its greater facilities for getting near its customers and consulting their individual wants.

Marshall stresses that in service trades in which face-to-face contact with the consumer is not important, and especially in some manufacturing business, 'the large firm can sell at a better price than the small one, the outgoings of the former are proportionately less and the incomings larger; and therefore, if profits are so reckoned as to include the same elements in both cases, the rate of profit in the former case must be higher than in the latter' (Marshall, 1890).

Critical Scale

Marshall is also quite explicit on the tactics which big business may adopt towards its smaller competitors. Thus he writes, in terms reminiscent of Marx, that 'large firms, after first crushing out small ones, either combine with one another and thus secure for themselves the gain of a limited monopoly, or by keen competition among themselves reduce the rate of profit very low'. He also admits (ibid., p. 507) that size may be a necessary condition for entry or start-up in a given market, allowing that 'there are many branches of the textile, the metal and the transport trades in which no business can be started at all except with a large capital. While those that are begun on a moderate scale struggle with great difficulties, in the hope that, after a time, it may be possible to find employment for a large capital, which will yield earnings of management high in the aggregate though low in proportion to the capital'.

Marshall further allows that a manufacturer of what he calls

> exceptional ability and energy will apply better methods, and perhaps better machinery than his rivals: he will organise better the manufacturing and marketing

sides of his business; and he will bring them into better relation to one another. *By these means he will extend his business; and therefore he will be able to take greater advantage from the specialisation of both labour and plant.* Thus he will obtain increasing returns and also increasing profit: for if he is only one among many producers his increased output will not materially lower the prices of his goods, and nearly all the benefit of his economies will accrue to himself. If he happens to have a partial monopoly of his branch of industry, he will so regulate his increased output that his monopoly profits increase'. [ibid., pp. 510–11, italics added.]

Increasing Returns

However, with reasoning which echoes Marx, Marshall claims that the improvement gained by the manufacturer of ability and energy may not be confined to one or two products. He therefore argues (p. 511) that when they arise from a general increase in demand and output, or from improved methods of production that are accessible to the whole of the industry, other firms in that industry and also subsidiary industries will gain increased external economies, reducing the costs of their inputs and also keeping the price of products close to a level which yields only a normal rate of profit to that class of industry as a whole. Indeed, Marshall admitted that 'when the production of a commodity conforms to the law of increasing returns in such a way as to give a very great advantage to large producers, it is apt to fall almost entirely into the hands of a few large firms', i.e. the trend to concentration claimed earlier by Marx. He also admitted (p. 329) that, in these circumstances, 'the normal marginal supply price cannot be isolated because it assumes the existence of a great many competitors with businesses of all sizes, some of them being young and some old, some in the ascending and some in the descending phase'.

Eddies and Tides

Nonetheless Marshall argues that when we are taking 'a broad view' of the causes which govern supply, we need not trouble ourselves with what he calls 'these eddies on the surface of the great tide'. In particular he admits that it may be that a wealthy firm may attain new economies, and obtain a larger output at a lower proportionate cost but he maintains (ibid., p. 314) that 'as this additional output will be small relatively to the aggregate volume of production in the trade, it will not much lower the price'.

Yet it is striking that when Marshall analyses what he calls the equilibrium of normal demand and supply, the key examples he gives of a tendency to diminishing returns are from the fishing industry rather than from manufacturing or services. Thus he claims (ibid., p. 308) that as fishermen take to their boats in increasing number, 'the source of supply in the sea might perhaps show signs of exhaustion, and the fishermen might have to resort to more distant coasts and deeper waters, nature giving a diminishing return to the increased application of capital and labour of a given order of efficiency'.

Marshall's resort to fishing is of more than passing interest. His famed preface quotation – *natura non facit saltum*, ('nature does not jump') – implies gradualism, continuity and also equilibrium. But apart from fishing, the examples on which he founds his theory come not from industry but from farming and agriculture.

Samuelson's Fixed Factors

But the real surprise is that nearly a century after Marshall's first edition in 1890 fishers and farmers still constitute the main examples of diminishing returns in market economy theory. Samuelson's treatment of the theory of the growth of the firm is punctuated throughout by frequent reference to farming, land and rent. Thus he stresses that 'if at first we have strong *increasing* returns we must at first have *declining*, rather than increasing, marginal cost'. But he then summarises what he calls the relationship between the productivity laws of returns and the laws of marginal cost by stressing that 'if at first there is increasing returns, there is at first declining marginal cost – but ultimately diminishing returns and increasing marginal cost' (Samuelson, 1976, Chapter 23, pp. 454–5).

Yet there is no supporting argument in Samuelson's Chapter 23 for the law of diminishing returns as such. We are cross-referred to his Chapter 2 where, as he puts it, 'the law of diminishing returns was defined [as] diminishing extra product for varying extra labour units added to fixed *land*', and similarly, 'land's marginal-product is the change in total product resulting from one additional unit of land, with all other inputs held constant – and so forth, *for any factor*' (ibid., pp. 539–40, italics added).

It is highly questionable in the last quarter of the twentieth century whether diminishing returns obtain in such a manner. When Samuelson addresses himself later in his text (ibid., Chapter 28) to the pricing of factor inputs, his argument is *exclusively* concerned with land rents and other agricultural examples rather than with modern industry or services.

Farming Fantasies

It cannot be assumed after some ten editions of his *Economics* that Samuelson's examples are due to inadequate reflection or revision. The striking feature of his argument is the extent to which he returns time and again to Ricardian or Marshallian examples from the non-industrial world. In this sense, although Samuelson formally presents arguments from perfect competition through imperfect competition to oligopoly, in practice he treats virtually all stages of the growth of the firm short of monopoly in a paradigm not of perfectly competitive firms but of perfectly competitive farms. Despite claims for 'positive' empiricism, his examples and evidence are bucolic rather than economic, and fantastic rather than real.

Lipsey on Land

Similarly, when treating the issues of competition and monopoly, under the subheading of 'The Drive to Monopolise Perfectly Competitive Industry', Richard Lipsey (1975, p. 292) gives examples essentially derived from farming and agriculture rather than services or industry. While recognising trades unions, his argument and examples in fact illustrate crop-restriction schemes for farmers and producers' co-operatives, with cross-reference to cocoa producers in West Africa, wheat producers in the United States and Canada, coffee growers in Brazil and (an example from mineralogy rather than manufactures) the Arab oil producers. Not only are manufacturing and services missing, but the argument itself stresses co-operation or collusion to raise prices rather than the dynamics through which the competitive process itself, by rewarding the competitive with a higher market share, may result in domination of the market by a few sellers.

Admitted Oligopoly

Lipsey does address himself at one point to the question of oligopoly, admitting that when we move from competition among the many to competition among the few the whole price-output problem of the firm takes on a new dimension. Yet rather than develop this dimension with reference to the 'positive' economics of 'developing testable hypotheses to explain actual aspects of observed behaviour', he simply disclaims the issues, stating (1975, p. 284) that 'we cannot enter into a detailed discussion of these elements in this book'.

With such a disclaimer, Lipsey gives (ibid., pp. 285–6) a shopping list of those hypotheses about oligopoly behaviour which qualify the perfect and imperfect competition model on which his text and argument are based. In summary these are:

(1) That the smaller the number of sellers, the greater the mutual recognition of interdependence and joint action to maximise profit by reducing direct competition.
(2) That the greater the dominance of the market by a leading firm or firms, the easier it is for firms in an industry by tacit agreement to raise price.

(3) That competitive pricing during periods of slack demand and excess capacity depends on uncertainty regarding the reaction of competitors, which will be reduced under conditions in which only a few firms command a given market.

(4) That prices will tend to be the more inflexible, the more effective is tacit agreement between a few firms, based on the established evidence that it is costly to change prices often, and that monopolists will change prices only infrequently.

(5) That non-price competition will tend to be more vigorous, the greater is the limitation on price competition.

(6) That an industry will be closer to a joint profit-maximising price, and thus further away from normal price and profits, the greater are the barriers to the entry of new firms.

(7) That with barriers to the entry of new firms, prices will tend to go up rather than come down, or be more flexible upwards and less flexible downwards.

(8) That non-price competition will tend to be greater, the weaker are other barriers to entry.

Key Issues

These are not only important questions. They are key issues in the political economy of the modern market. Nor is Lipsey unaware of the importance of big business. Thus he admits that concentration in the American economy lends support to the hypothesis that the largest corporations (a) tend to dominate the economy, (b) largely control market demand rather than being controlled by it, (c) co-opt governmental processes instead of being constrained by them, and (d) utilise their substantial discretionary power in ways that are against the interests of society.

Lipsey (ibid., p. 334) allows that one per cent of manufacturing corporations in the United States own over 85 per cent of manufacturing assets, while the 200–250 largest corporations – in his own words, less than one-tenth of one per cent of all manufacturing corporations – control approximately 50 per cent of such assets.

Yet Lipsey admits that his testing of the evidence of big business is 'superficial, at least'. He allots only some five pages of generally sceptical observations to the issues raised; while of the eight key hypotheses (listed above), only the question of barriers to entry is considered in any detail (ibid., pp. 287–90).

Inapplicable Supply Theory

Thus, like Samuelson, Lipsey discounts the domination of the market by big business and neglects its implications for the general theory of demand and supply in a market economy. As he puts it: 'We have now studied the theory of production sufficiently to realise that we cannot in fact apply our simple demand and supply theory to the whole economy.' The reason is that: 'This theory is a theory of *competitive* markets, i.e. markets in which there is a large number of buyers and sellers. Most manufactured goods, however, are produced under conditions of oligopoly in which there are a very few firms.'

Ending his brief treatment of the main hypotheses on oligopoly and barriers to entry with what he calls 'the final word', Lipsey (ibid., p. 290) writes:

> Of course, there is a great deal more to the theory of oligopoly than can be summarised here, but enough should have been said to show that the counsel of despair 'you will never explain something so complex as small-group behaviour' should be rejected. The assertion that something is impossible is a powerful challenge to the creative mind. Enough has already been established in this field to show not only that we can already explain and predict some parts of oligopoly behaviour, but also that *twenty years from now we shall probably be able to explain and predict much more.* [Italics added.]

4.3 Limits to Growth?

So are there limits to the growth of the firm? The theorists fall into two main categories. First, are those who assume that the free working of the market mechanism will assure a structure of more or less perfectly competitive enterprise, and that if monopoly trends occur, this will be due to interference by government or collusion. Typified by Milton Friedman, we call this the 'off-limits' school. Second, there are those who recognise that the mechanisms of returns to scale and gains from size have indubitably increased concentration, but argue that there are limits to the rate of growth of market share for big business. We call this the 'relative limits' school.

Friedman: Off-Limits

Milton Friedman admits the possibility that an individual firm may gain an outright domination of an individual market. Thus he allows (1976, p. 210) that if there are constant returns to scale, or an L-shaped long-run average cost curve, 'then there is nothing on the supply side that sets a limit to the size of firms; either monopoly will result, or the division of the output among firms is arbitrary and capricious or the meaning of a firm disappears'.

The unacceptable result, for Friedman, would be the increased market share of the leading firm or firms represented in our Figure 4.6, where the rate of growth – on either the solid or broken line – results in a trend to market dominance or outright monopoly. He avoids the problem by assuming (1976, p. 96) that the expansion of the firm will impose diseconomies, reflecting inadequate supply of entrepreneurial capacity and other factors, the amount of which the individual firm is not free to vary – in other words, the 'managerial diseconomies' case that was illustrated in Figure 4.4(a).

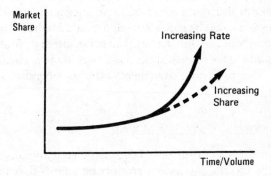

FIG. 4.6 Increased rate of growth and increased market share

Such an argument is highly implausible. Friedman claims that for any one firm, entrepreneurial capacity will be limited and that this is sufficient to explain why there are limits to the size of individual firms. But this will not be the case if the expanding firm can hire management to cope with the production, marketing, etc of the additional output.

He also confuses the short and long run. In the short run, there may be constraints on hiring additional managers to cope with new demand. But the issue of whether there are inherent limits to the growth of individual firms is a long-run argument. And in the long run, as shown later in analysis of Marris' argument later in this chapter (Marris, 1964), there are no such constraints unless the market has stopped offering management for hire.

Mistaken Big Business

Friedman's lapse is remarkable since he follows it directly with the claim (1976, pp. 105–6) that: 'it is, of course, precisely because we want to rationalize observed phenomena that suggests that the size of firm is not capricious or arbitrary or irrelevant that we have introduced this unknown something, which we have christened *entrepreneurial capacity*'. This is precisely what he fails to do, since his 'limits' case conflicts with the clearly observable and as yet unrestrained growth of big business in the world market economy as a whole – illustrated in some detail in Chapter 8.

So how does Friedman account for the trend to concentration and big business dominance? At a key stage in his argument he comes close to suggesting that the rise of big business is 'a mistake', or a phenomenon which should not have occurred. Thus he argues (ibid., p. 150) that 'if the distribution [of firms] tends to become increasingly concentrated, one might conclude that the extremes represented mistakes. . . . Whether, in fact, such deductions will be justified depends on how reasonable it is to suppose that the optimum scale or distribution has itself remained unchanged and that the emergence of new mistakes has been less important than the correction of old ones.' He adds that 'none of this can be taken for granted; it would have to be established by study of the empirical circumstances of the particular industry, which is why the preceding statements are so liberally strewn with "mights" '.

Foolish Questions – Foolish Answers

Apparently unconscious of the irony, Friedman then maintains that 'foolish questions deserve foolish answers'. Certainly he admits that there may be external circumstances which affect the size distribution of firms within an industry. One example might be assembly and distribution costs rising with the size of plant, although manufacturing costs decline. He also admits (ibid., p. 151) that differences in geography and location may play a role in the rise of big business. But his argument on such crucial issues for big business is interrogative rather than positive.

If this is the microeconomic basis for Friedman's much-vaunted macro-economic theory, then monetarism offers only queries rather than answers. It is a house built on mere assumption.

Penrose: Relative Limits

Edith Penrose (1963) introduced a welcome degree of realism into the debate on limits to growth through problems of entrepreneurship by explicitly admitting that any 'managerial limit' was relative rather than absolute.

Penrose stressed that managerial diseconomies come into play only if it is assumed that there is no change in knowledge and no change in the quality and type of managerial service. She contrasts (1963, pp. 53–7) these 'static' assumptions, which in effect interpret limits to management as limits on *output*, with dynamic assumptions in which it is possible for firms to effect a progressive subdivision of functions and decentralisation of operations where management becomes an *input* into the operations of the enterprise capable of specialisation and gains from size.

Indeed, in contrast with the 'off-limits' school, Edith Penrose also allows that large firms are for the most part multi-plant firms in which 'managerial economies' similar to other economies of scale can in principle be gained. These result when the larger firm can take advantage of increased division of managerial functions and also of the standardisation and mechanisation of administrative processes. It can also make more intensive use of existing managerial resources by the 'spreading' of overheads, and in this sense obtain economies from buying and selling on a larger scale, using its reserves more economically, acquiring capital on cheaper terms and supporting large-scale research within the context of increased management specialisation (Penrose, 1963, p. 92).

Beyond Owner-Entrepreneurship

The point can be illustrated by referring back to Figure 4.5(a). When the firm is a family affair (including shareholders and directors) then the owner-entrepreneur divides time between production, sales, finance, buying of materials, marketing, etc. Such management risks the negative fate which Adam Smith prescribed for the solo performance pin-maker – loss of business. By contrast, an enterprise which has achieved sufficient size for these tasks to be specialised in the hands of a production manager, a sales manager, a financial expert, etc on the lines of the multifunctional management in Figure 4.5(b) should gain efficiency and by implication lowered costs through both full-time attention to and cumulative experience in the individual roles concerned. Similarly, there is no reason in principle or logic why such efficiency gains from multifunctional management specialisation should not be replicated by multidivisional structures on the lines of Figure 4.5(c), whether for individual markets or different areas of the national or international economy.

Nonetheless, Edith Penrose (1963) maintains that 'it seems reasonable to deduce from the mere fact that organisation and coordination become such a central topic of discussion and concern for the larger firms that the stage of increasing returns, if it exists, does not last very long; and that after a point the firm had constantly to be alert to prevent a strong rise in the proportion of managerial services required to conduct current operations efficiently'. In other words while admitting that economies of scale through management specialisation are important to the growth of the firm, Penrose stresses that 'there seems no evidence that the problems of administration become progressively easier as the firm grows bigger and bigger'. Thus, the essence of her argument is qualitative rather than quantitative.

Necessary and Sufficient

What emerges from the Penrose analysis is her claim that managerial economies are a *necessary* but not *sufficient* condition for the growth of big business. Moreover, she claims that such studies as were available to her on changes in market structure over time lend support to the hypothesis 'that concentration tends to develop rapidly to a high point, increase fairly slowly thereafter, and eventually, when existing large firms become very large, to decline'.

In essence therefore, as illustrated in Figure 4.7, Edith Penrose claims a limit to the *rate* of growth of individual firms, which in practice could mean that their market share tended to fall relative to those competitors still in the full thrust of expansion. In other words, while she admits that some firms are bigger than others, and may grow bigger still, she nonetheless assumes either that their rate of growth will decline or that their market share will decline. If the claim were correct, then the essentials of the competitive market paradigm would be preserved.

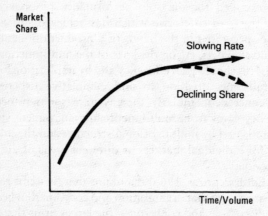

FIG. 4.7   Limits to the rate of growth and declining market share

On the other hand, the Penrose evidence is drawn from the United States alone, between 1935 and 1950. By contrast, as we shall see in some detail in Chapter 7, the dramatic concentration in markets in recent years has been since 1950 and outside the United States, for instance in Britain and continental Europe where US companies themselves have gone multinational on a major scale. Mrs Penrose prefaces her own conclusions with a warning about 'shaky evidence'. Certainly, while big business cannot necessarily increase its market share by virtue of size alone, neither managers nor policy-makers can assume that it will of necessity stop growing after it has gained some critical size at which diseconomies of scale set in.

Downie: The Transfer Mechanism

Jack Downie (1958) has been among the most articulate exponents of the relative forces working for and against concentration of markets among a few firms. He invokes two mechanisms to describe the factors involved: the 'transfer' and 'innovation' mechanisms.

The *transfer mechanism* is the process by which more efficient firms grow at the expense of less efficient. Downie stresses (1958) that it has considerable force. 'We must regard the relative outputs of today as the product, via the transfer mechanism, of the relative efficiencies of the past. If the transfer mechanism continued to be operated by an unchanged set of relative efficiencies, *the ultimate result could only be the concentration of the whole output of an industry in the hands of one, the most efficient, firm*' (italics added). In other words, like Friedman and Scitovsky, Downie is compelled to admit that either constant or increasing returns to scale lead to concentration. Moreover Downie (ibid., p. 60) maintains that such a process is not merely a theoretical curiosity, admitting that 'monuments to the self-immolation of the transfer mechanism are, in fact, not uncommon. Some industries are very largely dominated by a single firm.'

Nor does Downie underestimate the advantages of size: 'great size brings security. The bankruptcy of a small firm will, like the fall of a sparrow, in fact go unnoticed, except by the widows and orphans dependent on it and the creditors who have brought in the bailiffs. The death of a large firm, however, is so shocking an event as to be almost impossible. Someone, be it bank, insurance company, erstwhile rival, or government, will always be found to put it on its feet, and though the former owners or controllers may well be displaced in the process, they are likely to receive some financial consolation for their deprivation' (Downie, 1958, p. 64).

Downie also appreciates the effect of differences in cost. He considers two firms, A and B, whose conditions of production are identical apart from the fact that B has costs per unit 10 per cent below those of A, and concludes that 'B will make greater profits (or smaller losses) per unit of output than will A [and] it will also earn a higher rate of profit i.e. grow faster than A' (ibid., pp. 69–74).

The Innovation Mechanism

Against the force of the transfer mechanism Downie posits a counter process in the form of the *innovation mechanism*. In other words, innovators may offset the trend to dominant market share by big business through successfully entering the market. As Downie says, 'the successful innovator is he who can view the present practice with an objective as well as an imaginative eye, which neither finds change an end in itself, nor is wedded to the past by bonds of sentiment and habit'. Moreover, innovators may not be new-born entrepreneurs. They may be born-again entrepreneurs established already in a different activity. Indeed, in one sense, the outside firm may be in a better position to improve on the best present practice than is the firm which originated it.

Downie allows that large innovating firms may not maximise their potential, especially if they are not fully aware of possible competition of the kind which he stresses as important to the innovation process. As he puts it (ibid., p. 90), innovation will occur if the firm not only has the expectation of great gain from doing so but 'the fear of loss from not doing so'.

The Strong and the Weak

Downie observes that if the innovation mechanism does not work to reduce concentration, the 'rules of the game' are being interfered with and some firms are acting collusively. This may well be the case. But collusion reinforces the market power of big business.

Moreover, the arguments which Downie so fluently makes for the transfer mechanism contradict the force of his conclusion that 'in the carefree and complacent atmosphere of easy expansion there will be little incentive for managements to force themselves to the painful and difficult task of re-examining the fundamentals of their practice' (ibid., p. 91). This may or may not be the case for an individual firm. It may well be that an owner–entrepreneur decides at a certain stage that 'a quiet life' is preferable to continued efforts at profit maximisation through innovation. But it would be an error to assume that the concentration process through the 'transfer mechanism' is limited because professional managers, at a critical stage, slow down and go fishing.

Marris: Managerial Economics

Downie's case on the management of the modern capitalist corporation is in part reflected by Robin Marris (1964). Analysing what he calls the 'Disappearance of the Entrepreneur', Marris explains that once large-scale 'managerial' organisations appear, they can mould the environment to directions which suit themselves and 'soon find that, rather than competing perfectly in a given environment, it is better to strive to create conditions of monopoly, monopolistic competition or oligopoly.' Marris also forcefully stresses that 'until very recently almost all "micro" analysis implicitly regarded the corporation as a form of collective entrepreneurship, to be treated in much the same way as the one-man business' (ibid., p. 5). This is certainly the case in the microeconomics of Milton Friedman, and one of its key limits as a foundation for his macroeconomic theory.

Addressing the question whether there are inherent limits to the growth of the firm through either its ability to borrow or the willingness of lenders to invest, Marris emphasises that 'the limits on size can be penetrated by changing the structure of the firm. By corporate reorganisation the autocratic figure of the founder is replaced by a management team and the financing problem is eased by acquiring shareholders'.

The Management Team

On the issue of the internal limits to the rate of growth of the firm, Marris addresses himself to what he calls the 'Penrose theorem' and asks: 'why should not a firm at time t recruit large numbers of highly qualified managers amounting to a doubling of the size of its relevant team and then be able to expect to employ these people to bring about a very large increase in activity between $t+1$ and $t+2$'. In practice, he claims, the new member of an existing concern, however highly qualified, 'can almost never become fully efficient as a non-routine decision-maker on the instant he is recruited'. On the other hand he admits that there is no reason why a firm should not recruit large numbers of new managers or personnel at time t, await the completion of their training through $t+1$ to $t+n$, and then expand rapidly. Although qualifying the argument on the grounds that recruits learn better by personal contact with members of the company and that the capacity of such 'teachers' is limited, he stresses that so far conventional theory has been inadequate on the issue of managerial economies.

Furthermore, Marris is quite explicit on economies of scale and size, arguing that 'given large-scale organisation [and] provided a team of appropriate ability is employed, we assume the firm has no optimum size: if, when the scale of output is doubled, salary and all other inputs are doubled, the rate of return is constant. Management then become a factor of production behaving exactly like manual labour. . . . The larger the firm the more high-powered will be the team required, and by adjusting the team appropriately a firm could always obtain constant returns in expansion' (Marris, 1964, pp. 81–6).

Demand and Distribution

Marris makes it clear that the financial policies of faster-growing firms would mean that they were increasingly dependent on external capital, arguing (ibid., p. 248) that 'the faster you grow the less you earn on your capital and the less your utility from security'. He argues, following Kalecki (1954) and in a Keynesian context, that the rate of growth of the firm will be a function of the macroeconomic growth rate of the economy. But in considering this relation between micro and macroeconomic factors, he allows that it is possible that an economy may reach a situation where, 'until some major industrial or socio-economic revolution occurs, no quasi-natural rate exists. Disequilibrium states will then become chronic.'

Nonetheless, Marris (ibid., pp. 301–2) maintains that 'it also seems possible that, under other circumstances, there may exist within limits a continuous range of growth rates, all of which are quasi-natural', and he believes that three conditions can be distinguished: (1) there may be no quasi-natural rates; (2) there may be one quasi-natural rate; (3) there may be, within limits, a continuous range of such rates. He allows that in the first case, which he calls 'pathological', the economy is unable to find any kind of dynamic equilibrium until the position is somehow rectified. Yet in the summary of his analysis Marris also observes that 'the significance of the result is that the rate of growth is in a genuine causal sense determined not only by the growth propensities of the people who manage industry, but also by the distribution of income'.

4.4 Product Cycles and Growth

We have seen that Marris allows for the complacency of established versus unestablished management. As he puts it (ibid., pp. 246–7) there is 'a tendency for the laggards to take in organisational slack while the leaders become complacent'. This very much fits the image of competitive entre- preneurs, whose sling-shot skills in a world of corporate Goliaths enable them to fell giant firms.

Reality is somewhat different. One reason is the extent to which a fall in the rate of growth of larger firms may be associated with a decline in the rate of growth of those markets in which they operate, rather than supply-side or management constraints. Such a decline in the rate of growth of products has been identified by Vernon (1966) and others in terms of the so-called product-cycle model.

New, Growing and Mature

According to this model, during the first or new phase of the introduction of a product – illustrated in Figure 4.8(a) – its rate of growth is relatively slow.

This is a period when new processes and techniques are stabilised or standardised and – not least – quality control imposed on external suppliers. It also is a period when, through advertising and marketing, the consumer is both made familiar with the new product and encouraged to see the need for it. Thus it at first grows slowly as it becomes established in a new market.

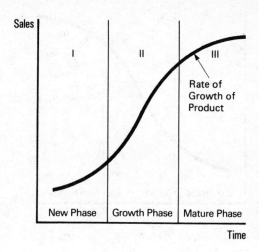

FIG. 4.8(a)   The three-phase product cycle

The second or 'growth' phase of the product cycle in Figure 4.8(a) represents the period when the product moves to a large-scale mass market or takes-off. In consumer durables there can be a clear social group or class dimension to this growth phase of the product cycle, reflecting the distribution of income of the kind stressed as important to enterprise growth by Marris. This was typical in Western Europe in the 1950s and 1960s for a broad range of household consumer durables (automobiles, refrigerators, washing machines, etc.), which in the inter-war period had been bought mainly by upper or professional social classes but which thereafter became mass markets proper.

The third or 'mature' phase of the product cycle in Figure 4.8(a) is the period when production has become standardised and the prevailing market saturated. In other words, demand for the product is no longer moving across boundaries of income or social class, but has stabilised as a replacement market.

Slowing Firms – or Slowing Markets?

Figure 4.8(b) relates the slow-fast-slower rate of growth for individual products through their 'life cycle' to the growth phases of a single-product or single-market firm. Thus Figures 4.8(a) and 4.8(b) have the same shape, but the former reflects *product* growth and the latter *enterprise* growth, where the firm concerned is concentrated on a single or limited product range.

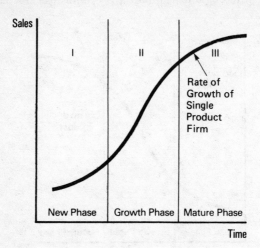

FIG. 4.8(b)   The product cycle and the single-product firm

The argument is essentially simple. If an enterprise is limited to one product or a limited product range in a single market, then its feasible rate of growth will reflect the rate of growth of, or the decline of demand for, the product itself. Thus the new, growth and mature phases of the product cycle will be reflected in new, growth and mature phases for the firm.

Such product-cycle analysis has been notably missing from much of the debate on the growth of the firm. Yet it gives a highly plausible explanation for the slowing rate of growth of firms which Penrose (1963) found in the top hundred US companies from 1935 to 1950. It also illustrates that while management organisation clearly is critical to market success, declining rates of growth for individual firms may be due less to internal or endogenous limits to management efficiency, and more to external or exogenous factors such as the rate of growth of and decline of demand for the product markets in which these firms operate.

In the long run, as technical progress or changing consumer demand takes effect, the third or 'mature' growth phase of a product may give way to a fourth phase of actual decline. Illustrated in Figure 4.8(c), this has been typified by the fate of iron in favour of steel construction, of gas lighting in favour of electric lighting, of electric trams in urban transport (with notable exceptions in San Francisco and Germany) in favour of petrol or diesel buses

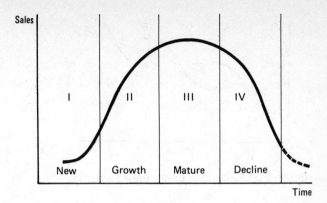

FIG. 4.8(c)   The four-phase product cycle

(with negative pollution effects), and of the valve in favour of the transistor in radio.

The fourth or decline phase of the product cycle may be relative rather than absolute, as in the energy sector where oil and to a lesser extent nuclear power (again with negative environmental effects) now compete with coal, where passenger shipping has been superceded by air transport, or where cotton and traditional textiles have in part been superceded by synthetic fibres. Such a decline phase of the product cycle underlies much of the problem of the decline of small firms in traditional industries in regions such as the North-East of the United States, the North of England and central Scotland, regions which established themselves in the new and growth phases of the product market but failed to adapt to changing demand and new product innovations by diversification.

Multiproduct and Multimarket Growth

Conversely, a multiproduct or multimarket firm may well be able to sustain its overall rate of growth of sales by staying abreast of the 'innovation frontier' and thereby introducing a range of successive new products.

This is illustrated in Figure 4.9, where the decline in the rate of growth of product A is compensated by the new growth phase of product B which in turn, as it matures, is compensated by the growth phases of product C. Thus while a microeconomic enterprise concentrated in a single product or single market may well find itself faced with slowing growth of sales and profits, there is nothing in principle which restrains the rate of growth of a multiproduct, multimarket firm.

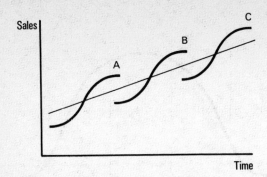

FIG. 4.9   Sustained growth of the multiproduct firm

This pattern of growth through diversification has been typical of the modern capitalist corporation in the twentieth century. Thus companies such as Krupps found themselves faced with declining rates of growth of demand for steel, but compensated by moving into primary steel-using industry such as heavy machinery and – classically – armaments. Companies such as General Electric diversified from power-generating equipment (in which they faced considerable constraints to growth – analysed later) into jet-engine production. Automobile companies such as FIAT shifted smartly between the wars from vehicles into aircraft, and thereafter into aerospace. Companies such as IBM have carefully planned the phased introduction of new products, whether (a) peripheral computers complementing its main-frame computer dominance, or (b) other office machinery such as the 'golfball' typewriter, followed by word and data processors, and (c) electronic telephone exchanges with, more recently, the satellite tele-communications market, corresponding with the A-B-C product phases or cycles of Figure 4.9.

Some companies, such as Vickers in Britain, started as armourers but failed to diversify successfully into civilian production. Their ventures into passenger cars (such as Hawker Siddeley) stayed stuck in the psychology of staff cars for 'top people'. Their heavy tractor (based on tank technology) proved both too slow and too heavy for civilian agriculture. Other smaller companies such as Schreiber in the UK encountered limits to its rate of growth in the furniture industry and were ripe for takeover by GEC which, after the Second World War, was looking for diversification out of heavy engineering.

Innovation, Costs and Pricing

Such arguments are relevant both to consumer and intermediate goods and also to new processes and products bought in by firms for their own use. These have a relatively slow initial phase, followed by a rapid growth phase as their application becomes more acceptable, and a mature phase in which their sales take mainly a replacement form. This has major implications for both costs and prices.

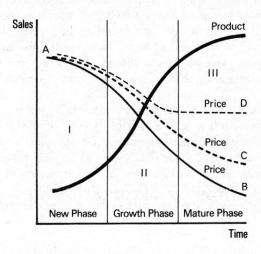

FIG. 4.10(a)   The product cycle and price cycles

Figure 4.10(a) illustrates the extent to which the introduction of a new product can be associated initially with a high price in phase I, followed by a declining price in phase II and a relatively low price in phase III. Such price falls in real terms are characteristic of many of the markets in which new products are introduced, especially those products with a high technology component where increases in productivity are associated with a cheapening of the cost of production, as has been the case with consumer hi-fi, video equipment and micro-electronics. In the latter field, as has been well illustrated by Edmond Sciberras (1977), a fall similar to that of AB is very possible. In some areas a fall in price in real terms more similar to the line AC may well be probable. In other markets, by contrast, for example in the automobile industry which achieved maturity in the 1930s in the United States and in the 1950s in Western Europe and Japan, prices may stabilise in the mature phase on the line AD.

Superficially, such price reduction following innovation appears to conform with the classic model of market competition. But the classic model is outdated. The survival of small microeconomic firms depends in large part on the extent to which larger mesoeconomic enterprise is either interested or already established in the new market.

Selective Survival

Thus, in terms of the standard product-cycle model as illustrated in Figure 4.10(a), a variety of firms could try to enter the market in its new phase I. But this would be followed by a period of relatively high mortality for those who failed to achieve the transition from innovation to the growth phase of the product, i.e. phase II of the product cycle. In phase III, the earlier rapid growth of firms tends to give way to a declining rate of growth as a degree of saturation – at prevailing levels of income distribution – is reached in the markets concerned.

Associated with this, with a decline in price per unit, profits would fall, leading to a relative decline in the rate of growth of the firm. Recent experience in the home computer market demonstrates that in phase II the industry often experiences a 'shake-out'. Numerous small computer firms have been the casualties of an inability to move from bright ideas to on-going commercial viability. Frequently it has been the inability of the owner-innovator to become a successful entrepreneur. It is in these micro cases that there is a limit to managerial capacity, rather than in the mesoeconomic company.

Typically, the transition between the first phase of the product cycle and the second growth phase is associated – for the surviving firms – with successful transition from an owner-entrepreneur or vertical management structure to the multifunctional or multidivisional management structure of the kind already illustrated in Figures 4.5(a) through to 4.5(c) and its related argument.

Early and Late Entrants

However, as illustrated in Figure 4.10(b), even if two or more firms may in principle achieve the same technical and management economies, as indicated by the long-run average cost curve declining through three phases of the product cycle, a later entrant to the market may find itself out-manoeuvred at each phase of the cycle by 'stepped' rather than 'smoothed' price reductions which are possible for the earlier entrant but with which the later firm cannot compete. By phase II of the product cycle, a later entrant would find its initial price level of 70 undercut by the price level 50 feasible at phase II for the earlier entrant to the market. Similarly at phase III of the product cycle, if the late entrant is successful enough to persist to such large-scale production, it will find itself competing with an earlier entrant which has already been able to achieve the price level of 30 units.

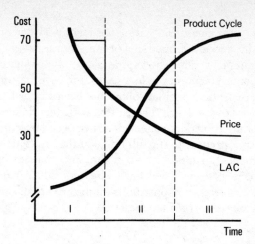

FIG. 4.10(b)   The product cycle and stepped price adjustment

To survive such competitive pricing over the successive cost-reducing phases of the product cycle, the late entrant would need to be able to sustain substantial losses. Small firms typical of the textbook microeconomic model may not make the transition to phase II unless they have either significant venture capital or stock market success, or state support (as in the case of Sir Clive Sinclair's nascent electronic companies in Britain in the 1970s). Any firm making it from phase II to phase III would need either substantial financial backing from creditors or institutions persuaded of its long-term chances of survival, or cross-subsidisation from other profitable activities. In either case, such a firm is likely to be large and mesoeconomic rather than small and microeconomic in character.

There also are other penalties from late entry. The video market provides an example. Early successful entrants could impose industry standards – such as was done by Sony-Beta and JVC-VHS. This meant that consumers could only change brands later at some cost, and unsuccessful entrants using different 'standards' failed (for instance Philips/Grundig with their V2000 model). This is especially true in high technology industries like tele-communications and computers.

Barriers to Expansion

Thus with few exceptions, expansion from the 'new' to the 'growth' phase of the product cycle is likely to be open only to a firm which manages to transcend the limits of the owner-entrepreneur paradigm of the textbook microeconomic model, or which has established itself early in the new product cycle.

The difficulties for a small firm with a vertical management structure in making the transition to multifunctional or multidivisional management are illustrated in Figure 4.11. This shows that a firm under successful owner-entrepreneurial management may at first see its unit costs fall and, by the end of production phase I, after an initial volume has been attained, unit costs will have reached their lowest level. Thereafter, with the change to a multi-functional or multidivisional management structure, gains from the original attention of the entrepreneur to the full range of the firm's activities may be offset by adjustment difficulties in expansion. Such barriers to expansion (rather than the barriers to entry which will be examined in Chapter 5) are not insurmountable, nor necessary constraints on the growth of small firms. But in practice they can prove considerable.

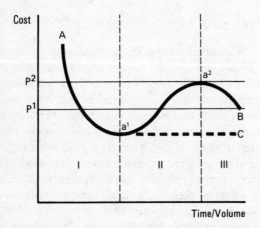

FIG. 4.11   Rising costs in transition to growth: the microeconomic firm

For instance, in Britain the Lotus car company in the 1960s achieved considerable market penetration through classic innovations, similar to phase I of the product cycle. Colin Chapman, an innovating entrepreneur of genius, had developed a 'monocoque' body which eliminated the need for the classic vehicle chassis. This weight reduction resulted in dramatic success on racing circuits. Chapman also sold his cars well on the domestic market by shrewd commercialisation of their 'grand prix' image. His Lotus cars, and in particular the basically simple *Elite*, gained a very considerable increase in volume sales. As a result, within a few years, the market penetration of Lotus had achieved nearly half that of the entire Rootes group (later Chrysler and later still Talbot-Citroën-Peugeot). However this 'growth phase' imposed very considerable demands on the entrepreneurial capacities of the company. In terms of Figure 4.11, in order to expand further than point a^1, Colin Chapman was forced to seek external finance, to delegate responsibility for design and production, and to enlarge his access to distribution retail outlets. Despite the genius of his design and the growing demand for Lotus cars, costs rose and the firm faced short-term profit difficulties. By the mid 1980s, Lotus had been taken over by General Motors, who planned to locate more of its production outside the UK.

Transitional Costs

Thus, a successful entrepreneur in phase I of a product cycle may find by the end of phase II that unit costs have risen from a^1 to a^2 in Figure 4.11, and above prevailing market price, p^1. In product areas less 'differentiated' than Lotus, there is only limited scope to raise the prevailing price p^1 to p^2 in such a way as to offset the rise in costs.

As a result, a small firm typical of the microeconomic model which seeks to expand into a multi-product market (in Chapman's case, a range of passenger cars rather than the basic Lotus model) may well face elimination from the market through the simple phenomenon of unit costs exceeding unit price, i.e. negative marginal receipts. From a different initial base, earlier in the twentieth century, and a different market share, Ford faced a similar problem of transition to modern management structures. Henry Ford innovated the entire mass-production automobile market in the United States. But he also refused to offer product variation ('you can have any colour you like so long as it's black'). In other words, the owner-entrepreneur found it difficult to delegate responsibility, constantly intervened himself in production or sales, obstructed management, and allowed General Motors to take over market leadership.

In principle such a firm may transcend the difficulties of phase II of Figure 4.11 and achieve a further reduction in costs in phase III of what we might call the *management cycle* rather than the product cycle. Thus, the enterprise may experience a decline in unit costs at a higher volume of sales in such a way that it transcends the S-shaped cost curve of Figure 4.11 and re-establishes itself at a level where its unit costs are lower than the prevailing market price. But if the firm achieved this transition it would have translated itself from the microeconomic structure of the owner-entrepreneur into the structure of a multifunctional, multidivisional company typical of the mesoeconomic sector.

Evidence and Evaluation

The theoretical case on barriers to expansion for small firms can be illustrated not only by the case of Lotus, but also by overall evaluation of US and UK evidence. For instance, Graham Bannock (1971) found in an assessment of the scope and limits of growth of small and medium firms that such enterprise 'ran out of steam' at an employment level of some 250 persons in the US and 100 persons in the UK.

In a more recent study, Doyle and Gallagher (1986) found even lower 'barriers to expansion' in the UK economy. Using database files for a range of firms for 1982–84, they found that the limit to expansion began as low as 20 employees. Certainly, smaller firms were the main creators of new jobs. In the category of firms with less than 20 employees, nearly one job per year was created, against a job loss of six per cent per year for firms employing more than 1,000 people. But after gaining an average of 20 employees apiece, the small companies encountered limits to their growth.

Doyle and Gallagher stress that there are differences between firms and regions behind their average figures. They offer no theoretical explanation of the limits to the rate of growth of such small firms. Nonetheless, they observe that: 'there is cause for concern in the rather low point on the size-distribution of firms at which net job gain becomes net job loss'.

Commenting on their findings, Clive Woodcock (1986) observes that they underline 'some of the doubts expressed whether the [small firm] sector can deliver all that is promised on its behalf by political and other promoters'. Woodcock also comments with reason that:

> The lack of new larger firms can also in the longer term have an effect on the ability of small firms themselves to survive as it has been observed that the successful growth of smaller firms often depends on there being a larger organisation around which they can cluster.

Such an observation excellently illustrates our argument on the unequal relations between the meso and micro sectors of the economy. The product cycle is unequally available to big and small business.

Product and Process

The above argument is relevant not only to *intra*-sectoral dynamics within the market economy but also to *inter*-sectoral growth. Moreover, the product-cycle case obtains not only for products themselves but also for processes of production, whether in agriculture, industry or services.

In agriculture, the innovation of high-yield seeds into grain or rice production in Third World countries may first be slow, then speed up during a growth phase, but thereafter face limited growth. In India, only some 200 hectares had been planted with the new high-yield seeds by the mid 1960s, but by 1970 some 24 million hectares had been planted with the new seed varieties. As with industrial product growth and income distribution, the social ownership of land played a key role in the 'growth phase' of the new seed products, with the gains accruing in large part to those landlords who could afford resources for project planning and irrigation. Moreover, a 'mature' phase or plateau was achieved in the new seed varieties before government intervention opened new water resources for a further phase of planting (Malloch Brown, 1984).

In industry, in the advanced market economies, new products such as assembly-line robots have transformed the production process, both increasing efficiency and decreasing costs through the displacement of labour. The result has been compromised in countries such as Britain and the United States by the resulting unemployment of industrial labour. In countries such as Japan, company management in association with the Ministry of International Trade and Industry have been concerned to ensure that the 'decline' phase of employment in the product cycle caused by the introduction of robotics has been offset by the introduction of what Perroux (1965) has stressed as 'entirely new' technologies, products and markets, enabling Japanese companies to maintain their commitment to the lifetime employment of their labour force.

In services, the introduction of new technologies such as word and data processors is only beginning to register a significant effect on employment in the 1980s. But one result has been computerised check-out systems in hypermarkets, reinforcing customer self-service with a reduction of staff per unit of turnover and increasing concentration in favour of multiple outlets versus corner stores. In office employment, including financial services and banking, computerisation and self-service is beginning to reduce counter staff and has already resulted in many cases in an end to employment growth. The new technologies of word and data processing have also promoted an increase in home-working versus office work, which in turn has indirect effects on the demand for office space in central urban areas, and thereby on the construction industry.

Public Intervention

The implications of the product cycle and technological innovation on public policy have been considerable. Virtually all governments in the advanced market economies have been concerned to offset the decline of agriculture or traditional industry through policies for the public support of prices or production.

In agriculture, the struggle of smallholders in the United States to establish their rights against the big ranchers and bank-backed barons of cattle rearing has formed the stock-in-trade of Hollywood producers for half a century. Earlier this century, the plight of the smallholder and the imperative need to get 'the farmer out of the mud' was the basis of Roosevelt's New Deal. In Europe, governments have offset the social trauma of a fall in working population in farming, from a quarter to less than a tenth over thirty years, by price support. Milton Friedman may criticise such subsidy. But he cannot have it both ways. Small farms survive through state support rather than managerial diseconomies in big farms.

In industry, some of the countries with the most committed public image of market economics have been the most active in formulating policies to support small versus big business. In West Germany this has taken the form of *Mittelstandspolitik*, the support by government through loans or grants for medium-sized enterprise. In Italy, a plethora of state agencies has been devised to achieve the same effect, including the state holding company, EFIM. In France, the policy of support for PME (Petite et Moyenne Entreprise) versus big business has been a key aspect of formal government policy, despite the fact that the main accent has been on support for 'national champions' which in practice has meant aid to mesoeconomic rather than microeconomic enterprise.

Government intervention in services such as education, health or transport has been mainly on social grounds. Until recently the expansion of services has posed few problems in terms of overall employment creation. Enthusiasm or euphoria has accompanied the claim that the advanced market economies could move painlessly into a post-industrial or service-orientated economy. But in reality, as we will see in Chapter 7, the dynamics of unequal competition and the dual market economy affect the services sector as much as any other.

4.5 The Surviving Small Firm

There are a range of reasons which explain the survival of the small firm against the dynamics of the trend to big business in the modern market economy. These include: (i) the unavailability of full capacity use by big business if they undertake additional investment at the restricted edge of given markets, and (ii) the price umbrella effect by which big business is content to gain super-normal profits while enabling smaller firms to survive with a lower profit mark-up. There is also (iii) the 'satellite' effect by which small firms survive as suppliers to bigger business, and (iv) the survival of small firms in traditional markets which are of no major interest to leading firms since their long-term potential is limited, or because they are in relative or absolute decline. In addition, there is (v) the role of public purchasing, and especially defence contracts, in sustaining both big and small business in a key growth market, and (vi) the role of the small innovating firm which is first into an entirely new market and which may well flourish there for some time before the big-league firms have entered on a scale sufficient to start the standard sequence of concentration and centralisation of activity in their own hands.

Only the sixth of these factors has been considered in recent literature, which has claimed a renaissance of the small firm. This has been combined with the claim that small business is the job-creator of the future, and the associated philosophy of 'small is beautiful'.

Small is Beautiful

'Small is beautiful' is identified with E. F. Schumacher. But Schumacher's argument was in no sense a simple foretaste of 'Thatchernomics' or 'Reaganomics'. Schumacher was a subtle and sophisticated man with a shrewd grasp of both the realities and limits of market forces. Coming from a culture in which the role of the small firm was considered an important aspect of government policy through *Mittelstandspolitik*, he nonetheless knew the realities of economies of scale and spent much of his life analysing their consequences as economic adviser to one of Britain's largest nationalised industries.

Schumacher's argument was not so much that big business should be broken up in favour of more beautiful, smaller enterprise, but that it risked being monolithic and bureaucratic and should try to recreate within its own structures the virtues of small size which gave direct responsibility and personal attachment to the management of many smaller firms. His emphasis was therefore sociological as much as economic, and his claims were for an economics in which 'people mattered'. Thus, 'small is beautiful' did not mean 'small is best'. He stressed (1974, p. 54) 'the *duality* of the human requirement when it comes to the question of size: there is no *single* answer. For his different purposes man needs many different structures, both small ones and large ones, some exclusive and some comprehensive. . . . For constructive work, the principal task is always the restoration of some kind of balance.'

'Small Means Jobs'?

In the United States in the late 1970s, much attention was given in business and political circles to the findings of Professor David Birch of MIT in his study of job creation among small and big business in the United States, *The*

Job Generation Process (1979). Professor Birch claimed to show that between 1960 and 1976 no fewer than two-thirds of the new jobs created in the private sector of the US economy were generated by the tiniest firms, those with fewer than 21 employees. Larger firms with more than 50 employees, by contrast, showed large net job losses. Very large firms stopped being net job-creators, losing on balance as many jobs through closures or contractions as they created.

Birch's main conclusion was that it was a waste of money for government to pump resources into larger firms as a method of job creation, and that it should focus instead on encouraging a fabric of small entrepreneurs.

Or Services Means Jobs?

Some support for one aspect of the Birch findings emerged from a study published in Britain by Steve Fothergill of the Centre for Environmental Studies and Graham Gudgin of the Cambridge Economic Policy Group, who found that in the East Midlands of the United Kingdom firms with fewer than 26 employees increased their employment from 1968 to 1975 by over 11 per cent, while jobs contracted in all other groups of firms (Fothergill and Gudgin, 1979).

But Fothergill and Gudgin parted company from Birch in two key respects. First, they found that the very small British firms which increased employment in manufacturing created very few jobs. Their total job creation over seven years was only just over one-fifth of one per cent a year. Second, the so-called shift of job creation to small firms was in fact a symptom of de-industrialisation and a structural shift of labour from manufacturing into services. This also was found to be the case with the Birch study for the United States where, although the smallest firms created 66 per cent of new jobs, only 8 per cent of these were in manufacturing.

Structural Shifts

The result is disappointing for those, like former British Chancellor Geoffrey Howe or the then Industry Secretary Sir Keith Joseph, who accepted the Birch study at face value and expected a regeneration of British industry through small business. The *intra*sectoral conclusions drawn from the Birch argument – that small firms are tomorrow's job creators – masked an *inter*sectoral shift in the structure of employment from industry into services. Not least, as shown by the trends to concentration and centralisation in the service sector in Chapter 7, major net job creation by small firms in services may prove to be relatively short-lived as job displacement through concentration, centralisation and the effects of new job-saving technology proceed apace.

Also, the broad-brush approach taken by the Birch study and the misleading conclusions drawn from it by policy-makers indicate the importance of distinguishing the intrasectoral dynamics of equal and unequal competition between big and small business. For instance, Birch's evidence cited three categories of firms: (1) large firms with no net job creation, (2) smaller firms with large net job loss, and (3) the smallest firms with some job creation.

As will be argued in more detail in Chapter 6, big business has tended to internalise hitherto external economies of scale. This means that the second category of Birch's firms may well include former 'satellite' suppliers who are no longer pulled along by external demand from leading firms. Some of Birch's third category of the smallest firms may either be in declining sectors or in segments of markets of no interest to larger firms. Moreover, big business still dominates the innovation process, both in Europe and the United States.

Micro and Meso Innovation

One of the most comprehensive international studies of innovation in small and medium firms has been undertaken by the OECD (OECD, 1982). This reveals both the scope and limits of innovation in the microeconomic sector and confirms the need to distinguish intrasectoral and intersectoral dimensions of innovation, as well as what we have called meso-micro linkages in the innovation process.

The OECD report shows that firms of less than 1,000 workers accounted for more than 40 per cent of major innovations in the United States. But nearly 50 per cent of industrial research and development expenditure in the OECD countries as a whole was represented by only 40 large firms. The report argues that large firms are not necessarily the first to innovate, tending to increase profits by perfecting existing lines while small firms try to exploit gaps in the market. But while small firms may be the first into new markets, 'the main innovation is likely to be the introduction of new materials and components by suppliers or technical centres serving the industrial branch. In sub-contracting and intermediate production, innovation by small firms is very much conditioned by the strategies of the large client industries' (OECD, 1982). In other words, the satellite role of micro firms is crucial and they tend to be meso-dependent innovators.

Moreover, the OECD report found that in established sectors where large and small firms exist side by side, 'the latter face competition from considerably more powerful competitors better equipped for R & D and marketing; here the big firms usually retain the initiative in radical innovations which change the technology of the sector while the smaller firms adapt by applying these innovations in the niches which they have filled and by specialising so as to keep clear of their powerful competitors'.

Similarly, a study of innovation in the British economy from 1945 to 1980 found that over half the number of innovations in this period were undertaken by firms with more than 10,000 employees, and over three-quarters by firms with more than 1,000 employees. Small firms with less than 200 employees represented only about a sixth of the innovations over the period concerned, while big business with over 10,000 employees had increased its share of innovations by a fifth of the total registered from 1945 to 1980 (SPRU, 1982).

The Dual Market

Thus the dual market of meso and micro enterprise applies in innovation as elsewhere. This is reflected in the minimal share of small and medium-sized firms in the innovation of what Perroux has called 'entirely new' products – from 10 per cent to 20 per cent for OECD countries as a whole. One reason, according to the OECD report, is that innovation 'is a means and not an end in the strategy of small firms'. They are driven to it by rising costs rather than consciously extending the technological frontier. In real terms they are mainly adapters and reactors in the innovation process. A second reason, according to the same report, is the lack of a sufficient 'innovative culture' among smaller firms, reflecting their relative lack of a long-term forward-planning capacity (OECD, 1982).

The result is that 'few new innovating firms are being set up, no more than a few dozen a year in the European countries' (and several of them, it might be added, with state subsidy and support rather than unaided entry to new markets). In Japan, Canada or the United States itself – allegedly the spawning-ground for new firms through a combination of wider access to venture capital and larger defence and high-tech federal purchasing – the OECD report states that 'there has been a disquieting *decline* which is reflected in the *decreasing* number of small technological firms registered on stock exchanges'. The OECD figures show a decline from some 100 to 200 new small firms in the 1960s, to 'almost zero' in the mid 1970s. Thereafter, with the largest-ever US armaments programme undertaken by the Reagan administration, the satellite-supplier effect temporarily re-appeared in the United States. But this had more to do with the role of government and the military-industrial complex than with the survival of the smallest and fittest for innovation through the free working of the market.

4.6 Summary

(1) Long-run average cost curves have multiple forms, ranging from exceptional U-shaped through rising or falling J-shaped, to so-called L-shaped.

(2) The same principle of increased efficiency and lowered costs through division of labour likewise applies to division of management responsibilities in the multifunctional, multidivisional or multinational company.

(3) The level or height of the cost curve as well as its shape is crucial in the competitive process.

(4) Major disparities in the level of costs have emerged for companies with otherwise comparable levels of management efficiency in the world economy. This occurs either because technical progress displaces labour and reduces wage costs through automation, or because of multinational access to cheaper labour for components production/assembly in less developed countries.

(5) While rising long-run average cost curves may be relevant to mining or agriculture (see further Chapter 7), their application by analogy from fishing or farming to industry (as by Samuelson and Lipsey) is invalid.

(6) Where managerial diseconomies do occur, they may be offset by technical or production economies of scale. Constant returns to scale may be offset by reduced overall costs through managerial economies. The efficiently run enterprise may benefit from both managerial *and* technical scale economies.

(7) There is no necessary limit to either the rate of growth or the absolute market share of a successful enterprise.

(8) Where slowing rates of growth of leading firms have been observed, this may reflect the mature or saturated phase of the product cycle rather than any inherent limits to the growth of the firm.

(9) Where relative stability is observable in the market shares of leading firms in mature economies, this may reflect non-competitive pricing between oligopolies which have transferred their main competitive thrust into export markets or foreign direct investment and production, rather than inherent limits to their size or rate of growth.

(10) The multi-product or multi-sectoral firm may sustain or increase its overall rate of growth by diversifying production into new markets.

(11) Limits to the growth of smaller firms may be imposed by raised costs and falling profits during the period of transition from owner-entrepreneurship to multi-functional or multi-divisional management structures.

(12) Small firms do not have a higher innovation record than bigger business, and their job creation is much less significant in industry than in services. Many small and medium firms rely on 'satellite'-type pull from big business or government for their survival or growth.

5 From Equal to Unequal Competition

Conventional market theory applauds rewards for winners and penalties for losers. But it also predicates competition between equals. It is reluctant to admit the outcome of unequal gains for winners, or the domination of modern markets by big business.

In reality, modern markets are closer to the paradigm of St Matthew (or Karl Marx) than to Milton Friedman. With only some exceptions, to firms that have shall be given and from firms that have not shall be taken away. As Joan Robinson (1971, p. 100) put it: 'the essence of the competitive process is that some firms take business away from others'. The 'takeaway' may well be takeover in the process of centralising market power in the hands of already bigger business. It may well be asset-stripping and elimination. For, in practice, modern markets are subject to unequal competition between big and small business rather than the competition between equals posited by traditional market theory.

On the other hand, the process of unequal competition has not led to the outright monopoly domination of all markets. Even when some of the Marxist theorists of 'monopoly capital' saw national markets dominated by giant holding companies or trusts, they only envisaged a world market dominated by a single giant combine as a logical rather than a probable outcome of the trend to monopoly. In reality, a fabric of smaller national firms continues to survive, and sometimes to flourish, in developed and less developed economies alike.

Some reasons for the continuance of smaller firms have already been given in Chapter 4. Inability to maximise technical economies of scale may mean that it is not worthwhile for mesoeconomic leaders to 'mop up' the micro end of a given market. At the same time, while few local or national firms can challenge the multinational majors, they may nevertheless mount a challenge to their equals in the microeconomic sector in a manner which more or less approximates to the conventional competitive model. We can describe such conditions as equal competition, bearing in mind that the equality is by and large within meso and micro markets rather than between them. Allowing for this qualification, various textbook categories of competitive strategy are still relevant to market behaviour.

5.1   Maximisers and Minimisers

In conventional theory, the aim of the firm is to maximise profits. According to William Baumol (1959), its aim is to maximise revenues. For Joan Robinson (1953), 'the most valid simple generalisation is that the aim of the entrepreneur is for the firm first to survive, and secondly to grow.'

Joan Robinson's observation is especially relevant to unequal competition between big and small business. Mesoeconomic firms may not be the first to pioneer a new product or technique, but they tend to be the leaders in the mass-production transition from its 'new' to its 'growth' phase. Leading in major innovations and investment projects, they also use their gains from size, their hold over buyers and suppliers and their access to finance to employ two main strategies of unequal competition. The first is the defensive strategy of imposing barriers to the entry of challengers. The second is the offensive strategy of setting prices which so reduce other firms' profits as to soften them up for takeover or eliminate them from the market.

Such mechanisms are analysed later in this chapter. But they have relevance for the issue of which firm can maximise what profits under whatever conditions. Microeconomic firms may prefer minimal or limited revenues rather than invite retaliation by challenging the market share of big-league firms already dominant in the market. They may well seek to defend their corner of the market, aiming to survive rather than maximise profits. With some exceptions in 'entirely new' markets, they will tend to be price-followers rather than price-leaders.

Price-Makers and Price-Takers

The result of such unequal competition between big- and small-league firms qualifies and revises the sequence of pricing in the conventional market model. For a generation of orthodox theorists, the price-making power of enterprise was limited essentially to imperfect competition through product differentiation, on the lines analysed in Chapter 3. For Baran and Sweezy (1966), price-making power by big business was considerably greater and amounted in effect to a form of producer sovereignty.

This theme has been developed particularly by Galbraith, who has also transformed the orthodox distinction between sovereign consumers expressing choice and firms as capacity-adapters responding to changes in demand. In *The New Industrial State* Galbraith describes this change as 'the revised sequence', contrasting his own arguments with those of Samuelson who maintained that 'the consumer is, so to speak, the king'. Galbraith argues (1967a, pp. 211–12) that the revised sequence means reversal of the signals and instructions from the consumer to the producer, maintaining that 'the producing firm reaches forward to control its markets and beyond to manage the market behaviour and shape the actual social attitude of those whom, ostensibly, it serves'.

But the revised sequence also implies further reversals of the competitive model. In its cruder versions such as Milton Friedman's *Free to Choose*, the model implies that what will be sold, in which quantity and at what price depends on the sovereign consumer. But even quantity can be influenced by advertising and 'induced' demand. The kind of product or service, at what price, now depend less on the so-called sovereign consumer and more on the market strategy of leading big business. In setting prices or proffering new products, modern enterprise looks as much or more to the anticipated reactions of other firms as to the market provided by final consumers.

Markers and Leaders

In practice, this corporate awareness of the realities of unequal competition transforms the context of 'cost-plus' pricing analysed in Chapter 3. 'Cost-plus' still remains the long-term marker for price determination. But the plus may be normal or super-normal profit, reflecting unequal cost structures between micro and meso enterprise and unequal power to set the prevailing price level.

One result has become known as 'rule-of-thumb' price-markers. In other words, market leaders will give a broad 'rule-of-thumb' indication that cost-plus or full-cost-plus pricing by smaller firms will be acceptable to them without retaliation. Alternatively, when costs are unequal, meso leaders may offer what Penrose has called the 'price umbrella' to micro firms, allowing them normal cost-plus margins while the leaders reap super-normal profits.

Scherer (1978, pp. 49–50) has observed that when costs vary widely between firms, co-ordination of the market through the issue of rule-of-thumb or full-cost pricing becomes more difficult. Classically, the trade associations of which Adam Smith himself was so suspicious help avoid 'cut-throat competition'. This can work either through direct recommendation or indirectly, as when trade associations develop standard cost accounting systems for 'the benefit of members'. Leading members of such associations are likely to play a leading role in recommended practices.

Leaders and Indicators

Focal-point pricing has been suggested by Schelling (1960) as a means of overcoming uncertainty in a market where a variety of firms may not be able independently to determine a standard price. Schelling gives the example of an invitation to meet somebody in New York City when no information has been given as to where or when to meet. Putting the issue to various people, Schelling found that a majority chose the information booth at Grand Central station and that nearly all had chosen to meet at twelve noon. The station is central within New York and noon is literally the central time of the day: in this sense, in Schelling's argument, they both constituted focal points for the otherwise uninformed individual. Alternatively, a leading firm may make lesser firms a godfather offer which they cannot afford to refuse, such as 'See you at Grand Central station at twelve'.

Laggard Pricing

Some firms are unable rather than unwilling to follow the price leaders. They may find through diminishing market share that they need to charge either a higher or lower price for particular products. Higher prices may be possible through brand attachment and product differentiation. Lower prices may be necessary as 'loss leaders' to increase consumer attachment or prevent a decrease in market share. But some price followers are simply laggards who have difficulty either in catching up or in surviving in the industry at all.

The case of American Motors has been a classic example of the laggard-pricing effect. In the mid 1960s, facing declining market share, the company reduced its list prices substantially relative to the Big Three market leaders – General Motors, Ford and Chrysler. The leaders did not retaliate partly because American Motors, with only some 2.5 per cent of the US market, represented no significant threat to their own market share. However, the leaders may also have seen indirect advantages in allowing American Motors to pursue its own price policy – the reduction of US motor manufacturers from four to three would possibly have initiated an enquiry under anti-trust legislation. The fact that American Motors was able to lower prices without retaliation reflected less the price challenge of the neoclassical competitive model than tolerance of maverick behaviour in their own interests by the market leaders.

Revenue Maximisation

Baumol (1959) has claimed that instead of maximising profits – either in the short term or long run – firms will tend to maximise sales, subject to the condition that their profits do not fall below some minimum value.

Baumol does not claim that profits play no role in the pricing decisions of firms but rather that they are secondary or subordinate to sales maximisation. Figures 5.1 and 5.2 represent the essentials of the revenue versus profit-maximisation case, in terms which are broadly compatible with Baumol's

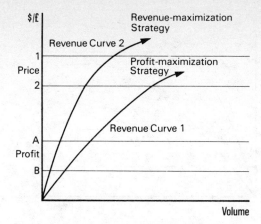

FIG. 5.1   Revenue versus unit profit maximisation

own exposition. Both figures represent total revenue curves.

In Figure 5.1, the firm pursuing a profit-maximisation strategy (revenue curve 1) charges price 1 and makes profits equivalent to level A. This gives it a lower rate of growth of total revenue and lower revenue overall than the firm pursuing a revenue-maximisation strategy (revenue curve 2), which charges the lower price 2 and makes lower profits equivalent to level B. This exposition makes sense in terms of the standard theory of the price elasticity of demand, i.e. that the lower the price the higher the sales and revenue, and vice versa.

On the other hand, the revenue-maximisation strategy, which yields a lower *rate* of profit in the short term may make possible a higher total *volume* of profit over the long run. As shown in Figure 5.2, due essentially to the lower price than that charged than in the profit-maximisation strategy, the revenue-maximising firm is able to incrase sales and revenue indefinitely. Thus, over the long run, the profit levels for the respective strategies in Figure 5.1 are reversed in Figure 5.2. Where the revenue maximiser with the lower price at 2 makes a higher rate of profit at B, the profit-maximising firm ends with lower revenue growth and lower profits (at A). The precise outcome is of course relative and depends on different short- and long-run factors.

The Short and the Long Term

A short-run revenue-maximisation strategy could well involve:

(1)   market penetration through either lower price or 'loss-leading';
(2)   promotional discounts on sales which are higher than would be pursued under the profit-maximisation strategy, thereby lowering the profit rate;

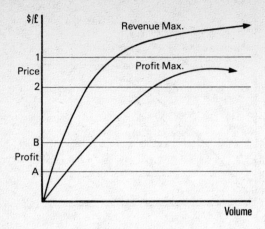

FIG. 5.2   Revenue and volume profit maximisation

(3)   higher advertising and other promotional expenditures devised to achieve a more rapid customer attachment to the brand or product or service concerned.

By the same token, however, these factors are also compatible with:

(1)   later price rises once consumer attachment and market penetration have been achieved;
(2)   a longer-term reduction of discounts away from 'loss-leading', and a more normal pricing practice designed to maintain market share;
(3)   lower advertising expenditure aimed at maintaining brand attachment rather than seeking a high profile and further penetration of the market, and thus inviting retaliation from other firms.

Market Power

The point is not that revenue maximisation does not occur, but that its role may be short rather than long term, depending on the relative market power of the company and the compatability of revenue maximisation with other aspects of overall corporate strategy.

Baumol was encouraged to break from the conventional assumptions of profits (versus sales) maximisation through his work as a consultant for a marketing research firm. He observed that marketing managers were preoccupied with the level of sales rather than current profits. Suggesting several reasons for this, Baumol argued that firms were in a weaker position to compete when sales either were not growing or were declining; that banks were less ready to finance companies which were faced with slow-growing or declining sales, and that personnel relations were eased by growth of revenue and sales while they were aggravated by low growth or contraction.

Clearly a successful rate of growth of sales and market share breeds success in a 'virtuous circle', generating optimism and higher 'animal spirits' among investors. In contrast with this optimism, both a low rate of growth of revenue and sales or a declining market share may encourage scepticism among investors and persuade them that a 'vicious circle' has gripped the company.

Sales and Personnel

The further factor stressed by Baumol (1959), the easing of personnel problems with revenue and job expansion, is self-evident. Sustained growth of sales implies both job creation for relevant management and also promotion mobility. In these respects, Baumol's case is compatible with Galbraith's argument that the technostructure is less concerned with profit maximisation in the short run than job fulfilment, promotion mobility and related salary increases. But, again, this may complement rather than deny the principle of maximising volume profits, subject to a minimum profit rate, over the long run.

While marketing executives stress sales, those in production emphasise output, finance executives accent the cost of borrowing, executives in foreign trade divisions highlight exchange rates, and foreign production managers in multinational companies are concerned with local conditions and the scope or scale of transfers between subsidiaries. These factors, like the divisions which they represent within the mesoeconomic company typical of the modern capitalist economy, form a part of multiple corporate strategies (elaborated in more detail in chapter 9).

Capacity Maximisation

One of the standard rules of thumb prevalent in an industry where firms have similar plant size and scale, concerns the profit break-even point at some percent of capacity, with profits made above or losses incurred below that level. Kaplan, Dirlan and Lanzilloti (1958, pp. 48–55 and 131–5) drew attention both to capacity maximisation as a corporate strategy and to its compatibility with full-cost or cost-plus pricing techniques.

General Motors, for example, for many years aimed at a return of some 15 per cent on total invested capital after tax, estimating its costs on an assumed standard volume operation of 80 per cent of capacity. Standard price was determined by adding the 15 per cent post-tax profit mark-up to this assumed standard volume of capacity use. In other words, in contrast with conventional marginal analysis, even General Motors could not know for certain how many automobiles it will sell in a given year. It therefore estimated cost as the basis for a full-cost or cost-plus profit mark-up on an assumed production capacity basis. A top-level prices policy committee within the corporation made adjustments to the standard price to allow for actual market circumstances, long-run strategic objectives in individual product markets, etc. But such additional long-run goals were secondary or sub-ordinate to the primary basis of capacity utilisation plus standard profit mark-up.

Multiplant Capacity

The rationale of capacity utilisation is simple enough. If a normal profit can be made by a standard profit mark-up on the basis of 80 per cent capacity use, and given the evidence that marginal cost either does not rise or may continue to fall until 100 per cent capacity utilisation, then higher than normal or super-normal profits will be made through full capacity utilisation in individual plants. Thus profit maximisation through plant maximisation becomes possible for the mesoeconomic multiplant company.

Such a capacity criterion is increasingly relevant in an era of multinational versus national companies. Tugendhat (1971) found that the Swedish SKF engineering corporation not only operated its pricing strategy for different plant in different countries on the basis of capacity utilisation but also worked, as a priority strategic aim, for capacity maximisation in different countries.

The different options open in this respect to mesoeconomic and micro-economic enterprise are very plain. A small company operating a single plant in one country where it is a market follower rather than a leader will not be in a position to operate a capacity-maximisation strategy. By contrast, a multinational company such as Ford is in a position to maximise capacity use for its plant worldwide and minimise losses in a recession by temporarily closing its least efficient plant. (See further Holland, 1987.)

The contrast can be illustrated in simple numerical terms. A single-plant microeconomic company may find that it is making no profit at all at 80 per cent of capacity utilisation. But a mesoeconomic company with either five plant in one country or five plant worldwide each of which, for the purposes of illustration, constitutes one-fifth of its overall production, can continue to operate four plants at full capacity while closing the fifth. Given that in real terms plant tend to be constructed over a number of years, the mesoeconomic company could withdraw the least efficient of its plant, thereby raising productivity in the others. It also could modernise capacity through an entirely new plant when and if economic conditions recover.

Maximise and Minimise

Thus for the mesoeconomic enterprise the strategic aim of capacity maximisation need not contradict a strategy of profit maximisation, but over the long run may fulfil it. By virtue of its multiplant capacity, the mesoeconomic company can minimise unit costs by maximising capacity, and thereby simultaneously maximise both profits and overall revenue.

In reality the growth, range and structure of sales in different national or multinational markets will constitute but one of several objectives which big business needs to accommodate in its overall corporate strategy. Not least among the attractions of low-price revenue maximisation is its compatibility with pricing strategies designed to deter entry of competitors into one's own market.

5.2 Dominance and Deterrence

The concept of barriers to entry was pioneered by J. S. Bain (1956) in his *Barriers to New Competition* (and also by Fellner (1949) in his *Competition Among the Few*). Bain broadly defines four categories concerning the ease of entry to markets and the tactics which can be employed by established firms to prevent it.

Easy Entry

On the first category of easy entry, Bain allows that conventional price theory has tended to exaggerate the freedom or ease for firms to realise the competitive assumptions of conventional neoclassical theory. Free entry assumes that existing members of the industry or service have no cost or other advantages over potential entrants. While Scherer (1978, p. 89) argues that empirical study suggests that continually declining long-run cost functions are exceptional in American industry, it is typical for long-run average total cost schedules to prove horizontal, rather than to rise. In other words if a downward-sloping J-shaped curve of the kind hypothesised in Chapter 4 is uncommon, the standard L-shaped cost schedule is more typical. In this case there are advantages from 'early entry' and disadvantages from 'late entry' into markets. Moreover, gains from size or economies of scale concern not only production economies but also finance and credit and hold over buyers and suppliers (oligopoly or oligopsony). All tend to impose barriers to entry for new firms into the market.

Ineffectively Impeded Entry

Bain's second category is 'ineffectively impeded entry'. He argues that the dominant firms may have an advantage over potential entrants and can in principle deter entry by price restraint or reducing prices. But because the period of contested entry may be long, with forgone cash flow and profit, the already established firms may find it preferable to let new firms into the market by raising prices above the entry-deterring level. This has the additional advantage to them of increasing cash flow or revenue so that the joint survivors accept the higher price levels set by already established firms to their mutual advantage.

Effectively Impeded Entry

Bain's third category of effectively impeded entry describes conditions where dominant firms have absolute cost advantages over smaller firms or potential entrants. Such advantages may arise from:

(1) control of production techniques by established firms, via either patents or secrecy;
(2) imperfections in the market for hired factors of production (labour, materials, etc) which allow lower buying prices to established firms;
(3) significant limitations on the supplies of productive factors in specific markets or sub-markets due to relative shortage of capacity in supplying firms, where new entry and an increase in output will perceptibly increase factor prices;
(4) money-market conditions imposing higher interest rates on potential entrants than upon established firms.

   Bain also stresses:

(5) the role of product differentiation through the cumulative preference over time of buyers for established brand names and company reputation, either generally or except for a small minority of buyers;
(6) large-scale advertising. A potential entrant might be able to sustain this for a period of time, but the cumulative effect of such advertising over decades identifies the product itself with the brand name of the established firm (such as Hoover for vacuum cleaners or Frigidaire for refrigerators), with considerable deterrent effect on new entrants.

Blockaded Entry

Bain's fourth category (blockaded entry) describes a situation in which

Hall-Hitch 'cost plus' prices lie below the entry price in such a way that a would-be entrant could not realise the kind of normal profit available to an established firm even in the long run. In practice, if established firms are price-makers, they may lower price in the short term so that the would-be entrant never enjoys a long run.

Bain allows that diseconomies of large scale may in principle prevent entry-deterring tactics by already established firms, but argues that 'we neglect this possibility as improbable, and will assume approximately constant unit costs as firm size exceeds the minimum necessary for those costs'. (Bain, 1956, pp. 1–20)

Crucially, Bain stressed the importance of the degree of concentration among already established sellers in the capacity to forestall or prevent entry into markets. The degree of seller concentration was important because it could be expected to determine whether or not, or to what extent, the established sellers in the market will in effect act collectively in determining their prices. He also argued that in concentrated industries collusion allowed a strategic escalation of prices where entry barriers were high.

Unequal Finance

Unequal access to finance and unequal borrowing costs for big and small business are a key part of unequal competition and barriers to entry. It is clear that a micro firm starting from scratch in the way envisaged by conventional market theory, would need external finance on a sizeable scale. To gain this it would need to persuade venture capitalists, the stock market or banks that it could penetrate and survive in markets already dominated by very much larger firms. Investors do not need a sophisticated theory of the firm to recognise that the financial and economic muscle of big business is likely to be used to restrain entry or eliminate small-scale business from new markets.

Moreover, it is evident that bankers in general have a clear idea of the different creditworthiness of big and small business, based on their relative chance of long-term survival. Kumar (1984) has shown that large business with bigger borrowing can gain a lower price or interest rate on its external funds from banks. In other words, banks are in the market for big borrowers and are prepared to offer lower terms on their lending. As illustrated in Figure 5.3, the micro entrant to the market borrows less at volume x and pays more at cost level a, while the meso firm borrows more at volume y and pays less at cost level b. Granted that the micro firm on entry could not have achieved the long-run scale economies and lower average cost of the already established meso enterprise, this combined penalty of higher cost of borrowing with a higher unit cost of production should in itself be sufficient to deter micro entrants from challenging established meso enterprise. As will be shown in some detail in Chapter 7, such dual financial markets and discriminatory borrowing structures are an increasingly important part of the mechanism of unequal competition since both mesoeconomic borrowers and lenders have increased their size and market share in recent years.

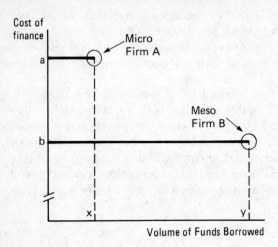

FIG. 5.3   Unequal costs of finance

The Edge of the Market

Shepherd (1979, p. 34) has usefully distinguished 'typical' and 'a-typical' degrees of concentration in the size distribution of firms in his analysis of market entry. In Figure 5.4 he shows a typical size distribution of firms in the order of their market shares, starting with the top and dominant firm, and reflecting the concentration and 'cut-off point' of the top four companies. These represent an 'oligopoly group' – distinguished from 'fringe' firms – in his own words, 'similar to the US automobile market'. Shepherd then argues that 'at the edge of the market – at the end of the array of firms – there may be barriers to entry which keep out whatever potential competitors there might be'. Stressing that the height of the entry barrier ranges from low to high enough to prevent any entry, Shepherd also admits that the group of most likely potential entrants 'may be large and strong or, instead, small and weak'.

Micro Edge and Meso Barriers

Shepherd's distinction between the 'oligopoly group' and 'fringe' firms directly parallels our categories of meso and micro enterprise. However, his

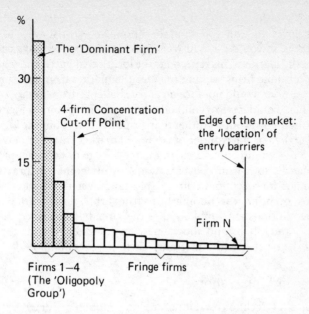

FIG. 5.4   Edge-of-market entry barriers (from Shepherd, 1979)

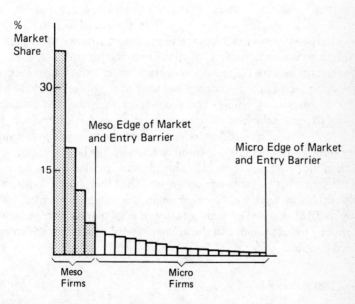

FIG. 5.5   Meso and micro barriers to entry

argument does not fully follow through the unequal entry prospects of big and small business. In reality, if a microeconomic enterprise were to seek to enter the market, it would do so at what – in Figure 5.5 – we have called the micro edge of the market. This represents the location of *micro entry barriers*.

But mesoeconomic firms seeking to enter the market from an established base in other sectors would not face an entry challenge from microeconomic enterprise. They would have to contend with firms one to four in Figure 5.4 – Shepherd's 'oligopoly group' – rather than firms five to *n*. Thus the location of *meso entry barriers* or the frontier of contested market entry for new firms – as in Figure 5.5 – would coincide with the meso edge of the market and the line of Shepherd's four-firm concentration 'cut-off point'. In practice, the entry of a major mesoeconomic firm could take over the market share of several or most of the microeconomic firms from firm five to firm *n*. But under competitive conditions it is unlikely that the already established oligopoly group would stand idly by and allow a new 'major' to enter and mop up the micro end of the market without strong reaction or retaliation.

Dominance and Innovation

Where barriers of technology alone are not enough to deter entry into markets, market leaders can employ a variety of non-price strategies which perpetuate unequal competition and indirectly ensure the exit of earlier entrants. One tactic in such a strategy is accelerated innovation. Thus a mesoeconomic company can upgrade the performance capability of a product such as a computer before it has fully amortized its cost. It thereby outmodes the products of micro competitors before their own investment has been paid off or has reasonable prospects of paying for itself.

Such a strategy becomes especially important when we no longer focus on a single product, such as the microchip, but look at the overall package of the computer industry as a whole. For a company such as IBM to be able successfully to pursue the kind of strategy just described, it is important for it to be able to dispose of a considerable range of computers rather than simply one computing component or one computer. Even quite large companies can stay stuck at the lower end of an individual product market in volume terms, such as Olivetti with its table-top computer. Thus they can find themselves seriously disadvantaged by the economies accruing to such a leading company as IBM whose key scale advantage is its market share combined with a wider product range and the greater spread of services which it can offer the consumer.

Leasing versus Sale

Similarly, there is no way that smaller companies can be guaranteed the volume of sales sufficient to enable them to match a company such as IBM in the leasing of computers to users, rather than direct sale. Such leasing of computers was one of the key means whereby IBM was able to establish a dominant position in the computer market, since it meant that the user companies were not required to meet the total capital outlay for the purchase of a computer. IBM could only afford a lower initial cash flow from leasing rather than sale because of its already established position in the market, and its anticipation that it could employ its mesoeconomic muscle to accelerate innovation and render redundant the models of other computer companies.

'Phantom' Entry: IBM and Control Data

The extent of IBM's market power is shown by the effects on its competitors of its intended entry into a new computer market. In the mid-1960s Control Data Corp of the US – a small-to-medium-size company – advertised a new supercomputer at the top end of the market. IBM followed by announcing one of its own. So great is IBM's dominance that it took all the orders for this new market. But whereas Control Data had a real machine, IBM's merely existed on paper. *IBM destroyed CD's chances without any product of its own yet on the market.* The matter was subject to an anti-trust case and settled out of court, with IBM relinquishing some of its operation to Control Data. This is an extreme example of unequal competition offset in the last instance by state intervention (see Locksley, 1981).

Apple and IBM

However, in 1981 IBM entered the microcomputer industry for real. By then the worldwide small business computer market was at least $1,250 billion and growing at up to 50 per cent per year. But IBM did not enter in the orthodox micro manner. Its entry changed the whole market, and by the end of 1983 IBM was selling nearly a third of the world's business micro-computers. From its initial entry, IBM has extended its model range both up and down market. In Europe in 1983 IBM microcomputers overtook and reduced Apple's market share, despite the fact that, just a year earlier, IBM had virtually no presence in Europe and Apple had nearly 30 per cent of the market.

In early 1984 IBM cut the price of its IBM PC range by between 7 and 20 per cent as it achieved full plant capacity utilisation. Dealers were astonished at the move because they could sell as many IBM personal computers as they could get their hands on at the going price. But with IBM's price cut, Apple's market share, profits and stock market price plummeted.

Some firms have reacted to IBM's entry with new models and price cuts.

IBM's rapidly achieved dominance of the microcomputer market to over 40 per cent was cut by 1986 to just under 30 per cent. But most of the new models produced to compete with IBM relied on their being compatible with IBM software programmes. In other words, such companies took IBM's market leadership for granted and produced what amounted to 'clones' of IBM's machines. Such a 'piggy-back' effect could in principle achieve a much reduced market share for IBM in personal or business microcomputers if anti-trust and competition agencies prevent IBM's own retaliation. But in terms of the model of competition on which such agencies rely, it is difficult to see the principles or precedents on which they could do this.

Meanwhile, IBM is staging a comeback. In April 1987 it launched an entirely new personal or business microcomputer, which is lower in price, harder to copy, and uses new software which is incompatible with the clones. Thus the terms and conditions of survival in the market are still being set by the market leader, whose own survival is not yet in question.

5.3 From Defensive to Offensive

In a significant analysis some quarter-century ago, Alexander Lamfalussy (1961) distinguished between what he called 'defensive' and 'enterprise' investment. Deriving his findings from the Belgian economy, Lamfalussy stressed the difference between the investment strategies of firms in growing or declining markets. As he put it: 'enterprise investment, as opposed to defensive investment, will rely mainly on "major" innovations . . . entailing the complete overhaul of production processes'. By contrast, defensive investment means 'sticking to minor processes or product innovations' (Lamfalussy, 1961, pp. 77–8 and 88).

Extending the polarity of Lamfalussy's categories, it could be said that a *defensive* corporate strategy means hanging onto markets one already has, and adapting as best as possible to challenge to them. *Offensive* corporate strategy means breaking into new products or markets and adapting to new opportunities through major changes in investment, production or marketing techniques.

Such a distinction is relevant to the important distinction made by Lamfalussy between growing and declining markets. It is also typical of differences between defensive or offensive strategies pursued by different firms within the same market. Lamfalussy's enterprising or offensive company may be microeconomic and the defensive firm mesoeconomic in character. But the winners in offensive strategies for increased market share are mainly meso enterprise. The losers are the micro enterprise which, after unequal contest with big-league firms, either shelter in a corner of the market or seek new client relationships – on unequal terms – with already established enterprise.

Entry – and Exit

The IBM example illustrates that mesoeconomic majors not only can force entry into markets, they can also thereby focus the exit of micro competitors through 'elimination pricing'. This concept was developed by Paolo Sylos-Labini (1962). How does it work in practice, and how does it relate to the theory of both offensive and defensive pricing?

The properties of symmetry, equilibrium and elegance characteristic of the neoclassical theory of the firm imply what can be called an 'entry bait'. In Figure 5.6 firm A in period 1 has pioneered a new market and achieved a super-normal profit at price level p^1. If there are no barriers to entry such as institutional monopoly, patents or techniques of production which are not readily available to other firms, it is likely that another firm, B, will enter the market in phase II and establish its price at level p^2, thereby attracting trade from firm A while earning itself a normal profit. As a consequence, the entry of firm B would force firm A to reduce its price in phase II from p^1 to p^2 to avoid loss of sales and market share. Thereby, according to the theory, the concepts of both normal profits and a prevailing industry price would be guaranteed through consumer sovereignty. This is the essence of the competitive process from Adam Smith to Milton Friedman.

Equal and Unequal Costs

However, conventional market theory is weak even at this elementary level of

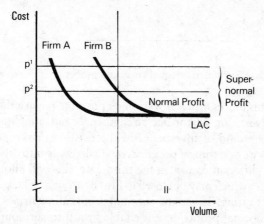

FIG. 5.6   Super-normal profits: the entry bait

normal profits and a prevailing price. For instance, the consequence of imperfect competition (as analysed in Chapter 3) is that consumer attachment or brand loyalty allows an established firm to charge a higher price. Therefore, in terms of Figure 5.6, firm B may be able to enter the market but only at price p^2, while the established firm A may be able to continue to charge price p^1. Thus while the later entrant, firm B, may be able to earn a normal profit, firm A gains a super-normal profit.

Alternatively, as shown in Figure 5.7, firm A may be earning a super-normal profit and attract the entry of firm B during phase I, even though B has a higher long-run average cost curve (LAC^2) than does firm A (LAC^1). In other words, it is possible that firm A chooses not to reduce price and continues to earn super-normal profits of ac, while allowing the new entrant B to survive earning a normal profit of ab. This represents an explicit case of what Edith Penrose (1963) has called the 'umbrella' price effect, whereby established lower-cost firms tolerate rather than eliminate higher-cost firms in the market since they thereby gain higher unit profits.

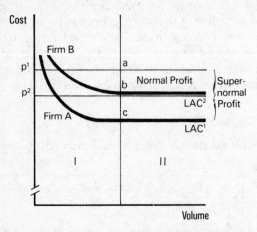

FIG. 5.7   Differentiated product: unequal costs and profits

In both cases this places firm A in a stronger position. It can either (1) spend yet more on advertising to further strengthen brand attachment, or (2) undertake a new round of investment in the existing market, embodying production gains from technical progress, or (3) diversify into other products in the same or a different sector. In the third case, this will allow firm A to enter a new market which may be closed to firm B through its lack of sufficient earnings or credit rating. Thus super-normal profits allow firm A to grow or diversify, while normal profits do not enable firm B to surmount the entry barriers to further new markets.

Entry and Elimination

However, with unequal costs, as in Figure 5.8, it is open to firm A (whether it is an already established and dominant firm or a later entrant, as in the case of IBM in the microcomputer market) to reduce price to p^2 in such a way as to signal to firm B (and other would-be entrants) that it will make no profit if it tries to enter the market on LAC^2. This amounts to a 'no-entry' barrier (or entry penalty), represented by the shaded area between price lines p^1 and p^2 and volume x and y in phase I of Figure 5.8. The argument on such 'no-entry' pricing is valid so long as firm A is an enterprise already established in the market, with lower overall costs than the would-be entrant, B.

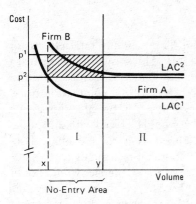

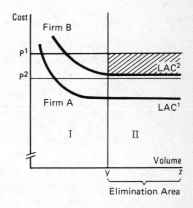

FIG. 5.8   No-entry pricing   FIG. 5.9   Elimination pricing

Otherwise, as shown in Figure 5.9, the earlier entrant and more established firm A may allow firm B to enter the market – or be unable to prevent its entry – yet thereafter in phase II reduce price from p^1 to p^2, below firm B's long-run average cost LAC^2. It can afford to do so since its own long-run cost curve LAC^1 is lower than the costs of firm B, and permits it a normal profit when B is earning no profit at all. Such 'elimination pricing' is represented by the shaded area between price lines p^1 and p^2 and volume x and y in Figure 5.8. It gives an abstract representation of the fate which struck many micro-computer firms in the United States when IBM (i) entered the market at its 'meso' edge, (ii) achieved full capacity and the lowest feasible unit costs, and then (iii) reduced price by up to 20 per cent.

If fortunate, the challenged firms will be made joint-venture offers they cannot afford to refuse, or be taken over. Otherwise, they may be subject to pressure on both long- and short-run costs, with the would-be eliminator reducing price below the variable costs (wage payments, etc) of the target firm, so that it cannot even meet its short-term commitments without access to external finance to ride out the challenge. As Sylos-Labini (1962, p. 40) puts it: 'a firm can remain in the market for some time if the price is so low that fixed cost cannot be recouped, but it can remain in the market for only a relatively short period if the price falls below variable costs'.

The results of such unequal competition – either for would-be micro entrants or eliminated competitors – are devastating for conventional market theory. Infant entrants may not make it to adolescence, far less adulthood. And this is the result of unequal competition within the market, rather than the state intervention – or interference – against which Milton Friedman inveighs with such vehemence.

Offensive Pricing

An example of such offensive pricing, and its potentially fatal effects for defensive or smaller firms, is given in Figure 5.10. This shows that as against a 'normal' price of p^1, a mesoeconomic company on LAC^1 can reduce price either to the 'no-entry' level p^2 or, if necessary, to the 'elimination price' equivalent to its own long-run average costs at p^3. In practice this would mean that the new micro entrant on its LAC would be faced with difficulties in amortizing or paying off its new investment as it entered phase II of production at price p^2. Also, while in the short term it might reach some accommodation on external finance, at price p^3 the challenger would not be gaining sufficient revenue to meet its variable costs, i.e. its weekly wage bill and its monthly or quarterly bill for inputs, components and raw materials. Meanwhile, the mesoeconomic company can afford to undertake a new

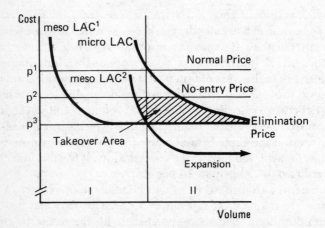

FIG. 5.10 Takeover, elimination and expansion

investment offensive, further reducing long-run costs through innovation and embodied technical progress, on the expansionary lines of meso LAC^2.

'Softening' and Takeover

Such a price and production response by the more established firm would either eliminate the new entrant from the market or 'soften it up' for takeover. The exceptions tend to be large companies able to ride out the elimination threat by countering with a lower price cross-subsidised from profits made from other activities. It is the microeconomic entrant of the conventional textbook neoclassical model which is most at risk from elimination pricing. The 'pick-up' price for the assets package of the eliminated micro company would be smaller than those for the takeover of a firm which had established entry but had not been rendered bankrupt. Frequently the predator firm is less interested in assets takeover than in picking up the eliminated company's order book to 'corner the market'. In both cases the 'takeover area' would be the shaded area in Figure 5.10.

The Unequal Impact of Inflation

There is also the unequal impact of inflation on micro and mesoeconomic enterprise. Conventional microeconomics both ignores this as exogenous or external to its model, and also assumes that competition will align capital-labour ratios for those firms able to survive in the market. However, bigger business tends to employ more capital and less labour in production than small firms, sometimes dramatically so. For instance, the cost of labour at Nissan by the early 1980s was under 7 per cent of total costs and less than 6 per cent at Toyota (Ohmae, 1985, p. 4).

However, fixed costs of capital tend to be less inflation-sensitive in the short term than variable costs such as those of wages, raw materials, components purchased from other firms or fuel and freight charges. In addition, because it has bargaining power over the price of some large-volume inputs of interest to other suppliers, big business typical of the mesoeconomic sector may be able to delay the impact of inflation on its variable costs more effectively than its microeconomic competitors.

The possible results are illustrated in Figure 5.11. This indicates that even if both micro and mesoeconomic firms were in the first instance able to achieve a similar long-run average cost curve LAC^1, and initially make a normal profit at price p^1, the impact of inflation would tend to raise the costs of the micro firm from its potential LAC^1 (indicated for both categories of firms by the broken LAC^1 line yz) to micro LAC^2. Even allowing for an 'industry'

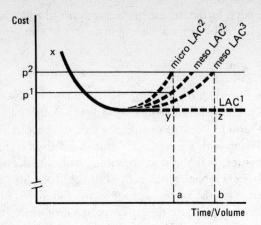

FIG. 5.11   The unequal impact of inflation

price rise to p^2, this would mean that at volume a the micro firm would go out of business (or make no profit for the product in question).

By contrast, even if the mesoeconomic enterprise were also hit relatively soon by inflation on a rising meso LAC^2, its lesser and later sensitivity to inflation would mean that it could still make some profit at the original price level p^1 for its sales up to volume a (thereby throwing the micro firm earlier into crisis). Alternatively, at the higher price level p^2, the meso enterprise could make significant if diminishing profits over the volume range ab until its meso LAC^3 reached price level p^2. Therefore an inflation which is critical for the micro firm is only problematic for mesoeconomic enterprise – not least since with price-making power and market leadership, the meso firm may be able to offset its rising LAC with yet further price rises (as elaborated in Figure 5.12).

Alternative Outcomes

Synthesising the previous analysis, Figure 5.12 represents the impact of inflation on the takeover or elimination of smaller by bigger business. The long-run average cost of a microeconomic enterprise (micro LAC) rises earlier than that of a mesoeconomic firm (meso LAC). During phase II, the shaded area abc represents that period in which the costs of the micro-economic enterprise increase and profits first decline and then are eliminated. During phase III, the shaded area cde represents the period in which the microeconomic enterprise is incurring costs well in excess of receipts, while the mesoeconomic company is merely suffering a profit reduction.

In other words, in phase III the mesoeconomic firm is facing profit decline

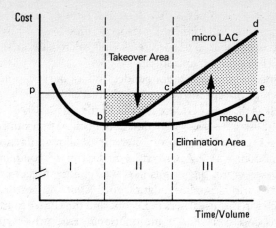

FIG. 5.12   Inflation, takeover and elimination

but the microeconomic firm is thrown into crisis. In terms of the foregoing analysis, phase II would typically be that period in which the microeconomic firm is liable to takeover on disadvantageous conditions by the meso-economic company. Phase III would include that period in which the microeconomic firm, in crisis, is liable to elimination by the mesoeconomic company.

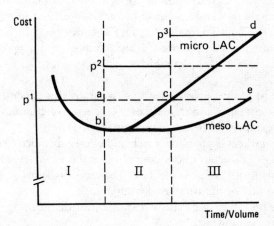

FIG. 5.13   Inflation and 'umbrella' pricing

Alternatively, as in Figure 5.13, the mesoeconomic enterprise, as an industry or sector leader, may choose to take advantage of inflation to raise price at the end of phase I from p^1 to p^2 so that the microeconomic firm does not expire at c but gains a new lease of life as a reborn survivor. In the same way, with continuing inflation, the mesoeconomic leader may again raise price at the end of phase II to p^3 so as to give the micro enterprise an after-life during phase III to point d, and so on.

This amounts to an application under inflationary conditions of the 'umbrella' pricing concept introduced by Edith Penrose. Under inflationary conditions such as those experienced in the 1970s and 1980s in several of the advanced capitalist countries, it is not unrealistic. For example, between 1968 and 1976 the annual real profit increase of all manufacturing firms in the United Kingdom was 0.7 per cent. For the top 25 companies it was 7 per cent, *ten times more*. Bigger business was making bigger profits during this inflationary period. Similarly, data from *Vision* and *Fortune* magazines indicate that the top profit-earners in Europe and the United States, with very few exceptions, are very large multinational enterprise typical of the mesoeconomic sector.

Baumol's Contestable Markets

Such an analytic framework of unequal market power and unequal competition is arguably more relevant to the late twentieth-century economy than the theory of 'contestable markets' recently developed by Baumol and others (Baumol, Panzar and Willig, 1982).

For instance, although the nominally new theory of contestable markets suggests the challenge and response of real contest for new markets and market share, the Baumol analysis in fact assumes away inequality in both actual and potential competition. Thus Baumol (1982, pp. 2–8) defines contestable markets as those in which:

(1) the concept of the perfectly competitive market is generalised;
(2) price exactly equals marginal costs (even for oligopolies), so that no product can be sold below its marginal cost;
(3) entry to markets is absolutely free and exit is absolutely costless;
(4) normal rates of profit obtain and abnormal profits never occur;
(5) no cross-subsidy is possible (e.g. between divisions or countries of multi-product or multinational companies);
(6) there are no increasing returns to scale (nor diminishing average costs with increased output).

It has already been shown that few or none of these conditions obtain for the central area of the economy dominated by mesoeconomic enterprise. Most firms price on a cost-plus basis with a range of rule-of-thumb variants, modified according to market tactics designed to defend or extend market share. Micro firms tend to be price-takers rather than price-makers, save in those sectors where rapidly changing technology makes possible short-term 'profit creaming' at high prices or 'piggy-back' effects from cloning market leaders. No-entry or elimination pricing is common for bigger business typical of the mesoeconomic sector. Focal-point pricing of the 'see you at Central Station at noon' variety represents either a spontaneous assumption by micro firms of what price the market will bear, or an invitation from price leaders to price followers which they would be ill advised to refuse. Constant technical economies of scale are typical throughout much of industry, and diminishing costs are obtainable either through technical progress or lower-cost multinational locations. Cross-subsidy is a common exercise employed by multi-product companies seeking to force an entry into other markets, and typical (through transfer pricing) for multinational companies between both product divisions and different countries.

Hypothetical Contest

One of the main aims of contestable market theory is to challenge the claim of oligopoly theory that firms pay as much or more attention to how rival firms set prices than to standard or given market prices which equate marginal cost with price. Baumol (1982) stresses that 'oligopoly models are heavily dependent on the assumed expectations and reaction patterns characterizing the firms that are involved'. By contrast he claims that, in the case of perfectly contestable markets, 'oligopolistic structure and behaviour are freed entirely from their previous dependence on the conjectural variations of *incumbents*'. Instead, 'these are generally determined uniquely and, in a manner that is tractable analytically, by the pressures of *potential* competition.'

Apart from the dubious status of a proposition which is claimed to be both 'general' and 'unique', the contestable market theory simply does not prove such a case. For one thing, in addition to the foregoing half dozen limiting assumptions, it also presumes that 'a contestable market is one into which entry is absolutely free, *and exit is absolutely costless*' (Baumol, 1982). Baumol contrasts the costs of entry and costless exit by claiming that 'we use "freedom of entry" . . . not to mean that it is costless or easy, but that it is a requirement of contestability that there be no cost discrimination against entrants'. This not only implies conditions of equal entry in terms of perfect competition rather than oligopoly theory, but is also incompatible with Baumol's claim in the same article that in contestable markets a new entrant can hit and if necessary run, 'counting his temporary but *supernormal* profits on the way to the bank'. As already stressed in this text, the essential condition for supernormal profits (abstracting from transfer pricing by multinational companies) lies either in higher prices through imperfect competition or in lower costs. Either of these imply unequal competition of a kind which violates Baumol's assumption of contestable markets.

Otherwise, Baumol's states that 'costless exit' means that any firm can leave a market in such a way as to 'recoup any costs incurred in the entry process'. He adds that 'if all capital is saleable or reusable without loss other than that corresponding to normal user cost and depreciation, then any risk of entry is eliminated' (Baumol, 1982). This is implausible on several grounds. First, re-sale of the capital implies that it can still earn a normal rate of return, in which case there is no clear reason why the contesting firm should have quit the market rather than stayed in it. Conglomerate predators might well quit after making a supernormal profit, and as profits with price competition returned to normal. But such price competition would have tended to increase the market share of contestants and reduced the re-sale value of assets, save in the case of asset stripping including sale of land, etc. Second, there are very few markets where the costs of entry are so low as to be negligible. Such costs include not only investment and production but also establishment of brand attachment, successful retail agreements and command over buyers and suppliers. Exit costs in most of the developed countries also tend to include redundancy payments to wage and salaried staffs. In the real world it can take years to contest entry to new markets, even for established firms such as Exxon, which has burned its fingers in food and computers. In such respects Baumol's 'costless exit' is little more than a theoretical curiosity.

Contest and Oligopoly

Within the contestable market paradigm, Baumol does confront the issue of duopoly or oligopoly. He assumes that duopoly does not exclude potential competition, but says little more on the subject. In practice duopoly is likely to be stable only with direct or indirect collusion of the kind analysed later in this chapter. Otherwise it will tend to (i) a monopoly outcome, if market forces are unrestrained by anti-trust or competition authorities, or to (ii) an oligopoly outcome for the world market as a whole if international competition is not contained by protection. In either of the latter cases state intervention rather than simply free-market forces are implied.

A more interesting aspect of Baumol's argument with that of Thijs ten Raa (1980) considers those conditions in which the optimum scale of production in a given market implies given 'indivisibilities'. In other words, following ten Raa, Baumol takes the case where a given market supports production of 4,000 units a year and the minimum output point on a U-shaped average cost curve is 1,000 units. From this he observes that it is obvious that four firms each producing 1,000 units can match industry supply and demand at minimum cost and with maximum consumer welfare (assuming perfectly competitive pricing).

But what if market demand is 4,030 units (or 4,300 or any figure which does not round up to 1,000). Following ten Raa, Baumol concludes that the welfare loss from massive spare capacity by all producers can be overcome if the long-run average cost curve is 'flat bottomed' (like a bowl rather than an egg), with the result that there is a margin of capacity at which the four firms can each produce a fraction of the additional 30 (or 300) units without a rise in cost. Thus, allegedly, potential competition (on price) and consumer welfare are preserved even in a four-firm market which would normally be considered a classic case of concentrated oligopoly (Baumol, 1982).

The issue of spare capacity and consumer welfare is for real. But the Baumol and ten Raa conclusions are not. For one thing, their outcome depends on U-shaped average cost curves of the kind which have already been shown in the critique of Samuelson (Chapter 4) to be hypothetical rather than real. In practice, long-run average cost curves tend to be either L-shaped or falling J-shaped in form. Further, by excluding the possibility of unequal production costs at a common market price. Baumol and ten Raa assume a four-firm oligopoly outcome rather than the possible outcome of four optimal cost producers plus a smaller higher-cost producer absorbing the extra 30 (or 300) units on the market. In other words, they ignore the forceful argument derived from Sylos-Labini (1969) that it is precisely technical economies of scale which may not make it worthwhile for oligopolists to squeeze smaller firms out of the market.

In practice, as suggested by our own argument in Chapter 4 and Figure 4.3, the continued survival of micro enterprise in sectors dominated by meso companies often depends on such indivisibilities as Baumol and ten Raa have correctly identified but wrongly interpreted. Moreover, if their neat four-firm division of a market were to occur in practice, it would be more likely in a planned economy – or as a freak outcome – than in a contestable market.

Facts and Fantasies

In fact one of the most serious indictments of contestable market theory comes from Baumol himself, who admits that in the case of multiproduct companies it is difficult to determine even average company costs. As he puts it: 'there is no way one can measure average cost for all output combinations in the multiproduct case' (Baumol, 1982). To get round the problem he devises what he calls a total cost function for the firm and industry, which amounts in practice to a three-dimensional form of the long-run average cost curves over time which we have given elsewhere in this text (Baumol, 1982, Figures 4–7).

While clearly interesting for its admission of the problem of identifying precise average unit costs in multiproduct companies (in his example a company producing both boots and shoes), Baumol's example only poses rather than answers key problems. The realism of taking what amounts to a cost vector rather than a simple cost curve is qualified by the fact that the analysis assumes that long-run costs for multiple-product firms shift in the same way, at the same rate, as for single-product companies. Otherwise, the stress on average rather than marginal costs and prices undermines the dependence of contestable market theory on the equation of marginal costs and price.

Further, confronting again the issue of spare capacity, and now introducing the possibility of scale economies, Baumol claims that 'because of economies of scale in the production of capacity the firm deliberately builds some excess capacity to take care of anticipated growth in sales volume.' This welcome realism qualifies his precondition for contestable markets that there are no increasing returns to scale. But it also contradicts the assumption of contestable market theory that there is an equilibrium condition (even for four-firm oligopoly) rather than ongoing disequilibrium in market structure. As Baumol puts it: 'here the invisible hand proves incapable of protecting the most efficient producing arrangement and leaves the incumbent producer vulnerable to displacement by an aggressive entrant'.

Baumol adds that he leaves to our imaginations 'what, if anything, this says about the successive displacements on the world market of the Dutch by the English, the English by the Germans and the Americans, and the Americans, perhaps, by the Japanese'. Which in turn shows the limits of contestable market theory in which such displacement, through unequal competition on the basis of unequal costs, is simply assumed away in the first place. If this were not sufficient to question the relevance of so-called contestable markets, Baumol's further observations might do so. For he also admits that:

> Real markets are rarely, if ever, perfectly contestable. Contestability is merely a broader ideal, a benchmark of wider applicability than is perfect competition. To say that contestable oligopolies behave ideally and that contestable monopolies have some incentives for doing so is not to imply that this is even nearly true of all oligopolies or of unregulated monopolies in reality [Baumol, 1982].

Baumol offers this observation as a response to those whom he anticipates might consider contestable market theory to be 'too Panglossian a view of reality'. Lest the allusion be lost, it may be worth observing that Pangloss, in Voltaire's *Candide*, was the figure who claimed that 'all was for the best in the best of all possible worlds' over the ashes of a city (Lisbon) which had been devastated by earthquake.

5.4   Competition and Collusion

The history of capitalist enterprise has shown a marked dualism between the pressures of competition and the pressures for co-operation and collusion.

Dual Market Structures

It is important to stress that unequal competition does not itself imply a trend to outright monopoly *per se* nor monopoly pricing and profits. There are several qualifications to the process. However, unequal competition changes the context of the imperfect competition analysis of Chapter 3. In other words, in a multiproduct company the differences between brand attachment for different products may be so great that they constitute essentially different markets in the product range of the same company rather than distinct products for different firms of the kind argued in the theory of imperfect competition. Thus Persil and Omo – household brandnames normally considered independent and competitive products by purchasers – are in practice both products of Unilever.

As we have already stressed in Chapter 4, it simply may not pay a large firm to eliminate smaller enterprise since the latter's share of the market may not justify minimal scale efficiencies in production. But in this case the restraint on the monopoly trend is due to technical economies of scale rather than the flourishing challenge to big business from small competitors. It qualifies rather than justifies the Friedmanite entrepreneurial myth.

Monopoly from Competition

This has several major implications for the analysis of unequal competition.

First, *monopoly may itself be the consequence of competition rather than its abuse.* The range of entry barriers, takeover and elimination-pricing tactics analysed in this chapter imply that big business does not necessarily collude to prevent competition. But the outcome of unequal competition is a bigger share of markets for already bigger business, (i.e. concentration) or the takeover of smaller firms, (i.e. centralisation). Big business not employing such tactics could itself be subject to takeover or elimination.

Moreover, it is axiomatic of success that it should bring with it higher profits or a bigger market share, or both. But the successful firm, following Joan Robinson's maxim of 'grow to survive', increases its size and market power at the expense of smaller and weaker competitors. This process in turn increases unequal competition and oligopolistic structures.

Competition Between Equals

Second, *those firms best able to enter a market dominated by big business will themselves be large firms*. In practice they can and do seek to penetrate each other's main markets. Thus Unilever allocates sizable sums of research to new product areas, including energy, while the oil companies such as Exxon allocate similar resources to the penetration of the food market.

Such entry may amount to vertical integration. Thus Exxon can introduce itself into the related motor-vehicle tyre market, taking advantage of its range of indirect retail outlets, whereas a small entrepreneur who may have developed the principle of the steel braced or radial tyre would not be able to do so. But such mesoeconomic companies also have the scale and market muscle to enter new unrelated markets such as electronics or microelectronics and data processing. Exxon has entered the 'electronic office' market through the acquisition of several firms in the field. In practice Exxon burned its fingers in the process. But a smaller 'new entrant' would risk being burned up. Such new entry amounts to classic horizontal integration but by meso rather than micro firms, analysed in more detail in Chapter 7.

Third, *the market power of big business may offset or countervail the monopoly trend among suppliers*. Normally classified as oligopsony, or the power of a few large purchasing firms, this is particularly evident in the large retail outlets in food, where companies such as Safeway and Tesco increasingly retail their 'own brands' of food and drink. The reason why they are able to persuade large producers with significant product differentiation and brand attachment to supply them with goods to sell under their own brands lies in the mesoeconomic size and scale of the retail outlets which they command. Microeconomic firms cannot command such countervailing power. A few large firms can do so.

Anti-Monopoly and Anti-Trust

There is, however, a further factor which may restrain the monopoly trend and promote co-operation between meso and micro enterprise. For some time there have been anti-monopoly agencies in the United States and Britain, with powers to restrict or restrain the trend to monopoly in given industries. In the United Kingdom this function has been performed by the Monopolies Commission and in the United States by the Anti-Trust authorities. Both bodies have exercised some deterrent effect on the takeover of micro-economic enterprise by mesoeconomic giants. Certainly, in the United States since the Sherman and other Anti-Trust Acts of the 1890s, big business, at least on occasion, have been broken up by the government and dispersed into smaller, nominally independent companies. A striking example was the break-up of Standard Oil and of the Morgan Guaranty and Trust Company early in the twentieth century. More recently, ATT has been broken up into separate operating companies in the United States.

Cosmetic Competition

What have such deterrents achieved in practice? One result in the postwar period may well have been the encouragement of the multinational trend of American enterprise. By extending their concentration and centralisation of capital to the global market, US enterprises have continued to expand while avoiding the teeth of anti-trust bodies.

Another phenomenon has been the encouragement of 'cosmetic competition', whereby big business typical of the mesoeconomic sector became concerned to ensure the survival of at least some smaller microeconomic enterprise. The reasons for this are understandable enough in view of the fact that, according to US anti-trust legislation, any company with 15 per cent or more of the market is automatically liable to an anti-trust suit if that share arises from the merger or takeover of two or more firms. The otherwise miraculous survival of the minuscule American Motors against the domination of the 'big three' US auto producers is an example. And even American Motors decided that the umbrella of a joint venture with Renault was in the long run preferable to the more readily removed cosmetic competition with General Motors, Ford and Chrysler.

The break-up of a major company such as ATT in practice divested it of less profitable intra-state communications for more profitable interstate and international business. Moreover, the breaking of ATT's monopoly in the US meant that it could move into computers, while IBM moved into tele-communications. The move therefore liberalised competition between mesoeconomic majors rather than facilitated the entry of micro firms into the market. Moreover, most of the companies divested from ATT stayed firmly within the top hundred US companies.

Paradox and Paralysis

Chapter 1 stressed the role of paradox in economic analysis. This is especially apparent in the extent to which increased competition for market share – especially between mesoeconomic companies – is accompanied by recent trends to cooperation in a range of economic activities falling short of merger. Alternatively, due to unequal competition, the merged firms are responding to offers from other companies which they cannot afford to refuse. In other cases, as in the international joint ventures between American, European and

Japanese companies, they are simply co-operating multinationally to avoid the worst rigours of international competition.

There also is a critical paradox for government competition policy implicit in the previous analysis. In effect, competition policy both seeks to prevent monopoly structures and monopoly pricing. But if an Anti-Trust or Monopolies Commission rules that a mesoeconomic company with a lower cost schedule than a microeconomic firm should reduce price to avoid super-normal profits, it thereby will tend to squeeze the profits of the micro firm – either exposing it to takeover or prompting its bankruptcy and elimination. In either case the mesoeconomic enterprise is the beneficiary.

A big business with major economies of scale may set price at a level in line with government inflation targets, but below that which would allow lesser firms any profit. Thus a mesoeconomic company may gain public accolade for price restraint while in practice extending its market share, increasing the trend to monopoly and ruining microeconomic competitors. Conventional anti-trust policy, based on an outdated model of equal competition, can no longer cope with such a perverse outcome from unequal costs and efficiency. In principle, the trust busters have razor teeth. But with only a handful of exceptions this century – notably the break-up of Standard Oil and of ATT – their bite is paralysed by the oligopolistic implications of unequal competition itself.

Cooperation

Clearly in a situation of outright monopoly, duopoly or a market dominated by mesoeconomic companies any of which is prepared to accept upward price leadership (with 'price umbrella' effects on microeconomic followers), such price increases may be determined independently in a manner compatible with the 'focal point' pricing or mutual market signalling of the kind analysed earlier in this chapter.

Alternatively, it may be that a varying degree of collusion may be necessary between mesoeconomic price leaders, or between themselves and micro-economic price followers, to achieve a price increase compensating for the decline in sales during a recession or crisis.

Classically, collusion – whether implicit or explicitly in the form of cartels – has occurred during periods of prolonged recession and crisis. At the minimal or soft end of the scale of collusion, affecting corporate strategy in individual markets, is what could be described as the difference between cooperative and non-cooperative enterprises. At this level, without resort to formal or explicit agreements on price and market share, it may well be that a certain firm or group of firms chooses not to follow the upward price leadership established by one or more mesoeconomic leaders, thereby threatening mutual corporate discipline and the feasibility of effective response to the crisis by the wider range of companies in the industry or sector.

In such circumstances, the market leaders may well choose temporarily to reduce price below the lower price already established by the 'challengers' in such a way as to either reduce their profits to an unacceptably low level or entirely eliminate them in the manner of the 'elimination-pricing' analysed by Sylos-Labini. Alternatively, a period of joint reduction of prices – in which mesoeconomic and especially multinational companies are able to reduce capacity by the closure or phasing-out of individual plant – may be sufficient to restore market discipline and the restoration of a higher level of long-term prices.

At the other end of the spectrum of collusion, governments or international agencies may be called upon collectively by both micro and mesoeconomic enterprise to achieve a degree of discipline in the restructuring of the market which a combination of unequal competition and pricing leadership cannot itself secure. This will particularly tend to be the case where the scale of minimally efficient production and the degree of capital intensity is very substantial – classically in chemicals and steel where minimal plant size may involve a production capacity of hundreds of thousands or millions of tons and where the capital/labour ratios involved can be as much as twenty to forty times as great as those involved in light engineering production or electronics (Holland, 1976a).

In the crisis of the European steel sector in the late 1970s and early 1980s, the European Coal and Steel Community was brought under sufficiently effective pressure from the major public and private steel-producers as actually to suspend its provisions stipulating competition in the Paris Treaty of 1952 and to introduce what amounted to a market-share and price cartel negotiated between different countries and different companies on a Community-wide basis. In the early 1980s the Commission of the European Economic Community was under similar pressure from companies in the heavy chemicals and derivatives sector to achieve a similar cartel. Despite considerable pressure over a number of years, however, no viable agreement was achieved.

Collusion

Between informal collusion of market leadership and indirect 'follow-the-leader' response, or the direct involvement of governments or international institutions to achieve cartel arrangements, lie a wider and more diverse range of strategies. This intermediate range of collusive practices is higher in risk and may well result in fines, penalties or worse for the managements and companies concerned.

One notorious case of a company landing in court was the Rockefeller empire of Standard Oil. John D. Rockefeller had made his original fortune not by producing oil, but buying up transport outlets for oil producers and creating a myriad of secret finance companies and trusts to foreclose and take over other companies. In general he put his talents as entrepreneur to establishing conditions of unequal competition, with himself as arbiter of fair play. The result was the break-up of the company before the First World War – among the last effective countervailance of monopoly power by the US government this century (Sampson, 1975).

A classic case, less renowned than Standard Oil, but significant in its own right, concerned an anti-trust action against executives of General Electric, Westinghouse and Allis Chalmers (respectively numbers one, two and three in the US power equipment industry in the 1950s and 1960s) and the managers of nearly forty other companies. Essentially, the market leaders in the electrical industry had learned the key lessons from modern management techniques and decided on 'profit centres' and target rates of return from their individual product divisions. As a consequence, on good 'cost-plus' grounds, they demanded an 'x' per cent return per year from product divisions such as switchgear equipment for power stations. The managers in charge found this initially hard to understand and later hard to tolerate. Power-station equipment is different from Coca Cola cans. It can neither be bought off the shelf in batch numbers, nor produced without major forward planning of capacity. In line with the principles of capacity maximisation, it occurred to several among them that the most rational forward planning for the industry as a whole would be an organised bidding system which matched probable demand with potential supply.

Companies in Court

The result was collusion. Coming together gradually, through informal discussion of the problems of the industry, executives took to meeting on golf courses and in hotel rooms to discuss a system for a new variant on 'focal pricing'. In other words, one company would underbid the others by a clear margin, which in this case would not be followed by the others. 'Discount' pricing, whether round number or fractional, would be mutually disallowed. The 'rule-of-thumb' marker in such cases was entered by each of them in a notebook indicating whose sale in turn was due to be met in bidding by electricity companies. The 'code' was to be known to them only, rather than to the top executives of their companies.

In due course, after a happy interlude in which supply matched demand quite adequately in the industry, a bright minded executive in one of the client companies worked out a consistent pattern in the bidding by power-plant companies. He checked with others and found that there was a remarkable unwillingness among suppliers to consider any normal discounts. Cracking the code in principle, he informed the anti-trust authorities, who in turn employed the FBI, who found one of the involved executives ready to talk under 'minor' pressure. The collusion was broken open and some key executives were charged and sent to gaol, after which several of them rejoined their companies.

Ironies

The irony of the US power-plant case is that such collusion revealed key limits in competition policy, for both companies and government. It had for some time become the maxim of the mesoeconomic corporation that profit targets should be a measure of divisional efficiency. It was the pursuit of such targets irrespective of the disproportion between possible demand and probable supply which led several executives into error. Five new power-plant orders in one year was more than any of them could cope with. None at all heralded divisional disaster. The result for those concerned was highly imperfect. They needed a mechanism which could supercede the uncertainties of the market.

In principle, this might have been provided by government itself, through a mutual planning and market allocation policy. In the event, breaking the informal cartel not only brought personal humiliation to those involved but also reintroduced the incoherence of the market into an industry which could not reasonably face competition without major penalties through the under-utilisation in some companies of potential capacity. Some of the executives concerned may since have read Milton Friedman's *Free to Choose*, and been amazed at his paradigm of perfectly competitive workers. In practice they might well have preferred an open and publicly accountable system of market sharing between companies which otherwise could not possibly fulfil potential economies of scale or reduce unit costs so as to provide electricity at the cheapest available cost and price. By their logic, 'normal profits' led directly to collusion. (See Smith, 1963 and 1966.)

5.5 Monopoly Capital

Conventional economic theory assumes that there is an inherent limit to the growth of the firm: whether absolute, or relative (in terms of slower rates of growth in larger firms which permit smaller enterprises to 'catch up').

Alternatively, as just illustrated, it is assumed that the rise of monopoly power is an abuse of competition by individuals who 'break the rules'. In this way, it is assumed that the objective working of the market mechanism would, at least in the long run, give rise to a relatively balanced and equal competitive structure. Distortion of competition, its abuse by cartels and monopoly power are seen as subjective factors which can be handled by taking individual managers to court.

The Marxist Rationale

Marx, by contrast, realised that competition itself gave rise to concentration. He was impressed by the dynamism of mid-nineteenth-century capitalism, stressing in volume I of *Capital* what he called the 'cyclopean scale' of the techniques of 'modern industry'. With arguments echoed a hundred years later, he referred to the capacity of such modern industry 'to construct machines by machines', throwing workers concerned out of employment but also creating 'entirely new branches of production' through an 'extra-ordinary extension of the factory system'. As he put it:

> we know that in no other system of production is improvement so continuous, and the compensation of the capital employed so constantly changing as in the factory system. . . . this growth . . . is, besides, constantly interrupted by the technical progress that at one time virtually supplies the place of new workmen, at another, actually displaces old ones. This qualitative change in mechanical industry continually discharges hands from the factory, or shuts its doors against the fresh stream of recruits, while the purely quantitative extension of the factory absorbs not only the men thrown out of work, but also fresh contingents. [Marx, 1887, Chapter XV.]

This expansion of the means of production implied greater concentration. As Marx put it, every individual firm 'is a larger or smaller concentration of means of production. . . . Every accumulation becomes the means of new accumulation . . . with the increasing mass of wealth which functions as capital, accumulation increases the concentration of that wealth in the hands of individual capitalists, and thereby widens the basis of production on a large scale and of the specific methods of capitalist production.'

Marx makes two points about this trend. First, that the increase in concentration is limited by the increase of social wealth. Second, that accumulation of capital both concentrates the means of production in the hands of fewer firms and at the same time thereby expels other firms from the market.

Competition and Credit

In essentials, Marx is talking about gains from size and scale to successful firms through the competitive process. He argues that the two most powerful levers of centralisation are competition and credit. As he put it (referring to 'capitals' rather than 'enterprise', in a manner shared by Marshall):

> the larger capitals beat the smaller . . . with the development of the capitalist mode of production there is increase in the minimum amount of individual capital necessary to carry on a business under normal conditions. The smaller capitals, therefore, crowd in spheres of production which modern industry has only sporadically or incompletely got hold of. Here competition rages in direct proportion to the number, and in inverse proportion to the magnitudes, of the antagonistic capitals. It always ends in the ruin of many small capitalists, whose capitals partly pass into the hands of their conquerors, partly vanish.

In this context the credit system comes into play. At first, credit is the assistant of accumulation, drawing into the hands of individual or associated capitalists resources which otherwise would lie scattered in larger or smaller enterprises. But credit 'soon becomes a new and terrible weapon in the battle of competition and is finally transformed into an enormous social mechanism for the centralisation of capitals'. (Marx, 1887, chapter XXV).

Concentration and Centralisation

Marx distinguished between concentration and centralisation. Concentration represents growth of the market share of individual firms. Centralisation represents takeover of other enterprise. But he stresses that whether increased scale is the result of concentration or centralisation, the economic effect remains the same: 'everywhere the increased scale of industrial establishments is a starting point for a more comprehensive organisation of the collective work of many, for a wider development of their material motive forces – in other words, for the progressive transformation of isolated processes of production, carried on by customary methods, into processes of production, socially combined and scientifically arranged'. But Marx argued that accumulation is a slow process compared with centralisation: 'the world would still be without railways if it had had to wait until accumulation had got a few individual capitals far enough to be adequate for the construction of a railway' (Marx, 1887, ibid.).

'New Capitalisms'

Lenin, following Marx, argued that monopoly actually stemmed from the free working of an unequal competitive process: 'free competition gives rise to the concentration of production which, in turn, at a certain stage of development, leads to monopoly.' Claiming that 'today monopoly has become a fact', Lenin pointed out that in the United States as early as 1904 'almost half the total production of the country was carried on by one hundredth part of enterprise'. He realised that these giant companies were not single-product, single-industry concerns but combines where 'the grouping in a single enterprise of different branches of industry, represent consecutive stages in the processing of raw materials' – i.e. vertical and horizontal integration (Lenin, 1917, pp. 14, 15 and 18).

Lenin emphasised the extent to which the trend to monopoly and 'combination' had reversed the old competitive model by the turn of the century. In fact he puts it even more emphatically and writes of a 'new capitalism': 'For Europe, the time when the *new capitalism* definitely superceded the old can be established with fair precision: it was the beginning of the twentieth century.' (Lenin, 1917, pp. 18–26).

He also argued that when 'competition becomes transformed into monopoly . . . this is something quite different from the old free competition between manufacturers, scattered and out of touch with each other, and producing for an unknown market'. In other words, the consumer sovereignty assumptions of competitive small scale capitalism are transformed. He cites Kestner as revealing the essence of the case, i.e. 'the prolonged raising of prices which results from the formation of cartels . . . the increase in profits resulting from this raising of prices . . . and a *dominating position* . . . which did not exist under free competition.' (Lenin, 1917, pp. 24–5, 20 and 27, and Kestner, 1912, p. 254.)

Hilferding's Combined Enterprise

Hilferding (1910) profoundly influenced Lenin's approach. He explained how such giant 'combined' enterprises had modified the model of small-scale capital, that they had thereby transformed the assumption of 'normal' profit rates, and with it undermined the assumption that technical progress and innovation was a reward for pioneering entrepreneurship. Hilferding was also close to the concept of big business 'planning' and producer sovereignty. As he put it: 'First, combination levels out the fluctuations of trade and thereby assures to the combined enterprises a more *stable rate of profit*. Second, combination has the effect of *eliminating trade*. Third, it renders possible technical improvements and acquisition of *superprofits* over and above those obtained by the 'pure' (i.e. non-combined) enterprises. Fourthly, it strengthens the position of the combined enterprises compared with that of "pure" enterprises.'

Bukharin on Elimination Pricing

Bukharin (1927) also stressed the 'organic' elimination of small-scale capital by the trend to monopoly and described it in terms of monopoly control over price-making of a kind which strikingly predates more recent theory of oligopoly and market dominance by a few firms. In the context of what he calls 'changed sales conditions', he referred to 'sales made at a loss for "strategic purposes", i.e. for rapid conquest of the market and for the annihilation of competitors'.

This is a technique of 'elimination pricing' identified by Sylos-Labini and analysed earlier in this chapter. It implies that firms have the power to manage their prices in the interests of their own market domination, rather than in the service of a sovereign consumer (since they tend to raise prices to oligopolistic levels after the elimination or takeover is completed). As Bukharin puts it: 'the struggle of individually owned enterprises is usually conducted by means of low prices: small shops sell cheaper, reducing their standard of living to a minimum; capitalists strive to reduce the production costs by improving technique and lowering wages etc. When the struggle among individually owned enterprises has been replaced by the struggle among trusts, the methods of struggle (insofar as it is conducted in the world market) undergo a certain change; low prices disappear in the home market, being replaced by high prices which facilitate the struggle in the world market.'

Following Hilferding, and also anticipating later cost-plus pricing theory and the theory of elimination pricing in more contemporary oligopoly theorists, Bukharin argued that: 'the amount of profit depends upon the mass of commodities and the amount of profit accruing to one commodity unit, which amount is equal to the selling price minus production costs. . . . The cost of production, however, is lower the greater the volume of commodities brought into the market. Improved methods of production, expansion of productive forces, and consequently of the volume of goods produced, are factors decreasing the cost of production. This explains the selling of commodities abroad at low prices.'

Trusts and Cartels

The distinction between cartels and trusts is important in understanding the degree of relevance of the previous analysis to contemporary capitalism. As stressed by Hilferding, trusts entail the elimination of a conflict of interests between the enterprises which they control, while cartels do not (Hilferding, cit. Bukharin, 1927, p. 64). Cartels can be stable or unstable, forming, breaking up and re-forming according to circumstances and in particular the state of trade. They also can be explicit or implicit. Since the famous break-up of Standard Oil, few big corporations have presented open cases of abuse of textbook competition to the trust-busters, whether in the United States or Europe, as the EEC Competition Directorate has found to its disadvantage. Sometimes they try, as has happened in the European Coal and Steel Community. (See Maurice Bye, 1970, pp. 169ff.) But for the most part the cartelisation process has given way to concealed collusion or indirect price leadership, where firms 'follow the leader' (or leaders) in upward price rises. With the range of pricing techniques now open to multinational companies, fewer firms need to go underground with collusive agreements. Many can afford to stay in the open and allow the process of unequal competition to earn them the increased market share which is intrinsic to the market mechanism of rewards to winners.

Ends and Beginnings

The work of the 'second generation' Marxists on the competitive process was a major departure. When Lenin wrote of the 'new capitalism' of price-making monopolistic power, he showed a readiness to open up new ground. Deriving much if not most of his analysis from Hilferding and Bukharin (whose work he had read before it was published), Lenin showed that second-generation Marxists were respectful of Marx but not prepared to be hidebound by his powerful insights into an earlier phase of capitalist competition.

Such insights have been neglected by many allegedly orthodox Marxists since the turn of the century. Rather than applying and extending the insights made by the second generation, many later Marxists have almost entirely neglected the 'supply side' analysis of Hilferding, Bukharin and Lenin and returned to first base with assumptions of a price-competitive capitalism. There have been some notable exceptions, including Baran and Sweezy in the United States in their analysis of monopoly capital and the role of 'surplus' – with later critical, evaluative and enlightened perceptions made by Sweezy (1981). But many Marxist economists have ignored such insights in favour of theoretical discourses on the labour theory of value and the problem posed in Marx's theory of the transformation of such values into prices. One reason was obvious enough. Super-normal profits made possible by price-making power pose problems for the transformation of labour values into prices. Monopoly power gets in between. The result was that the economics of the firm and industry, which leaped forward with the second-generation Marxists, thereafter stayed in a cul-de-sac, unable to respond effectively to the counter-offensive from neo-liberal market theory.

It is only in recent years that a reappraisal of Marx and the second-generation Marxists has given rise to a new analysis by radical economists of the nature of both monopoly and multinational capital. At the same time,

Hilferding's main thesis on the nature of finance capital has come into its own with the internationalisation of capital markets and the rise of multinational banking (analysed in Chapter 9). Such a restatement, relates more directly to the preceding analysis of equal and unequal competition than do the metaphysics of perfect and imperfect markets or countervailance of market power by individual sovereign consumers, or the theory of so-called contestable markets.

5.6 Summary

(1) Competition is increasingly unequal between major mesoeconomic companies and minor firms more typical of textbook microeconomic models.

(2) Bigger business may combine a range of market tactics – from minimising risk through to profit or revenue maximisation – depending on the relevance of different strategies in different markets. Such tactics are less open to individual firms the smaller their size and the more limited the range of markets in which they operate.

(3) The gains from size typical of unequal competition do not depend exclusively on lower costs through production economies of scale but reflect the gains from the size of the firm itself, with its consequent hold over buyers and suppliers (oligopoly and oligopsony), plus higher stock-market rating and access to lower-cost external finance, indicating greater market stability and chances of survival.

(4) The case on mesoeconomic power is not that big business invariably raises price to achieve abnormal or monopolistic profit levels. Such pricing still operates in the classic sense as a bait to new entrants. Rather, size brings with it relative price-making power by which bigger business can raise, lower or maintain price as part of its strategy for growth or survival.

(5) Such multiple price tactics may qualify long-run cost-plus, mark-up, rule-of-thumb or focal-point pricing.

(6) The competitive imperatives for an established firm may variously include the need to (i) defend itself against new entry; (ii) extend its market share; (iii) eliminate smaller competitors; (iv) soften up competitors for takeover; (v) penetrate existing markets; or (vi) innovate into 'entirely new' markets.

(7) Successful entry to markets is now typically achieved by bigger business already dominant in other markets (or multinational companies established in the same market in other countries), and less

typically by small firms challenging bigger firms in the same market. The relevant barriers to entry differ for meso and micro companies in individual markets.

(8) Dominant firms may allow inflation to take its toll of smaller or higher-cost firms. Alternatively, the leading firms may extend a 'price umbrella' to smaller firms to prevent undue concentration of market share and distract anti-trust or anti-monopoly action. The result may be inflationary in some markets, with long-run average price levels established at levels permitting less efficient firms to survive.

(9) The allegedly new theory of 'contestable markets' in fact assumes the key conditions of perfect competition, which then are inappropriately applied to what are oligopoly structures in little more than name. Its assumptions of free entry and costless exit from markets deny both the principles of oligopoly dominance and most practice in the real world. Markets are indeed contested but under conditions which contestable market theory does not properly address.

(10) Varying degrees of inter-firm cooperation short of outright cartel arrangements can and do occur in modern markets, ranging from (i) mutual agreement not to erode 'imperfect' profits through brand attachment, through to (ii) informal agreements on price, profit and market shares and (iii) joint venture agreements on research, development or production.

(11) Marx and the Marxists have been either neglected or rejected by mainstream Anglo-American theory of the firm. But second-generation Marxists such as Hilferding and Bukharin anticipated much of what later was to emerge in mainstream oligopoly theory. Many of their insights are more relevant to twentieth century reality than revamped conventional theory of the firm such as that of 'contestable markets'.

6 From National to Multinational

Conventional market theory assumes small national firms to be represent-ative of a given industry. In fact, the real world economy is divided between small national firms which still correspond in part to the conventional model, and large multinational companies which dominate the national and international economy. The result is a dual economy of micro and meso-economic enterprise.

6.1 From External to Internal Economies

Firms buy from and sell to each other as well as to individual consumers. Such market relations are in part expressed through the concept of 'external economies', by which one firm gains from another's lower costs by 'buying in' components or other inputs rather than producing them itself. But the concept of external economies is over-extended in conventional theory. It under-represents the unequal power relations between big and small business in the modern economy.

Peaceful co-existence between small and big business is rare. Inter-dependence may result in external dependence, in which unequal competition between meso and micro enterprise disrupts the 'harmony of interests' assumed by market theory. It also may imply the 'umbrella' effect by which big business lets smaller firms live because technical economies or the low potential of traditional markets offer no incentive to their takeover or elimination.

Modern markets, moreover, are multi-dimensional. Their dynamics include not only the role of internal and external economies of scale, but also the trend to multiproduct, multiregional and multinational enterprise.

Central and Peripheral

The result is a dual market economy divided between big and small business. This has been noted by leading European and American economists for some time. Robert Averitt, for example, has analysed the different physiognomy of what he calls 'centre' and 'periphery' firms in the US economy (Averitt, 1968,

Preface). As he defines them, *centre firms* are not only large but tend to be vertically integrated (either through ownership or informal control); they are diversified in their markets, decentralised in their management structures and geographically dispersed (nationally or internationally). By contrast, *periphery firms* are relatively small. They are not vertically integrated, and typically produce only a small line of related products. Their management tends to depend on one or a handful of individuals not dissimilar in role from the owner-entrepreneur of conventional wisdom. Their location also tends to be local or regional, rather than national or international. Many periphery firms are 'satellites' of centre firms rather than entirely autonomous units.

National and International

Averitt's analysis of central and peripheral firms extends conventional oligopoly theory and advances a *gestalt* which mirrors earlier work pioneered in France by Lucien Brocard and Francois Perroux. Brocard, in a three-volume interwar study, wrote that to approach economics through the study of international trade 'is like starting construction of a building with the roof or the top floor' (Brocard, 1929–31, vol. 1, p. 11). His method was to start with the foundations of the local and regional economy, and to show how the initial concentration of firms and industries in particular growth centres, or *centres de rayonnement*, promoted spread effects by which regional and interregional growth in due course became international.

Leaders and Laggards

Francois Perroux later developed Brocard's approach in a framework which integrated the analysis of structural and spatial development. In a series of articles published in 1964 under the title of *The Twentieth Century Economy*, Perroux's broad-ranging analysis should have been made widely available to Anglo-Saxon economists. But through a failure of the market not unknown in international publishing, only one of his articles – on the concept of 'growth poles' – was widely translated, and well received.

Among Perroux's powerful insights was that into the role of leading firms (*firmes motrices*) in the process of structural and spatial polarisation. Such firms pushed and pulled some smaller firms with them in their own expansion. But they undercut other firms in such a way that the latter first lagged and then fell behind the leaders.

Spread and Backwash

Perroux's analysis is developed in section 6.4 of this chapter, as is the complementary analysis of Gunnar Myrdal (1957) on 'spread' and 'back-wash' effects. Myrdal analysed the destabilising effects of capital and labour flows on the various regions of the national and international economy. Like Perroux, he stressed the role of internal and external economies of scale in cumulative imbalance, arguing that 'the free play of market forces normally tends to increase rather than decrease the inequalities between regions of the national and international economy.' This growth of new enterprise in some areas leaves others 'more or less in a backwater'. The virtuous circle of expansion is thereby locked in a mechanism of cumulative and circular causation, with the vicious circle of backwash and decline for enterprise which cannot benefit from the original spread effects.

External Economies

Conventional market theory has largely ignored the asymmetry and imbalance of the Perroux and Myrdal analyses. It assumes that the process of external economies benefits smaller firms which are unable to achieve internal economies of scale through insufficient size. Undoubtedly, this is the case for those small firms which can achieve no significant scale economies in their own production, and which survive or grow in the main through assembly or inputs bought from larger firms which have achieved such external economies. Assuming that the lower external cost is reflected in lower prices, the purchasing firm will gain from a lower cost for its inputs than it could achieve by producing them itself. But meso and micro business gain unequal advantage even from external economies.

We can take a practical example from an industry with a relatively high

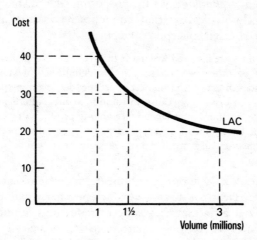

FIG. 6.1   Internal and external economies

degree of externalisation – automobiles. A major vehicle producer, whether Nissan, Renault or Chrysler, must now produce a million cars a year to achieve significant production economies of scale. Even at this level of output, it is not clear that it will be worth its while to produce all of the components which it assembles to make a motor vehicle if there is a significant declining slope in the long-run average cost curve.

For example, as illustrated in Figure 6.1, the unit costs of headlamps for a motor vehicle is equivalent to £30 at a volume of 1½ million units, as opposed to £20 for a volume production of 3 millions. This in part explains why a company such as Lucas company has made the headlamp units for many of the vehicles produced in Britain, as opposed to all the big manufacturers making their own. If Austin Rover were to produce its own headlamps, these would certainly be cheaper than if produced by a very small manufacturer such as Morgan. But the cost for Austin Rover would still be higher than that for an enterprise producing 1½ million units a year (or over 3 million units such as Toyota). This standard external economies argument is one of the reasons why even large firms both producing and assembling components for motor vehicles may gain external economies from buying from other firms.

From Indirect to Direct

Such external economies as illustrated for the motor industry involve an interdependence of purchases between firms, paid for on the market. This is one reason why Scitovsky (1954) has called them *pecuniary* external economies. But Scitovsky also identified another category of such economies, which he called *technological*. In proposing the distinction between pecuniary and technological external economies, he was attempting to clarify the use of an overloaded concept. As he put it:

> External economies are invoked whenever the profits of one producer are affected by the actions of other producers. . . . This definition of external economies obviously includes direct or non-market interdependence among producers. . . . It is much broader, however . . . because, in addition to direct interdependence among producers, it also includes interdependence among producers through the market mechanism. The latter type of interdependence may be called 'pecuniary external economies' to distinguish it from the technological external economies of direct interdependence.

However, Scitovsky's adoption of the term 'technological' is in part misleading. There clearly is a sense in which pecuniary external economies are also technological in that they concern reductions in unit costs for an individual producer in securing inputs from technologically related firms whose internal economies of scale permit them to produce the inputs at a lower cost than the producer who purchases them. There is a more evident 'technological' link here than for other external economies claimed by Scitovsky such as the availability of labour and transport facilities.

Locational Economies

But it is not only technology which distinguishes non-pecuniary external economies. There are also economies from location.

Probably one of the best ways to make this clear is to 'go back to Marshall'. In introducing the external and internal economies concepts, Marshall (1890, p. 221) stated that 'we may divide the economies arising from an increase in the scale of production of any kind of goods into two classes – firstly, those dependent on the general development of the industry; and, secondly, those dependent on the resources of the individual houses of business engaged in it, on their organisation and efficiency of management. We may call the former *external economies*, and the latter *internal economies*'. This statement – the most frequently cited – is clearly consistent with and can be held to support Scitovsky's emphasis on pecuniary external economies.

However, Marshall immediately continues by stating: 'in the present chapter we have been chiefly discussing internal economies; but we now proceed to examine those very important external economies which can often be secured by the concentration of many small businesses of a similar character *in particular localities*: or, as is commonly said, by the localisation of industry'. In the following chapter Marshall outlined the principal external economies from location – analysed extensively by the literature on location since his time – such as labour and employment availability, savings in transport costs and ease of communications (ibid., pp. 225–7). If we add socio-economic infrastructure, we have four of the principal categories of external economies from location recognised in later regional theory (Holland, 1976a).

Concentration and Dispersion

The terminology employed in identifying such external economies as labour availability, transport facilities, communications and infrastructure is not of crucial importance, provided the consequences of such economies are clear. For instance, Perroux (1965) later reduced the importance which he initially attached to external economies in contributing to the spatial concentration of activity. Some of his disciples have not followed him, and still argue that concentration alone can maximise economies and cost savings. But it is evident that some firms can gain greater economies by locating away from large urban concentrations rather than in them. Dispersion of this kind – both multi-regional and multinational – depends very much on the structure of firms and their stage of production. This process is analysed in some detail in section 6.4 of this chapter.

6.2   From Integration to Cooperation

As enterprise size has increased, many mesoeconomic firms have internalised production or services. There are fewer gains to them from buying externally as they increase their overall output. Not least, external buying means less control over the supply of goods and services. Design or production difficulties, or shortages of raw materials, may mean that the external supplier may not be able to satisfy the demands of the mesoeconomic enterprise.

The Biggest Business

Such internalisation of economies shows clearly in the overall figures for the world's biggest business. In an analysis of 830 industrial companies, Dunning and Pearce (1981, p. 6) assessed that 'firms prefer to internalise their competitive advantage whenever they do not think that they can capture the full economic rent of these advantages by selling them in the open market.' They call such internalisation a *market failure*, arguing that it 'tends to be greatest in the knowledge of intensive and resource based sectors, and

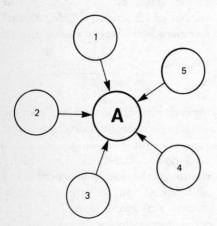

FIG. 6.2(a)   External economies

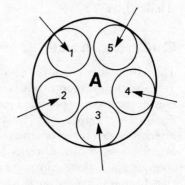

FIG. 6.2(b)   Internalised economies

wherever the potential buyer has not the knowledge or the skills to make as efficient use of the competitive advantage as does the firm possessing it'.

But in a clear sense, internalisation is less a market failure than a market success. It is through the successful application of internal economies of scale that most of the leading companies today have reduced their dependence on external suppliers, producing through their own subsidiaries rather than 'buying in' from other firms.

This process is shown in Figure 6.2. Figure 6.2(a) represents the textbook case implicit in neoclassical microeconomic theory of external economies, whereby an individual enterprise, A, will take advantage of the internal scale of economies achieved in firms 1 to 5, which are different and separate in terms of ownership and control structures. Figure 6.2(b) represents the situation in which the concentration of production has advanced to the point at which previously independent scale economies in five separate firms have been internalised in a single company. This transforms the interdependence of a large number of small microeconomic firms into the independence of a single large mesoeconomic company.

Micro and Meso Dimensions

Although Figure 6.2(b) overstates the probable degree of internalisation, such a process is an important part of the concentration of production among fewer firms. It also has negative effects for microeconomic enterprise. These can be seen as a structural dimension of Perroux's 'polarisation' or Myrdal's 'backwash'. In other words, the spread effects of extending production to activities formerly supplied by other firms is positive for the meso leaders, but negative for the micro suppliers who cease to be their customers.

Averitt's 'satellite' firms are also affected by the process. The 'satellite' relationship is the market link by which external suppliers to centre firms are dependent on them for much or most of their orders. With internalisation of scale economies by the centre enterprise, the satellites become detached. They are either consigned to the periphery of the market, or may succumb to the black hole of market concentration as bigger business takes over their market share.

Whether or not such firms disappear, big business certainly can combine the advantages of optimised internal economies with conditions of external supply which are dominated by its own market power. Thus Figure 6.2(c) illustrates the vertical integration and supply and outlet structure of the Toyota auto company in Japan. Although Toyota has not internalised all its component suppliers, the logic of Figure 6.2(c) is not far removed from the internalisation of Figure 6.2(b). All of the outlets of Toyota in Japan are directly controlled by the company. Some 60 per cent of supplied components

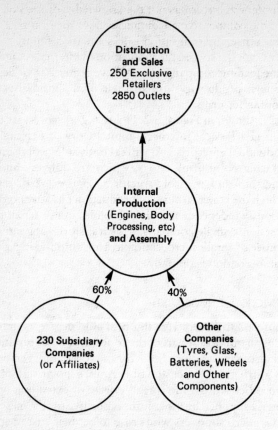

FIG. 6.2(C)   Toyota's internal and external economies

comes from subsidiary firms or firms with which Toyota has an institutional relationship. For the remaining 40 per cent of supplies, Toyota's bargaining position as a dominant manufacturer is sufficiently strong for it to gain supplies on terms and conditions it requires. The difference is that its 'satellites' are integrated into an expanding enterprise undertaking an 'offensive' global market strategy, unlike Averitt's 'satellites' which – through the vagaries of the open market rather than direct contractual links to a major company – risk being here today and gone tomorrow.

Vertical Integration

Such a process of internalising scale economies can involve vertical or horizontal or more circular forms of integration.

In the case of technically related enterprise, the cost savings from internalised scale economies are considerable. This obtains, for example, in the relation between basic petro-chemicals and downstream derivatives such as plastics, soaps and pharmaceuticals. It is also the case with iron and steel, where there are major scale economies from producing on a continuous basis in one integrated plant combining (1) blast furnaces with iron production from ore, through to (2) steel conversion, whether by oxygen or by another process, through to (3) rolled or pressed steel and (4) derivatives of plate, special steels, coils, tubes, pipes and wire. The technical imperatives to internalise various stages of production therefore have a logic which is more real than Scitovsky's 'technological' external economies.

One can see this process in practice in the recent concentration of steel production in single, shore-based, integrated plant – as at Dunkirk in France or Taranto in Italy. Shore-based plant thereby gain access to the lowest cost inputs of ore and coal from the cheapest world sources. This contrasts with the classic nineteenth-century pattern, where frequently separate enterprises tended to produce the iron ore, cooling it into ingots which were then transported to other enterprises which melted them down for steel conversion, with the steel then transported elsewhere for special processing. What were originally external economies for a range of independent producers, have now become internal economies for one enterprise in a single plant. The same obtains for chemicals, plastics and other derivatives.

Multi-Plant and Multinational

This does not mean that all the economies internal to a firm need to be concentrated on one site, in one region or in one country. As illustrated later in this chapter, the mesoeconomic enterprise, extending its activities on a multinational scale, may well disperse production on a global basis. For example, the Bulova watch company produces components in Switzerland, assembles them with low-cost labour in Taiwan, and then flies the product to the UK or the US for sale (Barnet and Muller, 1974). The key point, damaging for microeconomic theory, is the extent to which it internalises these stages within the ambit and framework of its own overall global corporate control.

The case for vertical integration is promoted by technology. But considerations of market security and control over the rate, scale, quality and flow of inputs have also encouraged firms to integrate production. In some cases, integration extends downstream through to distribution in both wholesale and retail outlets. This is now commonplace in automobiles, with your local GM, Ford or Toyota dealer, and in airline services, where companies such as Pan Am or British Airways frequently lease, license or otherwise control their own sales outlets. In financial services, building societies in Britain have recently moved upstream into competition with commercial banks and finance houses by offering instant cash withdrawals and credit-card facilities for general purchases.

Flexible Integration

Recently, Henry Ergas (1984) has revealed that many companies have responded to prolonged recession in the 1970s and 1980s by increasing the flexibility of their vertical integration, or the balance between in-house and out-house operations. Ergas points out that some firms are adopting a more selective attitude to vertical integration, through (1) limiting such a process to critical components which are unavailable in the open market and central to the firm's product strategy; (2) finding contractual alternatives to such integration for input requirements, with increased attention by top management to external purchases. Such increased specialisation or 'segmentation' of market strategy enables such business to reduce its risk of being 'locked-in' to internal supply, or avoid investment in innovation which, during a period of rapid technological change, may quickly become redundant.

Ergas' arguments relate both to market flexibility in recession and also to the changes in technology which have given rise to 'flexible automation' within given plant. One of the most impressive analyses of this process, resulting from a major international research project, has been given by Brankovic, who contrasts the *fixed* or 'hard' automation of the Ford model T mass-production line (where you could have any colour of car you liked so long as it was black) with the *flexible* or 'soft' automation of the period following widespread use of micro-processors and mini-computers into the production process (when you could have a car of any colour or custom mix you like). Such processors have now been introduced into equipment in not only manufacturing, construction, mining and agriculture, but also (through word-processing and data-processing variants) into a wide range of financial and retail services (Brankovic, 1987).

In practice, small firms or individuals can use micro-computers or word-processors (such as this author in the preparation of this text). But this no more helps a small firm become a global corporation than it helps a person of average height become a giant. It is the corporate context of the firm's size and the market power within which flexible automation is applied which counts. Not least there is the issue whether the firm commands enough market share either as a buyer or supplier to make it worthwhile to translate the production technique of flexible automation into vertical integration. As Brankovic himself observes:

> Revolutionary technologies never and nowhere appear as complete factory or other

functional systems ready for full scale and widespread application. This is in particular the case with the current industrial revolution, when especially intensive and large-scale research and experimenting proved to be a condition for successful application. . . . The needs for sub-contracting production components is tending to diminish [Brankovic, 1987].

Ford's European Integration

Thus the mini and micro technologies in the 1970s and 1980s have not essentially qualified the imperative of internalisation of economies for major companies. Ergas himself stresses that the degree of integration 'depends to a large extent on the size of firm and on its market position'. Table 6.1 shows the scale and range of vertical integration in its European operations of the Ford Motor Company. Rather than avoiding a vertical structure through buying in components (whether windshield glass, window winders, carburettors or distributors) on the lines of external economy theory, Ford produces not only these but also suspension components, fuel tanks, transmission, plugs, wheels and engines in individual plant in Europe (and in the case of windshield glass, in the United States), with the final assembly of the Fiesta model in three plant – at Valencia in Spain, Saarlouis in West Germany, and Dagenham in Britain. As Locksley (1983) points out, Ford treats Europe as a single production area but also 'segments the EEC as far as

TABLE 6.1   The Fiesta's Vertical Integration

Part	Sources
Suspension components	Wulfrath, West Germany
Fuel Tank	Saarlouis, West Germany
Window winder	Croydon, UK
Distributor	Belfast, Northern Ireland
Transmission	Bordeaux, France
Road Wheels	Genk, Belgium
Engine	Valencia, Spain
Bumper plating	Cologne, West Germany
Spark plugs	Enfield, UK
Windshield glass	Tulsa, Okla. USA
Carburettor	Belfast, Northern Ireland
Engine components	Leamington and Basildon, UK
	Cologne, West Germany
Final assembly	Valencia, Spain
	Saarlouis, West Germany
	Dagenham, UK

prices are concerned'. Thus with the UK price of the Fiesta in February 1983 equal to 100 (net of tax), its prices as set by Ford in Belgium are 70, France 74, the Netherlands 79, Italy 85, and West Germany 86. Thus the 'segmentation' stressed by Ergas is internalised both for products and prices by Ford through the range of its European production and markets.

Horizontal Integration

Horizontal integration within the same industry occurs when firms extend their operations either through (a) merger, (b) takeover, or (c) joint ventures and (d) market-sharing agreements. The mechanisms of takeover – mainly of micro by meso enterprises – have been analysed extensively in the preceding chapter. Through a variety of tactics, up to and including elimination pricing, larger and more strongly based firms can take over either the assets or order books of other enterprise. But horizontal integration also may involve joint ventures and other co-operative arrangements by which firms extend their activities within individual industry.

While takeover tends to be offensive in character, merger may well be either a defensive response to national or international competition, or the necessary condition for achieving minimal economies of scale.

Motor vehicles are a clear example of such volume thresholds. The research and development process for a new automobile can cost £20 million and take two to five years. To achieve profitability, full economies of scale need to be achieved so that fixed costs can be spread across as large an output as possible. As already indicated, the optimal production run for a new high-volume car is one million units per year – and the automation of car assembly may well increase this to two million in the near future. A bottom-line minimum of between a quarter and a third of a million vehicles is required to avoid serious financial difficulties. Such raised thresholds act as a decisive barrier to new micro entry into a market dominated by meso majors. They also prompt mergers and joint ventures between the majors themselves.

National Mergers

Figure 6.3 represents the extent of merger in the British motor-vehicle industry through the main part of the twentieth century. (It is worth bearing in mind that in the 1930s there were 137 vehicle producers in the UK (Watson, 1986).) Mergers in the mid-1930s between Lanchester and Daimler, and Morris and Riley, were undertaken with a view to rationalising joint production, but in practice this proved insufficient to achieve major economies of scale. The formation of the British Motor Corporation (BMC) in 1950, British Motor Holdings and Leyland in 1965, and the creation of the

British Leyland company merged over a dozen originally independent companies. But this was barely sufficient to achieve the minimum economies of scale for survival, partly through a failure to complement increased corporate size with a rationalised product range and sufficient standardisation of components to achieve greater technical economies of scale in production. As a result, the British Leyland corporation was brought into public ownership in the 1970s under the National Enterprise Board stateholding company, which pumped nearly £1 billion into the new joint enterprise, without which it would not have been able to replace basic models such as the Mini or undertake investment in successful new models such as the Rover and Land Rover.

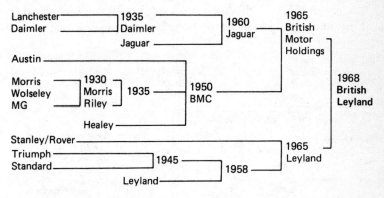

To avoid undue complication, dates are approximate and only major companies are shown

FIG. 6.3   Merger and concentration in the British motor industry (Source: *Barclays Review*, May 1983)

International Joint Ventures

When in the early 1980s British Leyland introduced their new Metro, Maestro and Rover models, they were to be its last genuinely British products. On the Maestro, by the time of its launch, sales of only one-fifth of a million units a year were regarded as probable – way below the minimum third of a million or the optimal million vehicles. Leyland then turned abroad for joint-venture agreements, and found them with Honda.

General Motors, the world's biggest automobile company, has not been immune from the pressure for international joint ventures. Under an agreement, also made in the early 1980s, between GM and Toyota, respectively the first and third largest motor manufacturers in the world,

Toyota produces small cars for the American market from a disused GM plant in California. Using common components and production techniques from multinational plant, it has already achieved the objective of the 'global automobile'.

No microeconomic car-producer on the lines of the competitive model can hope to challenge this mesoeconomic big league. Already, formal joint-venture links exist not only between General Motors and Toyota but also between GM and Izuzu, Ford and Toyo Kogyo, Chrysler and Mitsubishi, Nissan and Alfa Romeo, and Nissan and Iberica of Spain.

Figure 6.4 portrays the range and scale of the international links of British Leyland, including not only Honda for joint production of the Acclaim/Ballade but also gearboxes with Volkswagen, diesel engines with Alfa Romeo and Perkins, and links with Volvo, Volkswagen, Renault, Fiat and PSA in France through the European Automotive Engineering Research Association.

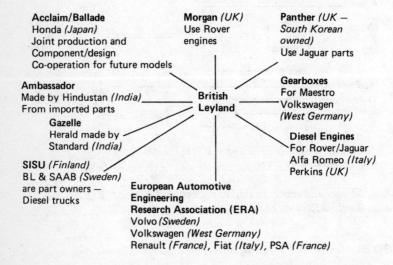

FIG. 6.4 International joint ventures: the British motor industry (Source: *Barclays Review*, May 1983)

In practice, the motor industry is now rife with collaborative agreements. By 1985, in a list of a hundred deals compiled by *Car Magazine*, 61 involved parts supply, joint production or licensed production, 22 were for research and development, and 17 covered financial and equity interests. Ignoring this imperative for concentration and collaboration, the British Conservative government in the 1980s attempted to solve the crisis of UK car manu-facturers by selling them off to the highest bidder (such as GM's bid for

British Leyland's truck division). Such an effort was defeated only by a revolt of backbenchers in the House of Commons.

Cooperation in Aerospace

Figure 6.5 illustrates the process of national concentration and cooperation in the British aerospace industry. In 1934, aircraft companies which had become world famous such as Gloster, Sopwith/Hawker, Armstrong-Whitworth and Avro were merged into the Hawker-Siddeley company, which in turn merged with Folland, Blackburn and De Haviland in 1960. In the same year, Vickers Armstrong, Bristol, English Electric and Hunting merged into the British Aircraft Corporation, and in 1977 this merged with both Hawker Siddeley and Scottish Aviation in the British Aerospace Corporation, under public ownership.

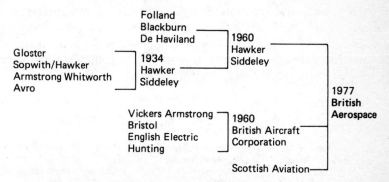

(To avoid undue complication, dates are approximate and only major companies are shown)

Fig. 6.5 Merger and concentration in the British aerospace industry (Source: *Barclays Review*, May 1983)

The penalties of late entry into a market make it increasingly imperative that even leading firms should be not only within reach but preferably on the frontier of new technology and new product innovation. For example, despite technical excellence, Lockheed's L10-11 failed to make any impression on Boeing's 747 share of the wide-bodied commercial airliner market, with the result that although Lockheed was not rendered bankrupt, it decided to cease commercial airline production altogether. Rolls-Royce was bankrupted by the failure of carbon-fibre blades in the early 1970s, and had to be salvaged by public ownership. By mid 1986 the Airbus A320 had some 440 orders and options, but needed to make 600 firm sales just to break even.

Security and Specialisation

The result, as in motor vehicles, has been a remorseless pressure for security through joint-venture collaboration between the major world aerospace companies, backed by increased state intervention at the national level. Figure 6.6 shows the international co-operation undertaken by British Aerospace with Air Italia in Italy, McDonnell-Douglas, Avco and Lockheed in the United States, Saab in Sweden, Aerospatiale and Dassault-Bregeut and Sud Aviation in France, plus Casa in Spain, Fokker in Holland, Belairbus in Belgium and Deutsche Airbus in West Germany. Airlines in the early 1980s were discussing the need for an apparently simple 500-mile range, 150-seater for the late 1980s or early 1990s. Rather than competing for the engine contracts, Rolls-Royce in the United Kingdom and Pratt and Whitney in the United States, together with three Japanese firms, Fiat of Italy and Motoren and Turbinen Union of West Germany, agreed to spend £100 million on the collaborative development of a suitable product. Against them, General Electric in the United States and Snecma of France collaborated on an engine for the same potential market. This pressure for joint ventures and collaboration between mesoeconomic companies in the developed countries follows the trend from regional to national and multinational capital in developed and less developed countries alike.

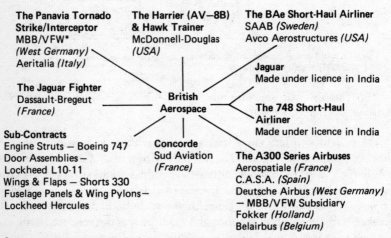

The Panavia Tornado
Strike/Interceptor
MBB/VFW*
(West Germany)
Aeritalia (Italy)

The Harrier (AV–8B)
& Hawk Trainer
McDonnell-Douglas
(USA)

The BAe Short-Haul Airliner
SAAB (Sweden)
Avco Aerostructures (USA)

The Jaguar Fighter
Dassault-Bregeut
(France)

British
Aerospace

Jaguar
Made under licence in India

The 748 Short-Haul
Airliner
Made under licence in India

Sub-Contracts
Engine Struts — Boeing 747
Door Assemblies —
Lockheed L10-11
Wings & Flaps — Shorts 330
Fuselage Panels & Wing Pylons—
Lockheed Hercules

Concorde
Sud Aviation
(France)

The A300 Series Airbuses
Aerospatiale (France)
C.A.S.A. (Spain)
Deutsche Airbus (West Germany)
— MBB/VFW Subsidiary
Fokker (Holland)
Belairbus (Belgium)

*Messerschmitt Bolkow-Blohm/Vereinigte Flugtechnische Werke

FIG. 6.6   International joint ventures: the British aerospace industry (Source: *Barclays Review*, May 1983)

6.3   From Multiproduct to Multisectoral

The categories of vertical and horizontal integration seem relatively clear cut. In practice, however, few firms operate within single industry or sector boundaries.

The key reasons are economic. But the perception is statistical. Standard industrial classifications in national accounts do not neatly coincide with company activities. Sometimes the definitions are too broad, sometimes too narrow – with the result that, in Shepherd's judgement, for the United States about half of industries in the industrial census 'depart seriously from correct market boundaries' (Shepherd, 1979, p. 199).

Another reason reflects technological change and innovation. Firms push forward their innovation frontiers into what Perroux (1965) has called 'entirely new' industries and sectors of activity. National and international accounting categories take time to catch up, for example when engineering or electrical sectors no longer represent the reality of electronics. Adding a new accounting column for an entirely new industry could solve the problem quickly enough if policy-makers could decide where the frontier lay, but international agreement may prove harder to gain and be delayed indefinitely.

Defensive and Offensive

The underlying reasons for the trend to multiproduct and multisectoral companies is the dynamic of competition itself. It reflects not only economies of scale in production, distribution and exchange, unequal access to finance and unequal hold over buyers and suppliers, but also the wider gains from size and scale made possible by diversification.

As with horizontal integration, such gains reflect either a defensive or offensive market strategy. A slowing of the rate of growth with product maturity in a given market may prompt management in big business to diversify offensively through forcing new entry, or the elimination/takeover of firms in other sectors. Alternatively, the management may establish profit-generating business outside its main market which can assist it in riding out a competitive challenge to its core or central activity.

Related and Unrelated

Such diversification no longer represents only technical economies of scale through reduced unit costs, but also financial economies of scale enabling big business to survive and grow through a range of activities.

Related diversification may include the mechanisms of internalised economies through vertical or horizontal integration, crossing conventional accounting frontiers. Unrelated diversification may bear no relation to technical or production scale economies, and conglomerate a range of diverse companies within the holding framework of the parent corporation. But many leading companies now defy such conventional categories and operate in both related and unrelated sectors.

TWA and Pan Am

Table 6.2 shows that in 1982 some two-thirds of the operating revenues of the Transworld Corporation were gained from its airline TWA and most of the remaining third from the Hilton International hotel chain, the Canteen Corporation and the Spartan Foods Systems company. In a clear sense these activities are related and reflect a vertical strategy whereby the Transworld Corporation has integrated hotels and food for customers using TWA airlines, as well as supplying itself in some cases. But it is also evident that such vertical integration is no longer within a single 'representative industry' on the lines of conventional theory. Not everyone using a vending machine in the Canteen Corporation, or the rooms and restaurants of the Hilton International, flies on Transworld Airlines.

TABLE 6.2   Transworld Airlines (US)

	% operating revenues 1982
TW Airlines	65.0
Canteen Corp	14.7
Hilton International*	13.9
Spartan Food Systems, Inc.	5.7
Century 21	0.7

*Divested 1987.

A multisectoral structure gave both TWA and Pan Am an unequal advantage in the early 1980s when faced with competition from classic micro entrants to the transatlantic air market such as Laker or Virgin airlines. The multi-national majors certainly were hard pressed when Laker and Virgin slashed fares with a view to forcing an entry and increasing their market share, with massive price gains for consumers. Because the transatlantic route was highly profitable, unlike many shorter hauls or long-distance routes with lower volume, both the majors were forced to reduce fares, profit margins and even sustain losses in the short run. At this stage, however, Pan Am was able to sell off its profitable Intercontinental hotel chain to the British Trafalgar House group and reinforce its financial position. TWA nearly sold its Hilton hotel chain to KLM, but when that fell through sold it in 1987 to United Airlines. Laker had no such assets on which to draw, and went bankrupt. In the mid 1980s Virgin airlines (perhaps well named) was hard pressed to maintain schedules with very few planes and was in considerable difficulties. The micro challengers are being squeezed – or squeezed out – by mesoeconomic and multinational companies.

Nippon Electric

Table 6.3 shows that over a third of the net sales of the Nippon Electric Company Ltd (NEC) of Japan in 1981 were in general communications, and just under half in computers and industrial electronic systems and electron devices, with most of the remainder in home electronics. Again, vertical integration theory explains much of this range of activities. Electron devices are directly related to computers, industrial electronic systems and communications. There is also a less direct link between industrial and home electronics. For NEC, vertical integration is still dominant.

TABLE 6.3   Nippon Electric Co. Ltd – Japan

	% net sales 1981
Communications	36
Computers & Industrial Electronic Systems	24
Electron Devices	23
Home Electronics	13
Other Operations	4

ITT

As shown in Table 6.4, the International Telephone and Telegraph Corporation also reflects a degree of vertical integration in its telecommunications, electronics and engineering products, which accounted for over half of its sales and revenue in 1980. On the other hand, nearly half of its activities were in the nominally less related sectors of consumer products and services, natural resources, and insurance and finance. ITT has even had a presence in the cosmetics industry and at one time ran the Sheraton Hotel chain and Avis car rental. It thus appeared part integrated and part unintegrated. But, as elaborated later in this chapter, ITT sought integration even in some of its nominally unrelated or conglomerate activities.

TABLE 6.4 ITT

	% of sales and revenues 1980
Telecommunications & Electronics	30.0
Engineered Products	26.0
Consumer Products & Services	16.0
Natural Resources	5.8
Insurance & Finance	22.2

Philips

Table 6.5 shows the range of activities of the Dutch Philips corporation, with Unilever and Royal Dutch Shell one of the three 'flagship' companies of the Netherlands. Philips clearly is both a multiproduct and multinational company. However, its range of activities is less diverse than those of ITT and more related to its 'core areas' of electrical and electronic goods. In this respect it compares directly with Nippon Electric, one of its key competitors on the world market.

TABLE 6.5 Philips

	% sales 1982
Lighting & Batteries	11
Home Electronics for Sound & Vision	26
Domestic Appliances & Personal Products	12
Products & Systems for Professional Applications	30
Industrial Supplies	13
Misc.	8

Holding Companies

In the late nineteenth and early twentieth centuries, new *holding* companies incorporating subsidiary *operating* companies became an important part of the trend to monopoly and financial trusts in the German and US economies. At the same time, similar centrally controlled holding companies, or *zaibatsu*, were fostered and flourished in Japan. Such multiproduct and multisectoral companies flourished in the era of dynamic growth in the US, German and Japanese economies. Their strategies were clearly offensive. They were actors and initiators promoting expansion rather than reactive adapters to decline.

By contrast, in the interwar period, holding companies were frequently defensive, responding to crisis, salvaging individual corporations and subsidising losses in the hope of better days to come. Several of them – precisely because of the costs – were public rather than private enterprises. The Italian Industrial Reconstruction Institute (IRI) was formed by the government in 1933 in response to the threatened bankruptcy of three of Italy's leading banks, inheriting from them a portfolio of unrelated holdings in a range of disparate companies (Holland, 1972).

After the Second World War, holding companies flourished in new forms in the US, Europe and Japan. In the United States, the financial *conglomerate* stole headlines and market ratings with pretax rates of profit growth five to ten times those of more conventional operating companies. In Europe, holding companies in the private sector achieved a renaissance in Germany after a period of tough postwar controls on big business by the Allied powers. Private banks exercised wide-ranging investment and management controls through *Aufsichtsräte*, or supervisory boards, in a pyramidic structure which gave them an overview not only of individual companies but also of the prospects of whole sectors of activity (Shonfield, 1965).

State holding companies, seeking to promote and reinforce success rather than salvage failure, flourished in the 1960s and early 1970s in Europe. The Industrial Development Institute (IDI) was established in France, the Society for National Investment (SNI) in Belgium, and the National Enterprise Board in Britain. These central holdings were also paralleled by local or regional holding companies on a wide scale (Minns and Thornley, 1978).

From *Zaibatsu* to *Keiretsu*

In Japan, offensive go-getting investment was the hallmark of postwar corporate strategy. While companies in other countries often waited for demand before planning supply, the Japanese thought forward to probable sales in five, ten or fifteen years and to the corporate structure which would be necessary to match demand expansion with appropriate supply.

Initially, as in Germany, the Japanese had to work within the constraints imposed by military defeat. The centrally controlled holding company dating from the nineteenth-century Meiji dynasty – the *zaibatsu* – had provided self-contained armaments industries for the Japanese war machine. Such *zaibatsu* anticipated by half a century what President Eisenhower was to warn against in his address to the nation as outgoing president – the power of the military-industrial complex.

But, with legendary ingenuity, the Japanese after the Second World War responded to the restrictions of the Allied Control Commission by developing

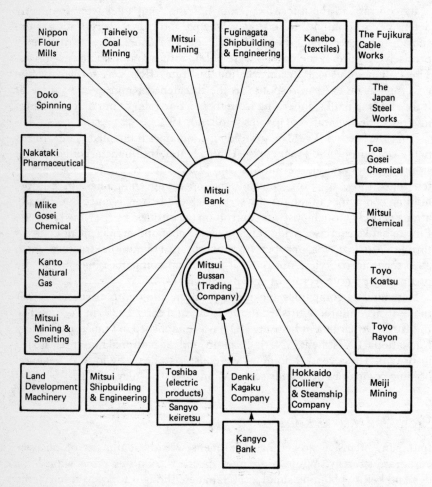

FIG. 6.7 Multidivisional conglomerate structure: the Mitsui Kinyu *keiretsu* (Source: Beida (1970))

a new multiproduct and multisectoral holding company which lacked apparent central control – the *keiretsu*. Figure 6.7 shows how the Mitsui combine is in a different world from the single-plant, single-product, single-market company predicated by conventional market theory. Ranging through mining, steel, engineering, chemicals, pharmaceuticals, electrical goods, electronic products, banking and distribution, Mitsui bears no relation to Samuelson's and Lipsey's cost constraints on 'representative' firms and industries.

Mitsui – From Sunset to Sunrise

A conglomerate such as Mitsui makes possible precisely the combined gains from scale in production, distribution and finance shown in Chapters 4 and 5 in the analysis of the rise of big business and unequal competition. Where constraints are imposed by plant size, they are transformed by the Japanese *keiretsu* by new capital-deepening and scale-widening investment which allows for under-capacity for up to five years in anticipation that when other companies in other countries are wondering whether to invest, Mitsui will be supplying worldwide demand at full capacity. Declining-sector activities such as steel, shipbuilding and textiles can be offset by building up growing sectors such as pharmaceuticals, electrical products and electronics, either in the same company's conglomerate framework, or through new mergers and joint ventures (such as are illustrated by Mitsui's links with Sangyo-Toshiba). Thus the sunrise-to-sunset syndrome depicted by US supply-side theorists as flourishing for different micro firms is also managed in reverse – from sunset to sunrise – within the giant Japanese combines.

Conglomerate Commotion

Despite claims that the *keiretsu* are not centrally controlled, it is notable that the Mitsui Bank lies at the heart of Mitsui Kinyu's operations. Banks have played a similar central role in the activities of trusts in several countries. In the United States, the rise (and, in some cases, fall) of leading conglomerates has not involved the same central role for an individual company bank as such. But the holding companies heading conglomerates have acted very much as financial centres for subsidiary enterprise. In principle, therefore, the conglomerate operates in a range of activities which are unrelated in terms of internal or external economies, or direct interdependence. But they are links in a chain of profit-centred operations, with subsidiary company strategy determined by the central holding company. Also, in key cases, the links have echoed the classic form of vertical integration.

It was in the 1960s that conglomerate companies began to attract major attention as high profit performers. Some US conglomerates jumped market boundaries and ploughed thereafter, such as Penn-Texas, Bellanca, Merritt-Chapman & Scott, as well as the Westec Corporation which was in oil and gas exploration, real estate, aerospace equipment and geophysical instruments at the time of its bankruptcy. Other conglomerates did well for years and sustained remarkable cross-market growth, including ITT and Litton. But few of these companies diversified on a random basis. Some consciously diversified from declining into growing markets, winding down or moving out of their 'home base' sectors.

Buccaneer Behn and ITT

The International Telephone and Telegraph Corporation was founded in 1920 by the buccaneer Sosthenes Behn, whose family had been sugar brokers. ITT began by selling telephone systems to a series of governments, starting with Spain under the dictator Primo de Rivera in 1923. Its major boost came through the acquisition in 1925 of the international holdings of the Western Electric Company, which was making telephones all over the world. Western decided to divest its foreign holdings under threat of an anti-trust action, and Sosthenes Behn thereby found himself with an 'instant multinational'. But he managed it much in the style of an owner-entrepreneur, wheeling and dealing with Goering and Hitler, and aiding the armaments industries of the Third Reich.

It was after the retirement of Behn in 1956 that ITT expanded from its base area of telephone and telegraph equipment and went conglomerate. This was in part due to the hiring of Harold Geneen, a former senior executive with Raytheon, who on taking over ITT was appalled at the lack of serious management in a company which 'was really no more than a holding company, investing in factories thousands of miles away and hoping for the best'. Anthony Sampson claims that ITT moved from taking over the Avis car hire company 'to buy anything, whatever it made, provided it was growing fast and profitably' (Sampson, 1973, pp. 70–81).

'Anything That Moves'

Within a few years, Geneen had bought up a range of new concerns. But many of his acquisitions were interrelated. These included the Bramwell Business College, the Nancy Taylor Secretarial School and the Speedwriting shorthand system. The purchase of Apcoa, a car-parking company, fitted well with the purchase of Avis, as did the acquisition of Cleveland Motels and also the more spectacular purchase of the Sheraton hotel chain. Likewise, the purchase of Levitt construction (which was into suburban housebuilding on a scale which made 'Levittown' a synonym for middle-class aspirations) fitted well with purchase of America's biggest glass manufacturer (Pennyslvania Glass and Sand). So did the takeover of Continental Baking (America's biggest bakery and food company) and that of the Canteen Corporation (then the world's leading vending machine company). A merger with the Grinnel Corporation (the biggest in the US fire protection business) made sense not only for ITT's property empire but also in relation to the successful bid for the Hartford Insurance Group. In turn, this made sense in relation to ITT's cluster of life insurance companies, including Hamilton Life, ITT Life, Mid-Western Life and Abbey Life in Britain.

Thus Sampson's judgement is both true and less than the whole truth. ITT did not simply pick off anything that moved, it crossed market boundaries *and* sought a degree of integration within them. It also sought to defend its corporate interests by contesting the democratically elected government of Chile, and attracted the attention of federal trust busters. The result was senate hearings and a degree of notoriety in which ITT – in the short run – was profoundly compromised.

Litton's Multi-Market Strategy

If ITT typifies a single-industry multinational which grew into a multimarket company, Litton more clearly conforms with the image of a 'pure' conglomerate.

An interview by *Fortune* magazine (Editors of *Fortune*, 1970) with Roy L. Ash, Litton's president during its 'long boom' years, provides an insight into its operations as a conglomerate and their relevance to some of the key principles of the growth of diversified big business. First, Ash was sceptical of the term 'conglomerate' and preferred to view Litton as a 'multi-industry' company of which technology was the common denominator. Second, the timing of innovation was important: new products 'cross their technical feasibility threshold before they cross their economic threshold'. Third, as a result, pioneering new products with success in markets does not mean being the first into them. Later entry may mean a better entry. Fourth, more innovation diversifies risk. Not every development programme succeeds, but more programmes increase 'a good batting average'. Fifth, heavy involvement in public-sector programmes, from housing through military technology to aerospace, provides the platform for ventures in the civilian market.

Super-Profits

For over a decade Litton achieved a rate of profit of around 30 per cent and refused to tolerate activities which earned substantially less. For its investors, from 1955 to 1965, Litton achieved an average rate on earnings per share, compounded, of 44 per cent a year. It thus seemed to combine the merits of a blue-chip or gilt-edged company with sensational returns untypical of secure but staid leading companies or government stock.

Many critics claimed during its boom years that Litton would go bust sometime in the future. And certainly Roy Ash's formulae for multimarket growth proved more difficult in practice than he anticipated. Some of Litton's purchases were hard to rationalise. They included Ingalls the shipbuilders, Hewitt-Robins in materials handling equipment, Royal McBee and Cole in office machinery and equipment, Monroe in adding machines and calculators, Royfax copiers, and others. By the later sixties, Litton was declaring a decline in profits for the first time in fourteen years. Early 1968 pretax profits dropped 30 per cent and its stock market rating dropped 50 per cent. Roy Ash remarked bitterly that US Steel's profits had dropped as much without similar stock market desertion. But the comparison was of like with unlike – of a multimarket flier with a basic single-sector stayer. With a reduced *rate* of profit – rather than actual loss – investors temporarily moved out of Litton and other conglomerate companies such as Teledyne, Gulf and Western and Ling-Temco-Vought.

The Conglomerate Trend

However, the conglomerates came back, restoring record profits and outstripping less wide-ranging companies. From 1978 to 1984 the total return to investors from conglomerates outstripped non-conglomerate companies among *Fortune*'s top 500 companies. Litton achieved a total average return, over the allegedly crisis-ridden decade of 1974–84, of nearly 40 per cent, Teledyne over 50 per cent, and the next eight top conglomerates an average of over 25 per cent. (*The Economist*, 15 June 1985).

Moreover, the trend was catching. New conglomerates in the United States now include some leading household names. Thus US Steel (against whom Roy Ash railed) has acquired Marathon Oil. Du Pont, the world's biggest chemical company, has bought the oil and coal corporation Conoco. Tenneco, which started as a gas company, has bought the agricultural equipment giant International Harvester. Ford, General Electric, General Motors, RCA and Xerox are among those who have added financial service companies to their former mainstream business operations.

General Motors has coolly swallowed the Hughes Aircraft Corporation and, with it, a range of activities including TWA, as well as the Dallas-based computer service company Electronic Data Systems, whose talents in turn have been applied to revolutionising GM's links between production, sales and auto finance (*Newsweek*, 17 June 1985).

The results are reflected in the trend to diversification in the mesoeconomic sector as a whole. According to Channon (1975), 80 per cent of the top 200 manufacturing and service companies in the United States are now in more than one line of business, against only 30 per cent in 1950. For Britain, 65 per cent of big business is now diversified, in contrast with only 25 per cent in 1950.

Implications

Such a trend represents more than mere conglomerate commotion. It has major implications for the theory of the modern capitalist firm. For one thing, it reinforces the argument in Chapter 4, where it was claimed that limits to the rate of growth of leading firms in single sectors – through product or demand maturity – could be offset by diversification into other products or other activities. Second, it confirms the force of the analysis in Chapter 5 of the dynamics of unequal competition. Competition still prevails, but new entry to markets is increasingly through the diversification of mesoeconomic enterprise already established as a dominant business in another sector. Third, it establishes that super-normal profits can not only be achieved by internal economies of scale but also by externalising the gains from size and security from an established base in one market into new higher profits in other areas. Fourth, much of the diversification is by takeover rather than organic market growth.

That is not to say that all multimarket diversification, by takeover or growth, is uncontested or successful even when the business is big or dominant in another sector. For instance, in the early 1980s Exxon – flagship of Standard Oil of New Jersey – had diversified into food products, office machinery and electronics. With global sales of some $100 billion, it could afford to invest $0.5 billion in fifteen new office and electronic equipment companies. But taking on IBM, the remaining 'core' of ATT and the Japanese was harder than anticipated, and by the mid 1980s Exxon had undertaken some sizeable disinvestments. Dow Chemical had done the same with some of its diversification, as had Philips and Thorn EMI. However, as *The Economist* (15 June 1985) commented: 'such divestments pale against the international trend towards still more diversification'. In a world dominated by a few dozen multiproduct, multisectoral and multinational companies, the microeconomic theory of the firm is not dead. But it has been transformed by the rise of the mesoeconomy.

6.4   From Multiregional to Multinational

Some companies such as ITT or British Petroleum — established by government *fiat* as the Anglo-Iranian Oil Company — either began life or entered corporate childhood as multinational companies. Others got there later – in adolescence or maturity. But many such firms grew from regional to national markets before they invested and produced abroad as multinational companies.

Multiregional Location

Orthodox market theory for the most part considers only single-product firms in specific regions, and self-balancing flows of capital and labour. It therefore assumes equality between regions as the result of rational location by profit-maximising firms. This implies the kind of symmetry represented in Figure 6.8(a). Given a more developed and less developed region (MDR and LDR respectively), it is assumed that labour will migrate from the more labour-abundant LDR to the more capital-abundant MDR (in order to gain either work or higher-paid work), while capital will migrate to the more labour-abundant LDR from the MDR (to gain lower-cost labour).

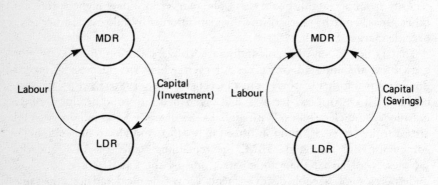

FIG. 6.8(a)   Interregional balance: self-adjusting factor flows

FIG. 6.8(b)   Interregional imbalance: asymmetric factor flows

However, as Myrdal (1957) has argued, and as is illustrated by Figure 6.8(b), the very fact of relatively more capital-intensive production in the more capital-abundant MDR will tend to mean a higher rate of return or profit. This in turn will mean that not only labour but also savings are attracted to the MDR from the LDR. Thus there is a basic asymmetry or inequality in interregional factor flows, which is only marginally offset by any 'trickle down' or spread-effect from the more developed to the less developed region.

Multinational Location

The rise of multinational capital in the later twentieth century has added a new dimension to this regional inequality. Relatively labour-intensive industry based in more developed countries has located plants in Latin America, Singapore, Hong Kong, Taiwan, South Korea, Thailand, Indonesia and the Philippines, countries where the cost of labour is a fifth, a tenth or even a twentieth of the cost of European and North American labour. Some of these countries offer the additional advantage, to such companies, of tax havens (with tax exemption for up to fifteen years) and union havens (in the sense of no normal trade-union freedoms, or no unions at all).

As a result, illustrated in Figure 6.9, capital investment in labour-intensive manufacturing has increasingly located in a newly industrialised country (NIC) or less developed country (LDC), rather than less developed regions (LDRs) of more developed regions (MDRs). At the same time, in Western Europe, at least until the post-1973 recession, labour tended to be drawn increasingly from peripheral countries in the Mediterranean area, or intermediate countries (IMCs). Much of it returned thereafter to under-

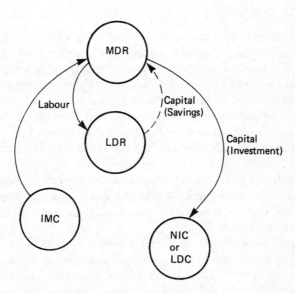

Fig. 6.9   Multinational versus multiregional location

employment or unemployment in the regions of original labour outflow. This pattern could be seen in the immigration to France of workers from Spain, Portugal and Algeria, and to Germany of workers from Greece, Yugoslavia and Turkey (cf. Castles and Kosack, 1973, part II).

Even during the period of sustained postwar economic growth, the location of investment in the less developed countries tended to be uneven and concentrated in the areas more attractive to capital, irrespective of the broader economic and social needs of the region as a whole. Regions such as western and southern France were relatively neglected both by French domestic capital and by foreign multinationals locating in France. Meanwhile most foreign multinational capital locating in the Italian south, or Mezzogiorno, has done so in the northernmost belt close to Rome or Naples. Italian leaders such as Fiat have, with minor exceptions, located increasingly in Spain or Latin America rather than less developed southern Italy. In West Germany, the central location of the country as a whole in Europe, plus the historical dispersion of administrative, social and cultural centres in the capital cities of the *Länder* – until 1871 independent states – has meant an exceptional degree of job dispersion. From Britain, with few exceptions, big business since the 1960s has tended to locate in continental Europe, the United States or less developed countries, rather than the less developed UK regions.

New Capital Flows

Such qualifications of the conventional market model of location are matched by others which reflect ongoing changes in the structure of postwar big business and its operations. Myrdal assumed that the syphoning of savings from a less to a more developed region would occur through the stock market and the banking system. But in several European countries share capital constitutes an insignificant fraction of total manufacturing investment. Bank finance for industrial companies is important in Germany, France and Italy (in the latter cases through both state banks and special credit institutes). But an increasing proportion of capital syphoned from less developed to more developed regions takes the form of pension and insurance funds placed by national financial intermediaries with big business, i.e. via the broken line in Figure 6.9. Much of this now goes abroad in the foreign investment made by multinational companies.

One reason, already stressed, is the extent to which most finance for manufacturing investment in a country such as Britain now comes through retained earnings or Eurodollar and Eurobond issues rather than through the stock market, deposit bank lending or pension and insurance funds. To the extent that this trend is matched in other developed countries, the less developed regions become increasingly peripheral to capital accumulation, even as sources of investment funds. In a country such as Italy, the less developed south has not been a net provider of funds for some time. The savings-syphoning or capital-depletion effect, rightly enough described for earlier stages of underdevelopment by Myrdal, has given way to net capital imports from the MDR, via public agencies and state intervention (Holland, 1971). Put again in terms of Figure 6.9, the LDR has increasingly been marginalised and bypassed on both the capital and labour migration accounts, substantially through the new financing and location patterns of multinational big business.

Certainly the postwar evidence for Britain, France and Italy shows that big business is hardly influenced in its routine location decisions in more developed countries by the incentives on either the capital or labour account offered by governments (Holland, 1976a and b). Nor are they significantly influenced by the assumed advantages of the spatial clustering of interrelated activity, as will be shown below. Both trends are critically important granted the extent to which (1) regional policy in developed countries tends to be based on incentives complemented by infrastructure provision; (2) big business and the multinational sector now dominates half or more of manufacturing output and employment in such countries (see further Chapter 7).

Polarisation and External Economies

In Perroux's original exposition, his growth-pole concept depended on externalities, as did Myrdal's analysis of cumulative spread effects in a more developed region.

The principle of externalities has already been made clear in Figure 6.1. This showed that a firm with a larger volume of output could produce components (e.g. headlamps) at half the unit cost of a firm producing only a third as many units. In location or regional theory it was assumed that firms would cluster or 'polarise' in particular areas to take advantage of such external economies, thereby saving transport costs for inputs in the manufacturing process (Perroux, 1964, ch. 7).

Without doubt such localised external economies played a significant role in the original clustering of small and medium firms in 'growth poles'. So also did the specific geography of coal or iron-ore deposits, and the availability of a pool or reserve of labour skilled in particular trades (miners, steelworkers, machinists, etc).

The 'polarisation' of such economies thereby played a key role in the first 'industrial revolutions'. This was the process which gave rise to the manufacturing of the British West Midlands, the *Ruhrgebiet* in Germany and the older industries of New England.

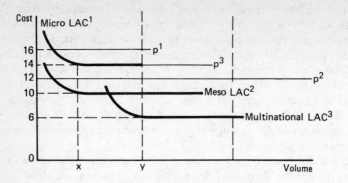

FIG. 6.10   Micro, meso and multinational cost schedules

However, the basic externalities case is profoundly qualified when one moves from the single-firm, single-market assumptions of the early expositions of growth-pole theory to the multiproduct, vertically integrated multinational of today. Essentially such companies are large enough to internalise most economies, if they so choose, in relatively large scale plant dispersed through several countries. The vertical integration of the Ford Fiesta model given in Table 6.1 illustrates the point. Ford produces a wide range of its own key components in different plant in seven countries on both sides of the Atlantic.

The production scale economies implicit in such location are illustrated in Figure 6.10. They include not only the volume of output on L-shaped coast curves, but also the lower cost schedules for meso than micro enterprise (LAC^2 versus LAC^1) made possible through combining more capital per worker and more technology than in smaller micro firms.

Thus a company such as Ford (or Toyota) can produce more cheaply at x on LAC^2 than a micro firm on LAC^1, while for other components using external suppliers. In general, production scale economies offset the additional transport costs arising from dispersed location. Where such companies choose a single main assembly plant (as Ford has recently done at Valencia), it still pays it to source components from subsidiaries in different countries.

Multinational Economies

But, in addition, especially since the 1960s, multinational big business has introduced an entirely new dimension to the issues of location and costs. For instance, in a case where labour accounts for half the production costs in manufacturing (which was not untypical for most of the postwar period), location in a less developed country, where its cost is a fifth of that in a developing country, could mean a reduction of total cost of 40 per cent. Assuming unchanged capital costs (in terms of Figure 6.10), this would reduce the overall cost of production at y for a multinational company on LAC^3 from 10 to 6.

Such a reduction of costs will massively outstrip normal transport costs arising from a more distant location, even circumnavigation of the globe. This is illustrated for a high-value, low-weight product such as watches by the fact that the Bulova company produces components in Switzerland, flies them to the Philippines for assembly by low-cost labour, and then flies them back to the United States for final sale (Barnet and Muller, 1975, Chapter 11). It is also illustrated by the phenomenal success of the labour-intensive industries of footwear, clothing, electrical goods, electronics and now increasingly mechanical engineering in South East Asian countries.

Micro, Meso and Multinational

The result has been that big business in the postwar period has tended to go multinational rather than expand on a multiregional basis within the parent country. It has also thereby reinforced the dynamics of unequal competition and increased the extent to which its competitiveness and price-making power can reduce the share of the microeconomic sector.

Even if we abstract from net price inflation in oligopolistic industry, we have seen in earlier chapters that leading firms can either undercut lagging firms through reducing prices temporarily, in line with cost reductions from larger-scale and multinational location, or alternatively can reap larger gains through self-financing by maintaining prices at a level which allows smaller, less efficient firms to survive, earning super-normal profits when smaller firms scrape by with lower profits nearer a profit norm.

For instance, in terms of Figure 6.10, the larger mesoeconomic firm with LAC^2 would reduce price to p^2 in a price-competitive situation. If it does so, the smaller microeconomic firm with LAC^1 and p^1 would go out of business. This would be an example of the 'elimination pricing' argued by Sylos-Labini (1969), whereby bigger business wipes out a smaller enterprise in the sector and picks up its market share. But the multinational company with LAC^3 would be earning super-normal profits. A variant of this price tactic is the 'no entry' pricing analysed by Bain (1956), whereby bigger business could raise price to p^3 to deter the entry of smaller firms at the micro 'edge' of the market, while in practice thereby gaining an even greater profit.

Multinationals and Unequal Competition

If we globalise the example and argue in terms of larger firms in more developed regions and smaller firms in less developed regions of the world economy, we can see a link between (1) the *structural* nature of unequal competition between meso and micro firms, and (2) the *spatial* distribution of unequal economic structures between more and less developed regions.

Chapter 1 stressed the role of paradox in economic analysis. A paradox or irony of the market economy is that the more a micro firm grows in terms of market share, the more it may line itself up for takeover or elimination by a more established and more secure meso enterprise. The micro national firm rarely makes it into the modern markets dominated by the multinational mesoeconomic enterprise. These dynamics of unequal competition between bigger and smaller firms are widely neglected in regional incentive policies.

In practice, as stressed in Chapter 5, under inflationary conditions mesoeconomic enterprise does not lower prices to exert no-entry or elimination effects. If it simply holds prices stable, absorbing inflation in costs by virtue of its higher profit levels, it can thereby eliminate the profit of smaller microeconomic firms. This is especially true of multinational enterprise. In terms of Figure 6.10, the lower-cost enterprise with a multinational location could eliminate the higher-cost micro company outright, while still making supernormal profits.

However, price stability has been untypical of big-league business in recent years. Also, anti-trust and anti-monopoly authorities take a dim view of the elimination of micro enterprise on a major scale (rather than their golden-handshake takeover). Partly to avoid the iron maiden of competition and anti-trust authorities, but essentially because it offers higher profits, big business in the multinational sector will frequently raise prices to allow medium-sized firms in the market to survive under inflationary or higher cost conditions.

Such mechanisms of price-making power, due both to new oligopoly domination and multinational power, certainly offset the pull effect of government incentives to locate in the less developed regions of more developed countries. They help to illustrate why problem regions in developed countries are increasingly marginalised in the location decisions of multinational enterprise.

Unequal Labour Costs

On the wages front, governments in MDCs might have to offer labour subsidies of between 80 and 90 per cent to compete with the costs of labour in some Third World countries. On the capital front, they might have to offer subsidies of more than the total cost of investment. If, for example, the price level is more than three times total LDC costs, and where capital cost is assumed to be only a fifth of total cost, the subsidy effect would need to represent more than fifteen times the cost of the capital concerned, rather than the fifth at present offered by UK or EEC regional incentives.

Of course, other factors enter into the calculus of multinational companies in their location decisions, including not only public relations with governments, but also the need to locate some plant in MDCs if governments are to award them contracts from public expenditure, plus the greater 'political stability' in MDCs and the lower threat – until recently – from nationalisation of capital-intensive plants. Nonetheless, even allowing for a wide margin of error in individual cases, the argument illustrates some of the reasons why firms in the mesoeconomic sector can gain more from either raising prices or going multinational – or both – rather than going multiregional within one country in response to regional incentives.

6.5 The Multinational Imperative

For these reasons big business, especially since the end of the Second World War, has gone multinational on a major scale. Its operations, including the elimination or takeover of other enterprises and thus its monopoly trend, tend to be understated by viewing only national data rather than international figures. One of the reasons why *Vision* and *Fortune* magazines have played an important role in the analysis of big business on a global scale has been the extent to which they collate and present figures on an annual basis, which make it possible to identify the multinational extension of market shares – even if some companies have recently disguised their overall concentration by registering only parent-company activities. Academic economists by and large have been remiss in tracing this trend.

Micro and Meso Dimensions

Not all multinational companies are large, but few large companies are not multinationals. The exceptions in the big-league sector tend to be nationalised or public enterprises in individual countries, concentrated in basic services and utilities such as gas, electricity, water supply etc., with only a few public-enterprise firms being multinational in operation. But even here the exceptions include Renault and Volkswagen, both in public or part public ownership, where extensive operations abroad have been built up since the 1960s.

Large-scale enterprise in manufacturing is typically multinational in character in the more developed countries. There are degrees of difference between the United States and the United Kingdom, on the one hand, and

Europe and Japan on the other. Both the US and the UK, as we will see in Chapter 7, have established sizeable foreign operations over an extensive period of time. Countries such as Japan and Germany, having failed through war to achieve direct foreign expansion, have been slower starting. Similarly French enterprise abroad, although extensive at the turn of the century, was set back by depression at home and changed political circumstances abroad, with only a recent increase in multinational operations. Further, it is important to distinguish foreign operations of companies through portfolio investment, i.e. shareholdings in the enterprises abroad, and foreign operations through direct investment, i.e. through subsidiaries of the parent company itself.

Portfolio and Direct

Portfolio investment is through the placing of shares, while *direct* investment is in plant or equipment. Historically, foreign investment has not always been through shareholdings or portfolios. In the colonial period, British investment in countries such as India, through the East India Company, involved direct investment and direct operations rather than indirect shareholdings or portfolio investment. Even when Ricardo was giving examples for his theory of the international division of labour and the advantage from trade between Portuguese wine and British cloth, British companies (mainly from Bristol) were investing substantially in Portugal through direct ownership of vineyards and control of the production, bottling and transit of Port wine. In this case, as with the East India Company, the multinational is not a latecomer to the scene. As indicated earlier, Ricardo missed its significance in his own key foreign-trade example.

Complexity

Moreover the rise of multinational capital has not been a simple transition from portfolio to direct investment by different firms in different countries. Acocella (1975) pointed out that the share of direct investment in total foreign investment was lower in 1914 for Britain than for France or Germany. This is a reverse of the current situation, and indicates that multinational investment is a complex and changing phenomenon.

Nonetheless, certain features are clear. Contemporary direct investment abroad is dominated by big business based in the most developed capitalist countries. As illustrated by the United Nations (1973, pp. 139–46 and 7), the United States in the early 1970s accounted for more than half of the world total of direct investment, and the US, UK, France and Germany for nearly 80 per cent. Such direct investment was also concentrated in a minimal number of companies. Between 250 and 300 American firms controlled more than 70 per cent of direct investment from the US in the early 1970s; in the United Kingdom 80 per cent was controlled by 165 companies, and in Germany 82 firms controlled 70 per cent of such direct investment. In this sense, multinational expansion through direct foreign investment represented the national mesoeconomic enterprise abroad and was a spatial extension of the activities of national big business (Acocella, 1975).

Classification

Further, there can be no simple classification of multinational direct investment by the level of development of the country of destination. In the era of multinational expansion at the end of the nineteenth and in the early twentieth century, most of the direct foreign investment of leading national companies was in less developed countries. By the mid-1960s, according to an estimate by the Economist Intelligence Unit (1971), some two-thirds of direct foreign investment was located in the developed capitalist countries. In the 1980s, two-thirds of the rest of multinational investment was located in intermediate or newly industrialising countries (IMF, 1985). US companies have tended to locate abroad to a greater degree in developed countries, and especially in Europe, while European and Japanese companies have particularly concentrated their foreign investment in Latin America and Africa (United Nations, 1973).

Colonial History

Historical factors are clearly important. While evidence from the 1960s and 1970s on the rate, scale and direction of foreign investment may reveal strictly economic factors, it is clear that the low share of foreign investment relative to exports of countries such as Germany and Japan reflects special historical circumstances.

It is reputed that when the Pan German League in the late nineteenth century pressured Bismarck to support direct foreign investment through state intervention on a wider scale in Africa, he turned to a map of Europe on the wall behind him, commenting 'here is my map of Africa'. Germany twice went to war in the twentieth century and its imperial war aims included direct economic control of major areas of Europe. Similarly, Japan attempted direct imperial control of major areas of South East Asia and China in the Second World War. Both countries were decisively defeated. As a result, their capital reconstruction was limited to their own national boundaries, quite apart from the fact that German and Japanese business in the period following the

Second World War was not necessarily welcome in several of the countries which they had recently invaded and occupied.

The Investment Imperative

A key question is why companies operate through direct investment abroad rather than indirectly through portfolio investment in shares and equity?

In practice, similar factors operate at a multinational as at a national level. As elaborated in Chapter 7, it is already part of the conventional wisdom of economic theory that the divorce between ownership and control has enabled management to secure a controlling position within a company without a majority of shares, depending on the degree to which equity was dispersed between individual shareholders. But more recently, multinational companies have used mutual share or equity agreements to underwrite joint-venture arrangements on research, innovation, investment or marketing. Also, the recent liberalisation of key stock markets such as London and Paris has meant greater scope for international portfolio investment by financial intermediaries such as pension funds and insurance companies.

As stressed by Rowthorn and Hymer (1971), the main factor in direct foreign investment is for big business to extend, and therefore also defend, its competitive position worldwide. As at the national level, this involves both centralisation through increased market share, and concentration by take-over and acquisition. There are various permutations on the theme, and they tend to change over time.

General Motors and Ford

In practice, multinationals can gain foreign companies by takeover and then rationalise their production to standardise components and achieve internal economies of scale. Thus General Motors took over the German vehicles producer Adam Opel before the Second World War, and the multinational imperative proved sufficiently strong for General Motors to be paid share revenue from its Opel subsidiary even after the outbreak of hostilities. But it took years for General Motors to rationalise production or raise the market profile of its other main European subsidiary of Vauxhall in Britain.

Ford, by contrast, from the start achieved greater coherence in its European operations through direct investment by the parent company rather than takeover of other firms, establishing itself quickly as a market leader among foreign companies in the UK. Ford also set the pace in Europeanisation of its vehicles, rationalising components production in individual plant, which then supplied Ford companies Europe-wide. Ultimately, as we saw in Table

6.1, Ford followed through the logic of internalised scale economies by producing components for the same vehicle for the European market from different plant in different European countries.

Chrysler in Crisis

Chrysler – number three in the US car market – was less successful with its European ventures. Trying in part to recoup through foreign investment what it could not achieve in increasing its market share at home, Chrysler bought up the Rootes company in the United Kingdom and Simca in France. But although this gave it a necessary condition for successful operation as a mesoeconomic enterprise, in particular access to a pre-existing market share in other countries, Chrysler did not manage to achieve the standardisation of components over a range of models that was typical for General Motors or Ford.

In the 1970s, with the major rises in the cost of oil, Chrysler was slow to accommodate its main product range to the new demand for smaller vehicles. For a time, it imported a model from the UK to the US – known in Britain as the Avenger and in the US as the Cricket. Later, as part of its attempt to gain a defensive alliance with Japanese competition, it imported a Mazda model from Japan under the Cricket brand name, in return for a minority holding in the Japanese company. But Chrysler still produced too many large cars. By the summer of 1979 it declared that it would need at least one billion dollars of US Federal aid. It was only by the mid-1980s that it had been turned round by a combination of market muscle and state aid.

Phases of Growth

The case of Chrysler illustrates that big business growth is not necessarily smooth, continuous or linear in the manner beloved by textbook theories of the firm. The same goes for countries as for companies. Thus Germany had more foreign investment at the outbreak of the First World War than Britain, whereas the situation now is the reverse. Moreover a description of the various categories of portfolio or direct investment abroad does not in itself explain the reasons why companies go multinational, nor when they do so. Part of the picture lies in the military and political power of the parent country of the multinational concerned. Another lies in the initial maturity of the product.

The Product Cycle

One of the most plausible explanations for the transition from exports to direct foreign investment has been provided by Vernon's product-cycle model (1966). This distinguishes between the new phase of the introduction of a product, the growth phase of its expansion, and a mature phase in which the growth of the now-established product declines. Such a model has already been used in relation to the dynamics of growth from small to big business. But it has also been applied by Vernon in the context of the multinational expansion.

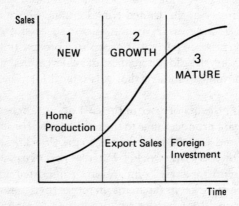

FIG. 6.11   The product cycle through domestic production to foreign investment

In simplified form, and represented by Figure 6.11, the company introducing a new product will tend to do so in its home market, possibly in a plant within or near to its main production base. This is due to the management problem of commanding appropriate inputs, sorting out teething problems in translation from research and development to production, and so forth. In the second rapid-growth phase of the product, as it becomes established on the market, Vernon argues that companies will tend to continue to locate in the parent country, serving foreign markets by export sales. It is only in the third or mature phase of production that companies will tend to undertake investment abroad.

In an area as complex as international investment and trade, one should not expect any single hypothesis to have more than a limited explanatory power. For instance, Vernon argued that it is evident that Otis Elevators' early proliferation of activities abroad was related to high transport costs. He also stressed a related 'proximity' factor, i.e. the need to 'know the market' by producing in it, as a motive for foreign investment.

Timing in Question

Vernon's argument has considerable force. Nonetheless, it is stylised and ultimately over-simple. While the curve of the product cycle as described in Figure 6.11 may be unduly symmetric, it is quite clear that the first and second phases of the Vernon product cycle may be more closely drawn, as represented in the case of Figure 6.12. In practice this was very much the case for some of the first multinational direct investment in the twentieth century. Companies such as Ford and General Motors began direct operations to produce vehicles in Britain very shortly after their introduction in the United States.

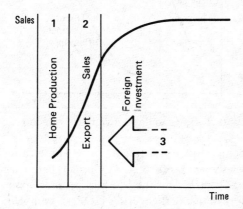

FIG. 6.12   From national to multinational: the accelerated product cycle

It is clear that in some advanced-technology products such as electronics, American companies still first innovate and produce at home rather than immediately producing abroad. Nonetheless, it is increasingly plausible for multinational companies to conjoin phases 1 and 2 of the product cycle, i.e. to export as soon as the product is produced in the home market, and then proceed to Vernon's stage three of production through direct operations abroad in what amounts in practice to a second phase of expansion.

The Multinational Triad

International competition also qualifies the Vernon product cycle. It has been stressed by Rowthorn and Hymer (1970) that the so-called American challenge of direct investment in Western Europe by US multinational companies in the 1960s was in fact less an offensive than a defensive response to the success of postwar European companies in exporting to the American market. In this respect, as illustrated in Figure 6.13, there is a preliminary phase to the product-cycle model and its stages, represented by phase 1(a) of the foreign export challenge, followed by phases 1(b) and 2 in which the companies in the challenged market respond by counter innovations, production and export, followed in turn by phase 3 – direct investment.

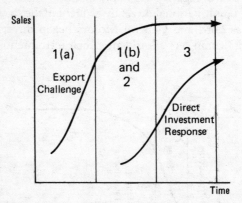

FIG. 6.13   From export challenge to direct investment response

However, as competitive pressures increase, the location pattern of the product cycle is telescoped yet further. As Ohmae (1985) argues, the key role played by the 'triad' markets of the US, Europe and Japan – between them accounting for more than half the world's GDP – is compelling multinational companies to innovate simultaneously in all three markets. The high costs of research and development and the swiftness of competitors' reactions in the global big league increase in turn the speed with which such R and D costs have to be amortised or paid off. Thus the markets of the 'triad' cannot be developed from home, followed by exports and then foreign investment. They have to be assaulted simultaneously, with products designed and made from the start for a global market (Bell, 1985).

Each case of multinational expansion clearly needs to be assessed rather than presumed. Nonetheless, common elements combining economies of scale and vertical, horizontal or conglomerate expansion are evident in the trend from national to multinational enterprise.

In reality, it is the multiproduct, multisectoral and multinational company typical of the mesoeconomic sector which dominates the innovation process in the modern market economy. Small firms still have an important role to play as satellite suppliers or edge-of-market innovators, especially in modern manufacturing and 'entirely new' industries. But as technology and techniques of production are stabilised or standardised, and as it becomes apparent to meso enterprise that there is more to be gained through internalising production or distribution than relying on external micro suppliers, the dynamics of unequal competition re-establish the dominance of big business. Neglected by mainstream market theory, this is as true of agriculture and agribusiness, and of services and finance, as it is of manufacturing industry.

6.6 Summary

(1) Uneven development in the regional and international economy is in part related to unequal competition between central and peripheral firms.

(2) The growth of external or locational economies originally favoured the concentration of production, employment and income in specific urban growth centres, but these were increasingly offset by (i) the reduced share of transport costs in total costs and (ii) internalisation of formerly external economies in bigger business.

(3) The spread effects from the growth of successful or leading firms is not neutral but tends either (i) to generate dependency relations in satellite suppliers or (ii) to backwash smaller enterprise.

(4) Big business grows bigger either through (i) concentration of a larger share of the market in its own sales, or (ii) centralisation of market share through takeover of other firms. Concentration is consistent with the combination of extended market share and elimination of competitors. Centralisation can combine contested or uncontested mergers and takeovers. Both embody the dynamics of unequal competition.

(5) Either vertical or horizontal integration are served by internalised economies of scale within the same company. Such internalised economies accompanied the high period of mass production and gave relative security of supply to major producers. Total internalisation in integrated plant (from iron ore to finished steel, or chemicals to plastics) is exceptional.

(6) The trend from multiregional to multinational location has extended the scope for internalised economies in big business, making possible the combination of modern technology and low-cost labour for the production of components or the assembly of finished products for global markets.

(7) Since World War Two complementary moves have been made by leading firms to minimise risk and stay within reach of the 'innovation

frontier' by undertaking joint ventures in research, development and components production with foreign firms. Such new joint ventures between multinational companies extend global mesoeconomic co-operation rather than restore the former micro model of internal and external economies.

(8) With the recent combination of recession and more rapid change in technology and techniques of production, some firms have reduced their dependence on vertical or 'in house' integration, with the aim of gaining more flexibility in the sourcing of inputs.

(9) Major multinationals such as Ford also achieve flexibility through both component production and final assembly in several countries. *Inter alia*, such spatial dispersion of what remain internal economies for the company as a whole, reduces the bargaining power of organised labour in any one country *vis-à-vis* the multinational company.

(10) Multi-product and multi-sectoral companies can flourish either on the highly integrated model of the Japanese group Mitsui, which combines finance and industrial capital, or on the unrelated diversification model of the conglomerate. Conglomerate growth is subject to more risk the greater its market range and the faster its growth.

(11) Leading and successful conglomerates have achieved relative degrees of integration within their main activities. Japanese companies have both specialised in specific international markets, and managed the transition from sunset to sunrise industries within their combine or conglomerate structure.

(12) The original product-cycle model of innovation and growth in the home market followed by export and foreign investment is being compressed by international competition into simultaneous innovation, production and sales for a global market.

7 The Dual Economy

The dominance of big business in the world economy is starkly illustrated by the UNCTAD study of Clairmonte and Cavanagh, which shows that in 1982 the combined sales of the world's top 200 corporations exceeded $3 trillion, equivalent to nearly a third of the world's Gross Domestic Product. More than three-quarters of the world's top 200 corporations (166) have their headquarters in just five countries – the United States (80), Japan (35), the United Kingdom (18), West Germany (17) and France (16). Concentration within the top 200 world companies is very marked, with the top 100 representing 85 per cent of the sales of the top 200 in 1982. Over half (118) of the top 200 companies are based in manufacturing, and two-fifths (82) were in services, representing also some two-fifths of the combined revenues of the top 200. Some three-quarters of these revenues were represented by companies based in only two countries – Japan (41 per cent) and the United States (33 per cent). (Clairmonte and Cavanagh, 1984, pp. 215ff.) Smaller-scale microeconomic enterprise both survives and, in some cases, flourishes. But it does so in a dual market structure increasingly dominated by mesoeconomic enterprise.

This chapter looks at the multisectoral and multinational structure of the modern mesoeconomy. It does so – with some qualifications – in terms of the three main sectors identified between the wars by Colin Clark and accepted as the main basis for sectoral classification in national and international accounting. Essentially Clark (1940) divided the economy into three broad sectors: (1) the *primary* sector (agriculture and fishing), (2) the *secondary* sector (mining and manufacturing) and (3) the *tertiary* sector (services). The empirical data shows the extent of intra-sectoral dualism, with the dominance of leading firms within individual sectors. It also shows the inter-sectoral scope and scale of the same mesoeconomic companies operating through direct or portfolio investment in a range of subsidiary companies and countries.

7.1 From Agriculture to Agribusiness

In parallel with the conventional dualism between traditional and modern sectors viewed as a whole in the conventional paradigm, a further dualism between meso and micro enterprise ranges across sectoral frontiers. Thus there is a traditional agriculture of microeconomic farms (rather than firms) – typical not only of Third World countries but also of the European and US economies. But in agriculture there is also the new vertically integrated 'agribusiness' sector of large multinational companies whose scope and range of production, processing, distribution and exchange is entirely different in scale and quality from the peasant or homesteading family farm of conventional wisdom.

Agricultural Dualism

The dualism between the rural and urban sectors of the economy – broadly between agriculture on the one hand and industry and services on the other – underlies some of the most crucial problems of development. For twenty years following the war, one of the primary fashions within development economics was the aim of achieving industrialisation sufficient to shift population from agriculture into industry or services, and thereby from over-populated rural areas into cities and towns. Based in many cases on aggregate models of the economy distinguishing between the main sectors rather than on dualism within them, much less attention was paid to the structure of ownership and land tenure than has been the case since the early 1970s.

  However, it is particularly in the area of ownership and land tenure that the intra-sectoral dualism within global agriculture is most apparent in less developed countries. In such countries, it is not untypical for a fraction of one per cent of the population to control a half to two-thirds of arable land and for a fifth to a third of the population to be literally landless.

  In Third World countries, the ownership of land is divided between a micro sector of small farms and a meso sector of large landholders, whose archetype is the *latifundia* or large estates of Southern Europe and Latin America. Such latifundia, often owned by absentee landlords, date from the neofeudal epoch, and entail a range of outdated leasing practices such as sharecropping – i.e. the *métayage* abolished in France during the French Revolution. But at the same time their produce tends to be purchased, exported, processed and distributed by modern multinational companies.

Concentration and Centralisation.

The process of concentration and centralisation is not only as typical of agriculture as of industry, but predated it.

In England it began in the sixteenth century with the enclosures, by bigger landlords, of the common land which had dated from Saxon times and on which smallholders or landless peasants had been able to graze their animals. Backed by their own votes in parliament and their own judgements in magistrates' courts, the bigger farmers and local aristocracy throughout the eighteenth century drained and appropriated hitherto unarable land. It was against this background of creating bigger farms, or units of ownership, that the industrialisation of agriculture 'took off' in the later nineteenth century. Introducing steam-driven tractors and combine harvesters – frequently leased to their larger tenants – the bigger landowners were able to reduce farm labour and increase productivity and profits in an increasingly competitive and commercial environment.

In the United States, many colonists saw themselves as appropriating God's Own Country, while in reality expropriating the nomadic Indians. As we have seen in Chapter 2, the dual American economy before and after Independence was divided between small entrepreneurs and a state capitalist nexus in industry and commerce. So with agriculture, where neo-colonial estates in the North East were complemented by the big slave-based plantations of the South. It was the Homestead Acts which were to bring the small family farm into its own for an interlude before the 'free land' ran out as the United States reached its present frontiers with Canada, Mexico and the Pacific coast. This was accompanied by major foreclosures and bankruptcies of small farms in the later nineteenth and early twentieth centuries, caused by both recession and competition in export markets in Western Europe from cheap wheat imported from Tsarist Russia.

State Intervention

The free working of the market was not enough to ensure a living wage for those small farm workers who survived the concentration and centralisation of farming in the States. Roosevelt's New Deal programme was designed in large part to offset this deficiency in the market and to 'get the farmers out of the mud'. Certainly US agricultural policy since the New Deal has been based upon comprehensive government intervention rather than the free working of market forces.

The same syndrome occurred in Western Europe. In Britain, until the United Kingdom joined the European Community, government assistance to farming was based upon a production quotas' system whereby subsidies would be given for an agreed level of limited production. In contrast, the Common Agricultural Policy of the EEC is a price-support system, with guaranteed prices at which the Commission of the Community will intervene to purchase surpluses without limits to production.

Heavily criticised for resulting wine lakes and butter mountains, the Common Agricultural Policy in fact reflects both a problem of differing efficiencies between the agricultures of different countries and also the internal dualism between micro and mesoeconomic farms.

Micro and Mesoeconomic Farms

The unit cost of production for farms clearly is similar in form to the long-run average cost curves for industrial firms. In the continental economies of the EEC a small farm of some ten to twenty hectares may employ a family, although at high real cost with disguised unemployment and unpaid family labour. Allowing that the size-cost relation will depend on the nature of the product, and allowing also for exceptions in viniculture and horticulture, it is mainly in farms approaching fifty hectares or more that significant economies of scale in production can be achieved, with extensive economies possible only in farms of several hundred hectares.

Thus the same principles concern the survival of micro and meso farms as apply in micro and meso firms in industry or services. In other words, with a price set at p^1 in Figure 7.1, all farms of less than twenty hectares would go out of business; farms between twenty and fifty hectares would gain first a low rate of return, then a normal profit, while farms of 500 hectares or more would be gaining super-normal profits. Granted that some half of the working population in agriculture of the European Economic Community – and a significant share in the United States – is employed in micro farms or smallholdings, and that this represents several million voters, it has been unacceptable to most European and American governments that such a collapse of small-scale farming should occur. As a result, they have set price at a level equivalent to p^2 in Figure 7.1. But while this is sufficient to enable micro smallholdings to survive, it makes possible super-normal profits for larger-scale mesoeconomic agribusiness and higher prices to consumers.

Typically, without policies for farm price support, 'surplus' population will migrate from farming. This sometimes happens by farmers and their families moving off the land, but more usually, in Western Europe and the United States, by the young not following their parents 'onto the farm' and going instead into urban industrial or services employment. There clearly may be welfare effects from such out-migration – between rural and urban areas, and between agriculture and other sectors of activity. This will especially be the case when the out-migration from farming is voluntary,

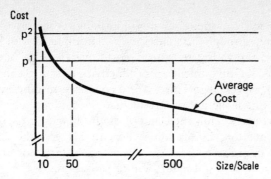

FIG. 7.1   Size of farm and rate of return

reflecting the pull-effect of higher education, increased income and widened opportunity. There would also be considerable welfare gains for consumers of farm products if prices actually were set at level p^1 in Figure 7.1.

Involuntary Migration

However, much migration out of agriculture is involuntary rather than voluntary. Rather than reflecting the pull-effect of demand for labour in towns or cities, it constitutes a push-effect off the land where incomes are seasonal and low, or negligible to non-existent where the labour is within the family rather than within a structured wage system.

In addition, even if farm prices do not actually fall, their rise relative to manufactured goods and services – some of them necessary as inputs for farming as well as for subsistence – may not be sufficient to maintain the real value of farm income. In other words, reflecting different efficiencies and productivity, the terms of trade of the non-farm sector may move against farming. The exodus of labour from small-scale farming – whether with Steinbeck's 'oakies' in the United States, from the 'campo' in Latin America, or the 'bush' in Africa – is frequently a testament to such involuntary migration. Thus such migration and the inability to sustain subsistence farming is a profound qualification of the so-called 'freedom of choice' stressed by Friedman and others. If laissez-faire policies were to be pursued in agriculture – on Friedman's lines – this would put millions of European and US farmers and their families on the dole. In less developed countries it adds them to the floating population of the migrant or urban unemployed without access to social security benefits.

Unequal Returns

The problems for 'micro farming' lie in diminishing returns in agriculture which occur not only through differences in the natural fertility of land, but also through (a) the inability to spread costs over a large output; (b) insufficient surplus for investment in productivity-raising technology or machinery, and (c), especially in Third World countries, insufficient income to purchase or maintain the use of intermediate technology such as water pumps or basic fertilizers. Thus the claim of diminishing returns, so widely misapplied by Samuelson, Lipsey and others to bigger industrial firms, applies very much in practice to the smaller marginal farm constrained by land size or traditional forms of tenure and organisation.

As illustrated in Figure 7.2 with its rising J-shaped cost curve, farms, mines or oil and gas fields in the more arable or accessible areas may allow large-scale exploitation and low costs. But the more marginal land, coal seams and oil or gas deposits involve reduced economies of scale or rising unit costs. Thus at price p^1 farms, mines or hydrocarbon fields 1 to 3 will be profitable whereas 4 and 5 will not. We return to this Figure, and its implications for state intervention and subsidy in mining and hydrocarbons, later.

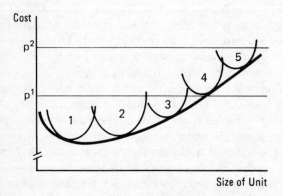

FIG. 7.2   Geography and geology: marginal and diminishing returns

Vertical Integration

Small and independent farmers are unable to achieve the economies of scale through vertical integration or 'forward linkages' of the kind open to large-scale multiproduct agribusiness. Thus small-scale microeconomic milk producers in Europe or the Third World are unable to follow through the process of pasturisation, bottling, dehydration, and 'long life' processing available to agribusiness. Also, while able to produce their own cheese and butter, they will not be able by themselves to deliver it to a wide market without a national or international transport network. Unaided, they cannot easily reach forward in the market to the wholesale distribution available to agribusiness. Nor can they achieve the product differentiation or brand attachment available to agribusiness 'majors'.

Cooperatives

Some small-scale farmers, especially in Europe, have been able to organise themselves into producer cooperatives and therefore achieve a degree of vertical integration which matches the economies of scale open to private agribusiness enterprises. Such cooperation has not been limited to the small-scale private sector. It has also involved intervention through regional or state agencies to achieve vertical economies of scale from production through processing, transport and distribution as well as the horizontal gains through sharing production equipment otherwise only available to agribusiness. 'Brand attachment' comparable with that of agribusiness majors has been offered to small farmers by national marketing and distribution agencies, such as 'Kerrygold' in Ireland. It is on such lines of mutual cooperation and state aid that unequal competition in agriculture between meso and micro farming has recently been countervailed, with some effect, in European countries. Flourishing cooperatives in Germany, France, Italy, Spain and elsewhere disprove Friedman's manichean opposition of competition versus cooperation, since the companies still have to compete – not least with agribusiness – in the final market.

Multinational Agribusiness

However, the relatively unequal competition between private producers' co-ops and national state agencies in agricultural products on the one hand, and private agribusiness on the other, is illustrated by the extent to which those food firms first achieving economies of scale have come to dominate the markets in the developed capitalist countries.

The same companies operating in different countries – Unilever, Heinz, Nestlé and others – typically dominate food production, processing and distribution. It is also notable that many such companies often choose to produce, process and distribute the bulk of their sales within individual national markets rather than to export between them.

The majors in the food industry not only dominate markets in the developed countries but also in some cases seek to sell such products in Third World countries where they can have damaging effects, which include raising infant mortality. This is notorious in the case of infant's milk powder sold to mothers in the Third World as a substitute for breast feeding their children. Introduced into an economy and society which lacks the medical inoculation of the developed countries, this frequently means that children fail to gain the natural antibodies from breast feeding which are essential for their survival. Some of the leading brand-name agribusiness companies are among the most miscreant in pushing such socially damaging sales in Third World countries.

More strikingly, as illustrated in Table 7.1, and as relevant to oil and mining as agriculture, less than half a dozen companies typically control between three-quarters and nine-tenths of the world's trade in food, agricultural raw materials and minerals.

TABLE 7.1   Corporate Control of Global Commodity Trade, 1980 (millions of dollars)

Commodity	Exports from developing countries	Percentage marketed by 3–6 largest multinationals
Food		
Wheat	16,556	85–90
Sugar	14,367	60
Coffee	12,585	85–90
Corn	11,852	85–90
Rice	4,978	70
Cocoa	3,004	85
Tea	1,905	80
Bananas	1,260	70–75
Pineapples	440	90
Agricultural raw materials		
Forest products	54,477	90
Cotton	7,886	85–90
Natural rubber	4,393	70–75
Tobacco	3,859	85–90
Hides and skins	2,743	25
Jute	203	85–90
Ores, minerals and materials		
Crude petroleum	306,000	75
Copper	10,650	80–85
Iron ore	6,930	90–95
Tin	3,599	75–80
Phosphates	1,585	50–60
Bauxite	991	80–85

Source: Clairmonte and Cavanagh, 1984.

7.2   From Mining to Manufacturing

Mining

As already indicated, diminishing returns apply not only in agriculture but also in mining. In the nineteenth century, successful coal mining was possible for a micro 'owner-entrepreneur' of the kind represented in Zola's *Germinal*, where the rate of exploitation of labour and the lack of safety conditions could be dramatic. However, with the reduction in transport costs through steam shipping and the increased penetration of European markets by cheaper, United States coal from larger scale, thicker or more accessible seams, major US mining companies with significant economies of scale undercut and lowered the rate of profit of many of the more marginal European producers.

In terms of Figure 7.2 this amounted to a reduction of price from p^2 to p^1, throwing British coal mining in particular into crisis. The result of reduced profits was increased downward pressure on wages, aggravated in Britain in 1925 by Churchill's decision as Chancellor of the Exchequer to revalue the pound, increasing the price of British coal abroad and decreasing export sales. With reduced cash flow and profits, private pit owners failed to undertake the modernisation and mechanisation necessary to achieve greater productivity. Nor were they able, because of insufficient size and resources as microeconomic enterprises, to undertake the search for new coal fields at greater depth – necessary to discover wider seams which would make possible greater economies of scale, higher productivity and increased profits.

Nationalisation

One consequence in Britain and elsewhere in Western Europe was state intervention. The postwar Labour government nationalised coal. It was only through this nationalisation programme that major modernisation and mechnisation were achieved. Far from penalising efficiency in the coal industry in the manner claimed by Milton Friedman, public ownership in fact achieved a massive increase in productivity as the labour force in mining was reduced from some two-thirds of a million workers in the immediate postwar period to less than 200,000 by the early 1980s.

Again in contrast with market mythology, it was only with the establishment of a National Coal Board and a massive injection of public funds that the search and research necessary to find and fund new coal fields was undertaken, including the two new major fields of Belvoir and Selby. At greater depth and demanding major pioneering technology, such seams compare with the best American fields and have enormous productivity and profit potential. Thus, in terms of Figure 7.3, technical progress has meant that coalfields 1–3 (such as Selby and Belvoir) have lower costs and could be profitable at price p^2, while fields 4 and 5 are profitable only at price p^1. This is one reason why a Friedmanite government, as in Britain under Mrs Thatcher, has tried to close some coalfields, and may try to open the new fields under private ownership, selling them to multinational majors in the mining or energy industries.

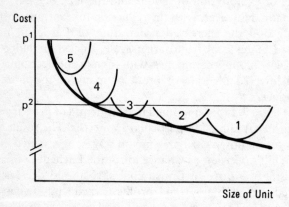

FIG. 7.3   Offseting geology: technical progress and increasing returns

Multinationalisation

Apart from, and in many cases despite, geological constraints, multinational companies like Rio Tinto Zinc or Alcan have developed through a combination of economies of scale and market muscle. The bargaining power of such companies in less developed countries has been dramatic. For instance, when the Manley government in Jamaica sought in the 1970s to ensure that the processing as well as the extraction of aluminium should be located in Jamaica, Alcan not only refused to do so but organised a boycott of Jamaican aluminium by the other leading world majors. Rio Tinto Zinc has generally had a subtler approach although they have also made offers to Third World governments which they 'could not refuse' on more than one occasion.

Oil and Petroleum

The failure of many microeconomic enterprises to survive unaided by state intervention is in striking contrast with the mythology of market forces. It has typified the oil industry in the country where the myth is most established:

the United States. It appears to millions of households watching *Dallas* that a single family firm such as the Ewings can flourish and survive in a competitive market through J.R.'s aggressive entrepreneurship. But the television series (like perfect competition textbook models) ignores the fact that the United States government, in association with the multinational oil companies, has operated a 'base point' price-support system designed precisely to protect relatively small-scale Texan and Mexican Gulf producers who would have been undermined by the economies of scale and much lower unit costs of Saudi Arabian and other Middle East competition.

As shown in Figure 7.4, the base point of this fixed price system was established at the equivalent of the price level p^2 rather than the price level p^1 which would have been possible if the Saudis and Kuwaitis had been able to penetrate the US market at a price sufficient to ensure them a 'normal' rate of return. In practice, the increased revenue represented by the difference between price lines p^1 and p^2 amounted for decades to a classic economic rent in the US oil industry not dissimilar to that which accrued to the land-owning aristocracy in Britain before the abolition of the Corn Laws.

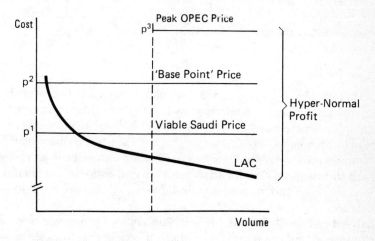

FIG. 7.4 Oil production costs and prices

The Producers' Cartel: OPEC

When the Middle Eastern and other Third World oil producers belonging to the Organisation of Petroleum Exporting Countries (OPEC) set in motion in September 1973 the first of the major increases in the price of oil, this temporarily gave some producers a hyper-normal profit equivalent to p^3 in Figure 7.4. Milton Friedman – falsely predicting that OPEC as a cartel could only survive against market forces for months rather than years – failed to draw the parallel between the 'rent' previously benefitting US producers through the Gulf base-point price system and the rent thereafter accruing to the oil-producing countries which in most cases lacked the range of alternative export markets in industry or financial services available to the United States.

Diminishing marginal returns in oil and petrochemicals are also clearly relevant to the exploitation of oil fields. For instance, Figure 7.2 represents with considerable realism the major economies of scale and low unit costs available in the North Sea from the initially exploited fields such as the 'Forties' in the first round of oil licensing by the state-owned British National Oil Corporation. In the second round of licensing, it was evident that marginal, less accessible and smaller fields would not have been viable at a price level of p^1 rather than p^2. In this case, rather than seeking to raise the price of oil on the UK domestic market, the British government agreed to lower petroleum revenue tax on the fields concerned in such a way as to encourage the oil majors to undertake their exploitation. Whether or not such tax concessions were necessary to persuade the majors to stay and undertake new drilling in the North Sea may be open to question. But, indubitably, state intervention offset the logic of diminishing returns.

The Seven Sisters

The oil industry has been dominated throughout the twentieth century by the multinational companies popularly known as the Seven Sisters. In early 1984 their number was reduced to six with the $13 billion 'friendly' takeover of Gulf Oil by Standard Oil of California (Socal). The process of concentration and centralisation involved less the cost cutting and returns to efficiency idealised in Friedman's competitive model than a ruthless combination of barriers to entry and outlets imposed by such buccaneers as John D. Rockefeller.

Analysed extensively in Anthony Sampson's book *The Seven Sisters: Great Oil Companies and the World They Made*, it is clear that Rockefeller made his multi-million fortune less from production than by controlling transport, distribution and finance in the oil industry. Employing not so much barriers to entry as barriers to transport outlets, Rockefeller realised that small oil producers could only distribute their product through access to railroads. Working through a variety of railway holding companies he therefore deprived small producers of adequate transport for their oil, reduced their cash flow, squeezed their profits, drove them into the hands of the banks – frequently his own – and forced or encouraged a takeover by Standard Oil or one of its subsidiaries.

Rockefeller's Perfect Information

Again in contrast with the alleged 'perfect information' of the perfect competition model, Rockefeller informed himself in detail about the market and potential competition. But he did so through employing his own 'secret agents' investigating the vulnerability of smaller enterprises which he then duly eliminated or took over.

This classic example of unequal competition – like the unequal competition in finance of Morgan Guarantee – led as is well known to the intervention of the US government and the break-up of both Standard Oil and Morgan Guaranty shortly before the First World War – the last break-up of a big business major in the United States until ATT in 1984. The survival of Standard Oil in its various component subsidiaries – including Standard Oil of New Jersey, Standard Oil of Ohio, Standard Oil of California, etc. – is also well known. The oil companies realised the consequences of antagonising public opinion and increasing political pressure for their accountability. In some cases they 'went underground' by a variety of means including reduced transparency in their operations through the techniques of transfer pricing, i.e. under or over invoicing prices – and thus declared revenues – on goods traded between their own subsidiaries. In other cases, as already indicated in Chapter 6, faced with limits to their increase in market share through anti-trust intervention, they were allowed to diversify into other sectors after divesting some of their original market share.

The moral is clear enough. The oil majors did not grow in the incremental manner assumed by perfect competition. Their growth in fact combined the full range of barriers to entry, cut-throat elimination pricing and devil-takeover-the-hindmost typical of the analysis of unequal competition in Chapter 6. Where new entry was forced at the 'meso' edge of the market, it was by state companies such as ENI in Italy in the 1950s.

7.3 Industrial Big Business

British and American Concentration

When five, six or seven firms dominate an industry, working out their market share is no great effort. Estimating the share of the top 50, 100 or 200 manufacturing or industrial corporations in the UK or US economy is more complex. This is partly because postwar national accounts largely measure what Keynes at the end of the war thought was important. This meant macroeconomic data on income and expenditure, savings and investment, trade, employment and prices. Data on the micro economy, for Keynes, was not especially significant – provided the state intervened to manage the level of demand, he believed that the processes of perfect and imperfect competition would by and large take care of the structure of supply. (In Chapter 9 we will consider proposals to remedy this through a more systematic accounting of the share of multinational big business in the modern economy, i.e. introducing the meso and micro dimensions to supply-side accounting.)

Part of the difficulty in estimating the size and share of US big business earlier in this century reflects the fact that until 1947 no census information was available on the subject. However, such census data was available for the United Kingdom, and in an important study Prais (1976) has sought to make a systematic reconciliation of US and UK data on industrial concentration.

The results are illustrated in Figure 7.5. In Britain the change was dramatic. The top 100 firms increased their share of manufactured output from under a fifth to over two-fifths between 1910 and the early 1970s. In the US the trend to bigness was also marked, with the top 100 increasing their share from a fifth to a third in the same period. Until the mid-1950s the top 100 manufacturing firms represented a greater share of net output in the United States than the top 100 in the United Kingdom. But as Prais (1976, p. 141) puts it: 'since the 1950s the position has been reversed; the much more rapid rise of the British giants has now given them a substantially greater share'.

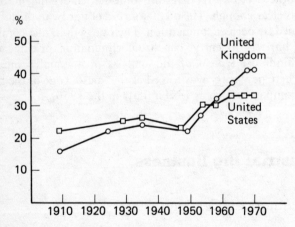

FIG. 7.5 Shares of the hundred largest enterprises in manufacturing net output, UK and USA (Source: Prais (1976))

Government Controls

The trend to bigness not only stopped but actually fell in both the UK and the

US during and immediately after the Second World War. Commenting on this, Prais (1976, p. 141) observes that the substantive reason is that 'both the US and the UK were subject to the same sequence of grave economic and political upheavals – the Great Depression, and then the war and the mobilisation of resources by the government'. In an article preceding publication of his book, he argued that 'the reasons lay in the wartime system of quotas and controls governing the allocation of scarce materials and the greater entrepreneurial intensity which gave them [small firms] a comparative advantage in times of scarcity' (*The Financial Times*, 21 March 1973).

A fabric of small and medium-sized firms was thus preserved during the wartime period, and indeed such firms increased their market share. The wartime evidence thus challenges those such as Milton Friedman who maintain that state intervention is inimical to the competitive process. Price controls operated in both the United Kingdom and the United States through the wartime period (in the latter case administered by John Kenneth Galbraith). Without recommending wartime controls as a model for a peacetime market economy, it is true to say that it was only after the war, once prices were liberalised and unequal competition could engage, that bigger business in both the UK and the US resumed its path to increased market dominance.

Drifts and Trends

Prais concerns himself with both special and general models of long-term trends, based in part on what he calls 'spontaneous drift'. As illustrated in Figure 7.6, his Special model passed through the observed share of the 100 largest firms in 1963. Only two pieces of empirical information were required to draw the Special curve: (1) the distribution of firms by size for a particular year, which determined its level; and (2) a measure of the dispersion of the growth rates of firms, which determined its slope. In other words, the slope in Prais's analysis has not been gained merely by deriving a curve to gain the best fit to the empirical evidence, but derived independently. A more simple extrapolation from Prais's actual concentration line from pre-1910 to the mid-1920s leads almost exactly to his observed concentration level in the early 1970s.

Prais's General model runs from the early 1950s through 1963 to a much higher level of concentration than observed in reality in the UK in the 1980s. On the latter basis, as he himself observes, 'by 1983 the 100 largest enterprises would produce 60 per cent of net output (instead of the 47 per cent implied by the Special theory) and by the turn of the century their share would rise to 80 per cent.' He comments that 'more disconcerting still is that half of all manufacturing net output could then be produced by no more than

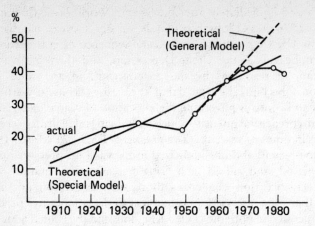

FIG. 7.6   Actual and theoretical shares of the hundred largest UK enterprises (Source: Prais (1976) and Parliamentary Questions, 14 June 1982 and 24 May 1985 (for post-1970 data))

the seven largest enterprises!', adding that 'it must, of course, be anticipated that society will intervene in various ways before such extreme levels of concentration are reached'. In general, he advises that his calculations should 'not be taken as predictions of what will happen, but rather as warnings that, on recent trends, the time left for manoeuvre is limited' (Prais, 1976, pp. 27–8 and 39).

TABLE 7.2   The Top Hundred UK Manufacturing Firms 1975–1983 (%)

	Net Output	Employment	Net Capital Expenditure
1975	38	36	37
1976	39	35	35
1977	37	35	39
1978	37	35	40
1979	37	35	40
1980	36	35	39
1981	36	34	37
1982	38	35	37
1983	38	34	37

Source: Annual Census of Production, and Parliamentary Questions, 14 June 1982, 24 May 1985 and 28 January 1986.

In fact by the early 1980s, as indicated in Table 7.2, the output concentration of the top 100 UK private-sector enterprises was below the lower trend of Prais's Special model rather than the more dramatic upwards trend of his General model. By 1977, output had fallen to 37 per cent, and stayed around that level through the early 1980s. The stability of employment for the top 100 private companies in the UK from 1975 to 1982 was quite marked, at 35 per cent. Net capital expenditure was higher in 1979–82 at some two-fifths of total capital formation in manufacturing, but this was more or less in line with the share of the top 100 firms in gross value added for the same years.

Mergers and Growth

The concentration which occurred in the UK economy from the 1950s was not simply a matter of technical economies of scale. As Aaronovitch and Sawyer argued in an article accompanying the publication of their study of big business (Aaronovitch and Sawyer, 1975, and *The Guardian*, 2 August 1975): 'undoubtedly there is a technical case for larger plants in some industries, but our own research suggests that the increase in the size of firm has not been matched by bigger plants'. Thus one needs to look elsewhere for an explanation of the scope and scale of concentration in the UK economy in the postwar period.

This does not mean to say that economies of scale are irrelevant. But it is the economies of overall size in production, distribution, access to buyers and suppliers, creditworthiness and the terms of finance which are crucial in determining who gains and who loses in the competitive process. As Aaronovitch and Sawyer (1975, p. 209) put it, economies of scale include not only division of labour but also the 'economies of massed resources'. They stress (p. 206) that 'in general large firms operate more plants of a larger size than small firms. Thus if they are reaping economies of scale then these could be both at plant and firm level'. But average plant size for larger firms actually diminished over time.

In fact over half the growth of the 100 largest manufacturing firms was accounted for by takeover or merger. The increase in part reflects the so-called 'merger boom' or 'merger mania' in the UK in the 1960s. But it was also a symptom of the unequal competition between big and small business analysed in Chapter 5. Aaronovitch and Sawyer (ibid., p. 189) found that 'most large firms made acquisitions at some time or another, and over 80 per cent of firms did so in the period 1958–1968. In addition large firms usually take over smaller ones.'

There is some evidence in the UK and considerable evidence for the US (Ansoff, 1972) that most firms undertaking acquisitions were initially in a 'low growth' category. Many such firms consciously sought to diversify, giving some support to our earlier argument that a falling-off in the rate of growth may reflect product saturation for single-industry firms, or firms with a high degree of specialisation. In other words, as already illustrated in Chaper 6, large firms at such a stage could and did diversify into other activities.

Finance and Takeovers

A marked feature of acquisition and takeover has been the preference of financial institutions for larger companies. As Kumar (1984, p. 179) puts it: 'Financial institutions such as pension funds and insurance companies hold a high and increasing proportion of shares in industrial and commercial companies. Since these institutions deal mainly in large blocks of shares, they have a preference for investing in large companies, which gives the latter favourable access to finance'.

This trend had already been observed by Prais, who stressed that the financial pressures brought into being by such vast transfers of capital have provided an incentive for company amalgamations. Prais noted the link between the rapid growth of intermediary financial institutions and accelerated industrial concentration in the UK, commenting that: 'the institutions are now set on a path which, if pursued, will in a matter of a further decade make them the owners of the greater part of the share capital of all quoted industrial companies' (Prais, 1976, p. 124).

Thus in access to external finance, corroborating the analysis of Chapter 5, mesoeconomic companies clearly have an advantage over microeconomic firms through their relative size and market share. Financial institutions are not slow to realise that smaller firms have a higher fatality rate and big business a better chance of survival. This is confirmed by Kumar's analysis of growth and acquisition in the UK economy, where some three-quarters of enterprise failures from 1966 to 1976 were due to takeovers. The incidence of 'death' declined sharply with an increase in firm size. While there was no strong relationship between growth and share issues, external borrowing increased almost uniformly with an increase in size. By contrast some 330 firms, about a third of his sample, and typical for the market share of the microeconomic sector, undertook no external financing at all (Kumar, 1984, pp. 48–9, 101 and 113).

International and Multinational

One of the key limits to many theories of the growth of the firm has been their restriction to individual national markets. Even Prais's sophisticated analysis of the trend to bigness in the UK economy suffers from this neglect. Yet the multinational trend of national big business abroad can profoundly modify the trend to monopoly in a given economy. It may in part explain why the upward trend of Prais's General model for the UK in Figure 7.6 has apparently not been fulfilled. It may also explain why the increased market share of the top 100 manufacturing firms in the US economy has been relatively restrained. Put simply, UK and US business got bigger still, but much of its expansion was in other countries.

By the early 1970s both British and American multinational companies were already well established abroad, with a foreign production whose value in 1971 was more than double UK visible exports and quadruple US exports. As shown in Figure 7.7, Japan and West Germany had a much lower ratio of foreign production to exports than the UK (or the US). In effect they were mainly exporters of goods rather than of capital for foreign investment and production.

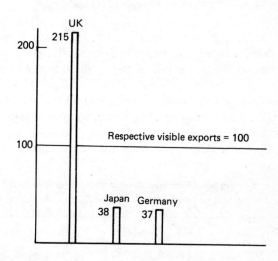

FIG. 7.7   Multinational production versus national exports (Source: UN, 1973)

Table 7.3 shows that some other economies have been catching up with the United Kingdom on foreign investment through the 1970s, with a relative fall-back of the United States. But abolition of exchange controls by the Conservative government in 1979 resulted in a massive capital outflow of some £50 billion between 1979 and 1985. This capital outflow from the UK was broadly equivalent to the value of British manufacturing investment in the 1979–85 period.

While not all of this outflow was in productive investment rather than

TABLE 7.3   Foreign Investment Trends: International Direct Foreign Investment as a Proportion of UK DFI

	1970	1973	1976	1979
West Germany	67	42	65	79
France	28	22	32	32
Italy	8	6	4	9
Netherlands	40	21	30	38
Benelux	12	4	8	19
UK	100	100	100	100
Ireland	0	0	0	na
Denmark	2	3	5	na
USA	561	330	306	411
Japan	27	48	53	48

Source: Derived from 'Balances of Payments Global Data 1970–79', SOEC, 1980, cit. Gareth Locksley 'The UK Economy 1969–1979: A Decade of Decline'.

portfolios in stocks and shares, or property, there is evidence that such foreign investment reduced investment in British industry. Table 7.3 shows that British firms consistently exported more capital than any other country except the United States through the 1970s, and Table 7.4 that the ratio of direct foreign investment to gross fixed capital formation in the 1970s was higher in the UK than for any other country. It was nearly double that of the United States itself, and nearly ten times that of Italy or Japan. Only the Netherlands approached the British ratio among the European economies.

TABLE 7.4   Foreign Versus Domestic Investment: International Foreign Direct Investment as a Proportion of Domestic Gross Fixed Domestic Capital Formation

	1970	1973	1976	1979	mean* %
West Germany	1.8	2.0	2.7	2.6	2.3
France	1.1	1.5	1.5	1.6	1.3
Italy	0.5	0.8	0.4	0.9	0.8
Netherlands	6.4	6.0	6.4	7.1	6.8
UK	5.8	11.4	8.9	8.5	7.6
USA	4.3	5.5	4.2	5.8	4.8
Japan	0.5	1.1	1.1	0.9	0.8

*Mean% industrial years 1970–79.
Source: Derived from 'Balances of Payments Global Data 1970–1979', SOEC and 'National Accounts ESA – Aggregates' SOEC, 1981, cit. Gareth Locksley 'The UK Economy 1969–1979: A Decade of Decline'.

Thus, even before the abolition of exchange controls British big business faced a trade-off between investment at home and abroad. Size was important in relation to foreign investment. In one of the few studies on the subject commissioned by the British government, surveying the activity of some 1,600 companies, Reddaway (1967) found that fifty-two companies accounted for more than 70 per cent of the net assets of the overseas subsidiaries of British companies in the mid-1960s. This evidence of the mesoeconomic dominance of foreign investment by UK companies is confirmed by the concentration of UK visible export trade in the hands of very few firms. A few dozen mesoeconomic companies literally dominate the UK's visible export trade.

In an exchange with the present author on the floor of the House of Commons, the then Industry Minister, Sir Keith Joseph, claimed in Friedmanite terms that once the burden of taxation had been lifted from the backs of British business, 'millions of entrepreneurs' would unleash themselves on world markets. The reality, as pointed out to him at the time, is very different. Only some 10,000 firms are regularly engaged in UK visible export trade. As shown in Table 7.5, from 1975 to 1981 the top 30 exporters have accounted for between one-third and two-fifths of total visible exports, the top 75 exporters for up to a half, and the top 220 exporters for some two-thirds of this trade.

TABLE 7.5   Big Business Dominance of UK Visible Export Trade 1975–81 (%)

	1975	1976	1977	1978	1979	1980	1981
Top 30 exporters	33	36	35	32	35	35	39
Top 75 exporters	46	50	47	44	47	47	51
Top 220 exporters	64	67	64	61	64	62	65

Source: Department of Trade's Annual Overseas Transactions Inquiry and Parliamentary Questions 28 July 1980 and 11 July 1983.

It is significant that in 1983 the Conservative government decided to stop publishing such data on the command by big business of UK visible export trade (formerly published in *British Business*). No doubt some official statisticians put up a fight for the figures. But the government could not tolerate them. This is not to say that governments alone are culpable. Some big business has stopped giving *Fortune* magazine consolidated figures for all subsidiaries and instead give only those for parent companies, thereby considerably understating the real market share of the mesoeconomy.

American Challenge?

One of the noted target areas for US foreign investment in the 1960s was continental Western Europe. Indeed, Jean-Jacques Servan-Schreiber opened his book *The American Challenge* by claiming that 'fifteen years from now the world's third greatest industrial power, just after the United States and Russia, might not be Europe, but *American Industry in Europe*'. With a journalist's panache, Servan-Schreiber also claimed that nine-tenths of American investment was financed from Europe itself and that innovation by US companies in Europe was frequently based on technical breakthrough by European laboratories (Servan-Schreiber, 1969).

There is no doubt that US business was increasingly attracted to continental Western Europe during the 1960s, in part due to the commitment of the original six signatories of the Rome Treaty to create a common market. In 1950, the total value of US investment in the UK was one and a half times that of the initial six members of the European Community, with a common language and common institutions playing a key role in the preference for Britain. But by 1966 this ratio had been reversed, with the Six accounting for one and a half times as much US direct investment as the UK. The switch dated from 1958, the first year in which the new European Community came into operation.

However, while there is little doubt that direct investment by US multinationals in Western Europe in the 1960s was encouraged by the opening of the EEC, it is arguable that Servan-Schreiber fell for a statistical illusion. Statistics on the activity of American firms abroad were more readily available at the time from US government sources than figures on European big business and its own multinational spread.

The Servan-Schreiber thesis has been challenged on a comprehensive basis by Robert Rowthorn and Stephen Hymer (1970 and 1971). They recognised an 'American challenge' to European firms in some sectors such as electricals and, to a lesser extent, engineering. But they found that in key modern industries such as chemicals, oil and motor vehicles, there was no American lead in the 1960s, and that through a broad range of industry continental European firms – albeit starting from a lower base – grew much faster than American companies in Europe.

Rowthorn and Hymer stressed that the crucial phenomenon of the 1960s was not so much the spread of US multinational capital as the multinational trend of European capital in general. As they put it (1971, p.2): 'International trade and investment have weakened the links binding firms to their national economies. Overseas sales, and to a lesser extent overseas production, now account for a substantial proportion of the total output of firms. This process of outward expansion has, however, been a two-way affair in which the firms of each industrial country have also lost part of their domestic economy to foreigners. The process has been one of inter-penetration.'

Europe's Bigger Business

Rowthorn and Hymer's findings have been confirmed by several analyses on the trend to bigger business in Western Europe during the 1970s and early 1980s. Jacquemin and Lichtbuer (1973) found a marked trend to bigger European business. Using mainly data from asset ratios, they established that: 'There is a convergence between the European evolution of overall concentration and industrial concentration. The growing weight of giant firms in the manufacturing sector as a whole is confirmed by their growing importance in each particular industry.'

Lawrence Franko also has challenged Servan-Schreiber's thesis, observing that since only a handful of firms in the 1960s were undertaking multinational mergers, 'it was sometimes thought that enterprises on the continent were becoming increasingly national'. By contrast, he argued, a closer examination of the record showed that 'multinationality has never been an exclusive characteristic of American and British enterprise'. Interwar cartelisation across frontiers was more marked than postwar mergers. But the majority of European firms went multinational on a major scale after the Second World War, and especially from the mid-1950s (Franko, 1976, p. 98).

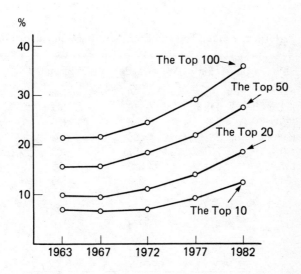

FIG. 7.8   The top hundred European companies: sales as ratio of EEC GDP (Source: OECD (1984))

As illustrated in Figure 7.8, the share of the top 100 European companies in the gross domestic product of the ten EEC countries (i.e. before the accession of Spain and Portugal) increased from just over a fifth to over a third between 1963 and 1982. The share of the top 50 companies over the same period increased by more than half, while that of the top 20 doubled.

TABLE 7.6   Europe's Bigger Business: Ratio of Sales of the Top 100 European Companies to EEC Gross Domestic Product

Number of firms	1963	1967	1972	1977	1982
C1	1.8	1.7	1.6	2.4	3.5
C2	3	2.8	2.6	3.7	5.7
C4	4.3	4	4	5.4	7.9
C10	7	6.7	7	9.2	12.6
C20	9.9	9.7	11	14	18.7
C30	12.3	12	14	17.3	22.5
C50	15.8	15.7	18.4	22	27.8
C100	21.2	21.5	24.3	29	36

Source: OECD, *Structures et Performances des Plus Grandes Entreprises Européennes*, 1984.

TABLE 7.7   Performance of the Top 100 EEC Industrial Companies 1969–80

	GDP*	Sales	Assets	Employment	Profit
1969	100	100	100	100	100
1970	112	115	116	106	92
1971	125	132	136	109	84
1972	139	157	156	108	85
1973	160	207	181	108	180
1974	181	281	229	108	199
1975	203	304	238	108	122
1976	233	326	273	111	182
1977	259	354	302	108	164
1978	287	416	378	110	199
1979	322	553	466	112	508
1980	365	664	491	116	340

*GDP at market prices. EEC nine (excluding Greece).
Source: Locksley (1984)

Table 7.6 sets out the structure of concentration from the largest (C1) to the top hundred (C100) companies in the European Community.

Mesoeconomic Structure

The trend shown in Table 7.6 and Figure 7.8 demonstrates the emerging structure of the European mesoeconomy. This is well illustrated by the fact that by the early 1980s the top 10 European firms contributed as much to the European Community's gross domestic product as its entire agricultural sector. Gareth Locksley (1984) has also shown that the growth of sales and assets in the top 100 European companies has outpaced EEC gross domestic product through the 1970s.

As indicated in Table 7.7, from 1969 to 1980 the sales of the top 100 industrial companies in the EEC grew more than sixfold, and their assets nearly fivefold, while their profits more than trebled. Sales per employee rose nearly six times and assets per employee more than quadrupled, while employment itself hardly changed (increasing by only sixteen per cent).

TABLE 7.8   Performance of the Top 50 EEC Industrial Companies 1969–80*

Employment	Sales	Assets	Profits†
74.1	77.8	78.0	80.1

*Mean share of the top 50 companies within the top 100 (%).
†Post tax.
Source: Locksley (1984).

Table 7.8 reveals the dominance of the top 50 EEC industrial companies within the top 100, accounting for nearly three-quarters of employment, more than three-quarters of sales and assets, and more than four-fifths of post-tax profits. As Locksley comments (1984, p. 34), for European business 'the fact of bigness and fewness is well established'.

7.4   Services and Distribution

The services sector includes commerce (both wholesale and retail distribution); transport and communications; finance (banking, insurance and building societies); property and real estate; professional services from advertising through to accountancy; and the whole range of government, from social services to the police and armed forces.

Although the focus of much conventional economics is on manufacturing, services is by far the biggest sector in the GNP of most countries. In 1980 it represented nearly two-thirds of world GNP, against less than a third for manufacturing and less than 7 per cent for agriculture.

Not only is the services sector bigger, wider ranging and more closed to statistical analysis than agriculture or manufacturing. In addition, as George Stigler has put it, there is 'no authoritative consensus on either the boundaries or the classification of the *service industries*', showing, by the words in our emphasis, that there is an ambivalence as to whether some services are industries or industrial (Stigler, 1956, p. 47). Nobel Prizewinner Simon Kuznets included transportation, communications and public utilities among services in 1958 but excluded them eight years later (Kuznets, 1958 and 1966).

Arguably, Kuznets' second choice was a better choice and might well be recommended for adoption in national and international accounting. A similar choice might be to classify the whole area of finance – banking, insurance and other financial services – into a new fourth sector, given not only the general distinctions between finance capital and industrial or services capital, but also the overwhelming role now played by international and multinational finance on a global scale.

The Underground Economy

If reclassifying financial services appears a major task, it may be less herculean than tackling what variously is called the underground economy, the subterranean economy, the informal economy, the unrecorded economy or – in terms predating racial sensitivity – plain black market. Arguing that Clark's (1940) and Kuznets' work is flawed in that it covers only recorded transactions, Clairmonte and Cavanagh cite marginal activities such as tax evasion, illicit currency transactions, illicit unrecorded work, prostitution, drug trafficking, larceny, theft and white-collar crimes (Clairmonte and Cavanagh, 1984, p. 222).

According to conventional wisdom, such unrecorded activities are typical of smaller business in the service sector. Clearly it is easier for many small service firms to evade tax than to avoid it, since as small operations lacking the multi-plant, multi-company and multinational reach of big business, they also lack the range of techniques and devices by which mesoeconomic business – whether in agriculture, industry or services – can overstate costs and understate profits on financial transactions or payments between its own national or international operations. Yet such tax avoidance by big business is big business in itself and certainly more significant in overall terms than the more conspicuous dependence of certain countries on illegal export of drugs, or of certain persons or groups on prostitution and larceny.

Services and the Market System

In his analysis of services in *Economics and the Public Purpose* (1974), John Kenneth Galbraith observes that

> services are rightly assumed to be the domain of the small firm and thus of the market system. In recent times there has been much talk in the United States and other industrial economies of the rise of the so-called service economy. This, in turn, has been taken by determined defenders of the market to prove that the market-controlled economy is not only surviving but resurgent. . . . On examination this development turns out to be a good deal more complex. Numerous service enterprises are the by-product of the rise of the large firm.

As on other occasions, Galbraith is being proved correct. Not only are services firms in large part external or satellite suppliers to established big business on a world scale. Concentration and centralisation through the dynamics of unequal competition are already as typical of services as the more highly publicised data on the industrial economy (especially manu-facturing). Moreover, as Clairmonte and Cavanagh have argued: 'whereas a hundred years ago, most services were transacted by highly specialised firms that provided single service lines, at present the boundaries between services are crumbling in consequence of corporate diversification and of the evolution of corporations that could be designated as financial super-markets'.

Multisectoral Services

The changing structure of services has been illustrated by Gershuny and Miles' detailed study of occupational data for France, Italy, the UK and Ireland. They found that: 'during the 1960s and 1970s, changes in the occupational distribution of employment have resulted more from changes in occupational structure within economic sectors than from changes in demand patterns between them. Increased demand for professional, tech-nical, clerical and other specialised service occupations relative to other employees within each sector accounts for much more of the increase of employment in these sorts of occupations than does the increase of demand for the products of services industries' (Gershuny and Miles, 1983).

Citing Gershuny and Miles' findings, Juan Rada observes that their assessment qualifies the purely 'sectoral shift' view. Identified with Rostow (1960), this argued that as countries develop they go through a simple process of transfer of employment and activities from agriculture to industry and services. As Rada (1984, p. 289) puts it: 'in fact, it implies that there is a certain integration within sectors, accompanied by an increase in the service content of the different activities. . . . This is critically important because it implies a strong organic link between the different types of activities. In other words, is it possible to provide, say, car design services without a car industry? Can an autonomous high value added service sector evolve without a manufacturing and agricultural base?'

Such questions have produced a simplistic answer from the British Conservative government since 1979, which has assumed that the UK can flourish as a service economy for world markets with a declining manufacturing base. But as Rada stresses, services are now multisectoral rather than simply tertiary, affecting the internal structure of agriculture and industry as well as the broader inter-sectoral distribution of activities.

Information Technology

Part of this process of increased 'white-collar' employment in traditionally 'blue-collar' sectors such as agriculture and industry relates to the increased sophistication of the conditions of production, distribution and exchange. For instance, white-collar employment in British manufacturing industry has more than doubled since the Second World War. However, the role of service inputs into the primary and secondary sectors has been transformed by the revolution in information technology. As Rada argues, this is a process whereby the information content of material production itself increases: 'Because of greater complexity of production, improved productivity, efficiency and specialisation, a greater amount of input is required for each stage of production.'

In an empirical analysis of the United States economy, Johnscher (1983) has shown that in 1972 some three-quarters of the information sector's output formed an input to the production of physical goods. Less than ten per cent went into final consumption of information services, and the rest amounted to an input to the information sector itself. Thus, while in nominal terms the information sector has been growing more rapidly than the production of goods, the most rapid growth in fact has been in the input of information services to the physical goods sector.

Drawing attention to the importance of Johnscher's findings, Rada (1984) has also analysed five main dimensions of the transformation of services by information technology:

First, improved productivity in services themselves through extensive digitalisation of all types of signals, which allows the use of interrelated networks to transfer, process and retrieve information through the interfacing of computers and telecommunications – what the French have called *télématique* – which itself is related to value added networks which process information while transmitting it.

Second, increased transparency in service markets, for instance where Reuters Commodity Services makes access to markets by non-established producers easier. At the same time, however, this shortens managerial decision-making cycles and accents rapid response times, which in due course makes it more likely that oligopolistic practices will assert themselves in this nominally open field.

Third, changes in scale economies within services, where in some cases the barrier to entry is lowered while in others it becomes much higher. Thus while individual self-employed programmers can offer their services through the telecommunications network and send their product through it at a relatively modest cost of entry, a critical minimum infrastructure is necessary to create both new activities and also employment. In services, information technology alone cannot transcend the barriers to growth experienced by the owner-entrepreneurial or small family firm, which we examined in Chapter 5. Certainly in the area of insurance, credit cards, databases and banks, and certain other types of software, information technology has raised this threshold barrier significantly.

Fourth, changed market frontiers between service providers, and between industry and services, with a trend to increasing self-service through (a) the use of remote entry terminals at home or in the office which allow telebanking, teleshopping and other forms of telebookings, as well as (b) the use of equipment to transfer the manual cost of transactions to users, as in the case of automatic petrol pump stations and automatic cash dispensers.

Multinational Services

The fifth main transformation of services by information technology, stressed by Rada, is the rapid internationalisation of services. Its implications have been extensively analysed by Clairmonte and Cavanagh, (1984), who have stressed the difference between three main variations, set out below, in the multinational service company.

Single-line services. The food retailer is symptomatic of the species. Although McDonalds already employs more people than US Steel, Clairmonte and Cavanagh argue that 'this grouping is actually on the road to extinction, owing to the enhanced power in finance and marketing and capacity for survival that conglomeration offers'. Certainly it is clear that the multinational spread of single-line or single-product service companies such as McDonalds can sustain corporate growth through a globalisation of the second growth phase of the Vernon product cycle. However, to offset the decline in the rate of growth of revenues and profits, as analysed in Chapter 4, even a pace-making and dominant single-line company such as McDonalds may need to merge or diversify in order to sustain its 'growth phase' rate of return on capital.

Integrated service conglomerates. If single-line or single-product firms have to diversify to sustain profitability, they usually expand into a complementary line that can build successfully on the firm's existing technical and marketing expertise. Such attempts at related diversification have already been analysed in the case of ITT and other American conglomerates in Chapter 6. Clairmonte and Cavanagh stress that in the case of services such complementarities mainly exist between banking, insurance and other financial services, and between advertising, public relations, the media and telecommunications. They believe that multinational conglomerates of this type can be expected to make considerable headway in the future.

Diversified conglomerates. Clairmonte and Cavanagh's third category represents what they describe as 'the supreme embodiment of modern capitalism', claiming that the logic of uninhibited corporate growth is nowhere more frankly stated than in a report by R. J. Reynolds Industries Inc. (1981 sales: $13.8 billion), which straddles manufacturing, plantation agriculture and service sectors:

'First, having captured one third of the United States cigarette market, the company could see a point of diminishing returns for growth potential. Second, significant cash was being generated which could be invested advantageously elsewhere. [Adopting] an unrestricted approach towards diversification, Reynolds moved into entirely new areas – shipping and petroleum, on the theory that it made sense, when appropriate, to supply cash to any strong, well established business'. (Clairmonte and Cavanagh, 1984.)

Distribution

The dynamics of unequal competition, including concentration and central-isation, barriers to entry and the multinational trend are increasingly evident in the distribution services sector.

Many personal services tend to be more price-competitive than industry, as they directly concern the individual consumer. There are various reasons. In some markets some people can 'shop around' for better quality or price. But the ability to 'shop around' depends either on transport availability and easy access or on the 'clustering' of retail outlets, such as food or shoe shops in the high street, or specialist hi-fi electronics companies, as in the Tottenham Court Road in London. Even in this case, the other side of such 'clustering' of outlets is the ease with which sellers can see what others are charging and their agreement in some cases on minimum prices. It also is worth observing that many of these outlets manage to change prices, under the guise of special discount offers, in such a way as to make a rational choice by the consumer more difficult. Special offers when employed rarely last for long. They tend to be the offer of the week or the offer of the month.

TABLE 7.9 Number of Firms in UK Representing Upper Half Retail Sales

1950	4,750
1961	1,700
1971	930
1976	350
1979	165
1982	138
1983	121
1984	107

Source: Parliamentary Questions, Dept. of Trade and Industry, 11 June 1979, 14 June 1982, 21 January 1985 and 28 January 1986.

TABLE 7.10 Packaged Grocery Sales, December 1983 – March 1984

	%
Sainsbury	16.7
Tesco	15.0
Asda	8.0
Sub-total (top three firms)	39.7
Dee Retail and BAT (International)	7.0*
Kwik Save	5.7
Sub-total (top five firms)	52.4
Argyll	5.4
Fine Fare Group	4.6
Safeway	2.0
Hillards	1.7
Waitrose	1.4
Other multiples	6.9
All multiple grocers	74.4
All co-op	14.9
All symbol group	5.4
Other independents	5.3
	100.0

*Excludes Lennons.
Source: The Monopolies and Mergers Commission Report (1985).

Concentration

Retail concentration has increased dramatically since the Second World War in the UK economy. As shown in Table 7.9, in 1950 4,750 main retail companies accounted for the upper half of trade. By 1984 this had been reduced to just over a hundred firms.

As might be expected, evidence on overall concentration in the retail trade is confirmed at the level of individual markets. For example, Table 7.10 gives an analysis of packaged grocery sales in Great Britain in the first quarter of 1984. This shows that the three market leaders, Sainsbury, Tesco and Asda, between them accounted for nearly 40 per cent of the total market share and that with Dee Retail and BAT International, plus Kwik Save, the top five companies represented over 50 per cent of the market.

The relation of the market shares of different kinds of companies to our previous analysis of meso and microeconomic structures is illustrated in Table 7.11. This shows that the multiple grocery retailing companies, typical of the mesoeconomic sector, increased their share of the grocery retailing market from just over two-fifths in 1971 to over two-thirds in 1983. Micro independent retailers correspondingly lost out, with a decrease in their share of grocery retailing from over two-fifths in 1971 to just over one-fifth in 1983.

TABLE 7.11 Market Share of Co-operatives, Meso-multiples and Micro-independents (%)

	1971	1975	1981	1982	1983
Multiples	44.3	48.9	62.2	64.7	66.4
Independents	42.5	37.4	23.6	22.2	21.2
Co-operatives	13.2	13.7	13.7	13.1	12.7
Total turnover (£m)	4,156	7,500	16,950	18,708	N/A

Source: A. C. Nielsen, cit. Monopolies and Mergers Commission (1985).

The co-operative sector managed to defend its market share against the offensive from the multiple stores, but still lost half of one per cent of the market, dropping from just over 13 to 12 per cent of total market share. Such a concentration indicates the greater economies of scale which can be achieved by supermarket or hypermarket distribution rather than the classic corner shop.

Convenience

Nonetheless, as is apparent to any shopper, the small store manages to survive, and sometimes to flourish. This represents the dualism in the retail market similar to that observed by Averitt and analysed in Chapter 6. In terms of the imperfect competition analysis of Chapter 3, the different types of outlet will be serving different kinds of consumer need. The clearest example is the case in which a consumer may do the week's main shopping in one stint at a major supermarket outlet, but nontheless use the corner shop or smaller outlet for either casual shopping or for meeting those needs which have been overlooked at the time of the main weekly purchase.

In this sense, there is a 'convenience' element in the smaller or micro-economic outlet versus the mesoeconomic or larger distribution centre. The Monopolies and Mergers Commision report on the proposed merger of *The Dee Corporation and Booker McConnell* (1985) found that an independent retailer cannot charge more than 10 per cent above the price of a multiple retailer without losing business. But within that margin the convenience factor (Scitovsky's product differentiation from location) seems to obtain.

And Class

There are related barriers to effective price competition in distribution which reflect less on consumer choice or short-term consumer need, and more on the socio-economic class of consumers. For one thing, while automobiles are common enough in the United States, even to the point of two or more to a family for some income brackets, they are not so common in Europe especially for some sections of the working class or for the more elderly and retired. Less than 60 per cent of UK households had access to a car in the mid 1980s.

At this point the weight-value ratio, which is of such considerable importance in transport theory, becomes significant in the economics of retail distribution. Elderly people without the use of a car simply may not be able to carry the weight of goods which would be involved in a big shop from a supermarket. They will be forced to purchase in smaller bulk at more frequent intervals, and will very much tend to do so from the nearer retail outlet, especially if this enables them to avoid paying the public transport fare to the larger outlet, or waiting for a public transport vehicle in possibly inclement weather or physically insecure circumstances in inner urban areas. The same kind of factor can obtain in rural areas where the consumers do not have private vehicle transport, and where the dispersed population or market does not validate a supermarket outlet.

Micro Suppliers and Meso Buyers

Nonetheless, of course, competition between micro and mesoeconomic

enterprise in the retail trade is very significant, as reflected in the concentration and centralisation figures already given in Table 7.9. When firms in the
retail trade have cost schedules as distinct as those analysed in Chapter 5, or
even cost schedules which are closer but significantly different, there is bound
to be pressure on the small retail outlet. This is aggravated by the extent to
which it will tend to be retailing manufactured goods, in the case of the food
trade, whose prices are determined by highly concentrated enterprises in the
food sector. In other cases, such as alcoholic drinks, minimum prices in micro
outlets are set by mesoeconomic brewers such as Watney-Mann or
Charringtons, who thereby restrict the price flexibility open to small off-
licence stores.

Cost increases imposed on microeconomic outlets by mesoeconomic
wholesalers or manufacturers can prove critical to their survival. Even if the
enterprise manages to survive, it will tend to do so at very low profit margins.
Meanwhile, mesoeconomic retail enterprises can exert a joint monopsonistic
(or oligopsonistic) effect on mesoeconomic manufacturers for a range of
products sold under their own brand names.

The Corner Shop

It is hardly surprising in this sense that many small corner shops in either
Europe or the United States complain about cost inflation, or constitute one
of the main vehicles for reinforcing the concept of a prevailing competitive or
competition ideology in the eyes and minds of the general consuming public.
They tend to be squeezed more severely by inflation than firms in the
mesoeconomic sector. The very problems which they face in part indicate the
limited relevance of wage inflation to inflation in general. For while part of
the inflation in their input costs may well reflect inflation in the manufacturing sector, the microeconomic corner shop or small retail outlets do not
typically use much paid or unionised labour. They tend to be family concerns,
where the labour is not strictly dependent in the sense of being paid a given
basic wage plus overtime. Not untypically in immigrant communities the
corner shop will service the public for very long hours including late or 'anti-
social' hours which are not paid at all.

In a real sense, many corner shops survive through the willingness of family
labour to work anti-social, unpaid hours. But they survive less under
conditions of equal competition, or even capitalist competition, than by pre-
capitalist or non-capitalist family modes of organisation. Thus, instead of
exchanging labour for capital in return for a wage, they survive by the
exploitation of unpaid labour. The total net revenue or profit accruing to such
microeconomic retail enterprises in any given period, whether a week, a
month or a year, may well be equivalent to an adequate wage or salary for

one person. But in many cases this will be achieved by the underpaid or unpaid employment of several persons, in particular the wife and in many cases the children of the owner-entrepreneur.

7.5 Banking and Finance

It has been observed, over time, that leading analysts such as Kuznets have changed their classification of individual sectors of activity. It has also been noted that there is a strong case, on these lines, for reclassifying the role of finance in the modern market economy. Normally included in the tertiary or services sector, the scope and scale of finance – from services into industry and agriculture, and also its new multinational spread of activities – justifies its consideration as a new fourth or quartery sector of economic activity.

TABLE 7.12   Profile of Top 100 Banks, 1982

Headquarters	Number of banks	Assets (billion dollars)	Percentage of total assets
Japan	24	1,161.0	25.8
USA	15	743.9	16.5
France	8	514.3	11.4
Germany, Fed. Rep. of	11	466.1	10.4
UK	5	355.6	7.9
Italy	8	263.3	5.9
Canada	5	247.5	5.5
Netherlands	4	154.5	3.4
Switzerland	3	138.6	3.1
Belgium	4	91.7	2.0
Brazil	1	61.7	1.4
Hong Kong	1	57.1	1.3
Australia	2	49.1	1.1
Israel	2	42.6	1.0
Spain	2	41.6	0.9
Iran	1	27.1	0.6
India	1	23.6	0.5
Austria	1	19.6	0.4
Sweden	1	19.1	0.4
Iraq	1	18.6	0.4
	100	4,496.6	100.0

Source: Clairmonte and Cavanagh (1984).

Stressing the mesoeconomic conceptual framework, it is clear that finance is now big business on a world scale and that its dominant command of individual financial markets corroborates the earlier analysis of concentration, centralisation and oligopoly structures.

Global Dominance

The global dominance of the world's top banks is now truly phenomenal. As indicated in Table 7.12, in 1982 their combined assets of $4.5 trillion were equivalent to almost half of global GDP and more than one and a half times the combined sales of the top 200 world corporations. Japan, rather than the United States, leads with nearly a quarter of the top 100 banks and over a quarter of their total assets, in turn worth over a trillion dollars. The United States comes second, and Japanese and United States banks together control over two-fifths of the total assets of the top hundred.

International and multinational operations have been undertaken by banks for several centuries. Geneva was an 'offshore' or more literally 'onshore' banking centre during the time of Louis XIV, while the banks of the Italian city states financed the crusades of the eleventh and twelth centuries. Multinational banking proper began in earnest in the 1870s. But the major global expansion which has resulted in the dominance of the top hundred banks occurred as recently as the 1970s, when they became the major intermediaries for recycling petrodollar surpluses. The dramatic consequence was that the share of profits from foreign operations for the top seven US banks soared from just over a fifth in 1970 to over a half in 1981, and approached two-thirds in the early 1980s.

Such an increase in the share of foreign invested domestic profits was not without its risks or potential penalities. By the early 1980s the debt of leading US and some UK banks to Latin America alone exceeded total shareholders' equity.

Barriers to Entry

Granted the risks of such exposure, politicians might be excused for asking whether international finance is too important to be left to bankers. Nonetheless, such banking operations on a world scale can only be undertaken by meso rather than micro banking enterprises. As the American insurance periodical *Best's Review* (July 1983) put it: 'the financial services world is an intricate one of competing conglomerates, interlocking directorates, foreign and domestic subsidiaries and spin-off companies, all interwoven with provincial and federal legislative policies that can present a daunting prospect for newcomers to the field'.

As Clairmonte and Cavanagh (1984, p. 236) comment on *Best's Review*: 'the conglomeration of financial services is being facilitated and promoted by the interaction of electronic technology, government deregulation and the corporate striving for the dismantlement of existing barriers'. They cite the colossal economies of scale now prevalent in commercial banking, with estimates of optimal bank size beginning at $15 billion worth of assets. Such economies of scale are clearly related to our earlier analysis on the dynamics of equal and unequal competition, with size bringing not only technical economies from large volume transactions, and managerial economies through specialisation, but also (with a caveat on recent big bank lending to Latin America) a spreading of risks between various markets and countries. Again, a contradiction emerges in the currently fashionable deregulation policies being pursued in countries such as the United States and the United Kingdom. While these in principle lower barriers of entry to smaller banks, the main beneficiaries of such deregulation have been the big financial institutions such as banks, insurance companies and building societies, which have increasingly ranged across each other's sectoral boundaries in search of new areas of profit. When smaller merchant banks have managed to break through, as with Warburg's in postwar Britain, this has been through financial services to big business in the mesoeconomic sector, rather than profits generated from services to microeconomic firms. Meanwhile, they are dwarfed by the Japanese.

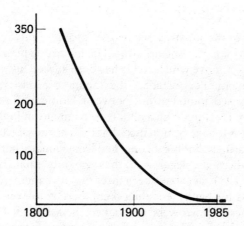

FIG. 7.9 Decline in the number of deposit banks in Britain

Mergers and Centralisation

It has been estimated that in the time of Ricardo in the early nineteenth century there were some 350 joint stock or clearing banks in Britain. By 1890, as Figure 7.9 illustrates, this had been reduced by more than two-thirds, to just over one hundred; by 1942 the process of concentration and central-isation had reduced the number further to twenty-five, and by 1973 only thirteen clearing banks remained. The largest five banks held less than a third of total deposits in 1900, but by 1953 this had risen to four-fifths. By the early 1970s the 'big four' of National Westminster, Lloyds, Barclays and the Midland – plus two small London clearing banks – accounted for over 85 per cent of the value of British current and deposit accounts (Boddy, 1980, p. 32).

Such national mergers have been paralleled at the international level. Citibank and Lloyds have acquired Grindlays Bank in the UK, the former taking nearly 49 per cent of Grindlays' equity and Lloyds being the other major owner. In 1980 the Midland Bank spent $820 million in acquiring the eleventh biggest bank in the United States, Crocker National of California, and in 1983 boosted its shareholdings to 57 per cent. (This was to prove very costly to the Midland, with losses which in 1985 led to major questioning of its overall management.) The Mitsubishi (Japan's fourth biggest bank) made a better judgement in its takeover of BanCal Tri-State Corporation, which itself owns one of the oldest banks on the Pacific coast, the Bank of California. This deal substantially enhanced Mitsubishi's service and manufacturing leverage in the United States.

The Japanese Challenge

Such penetration of the Japanese big league into the United States financial market has led to counter moves from US finance capital to break into Japanese finance – a move which so far has been successfully resisted by the Japanese government. For instance, the Japanese Ministry of Finance is hostile to a proposed joint venture between Nomnomura Securities and Morgan Guaranty Trust to set up a joint trust company in Japan. Clairmonte and Cavanagh (1984) have commented that these forms of corporate finance merger 'are increasingly finding a congenial legal climate, particularly in the United States, where the legal wall that separate financial services are crumbling.' Since 1981 there have been three major changes: (1) the abolition of interest ceilings for banks, enabling them thereby to exert their financial leverage on domestic borrowers to finance their foreign lending; (2) an elimination of the barriers between banking and other financial services so that banks increasingly may move into stockbroking and other financial services; (3) a suspension of the 50-year ban on inter-State branching, authorising stronger banks to take over weaker ones in other States in crisis – due largely to the forementioned failure of small farms. Meanwhile, as Japanse banks shrewdly penetrated the US market, American banks such as

Citicorp and Bank of America first sank capital into farmers' banks, and then submerged themselves in Latin American debt.

Banks and Building Societies

The liberalisation pursued by the Reagan administration in the United States has been paralleled by that of the Thatcher government in Britain. But in the same way it has served the interest of mesoeconomic finance rather than microeconomic competition in financial services. As set out in Table 7.13, the London clearing banks in 1951 had five times the deposits of UK building societies, whereas by 1984 this disparity had been reduced to parity, with the London clearing banks and the building societies each accounting for just over a third of total deposits.

TABLE 7.13   Share of Deposits: UK Banks and Building Societies

	1951 end-Dec	1961 mid-Dec	1971 mid-Dec	1981 mid-Dec	1984	Share of Total (%)
UK banks					180,146	65.7
London clearing banks	6,060	6,877	11,224	44,084	94,400	34.4
Scottish clearing banks	682	718	1,090	4,940	9,904	3.6
Northern Ireland banks	116	147	299	1,161		
Other banks	848	2,013	4,992	28,146	75,842	27.7
Building Societies	1,265	3,149	12,176	57,146	94,059	34.3
				Total:	274,205	100.0

Source: *Bank of England Quarterly Bulletin, Financial Statistics* and the Committee of London Clearing Banks, and Parliamentary Questions, 18 July 1983 and 21 January 1985.

Centralisation among the building societies has been as marked – and as neglected by conventional theory – as centralisation in banking itself. As shown in Figure 7.10 and Table 7.14, nearly 2,300 building societies flourished in the United Kingdom at the turn of the century. But 1930 this had been halved, by 1970 it had been halved again, and by 1984 less than 200 building societies operated in the United Kingdom.

Mesoeconomic centralisation in the building society market is illustrated in Table 7.15, which shows that in 1984 the largest three societies accounted for nearly half of deposits and loans, the top six companies for nearly two-thirds, and the top ten firms for some three-quarters of total deposits and loans in the sector.

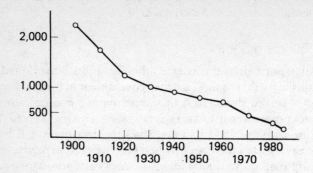

FIG. 7.10   The decline in independent Building Societies 1900–1984

TABLE 7.14   From Micro to Mesoeconomy: UK Building Societies

Year	Number of societies
1900	2,286
1910	1,723
1920	1,271
1930	1,026
1940	952
1950	819
1960	726
1970	481
1975	382
1980	273
1983	206
1984	190

Source: Parliamentary Questions, 23 January 1985 and 28 January 1986 and Royal Commission on Financial Institutions, op. cit.

TABLE 7.15   The Dominance of the Top Ten UK Building Societies in 1984*

Largest three societies	45
Largest six societies	61
Largest ten societies	74

*Percentage of total share of deposits and loans of all building societies.
Source: Parliamentary Question, 28 January 1986.

Insurance

World insurance markets in the last twenty years have increased almost eightfold from $40 billion to over $300 billion, while reinsurance premiums have risen from just over $5 billion to more than $40 billion. By 1983, worldwide insurance policies amounted to $5 trillion, the equivalent of nearly half of the world's gross domestic product (*Best's Review*, June 1983 and *The Economist*, 8 October 1983). Citing these astronomic figures, Clairmonte and Cavanagh comment that they 'reflect a prodigious growth in the insurance industry in all regions since the 1960s.' A regional breakdown of the premiums (direct insurance and reinsurance) indicates a decline in the share of US insurers, from almost three-fifths of the world's total in 1965 to under half today. This declining US share has been countered by a slight rise in the share of Western European insurers, while the rest of the non-socialist world doubled its share from 9 to 18 per cent.

As with both multinational services and banking, corporations based in five countries dominate the international insurance market: the United States, the United Kingdom, West Germany, Switzerland and France. Firms' headquarters in these countries have some three-quarters of all overseas insurance business. The other big-league insurance companies are based in five other countries who also are leading actors in the world market: Japan, Italy, The Netherlands, Belgium and South Africa. As with UK banking, the United States shows a relatively concentrated structure in insurance, with the top 42 life insurance companies accounting for over half of insurance policies issued in 1982.

Life, property and casualty insurance are dominated by three large mesoeconomic corporations which account for over half of the top ten companies' business. The US market illustrates the diversification analysed in earlier chapters, including the creation of captive insurance markets by companies such as Exxon and Mobil. Within the OECD countries, over two-fifths of such business is accounted for by life insurance; nearly 40 per cent by fire, marine and accident liability premiums, and the rest represented mainly by motor insurance. Foreign penetration of the domestic market of the United States is still relatively small – under two per cent for the premium volume in life, accident and health insurance, and under five per cent for the property and casualty market. Nonetheless, assuming continuation of the commitment of the US administration to liberalisation during President Reagan's second term does not diminish, it can be assumed that the share of European and Japanese insurance companies on the US market will rise.

The dominance of a few leading insurance corporations is certainly evident in the United Kingdom, West Germany, Italy and Switzerland, which account for the headquarters of 36 of Europe's top 40 private insurance companies.

Virtually all of these mesoeconomic groups derive increasing amounts of their income from overseas. In Japan eight firms dominate insurance and all but one of these belong to the big six Japanese conglomerates.

Such a trend has not passed entirely without challenge. A counter movement is evident in the developing world. In Africa and Asia the number of countries which nationalised the insurance industry or restrict the operations of foreign insurance companies rose ten times from 1968 to 1982 (Clairmonte and Cavanagh, 1984, pp. 243–50), and in France in the early 1980s the socialist government took measures which in practice brought all domestic banking and finance into the public sector.

7.6 Summary

(1) Two hundred multinational companies now command nearly a third of the world's production. Smaller microeconomic enterprise survives and in some cases flourishes. But it does so within a dual market economy on terms set by mesoeconomic big business.

(2) The conventional distinction of primary, secondary and tertiary sectors should be complemented by (i) admission of the multi-sectoral role of the multinational company, and (ii) the increased importance of global finance as opposed to non-financial services meriting recognition as a new fourth or quartery sector of the global economy.

(3) The primary or agriculture sector is increasingly dominated by multinational agribusiness world wide. The dualism within agriculture between meso and micro farms parallels the dualism between town and country or the urban and rural sectors of the economy.

(4) In the developed countries, lower food prices cannot be achieved without involuntary out-migration from agriculture unless direct income support is sustained or increased for those in marginal farms. Inversely, in developing countries, food production cannot be sustained in many rural areas unless the price mechanism is supplemented by direct income support or other incentives.

(5) Multinational companies have leapt the frontier between the primary sectors of mining and hydrocarbons and the secondary and tertiary sectors of manufacturing and services. The international producers' cartel of OPEC was preceded by the national base-point pricing system which guaranteed given income levels to US oil producers.

(6) Relative stability in the recent market shares of industrial big business in the US and the UK has less reflected limits to the growth of American and British firms than their multinational expansion through investment and production in foreign markets.

(7) The near doubling of the market share of the top 100 UK industrial companies from 1950 to 1970 has been matched by a near doubling of the share of the top 100 European companies from the early 1960s to the early 1980s.

(8) The concentration and centralisation of non-financial services since the war has been more dramatic than in industry. The firms accounting for the upper half of UK retail distribution have been reduced from nearly 5,000 to just over 100 since 1950.

(9) Deposit banks face increasing competition from non-bank financial services in economies such as the UK. In the US, banking regulations sustain a plural banking structure. But when left to the free play of market forces, concentration and centralisation have reduced the supply of banking or building society services to a handful of giant companies.

(10) World insurance markets are similarly dominated by a few dozen companies in the global mesoeconomy.

8 Owners and Controllers

Who controls the giant capitalist corporation? How is such control changing, and what does this mean for modern society?

There are various claims. The conventional wisdom, well established since Berle and Means (1932), is that ownership is now divorced from control and that top management, rather than holders of stocks and shares, controls top companies. Galbraith (1967a) challenged this claim as too simple, stressing a key control role for a technostructure of intermediate management.

Just how management controls business is important not only in terms of efficiency but also accountability. Many governments are concerned to gain greater accountability over big business, and a better match between its performance and the objectives of macroeconomic policy. But big business management tends to claim that this would prove unworkable because of the complexity of multidivisional, multinational enterprise, and the devolution of internal decision-making. Thus the structure of decision-making in business is not only a matter of managerial organisation. It also defines the frontiers of public and private power.

Moreover, while Berle and Means tended to dismiss the power of the dispersed shareholder, the rise of pension funds and their management by major institutions has changed the role of hitherto passive shareholders. It has already been seen that big financial intermediaries prefer big operating companies, and thereby aid and abet the process of concentration in the mesoeconomic sector. But such financial intermediaries now are so large that they may either lever indirect change in the policy of operating companies, or force their takeover and the loss of management autonomy. This power of finance capital versus operating management has been increased by the international liberalisation of capital markets since the late 1950s.

In addition, there is a joker in the pack in the form of the rise of trades-union pension funds and the increased block power of workers' pension schemes. For some time trades unions have been prepared to allow financial institutions to determine by their own criteria the use to which such funds are put, in whatever companies. But increasingly trades unions have become aware of the scope and scale of their own shareholding interest, and some have reflected this in a challenge to conventional management. Moreover, as shown in the recent argument of Weitzman (1984), it is not only those on the radical Left who are proposing an extension of worker shareholding in the modern economy.

8.1 Ownership versus Control?

Marx: Joint-Stock Capital

Marx was well aware that changes in ownership and control through the rise of joint-stock companies had transformed the role of the owner-entrepreneur. In Volume III of *Capital* he wrote of the transformation of the 'capitalist into a mere manager and administrator of other people's capital, and the owners of capital into mere owners, mere money capitalists'. As he put it very clearly: 'in joint stock companies the process of production, of course, is entirely separated from ownership of the means of production and of surplus labour. This result of the highest development of capitalist production is a necessary transition . . . of capital into the property of the producers, no longer as the private property of individual producers, but as the common property of associates, a social property outright.'

Thus, while Berle and Means (1932) are credited with pioneering work on the divorce of ownership and control in the 1930s, their insight had been presaged by Marx in the mid-nineteenth century. Moreover, one of the most penetrating analyses of the implications of the rise of the joint-stock company for ownership and control had been published more than twenty years earlier than Berle and Means, by one of the leading second-generation Marxists, Rudolf Hilferding.

Hilferding: Finance Capital

Hilferding's *Finance Capital* (1910) exerted a major influence on Marxists in his time and was translated into several languages. However, due in part to delays in negotiation with the beneficiaries of his estate, his work was not translated into English until 1981.

Hilferding recognised the implications of the rise of the joint-stock company for ownership and control. As he put it: 'Up to the present, economics has sought to distinguish between individually owned enterprise and the joint-stock company only in terms of differences in organisational forms.' However, the joint-stock corporation involves 'the liberation of the industrial capitalist from his function as industrial entrepreneur. As a result of this change the capital invested in a corporation becomes pure money capital so far as the capitalist is concerned. The money capitalist as creditor has nothing to do with the use which is made of his capital in production. His only function is to lend his capital and, after a period of time, to get it back with interest – a function which is accomplished in a legal transaction. So the shareholder functions simply as a money capitalist. The shareholder is not an industrial entrepreneur' (Hilferding, 1910, pp. 107–9).

Hilferding stresses that the joint-stock corporation is no longer the individual enterprise or an owner-entrepreneur but an association of capitalists, formed by each contributing a share of capital, with participation, voting rights and degree of influence determined by the amount of capital contributed: 'Hence the control of the enterprise as a whole is in the hands of those who own a majority of the shares' (ibid., p. 118).

Minority Control

However, Hilferding also was well aware of the possibility of Minority Control through a system of interdependent companies. He describes the process in the following way. Suppose a capitalist X with 5 million shares controls company A, whose share capital is 9 million. Company A now establishes a subsidiary company, B, with a share capital of 30 million and retains 16 million of these shares in its own portfolio. In order to pay for these 16 million shares, A issues 16 million fixed-interest debentures without voting rights. With his 5 million, capitalist X now controls both companies, or a total capital of 39 million. Following the same procedure, A and B can now create other new companies, so that X, with a relatively small capital, acquires control over an exceptionally large amount of outside capital. 'With the development of the joint-stock system there emerges a distinctive financial technique, the aim of which is to ensure control over the largest possible amount of outside capital with the smallest possible amount of one's own capital.' He observed that 'this technique has reached its peak of perfection in the financing of the American railway system' (Hilferding, 1910, p. 119).

Hilferding not only anticipated the main analysis of Berle and Means, but also the major forms of control which they identified in the modern capitalist corporation.

Berle and Means: Management Control

Berle and Means described management control as that in which ownership is so widely distributed or dispersed that no individual or small group has an interest large enough to dominate the affairs of the company. As an example, when the largest single shareholding interest amounts to only a fraction of one per cent – the case in several of the largest American corporations in the 1920s which they studied – no shareholder is in a position through holdings alone to place what they call 'important pressure on the management' or to use holdings as the nucleus for accumulation of the majority votes necessary for control.

Berle and Means stressed that such management control did not rest on any legal foundation as such, yet appeared to be comparatively secure when the stock or shares were widely distributed. They nonetheless emphasised that a controlling minority of shareholders may be dependent upon the co-operation of the management of the corporation, and also that a controlling management may have to accede to the demands of a strong minority in order to maintain its measure of control. They also allowed that it was not unusual for two or more strong minority interests to enter into a working arrange-ment by which they jointly maintained control, or for a minority of shareholders and management to combine to achieve what they called 'joint control' of the corporation (Berle and Means, 1932, pp. 78–83).

Analysing the 200 largest US corporations in the 1920s by proportion of shareholding wealth, Berle and Means found that nearly half of all firms, and nearly two-thirds of the top 200, were controlled by managers rather than shareholders. Minority control and control by 'legal device' was typical in nearly half of the top 200 companies. The categories of Majority Ownership or Outright Ownership accounted for only just over one tenth of the top 200 corporations and just over one twentieth of the wealth invested in them (ibid., p. 109).

Admitting that their findings were in a sense only a still photograph of a dynamic and changing situation, and also based in many cases on careful guesses, they concluded that 'their cumulative effect is such as to indicate the great extent to which control of these companies rests on some factor other than ownership alone, and more striking still, the extent to which the management has itself become the control. That 65 per cent of the companies and 80 per cent of their combined wealth should be controlled either by the management, or by a legal device involving a small proportion of ownership, indicates the important extent to which ownership and control have become separated' (ibid., pp. 84–110).

Managerial Revolution?

Berle and Means knew that their findings were significant. Describing the new corporate sector in terms similar to Marx's comparison and contrast of different modes of production, they wrote that: 'on the one hand [the corporation] involves a concentration of power in the economic field comparable to the concentration of religious power in the medieval church or of political power in the nation state. On the other hand, it involves the interrelation of a wide diversity of economic interests – those of the "owners" who supply capital, those of the workers who "create", those of the consumers who give value to the products of the enterprise, and above all those of the *control* who wield power' (ibid., pp. 309–10).

They were also aware of the contrast between the modern capitalist corporation and the model of enterprise in Adam Smith and his followers, commenting that the concepts of private property, private enterprise, individual initiative, the profit motive, wealth and competition which Smith employed in describing the economy of his time have ceased to be accurate in describing modern enterprise.

Adam Smith himself had emphatically repudiated the joint-stock corporation as a business mechanism, holding that dispersed ownership made operation impossible and claiming that: 'the directors of such companies being the managers of other people's money than of their own, it cannot well be expected that they should watch over it with the same anxious vigilance with which the partners in private co-partnership frequently watch over their own. . . . Negligence and confusion, therefore, must always prevail, more or less, in the management of the affairs of such a company.' Challenging Smith's assumption that private property indissolubly combined ownership and efficient control, Berle and Means bluntly showed that such unity had been shattered in the modern corporation.

Active and Passive Control

Distinguishing between *passive* property, i.e. shares, or bonds, and *active* property, i.e. the organisation which makes up the enterprise, Berle and Means also echoed a Marxist distinction between money or finance capital and the means or forces of production.

This had major implications for legitimation of initiative and the profit motive within modern capitalism. Berle and Means argued that 'as private enterprise disappears with increasing size, so also does individual initiative. The idea that an army operates on the basis of "rugged individualism" would be ludicrous. Equally so is the same idea with respect to the modern corporation.' They concluded that 'the profit motive has become distorted in the modern corporation.' Rather than being substantially reinvested in industry, the dispersion of profits to passive shareholders prevents them from reaching 'the very group whose action is most important to the efficient conduct of an enterprise'. They also observed that 'more could be learned by regarding and by studying the motives of an Alexander the Great, seeking new worlds to conquer than by considering the motives of a petty tradesman in the day of Adam Smith' (Berle and Means, 1932, pp. 303–8).

Managerial Capitalism?

But what does this mean in the late twentieth century? Has the managerial revolution resulted in a 'managerial capitalism'? If so, is it comparable in its claims as a mode of production, distribution and exchange to the broad sweep of Marxist theory?

Berle came closest to arguing this case in the preface, written in December 1967, to a new edition of his work with Means. Claiming that the modern managerial corporation 'has become, and now is, the dominant form of organisation and production', he also argued that it 'has proved a vital, albeit neutral, instrument and vehicle' for the five main driving forces of the twentieth-century American economic revolution, which were: (1) an immense increase in productivity; (2) the massive collectivisation of property devoted to production, with an accompanying decline of individual control and decision-making; (3) the dissociation of wealth from active management; (4) a growing pressure for greater distribution of such passive wealth; (5) the assertion of the individual's right to live and consume as he or she chooses.

But even in this later preface, Berle refers to 'the institutional economic revolution' of which the managerial revolution is part. Opening up these wider issues (only partly discussed in his earlier work with Means), Berle argues that the future lies increasingly with state capitalism. In particular he claims that 'in notable areas production for use rather than production for profit is emerging as the norm. Education, scientific research and development, the arts, and a variety of services ranging from roads and low-income housing to non-profit recreation and television constitute a few illustrative fields. Health will probably be – in part now is – such a field.' He also argues that 'increasingly it is clear that these non-commercial functions are, among other things, essential to the continued life, stability and growth of enterprise' (Berle, 1968, pp. xxv–vi).

Soulful Corporations

Such claims for non-commercial media, arts, education, housing and health have recently been challenged by the monetarist counter-revolution. But for a while this case was echoed in a debate on the 'soulful corporation' in the 1960s and 1970s, mainly conducted by management itself. Over the years a number of billionaires have established charitable institutions through which some profits were ploughed into art, education or welfare projects rather than into the further expansion of the companies which they controlled. Foundations such as those of Mellon or Tate, Ford or Nuffield, Carnegie or Rowntree have promoted non-profit projects and organisations – and the reputation of their founders.

But where private companies respect the public interest in matters which *directly* conflict with their private interests, such as the environment, this tends to reflect public demand embodied in legislation. Many nominally non-profit activities simply promote public relations or evade restrictions on direct advertising (such as cigarette companies sponsoring concerts and Grand Prix racing).

Thus, the heart of even the soulful corporation pumps on profit. Moreover, a problem for 'soulful corporations' is who decides the frontier between the world of profit and the realm of social benefit? The further the corporation moves into welfare programmes such as Berle's low-income housing, or urban renewal, the more it risks being brought into the political arena. Members of the public or public agencies might challenge aspects of central corporate strategy, ranging from misleading advertising or low-nutrition fast foods through to major environmental issues such as toxic products, pollution and acid rain. In the 1960s in the United States, some 'soulful' managers in big business were the targets of protest against the chemical weapons used in Vietnam. Having claimed interest in a welfare society they were indicted for promoting a warfare state.

8.2   Technocrats and Technicians

Veblen: Industry versus Ownership

Thorstein Veblen highlighted such issues in the modern American corporation, and argued that its claims to merit were entirely arbitrary. Veblen maintained that wealth was created by technology, resulting from the applied skills of working people themselves rather than through the manipulations of entrepreneurs. Indeed, he claimed that such entrepreneurs had in large part 'sabotaged' the progress made possible by the application of skilled labour.

In Veblen's argument the vested interests of big business have the power to levy tribute from the rest of the system. In a 'free economy', big business is free to exert power without 'counteracting influence' from consumers or government. Unlike the Anglo-Austrian theorists or Milton Friedman, Veblen did not believe that small and medium firms could challenge big business in the modern economy in such a way as to counteract the trend to concentration and oligopoly.

Absentee Owners

In his *Absentee Ownership* (1923), Veblen stressed that those who amassed fortunes from the proceeds of industry during the early period of modern capitalism from 1760 to 1860 were not necessarily pioneering entrepreneurs but in large part made their gains by shrewd investment and conservative undertakings in other people's enterprise. Yet he admitted that the period from the mid-eighteenth to mid-nineteenth century exhibited so much of the 'spirit of initiative and adventure abroad in the conduct of industry . . . as to have enabled the *captain of industry* to find lodgement in the popular belief: a man of workmanlike force and creative insight into the community's need, who stood out on a footing of self-help, took large chances for large ideals, and came in for his gains as a due reward for work well done in the service of the common good.'

Entrepreneurial Myths

Veblen's absentee owners are similar to those Berle and Means later described as passive capitalists. On the image of an active entrepreneur, Veblen commented that 'it is by no means easy at this distance to make out how much of popular myth-making went in to set up this genial conception of the captain of industry in the popular mind, or how much more of the same engaging conceit was contributed towards the same preconception by the many-sided self-esteem of many substantial businessmen who had grown great by "buying in" and "sitting tight" and who would like to believe that they had done something to merit their gains.' Observing that economists had classified the captain of industry, under the title of the 'entrepreneur', as a fourth factor of production along with land, labour and capital, Veblen argued that the image of the captain of industry disguised the role of 'those absentee owners who control the country's industrial plant and trade on a restricted output' (Veblen, 1948, pp. 377–81).

Technical Management

However, Veblen recognised that as industry grew bigger, employing both larger-scale capital and more workers, its increase in size necessarily implied a new structure of supervision, contact and control, with new relations between the employer-owner and the workforce: 'the employer-owner, and ever increasingly impersonal business concern, shifted more and more to a footing of accountancy in its relations with the industrial plant and its personnel, and the oversight of the works passed by insensible degrees into the hands of technical experts. So the function of the entrepreneur, the captain of industry, gradually fell apart into a two-fold division of labour, between the business manager and office work on the one side and the technician and industrial work on the other side. . . . The tangible performance of so much work as the absentee owner considered to be wise, fell increasingly under the management of the technicians' (ibid., pp. 381–2).

The Power System

Veblen was highly critical of what he called the cleavage between industry and business, and between technology and ownership. He argued that the price system had been taken over by business as part of the power system by which the process of concentration and centralisation occurred.

Veblen anticipated that the main potential countervailing influence within the system would come not through the process of competition between small and big business but by a transformation of the power system by those who directly served it. He saw this counteracting power emerging from those he called 'engineers', by which he meant technicians with the technological experience, information and skill indispensable to the everyday work of the economy (Veblen, 1921, chapter 1).

Contrasting so-called 'captains of industry' or top managers in big business with the 'engineers' on whom their entrepreneurship and profits depended, Veblen argued that the future of the modern capitalist economy depended on the question 'whether the direction of responsibility in the management of the country's industry shall pass from the financiers, who speak for the vested interests, to the technicians, who speak for the industrial system as a going concern'. He claimed that there was no third party qualified to make a bid to challenge the technicians' power, to redress the imbalance between big business and the mass of the working people as a whole.

Galbraith's Technostructure

The parallels between Veblen's 'technicians' and John Kenneth Galbraith's concept of 'the technocracy' are striking. In his *New Industrial State*, Galbraith stresses that the enemy of the market is not ideology but the technician, and much of his later analysis focuses on the role of what he calls the 'technostructure' in exercising a 'countervailing power' against the structures of big business. As he puts it, 'power has passed to what might be called a new factor of production, i.e. the association of men of diverse knowledge, experience or other talents which modern industrial technology and planning require' (1967a, pp. 33–59).

Galbraith's extension of Veblen's concept of 'counteracting tendencies' was indirect. In his earlier analysis of the American economy (Galbraith, 1957) he had held that organised labour could exert a countervailing pressure on organised capital. But by the 1960s he was persuaded that trades unions would not be able to countervail big business, especially in its privileged relations with government. Instead, he increasingly developed his analysis of the role of technicians or the 'technostructure'.

For Galbraith, technology and the technostructure both cause and respond to change in the economy. With new technology, demand grows for specialised manpower and an organisation capable of planning the introduction of sophisticated products or techniques of production necessary to command sales on modern markets (Galbraith, 1967a, pp. 13–20). For the small and medium firm, technology is simple and capital need not be large. But with growing size and complexity of operation, smaller owners tend to lose their power of decision-making to the technical experts within the enterprise and increasingly play a passive rather than an active role.

Technocratic Structures

In certain respects, Galbraith's technostructure does not differ from some arguments put forward by Berle and Means. But Galbraith sees the technostructure as qualifying the role of management executives in the planning of big business. He describes concentric circles of shareholders, production workers, lower-grade white-collar workers, executives, management and technicians in a way which lodges the power of decision in the inner group and especially with the technicians themselves.

Changing his metaphor, Galbraith describes the organisation of the new industrial system in the shape of a tall urn, widening below the top to reflect the need of the technostructure for administrative, co-ordinating and planning talent, for scientists and engineers, for sales executives, salesmen, advertising personnel etc., and widening still further for white-collar workers, and then narrowing towards the base for those qualified only for what he calls 'muscular and repetitive tasks' (Galbraith, 1967a, p. 149).

According to Galbraith the technostructure are not shareholders rewarded by performance through a share in profitability in the manner assumed in the conventional competitive model. He allows that pecuniary compensation becomes generous as one moves towards the inner circle of the corporate control structure, and that for senior executives in large corporations it can on occasion be spectacular. But he claims (ibid, p. 158) that 'few things are so certain as the absence of any close relationship between compensation and effort in the inner circles of the mature corporation. At the centre of the corporation, compensation is only a part of the larger motivational system'.

The Military-Industrial Complex

Galbraith stresses that one of the crucial roles played by the technostructure is in relation to government spending and in particular to military spending. This is 'the fulcrum on which the public expenditure system rests' (ibid., p. 229). His recognition of the importance of the relationship between big business and the government – derived in part from his experience as the key price controller during the wartime period – is both more extensive and more explicit than found in most economists in the United States. In a real sense his *New Industrial State* and his *Economics and the Public Purpose* (1973) develop not only a theory of big business but also a theory of the modern capitalist state and its role in the United States economy. These issues and the increased role of the military-industrial complex will be examined in detail in *The Political Economy* (Holland, forthcoming).

8.3 Active Control

As already indicated, how managers manage is not only relevant (a) to internal efficiency, and (b) to the range of strategies and tactics which the corporation can adopt at home or abroad, but also (c) to the accountability of private to public power.

Role and Control

To clarify the nature of control we need to specify who takes what decisions in the modern capitalist corporation. Broadly, the activity of any enterprise can be broken down into decisions about the following:

- Which product, service or sale.
- Why and by what criteria (market share, revenue or profit maximisation).
- When – including timing in relation to the business cycle.
- Where – including local, regional, national or international markets for traded goods or the location of investment.
- With whom – including joint ventures with other companies or on government contracts.
- What price – including initial market-entry pricing or profit creaming, price reductions during the growth or mature phase of the product, and transfer prices in trade between subsidiaries.
- How – including technology and labour process, plus the source and scale of external finance or internal funding allocation.
- What cost – including labour costs and whether the location of production is in a more or less developed region or a more or less developed country, as well as promotional costs, advertising, etc.

Top Managers and Technocrats

It is already evident that the larger the company the greater the range of organisational structures available to it in the direct or indirect control of its operations. It is clearly unlikely that a modern multiproduct, multidivisional or multinational company of the kind analysed in Chapter 4, would allocate strategic decisions to technicians or technocrats rather than the most senior management level. This distinction between who manages at secondary levels and who primarily controls such secondary management, from the top, may become clearer through considering individual decisions and their control implications.

Top managers depend on a technostructure of other managers and technicians for provision of information, research and development, the design or drafting of products or services and their market profile, analysis of the current state of the market and projected future trends, evaluation of future options at home or abroad, interfacing with government and its departments, labour relations, etc. Much of this information is both technical and complex, involving sophisticated evaluation of the costs and benefits under different circumstances.

Nonetheless, strategic decisions affecting either the company as a whole or subsidiary divisions and activities in different sectors or regions of the world economy are still taken, monitored, cleared or vetoed by a very few people at topmost board level. Certainly, the more important the quantitative impact of the decision for company finance or performance, the closer decisions will be taken to the top, either of the area, division, or the head office itself.

Defensive Management

Obviously practice differs from company to company and depends on the activity concerned. In a large undiversified corporation in an established market, where there has been little long-term variation in technology or market share, the senior controllers of corporate strategy may concern themselves mainly with financial control and supervision. If they do so, however, they risk forgetting to modernise or diversify, and may join those at the bottom of the industry class whom investors and financial intermediaries recognise as having gone to sleep. Such sleepers, on waking, may find themselves confined to a defensive market strategy, hanging on for life to what they have, rather than being able to break through to new ventures or new markets.

Offensive Management

At the other extreme, in a conglomerate company operating in unrelated activities, senior controlling management may demand detailed evaluation of the full range of the eight main criteria outlined on page 286 before deciding whether to take over an existing enterprise or seek to penetrate a new market. Such 'offensive' go-getting intervention was typified by Litton in its heyday. According to Roy Ash, Litton's president, 'our kind of man is the kind you usually think of as an entrepreneur – he thinks and acts as though he's in business for himself'. But that did not mean for Litton that they were in their own independent business. Moreover, when Litton ran into problems in the 1960s these may have been due to too long rather than too short a rein from head office.

Target Management

In a well-structured multidivisional company, overall control may be exerted at senior level on supervisory evaluation of profit and loss criteria, target rates of return on capital, and market share. But when this happens in the big league, things can go badly wrong at the divisional level, as seen in the market-sharing ring organised in General Electric, Westinghouse and other companies in the US power-generating sector, and cited in Chapter 5.

Further, the limiting of key decisions to senior executives does not imply abdication of top-level control. When IBM faced an anti-trust suit on its activities, it is alleged that it daunted the trust-busters by offering them access to several buildings filled with computerised records. But senior executives do not cart such tapes into the boardroom for key decisions. Indeed, they pride themselves on conspicuously smaller files, carried in slim attaché cases. An executive summary of the key issues, after preliminary and secondary evaluation, may well take only a couple of pages. In a sense, it should do so if the technostructure has done its job properly in servicing top management decision-making.

Products and Parents

It is clear that greater senior management resources are needed to introduce a new product or service onto the market, than when the product (or service) has become standardised, routine and mature. The ironing-out of initial difficulties, deciding which managers are best at divisional or operating level in new jobs, the terms of purchase of inputs, the decisions whether to internalise or externalise input provision, and the conditions of sale or leasing of output, call for disproportionately greater management involvement at senior level in the 'new' phase of a product cycle, than when the market is 'mature'.

However, especially under current conditions when many multinational companies produce more abroad than at home, the relation between subsidiary management and overall strategic control tends to be closely supervised by parent companies.

Permanent Monitoring

In the early days of multinational capital (as with international diplomacy), communications difficulties and the need to gain special knowledge of local conditions gave some autonomy to the managers of local operations. But today the electronic information revolution has transformed the situation. Permanent satellite time (as shown in *The Global Economy*, Chapter 6) is now booked by many multinational companies for the continuous transmission of highly detailed information from foreign subsidiaries to the parent company. Vice presidents of companies working abroad by broad world region such as Europe and Latin America ignore the parent board – and their presidents – at their peril.

Some multinational managers claim that their organisation is so complex and their activities so widespread that they seek to recreate the market within the multinational by allowing freedom of initiative to local management. But over the whole range of multinational companies, in industry, services and finance, the centralisation of information and the control process is increasingly evident.

For example, when Chrysler took over Rootes in Great Britain in the 1960s, the telex and telecommunications system was so centralised that even detailed matters concerning plant operation passed not between the Ryton plant in the English Midlands to Chrysler's UK head office in London, but direct via satellite to the United States.

Seniors and Subordinates

In addition, while it is clear that some freedom of initiative may be granted to the management of subsidiary companies over the prices charged on transfers of goods and services, or transfer prices, it is rare for the head office of the company to remain uninformed of the transactions. It is claimed, perhaps apocryphally, that Mobil once devolved so much on transfer pricing that it ended up believing its own declared losses, and its senior managers were then preoccupied for months with determining its true profit-and-loss situation. Certainly in leading multinational companies operating in the United Kingdom at the time of the November 1967 devaluation, it is well known that the UK subsidiaries were instructed not to change any transfer prices in trade with subsidiaries of the same company abroad, or follow through devaluation with lower prices in sales abroad to third parties without first clearing the price changes with the head office of the parent company outside Britain.

This is not to suggest that top management in modern big business constantly supervises what is done, why, when, where and how in each subsidiary in the national and global economy. It is precisely this role of supervision and evaluation which is performed by what Galbraith rightly calls the technostructure. But it is clear that the strategic decisions are passed or blocked, promoted or demoted, by a handful of managers at the most senior levels.

It could hardly be otherwise in any modern corporation which achieved strategic coherence or had the capacity for market initiative or response. For instance, if top management did not co-ordinate the activities of subsidiaries, the various area divisions of multinationals might actually start competing in price terms against themselves – good for some in the short run, but potentially catastrophic for the company overall.

Personal Incentives

In this context a new dimension of owner-management becomes significant. Criticism has been made of Berle and Means' argument, with claims that the top managerial class is still the largest single group in the shareholding population. Miliband (1969), for example, has shown that top-level managers in Europe and the United States tend also to be significant stockholders.

The argument does not challenge the claim that managers rather than shareholders control the modern capitalist corporation. But it does show that it is over-simple to assume that the most senior controllers of capital in mesoeconomic companies are not influenced by stocks or shares from which they directly benefit. In both Europe and the United States it is not untypical for the board members of leading companies to hold either tens of thousands or hundreds of thousands of shares in the companies they manage.

The salaries of top executives are increasingly linked to company performance. Such personal incentives, commonplace in the United States for some time, are also becoming typical in the UK. For instance, Table 8.1 illustrates the relation between personal and company earnings for the top 20 of a *Datastream* survey of the 100 highest-paid directors in British private companies. The survey showed that their salaries increased by around a fifth in 1983–4 against an average increase in the pre-tax profits of their companies of just over a quarter. Only ten per cent of the top 100 executives had rises markedly in excess of company profit increases, and when a company did not do well most directors' salaries were curbed accordingly. A PA Personnel Services study in 1985 also showed that, from a sample of 145 companies, 62 per cent now take account of individual managers' performance when fixing fringe benefit levels (*Sunday Times*, 19 May 1985).

TABLE 8.1   The Top Twenty Executives: Earnings and Company Performance

	Company	1984 salary £000	% pay increase 1983–84	% rise in pre-tax profits
1	BOC	772	48	30
2	BSR	526	8	29
3	Heron	446	2	53
4	Burton	348	75	44
5	Lonrho	323	22	19
6	Lex	308	62	24
7	STC	297	48	53
8	ICI	287	68	67
9	Plessey	248	6	20
10	BP	242	32	33
11	Hill Samuel	242	92	—
12	Shell Transport	210	4	32
13	BAT	200	33	43
14	LRC	200	28	25
15	Hawley	199	114	121
16	Tate & Lyle	198	46	21
17	Kleinworts	186	96	—
18	Ultramar	182	23	84
19	Hanson	177	26	86
20	Wedgwood	174	61	266

Source: Datastream and *Sunday Times*.

8.4 Passive Control

Ironically, while the personal earnings of British top executives are increasingly linked to company performance, real corporate growth and profits bear only a tenuous relation to stock-market ratings.

Listening to radio or watching television, one could be forgiven for assuming that the state of the stock market reflected the state of the real economy. In practice it does not. For most of this century, the British stock market has financed less than a twentieth of the investment needs of British industry. As shown in Table 8.2, by 1984 nearly 90 per cent of the source of funds for UK industrial and commercial companies was from retained earnings and only 3 per cent from ordinary shares. In the United States in 1983 such corporate self-financing from internal sources was 76 per cent; in West Germany 75 per cent, and in Japan a little less than 70 per cent. The percentage for small companies was lower (*The Economist*, 7 June 1986).

TABLE 8.2   Source of Funds in British Industrial and Commercial Companies (% of total funding)

Year	Total internal funds	Issue of ordinary shares for cash
1978	78	4
1979	75	3
1980	65	3
1981	64	5
1982	63	3
1983	78	5
1984*	89	3

* January/September.
Source: UK *Financial Statistics* and Parliamentary Question, 22 January 1985.

This increased independence from external finance has been part of the syndrome by which the boards of big business have achieved relative autonomy in their active management control.

However, the market ranking of stocks and shares can have a very considerable influence on the readiness of financial institutions to subscribe external funds, whether bank credit or bond issues. A leading company with a poor share rating is likely to find more difficulty in gaining major external finance than a 'triple A' company or corporation whose real rate of return and market dividend return is both positive and healthy. Thus, by fortunate coincidence for the senior management who are also shareholders, there is a mutual benefit to both their companies and themselves from a positive return on assets, just as there was for the classic owner-entrepreneur.

The Rise of Pension Funds

External funding posed no special difficulty for leading companies with proven market stability during the main period of postwar economic growth. But the negative control sanctions exerted by funding institutions over even major corporations has increased since the early 1970s with recession or depression in key markets. A degree of recession-proofing is available to dominant enterprise by the extent to which price-making power makes it possible to compensate for falling sales by raising prices. But in companies in sectors with chronic overcapacity or in leading companies with undue concentration in a narrow range of activities, pressure both from banks and pension funds can exert major influence over corporate strategy. As illustrated later, this is especially evident when major companies enter into crisis, such as Chrysler, British Leyland or Citroen–Peugeot in the 1970s or the major German combine AEG in the early 1980s. It also reflects the almost silent revolution in ownership and control represented by the rise of pension and insurance funds.

As shown in Table 8.3, at the end of 1957 the assets of self-administered pension funds in the UK had a market value of just over £2 billion. Within twenty years this had increased to nearly £30 billion, and by 1983 to over £100 billion.

TABLE 8.3   The Assets of UK Pension Funds

Year	£ billion
1957	2.1
1967	6.6
1977*	28.8
1982*	84.2
1983*	106.2

* Net of short-term liabilities and long-term borrowing.
Source: Parliamentary Question, 7 February 1985.

Although the growth of such funds in part reflected increased inflation in the 1960s and especially the 1970s, the value of pension funds increased some fifty times compared to a threefold overall price increase. While such funds certainly were not held uniformly by everyone in Britain, their value amounted to the equivalent of some £2,000 for every man, woman and child in the United Kingdom in 1983. By 1981 the inflow to pension funds of some £7 billion a year was equal to the total value of UK manufacturing investment.

As the Wilson Committee (Wilson, 1980, p. 92) observed: 'the explanation of the growth in pension funds, and in the pension business of the life assurance companies, lies largely in the improved level of benefits provided by occupational pension schemes'. While the majority of the schemes, as indicated in Table 8.4, are in the private sector, the share of local authority and other public-sector bodies has been rising fast. Moreover the private-sector schemes include trades-union pension funds which now represent a major share of private equity capital in the United Kingdom.

Concentration and Centralisation

Most pension fund assets are owned by a relatively small number of funds, typical of the mesoeconomic sector. For example, the top ten pension funds in Britain in 1984 owned a quarter of total pension assets, while the top 200

TABLE 8.4   The Source of UK Pension Fund Assets*

	£ billion		% of total	
Source of funds	1982	1983	1982	1983
Private-sector funds	48.9	62.5	58.0	58.9
Local authority funds	11.4	14.3	13.5	13.4
Other public-sector funds	24.0	29.4	28.5	27.7
Total, all funds	84.2	106.2	100.0	100.0

* Net of short-term and long-term borrowing; end-year figures.
Source: Parliamentary Question, 7 February 1985.

funds accounted for over half (Parliamentary Question, Trade and Industry, 7 July 1986). As the 1980 report on pension funds of the British Trade Union Congress (TUC) emphasised, although there were over 85,000 pension schemes with over 11.5 million members, nearly 70,000 of these had less than a hundred members.

Over half the pension funds' annual investments are in company shares. As illustrated in Figure 8.1, by the end of 1983 the pension funds, insurance companies and trust companies together owned 56 per cent of private company shares, with the pension funds alone accounting for nearly 30 per cent and trust companies (unit trusts and investment trusts) for 7 per cent. This confirms the simple extrapolation made in 1980 by the Wilson Committee that the pension funds, insurance companies and trusts could own more than 70 per cent of British industry by the year 2000.

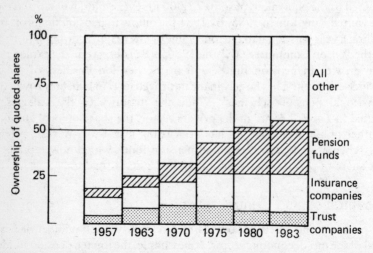

FIG. 8.1   Who owns British industry

The Multinational Trend

The mesoeconomic structure of the funds themselves is mirrored in the companies in which they invest. Altogether pension funds and other institutional investment in UK equities has predominantly concentrated on the shares of large national and multinational corporations. These large companies (the top 250) represented about four-fifths of the total market worth of all companies quoted on the stock exchange at the end of the 1970s.

As the 1980 TUC report stresses, since the abolition of exchange controls in 1979 the pension funds have increasingly invested in overseas equities at the expense of British companies or other investments. By the early 1980s, private-sector pension funds were investing more in overseas equities than in UK equities. This resulted in a doubling of the level of overseas assets in their portfolios. Moreover, nearly 90 per cent of pension fund equity investment has been in the top 250 companies, the largest 50 of which base nearly two-fifths of their total production overseas (GLC, 1984, pp. 49–50).

The US Pension Funds

American pension funds constitute one of the largest pools of private capital in the world. In 1984 the combined public and private funds' assets totalled some $900 billion, and estimates predict that they may increase to over $4 trillion – or nearly double the current GDP of Third World countries – before the end of the century. Public pension funds currently constitute about a quarter of these assets, and union-negotiated funds around a half, with the other quarter controlled by private employers.

There has recently been increasing concern from members of the public and of trades unions within the United States about the direction of investments by pension funds, particularly investments in companies operating in countries with repressive regimes or poor human rights' records. The AFL-CIO has established four principles for socially responsible investment: (1) to increase employment through reindustrialisation, including manufacturing, construction, transportation, maritime and other sectors necessary to revitalise the economy; (2) to advance social purposes such as workers' housing and health centres; (3) to improve the ability of workers to exercise their rights as shareholders in a co-ordinated fashion; and (4) to exclude from union pension funds any investment in companies whose policies are hostile to workers' rights (GLC, 1984, pp. 141–4). Such issues of 'socially responsible investment' are analysed in a wider context in Chapter 9.

Acquisition and Acquiescence

To what degree are financial institutions such as pension funds active or passive in their approach to decisions taken in operating companies?

While there is no doubt from the previous evidence that the top management controllers of capital also are significant owners, there remain the related questions whether and in what way either stock-market finance or credit availability exert a negative constraint on the operations of different kinds of companies. The issue is not simply a question of concentrated versus dispersed shareholdings in the manner analysed by Berle and Means. Nor is it simply a question of the extent to which share dispersion gives management relative freedom to pursue corporate strategies. It concerns the extent to which indirect, secondary or passive control can be exerted by stock markets or financial institutions on the operations of different kinds of firms.

The Private Entrepreneur

Clearly in the case of a microeconomic company, the influence of stock markets and financial institutions can be very considerable. This is mostly the case where the company is a growing enterprise in a new market, and seeking to expand its activity over and above the rate of self-financing available through retention of some profits from cash flow. In the United States the venture capital for such firms, especially in such markets as electronics or bio-technology, is highly developed. Financial intermediaries are prepared to take risks on the frequently plausible assumption of very high returns and rewards. However, the nature of the market and the firm, its chances of entry and survival are clearly related to the degree to which it can count on at least passive support from financial institutions. 'Go it alone' small firms tend to have less chance of gaining external finance or a high credit rating from banks than microeconomic firms which are, in practice, component suppliers to other enterprises.

The Sinclair Saga

The influence of the public sector and public purchasing is evident in some success stories of the growth of small to medium firms in both the United States and Britain in recent years. Many small firms in Silicone Valley in California have been able to flourish in a market sustained by public spending, whether straightforward defence or NASA contracts. A degree of certainty over the medium term has been introduced by the public and private contract procedure.

In a classic case in the United Kingdom, Sir Clive Sinclair – a pioneering introducer of low-cost miniature calculators, computers and television sets – managed to penetrate the market over a number of years and compete successfully with large-scale US multinationals and Japanese conglomerates. At one stage Sinclair held two-fifths of the UK home computer market. But this was not achieved by a combination of entrepreneurship and private risk capital. He could not gain sufficient private finance from the stock market to follow through his initial micro-calculators with the range of ZX80/81, Spectrum and QL computers. Through Sinclair, the Inmos and Nexos companies ran up substantial losses of some £50 million. It was the state as entrepreneur, in the form of the National Enterprise Board, which under-wrote the risk necessary to help gain the company's entry into the new market.

The incoming 1979 Conservative government gave Clive Sinclair a knighthood for his entrepreneurship, but took away the state support which had made possible his earlier market share. Sinclair's companies fell subject to predatory bids made by more established companies in the mesoeconomic sector such as ATT, which in 1984 offered the Conservative government some £45 million for Inmos. A year later, Sir Clive was under further pressure from the financial institutions to transfer control of his company from an innovator to a 'top manager'. By 1986, without state support, and with an inadequate financial base to 'ride out' to an effective multidivisional and multinational management structure, he was forced to dispose of his remaining assets to Amstrad for a knock-down £5 million cash.

Internal versus External Funding

It has already been indicated that share issues have only a barometric relationship to the performance of leading companies – in other words that they give an indication of market performance and credit rating rather than constituting a significant source of finance.

Berle, in both the later and early editions of *The Modern Corporation and Private Property*, stressed the changing origins of finance capital. Already, at the time he was writing, more than 60 per cent of capital was internally or 'price-generated'; 20 per cent was borrowed from banks, and less than 20 per cent was in the form of stocks, bonds, or personal savings channeled into the firm through insurance companies and pension funds.

While this indicates that internal finance is more important to the company than external finance, outside funds nonetheless may prove crucial either to its new investment, staying abreast of a new technological frontier, or simply surviving (in the case of bank credit, if it is a small company).

In such a context the distinction between passive and active control by financial institutions becomes especially relevant. With successful expansion, a major enterprise may be able to self-finance an important new venture in an entirely new market. In other circumstances it may find that an outright unwillingness by financial intermediaries to subscribe a major bond issue, or a qualified approval resulting in inadequate external financing, may prove sufficient to deter senior management from undertaking the venture concerned.

It also has to be stressed that there are considerable variations between countries and regional world markets in the relative degree of willingness of banks and financial intermediaries to undertake a positive role in the control of companies. In West Germany, bank representation on supervisory boards of companies means a considerable degree of control over corporate strategy. By contrast, British banks and pension funds have been mainly passive partners. In other words UK commerical banks and the managers of pension funds have by and large been prepared to invest or disinvest in companies, depending simply on financial performance in relation to other investment opportunities. It has been rare in Britain for either a major bank or a pension fund to seek to directly concern itself in the corporate strategy of an individual company.

Pension Fund Pressure: Vickers, Krupps and Others

Nonetheless, there have been important exceptions in the past which may prove tomorrow's new rule. For example, the Vickers company has established its record in armaments production for over a century. But Vickers' record in building ships and tanks (at one time providing a self-contained armaments industry to the British government much as Krupps did to the Third Reich) depended very much both on its professional competence and on high profit margins from military contracts. In the civil area, especially since the Second World War, Vickers failed to diversify effectively. After considerable success with the Viscount turbo-prop aircraft, it failed to manage the transition to pure jet aircraft. Similarly, its Hawker-Siddely luxury car, sold at a premium from the 1930s to the 1950s, was designed essentially as a staff car for military purposes with a civilian spin-off. The motor-vehicles division of Vickers failed to penetrate the civilian car market successfully and closed down.

By the 1960s, with sophistication in military technology favouring more modern and especially electronics-based companies, and without successful diversification into civil production or services, its key stockholder – a major pension fund – instructed Vickers that it needed to 'diversify' its activities on a rapid scale if it were still to invest its resources in the company. This sanction prompted Vickers to diversify into both the office equipment and property market, through Roneo-Vickers and office premises including the

Vickers Tower on Thameside in central London and office development and warehousing elsewhere. It also encouraged the company to divest and close down several of its manufacturing operations in the UK – despite the fact that they were still making a positive rate of return – in favour of purchasing existing, more modern and more profitable manufacturing facilities abroad.

Similarly, Krupps and other heavy engineering companies in West Germany have faced considerable difficulties with investing institutions and especially the banks, while chemical companies worldwide, faced with a slump in the demand for heavy chemicals and many of their derivatives, have found themselves under increasing financial pressure either from private financial intermediaries or state credit institutions. They have been told to diversify, or stop trading. Likewise, Thorn-EMI in Britain in 1985 was told by the financial institutions to divest or expect diminished funding.

8.5 Capital and Labour

Of the eight areas of control in the modern corporation identified on page 286, it is striking that only part of the seventh and eighth – the labour process and labour costs – are traditionally open to union negotiation in the advanced capitalist countries. Even in this area of wages and working conditions, direct bargaining scope has recently been reduced by the decline of traditional industry and the blue-collar labour in which trades unions hitherto have been best organised.

White Collar and Blue Collar

In general, white-collar workers are better paid with more secure conditions of work, salary and pensions than semi-skilled or less qualified blue-collar workers. They also have a closer relationship with the control structure of the modern capitalist corporation than blue-collar workers. The information revolution and computerisation of routine management processes demote many traditional management functions and promote the importance of the white-collar programmers and qualified data processors on whom the senior management in the modern corporation depend for the effective operation of the enterprise. Thus professional competence, expertise and the scope for initiative in new products and processes in the successful corporation in large part depend on the expertise of white-collar workers. In principle, white-collar workers can exert negative control, at least on some activities of the corporation.

Negative Control

The most obvious sanction, or negative control, of both white- and blue-collar labour in the modern capitalist corporation is the withdrawal of labour. With national microeconomic capital, and with protracted disputes, such action can frustrate and negate corporate policy objectives. Nonetheless, such sanctions tend to be limited to wages, working conditions, and – to a lesser extent – pensions and post-employment benefits.

Taking the broad range of the control categories previously described – ranging through what is produced, why, when, where, with whom, how and at what price – the negative control of either white- or blue-collar labour tends to be restricted to the remaining category of *what cost*. This covers (1) the wage or salary bill; (2) superannuation or retirement benefit; (3) salaries or wages; (4) hours worked; (5) vacation or holiday periods; and (6) the labour or work process (including the quality of working conditions, the extent of break or meal times, safety in conditions of work and, on occasion, the rate of the production process especially where assembly-line production is concerned).

The Labour Process

The innovators of the professional white-collar sector, whether in pharmacology and genetic engineering, avionics or electronics, provide a qualification to this picture. Leading designers, technicians or research scientists can withdraw labour not only by collective industrial action but also by taking up their bed and moving to another company or starting their own enterprise. But this section of the white-collar working population is an exceptional elite able to negotiate its own terms and conditions of work. Its 'control' is a personal sanction, concerning job prospects or mobility, not a collective sanction over the company's corporate plan or strategy.

Similarly, the upper echelons of white-collar workers in the Galbraithian technostructure undoubtedly are able to confine, refine or expand the terms of reference by which the most senior controllers of leading corporations are able to determine what shall be done, why, when and where, by virtue of a considerable degree of control over the information process on the basis of which top-level decisions are undertaken.

'Fordism'

Nonetheless, for most white-collar workers and certainly for blue-collar workers, the labour process is standardised and routine. Mass production implies its own rate, speed and scale of production, with co-operation from a labour force whose process of work is determined by machinery rather than themselves. Widely known as 'Fordism' after Henry Ford's pioneering introduction of mass production with the Model T ('any color you like so long as it's black'), such a mechanised labour process leaves blue-collar labour little sanction or countervailance of management other than stopping the machines themselves. It is the elite of the white-collar technostructure who are called upon to prepare memoranda for top policy decision-making in the corporation and who have some prospects of upward mobility. For blue-collar and most white-collar workers, theirs is less to reason why the corporation functions than to accept or reject decisions and working conditions taken for them by others in the management hierarchy.

Limited Control

Moreover, for both white- and blue-collar workers the negative sanction of industrial action may have limited returns. If the industrial action concerns what is known as a 'work to rule', then the dispute with management may not involve loss of basic earnings. However, if it involves strike action and the withdrawal of labour then both white- and blue-collar workers forgo the earnings which they otherwise would have gained through employment and also may face the risk of dismissal. While trades-union organisations in both Europe and the United States have developed considerably in the twentieth century, especially in the postwar period, strike pay and unemployment benefits for the families of those engaging in withdrawal of labour tend to represent a fraction of that income which could be gained from full-time or overtime employment.

It is exceptional for industrial action through the withdrawal of labour – such as the British miners' strike of 1984–5 – to last more than a few days or a few weeks. In those cases where the action runs into several months, it is possible that the management of the enterprise will agree to settle the dispute on terms which are favourable to those who have withdrawn their labour. But a multiplant national company may close down the factory or branch which is experiencing the dispute. A multinational company may simply go abroad. A nationalised industry backed by the government, like the National Coal Board in Britain in 1984–5, may simply gain a subsidy for its losses and, with whatever difficulty, ride out the dispute.

Constraints

In other words, negative control by either white- or blue-collar labour tends to be limited to wages and working conditions. These mainly impact on the 'how' of production. If they prompt management in the multinational big business sector to go abroad, it may locate an increasing share of investment and employment in those countries in Latin America and South East Asia – or South Africa – where corporate freedom to decide on what is done, why, when and how is not circumscribed by free trades unions and is aided by much lower wage costs. In many such countries the existence of trades unions – quite apart from industrial actions, stoppages or strikes to improve wages and working conditions – is illegal and enforced by the courts, the police or the armed forces.

Thus, the sanctions exerted by either white- or blue-collar labour on multinational corporations is relatively limited. For the elite in the white-collar sector prepared to spend time abroad in order to gain access to the higher rungs of the management echelons in the home country, industrial action or the withdrawal of labour is virtually non-existent. Individual problems by and large can be ironed out by the 'career planners' of the personnel departments of multinational companies.

Blue-collar workers can expect considerably more leverage in those sectors of activity where the capital intensity and scale of investment by multi-national corporations poses a risk if located in less developed countries liable to political instability. The short-term advantages of location in such regions of the world economy may be offset in the longer term by an overthrow of the existing order and nationalisation. This is one of the factors which has led multinational organisations to divide production among different countries in global markets. There still is considerable scope for multinational management to trade off unfavourable labour relations in an individual economy in the developed regions of the world system against other economies and countries. A period of poor labour relations in some developed countries may prompt a multinational company to locate its next major plant elsewhere.

Owner-workers

Ironically, while the workers in the developed capitalist countries have seen the decline in recent years in their means of direct control over the activities of big business – especially in the multinational sector – as well as a weakening of their bargaining position since the mid-1970s in terms of the rise in unemployment, they nonetheless gained an indirect benefit in the postwar period in several developed countries, especially from a silent revolution in the funding of big business. In countries such as Britain this has taken the form of the rise of pension funds, whose major share of equity finance has already been described. In principle, this means a new dispersion of individual shareholding between social groups and classes. However, in practice the dispersion is limited, while in cases of privatisation as in Britain in

TABLE 8.5 Privatisation and Concentration: Public Enterprise Sold in the UK Economy Since 1979

	Issue price p	High/low p	No of shareholders	No of shareholders at float
Amersham (1982)	142	392/186	6,600	63,800
Assoc British Ports (1983)	112	625/129	n/a	n/a
British Aerospace (1981)	150	608/170	130,000	260,000
British Telecom (1984)	130	278/180	1.6 million*	2.1 million
Britoil (1982)	215	208/160	245,500	452,000
Cable & Wireless (1981)	168	369/284	211,000	218,500
Enterprise Oil (1984)	185	154/128	14,200	13,700
Jaguar (1984)	165	578/171	43,000	125,000

1 Figures for BT may exclude the joint holders and employees in the employee share scheme.
2 High/low share prices from first dealings to 30 September 1986.
3 Issue prices are fully-paid. The following sold further tranches: Assoc British Ports (270p, 1984), British Aerospace (375p, 1985), Britoil (185p, 1985), Cable & Wireless (275p, 1983 and 587p, 1985).
Source: HM Treasury and *The Observer*, 26 October 1986.

the 1980s, workers tend to sell shares for their cash value rather than seek to exert control through collective ownership.

Table 8.5 shows the results by 1986 of the purported share dispersion intended by the Conservative government in its privatisation of public enterprise from 1981 onwards. The number of shareholders at the time of flotation had shrunk tenfold for Amersham, by half for British Aerospace, by nearly a half for Britoil, by a third for British Telecom and by nearly two-thirds for Jaguar. Thus individual employees had sold their shares after issue for cash, while control of major shareholdings had passed to institutions or other private investors. In contrast with the mythology of widened share ownership embodied in Conservative ideology, the classic mechanisms of centralisation had begun to take effect. As shown by the difference between the issue price on privatisation and the subsequent stock-market valuation (both high and low), most employees had benefitted from short-term cash gains. But ownership had become centralised in other hands.

Unequal Participation

The reality can be put in a historical context by considering the changing structure of ownership and control through the evolution of the modern capitalist corporation. The founder's capital and total control of the owner-entrepreneur gave way increasingly from the mid-nineteenth century to joint-stock companies in which the shares of either dispersed or concentrated ownership expanded the capital of the enterprise. Then, from the later nineteenth to earlier twentieth century, with the rise of the modern corporation, the expanding stock of capital was complemented not only by stocks and shares but also by pension funds.

The role of various categories of labour in production and distribution and the form of ownership in companies (direct or indirect) bears an analytic relation to social class. It is clear that the controlling board of the modern corporation gains access to preference shares and stock options not available to middle and junior managers, let alone white- and blue-collar labour. In a real sense, such 'top managers' are also part of the upper class within the economy and society.

While the technostructure within the administration may not have access to certain grade A or level 1 preference shares, it is nonetheless likely to invest in pension funds and investment trusts. But this may not be the case for lower, middle or executive white-collar workers. These tend to be eligible for company pensions, but unable to get into the 'surplus shifting' or surplus disposal exercise available to the middle and upper echelons of the technostructure and board.

Semi-skilled and unskilled labour whether or not hired by large companies (for instance in the construction industry) tends to be lower-working-class in status and also to be excluded from company pension schemes. In principle such workers should have their national insurance paid for them by the company. In practice, as is well known in an industry such as construction in Britain through 'lump' labour, not even the national insurance contribution may be paid by the employer.

From Passive to Active?

In Britain, where trades-union pension funds by the later 1970s already totalled some two-fifths of total corporate equity and were still rising in the early 1980s, the argument was made in a debate in the House of Commons on his report on financial institutions (Wilson, 1980) by former Prime Minister Harold Wilson that there was no need to press for nationalisation of financial institutions since the public already controlled them. Sir Harold was followed by the present author, who pointed out that ownership does not necessarily imply control for individual shareholders, or the workers, for the foregoing reasons. (*Hansard*, vol. 997, 23 January 1981, cols 604–10.)

Nonetheless, while control over the portfolios of trades-union pension funds is largely passive at present, union fund managers are showing interest in a more active control in Britain to restrain the massive foreign outflow of such funds such as occurred following the abolition of exchange controls by the 1979 Conservative government.

Such issues relate to broader questions on the relative control of resources in modern capitalist society. Many managers and owner-entrepreneurs in micro companies oppose trades unions outright. Others, especially in mesoeconomic companies, recognise that big business may benefit from big unions, representing the broad range of their workforce. Negotiation on wages or the work process may be tiresome but also tends to be more efficient than a series of individual agreements with groups of workers, or dealing with problems from the shopfloor as they arise. But when unions are recognised in private enterprise, managers tend to view their role as that of a parliamentary opposition. They may concede the union's right to *oppose* management on wages and working conditions, training or pension rights. Yet managers rarely agree that unions should be able to *propose* changes in corporate policy, and negotiation stays mainly in the area of wage bargaining. Moreover, unlike the principle of parliamentary or political opposition, managers do not concede the right of unions periodically to change the board and run the companies themselves.

Beyond the Wage Bargain

Some unions in the advanced countries have challenged such exclusive management control, and demanded an increased say in how resources are allocated by big business. In the United States this has been seen in a series of new demands by the United Auto Workers. In West Germany, unions in many cases have the right by law to membership of supervisory boards of big business, with the right to contest the policy of the executive board. In Belgium and France, governments have also challenged exclusive management control, insisting on bilateral agreements or contracts especially where significant public money is involved in either aid to investment or public purchasing. In some cases governments, as in France since 1982, have insisted that such Planning Agreements or Planning Contracts be tripartite rather than bilateral. In principle this means the involvement of unions, as well as management and government, in negotiation of changes in corporate plans.

Some such tripartite agreements, as in both France and Italy in the 1980s, have involved regional planning bodies, and affected location decisions which otherwise would remain the exclusive prerogative of management. On occasion also, both central and local governments have required public shareholdings in the equity of aided enterprise, as part of the process of gaining a trade-off for the use of public money in the private sector. In many cases, they are thereby giving private companies a capital infusion which they could not gain from private institutions or on stock markets. This has proved especially significant in smaller firms in declining sectors of activity, which lack the profit rate or growth to attract private capital. Public funding, and sometimes shareholding, has been their best chance of shifting from a 'defensive' to an 'offensive' market strategy. But it has also been resisted by many management representatives who appreciate that minority state ownership may in effect mean major state control, paralleling the indirect control through holding company structures analysed by Hilferding and Berle and Means, and cited earlier in this chapter.

Relevance to the Planning System

In effect, the issue of ownership and control no longer simply concerns the relation between private shares and private corporation managers. The dynamics of unequal competition between micro and meso enterprise, and the problem for smaller firms of transition from traditional to modern markets, has involved increased funding, ownership and control by a range of government or para-governmental bodies. Similarly, big business in what Galbraith has with reason called the 'Planning System' has found it increasingly hard to plan its own corporate strategy without co-operation from trades unions in the labour process, and from government in public purchasing or capital assistance.

This does not mean an uncontested forward march of labour or government into the boardroom. In Britain since 1979, there has been a government counter-offensive against both the rights and roles of trades unions, and against government intervention in ownership or control. Moreover, when the post 1974 Labour government sought to introduce Planning Agreements in the meso sector, the Confederation of British Industry fought a successful battle against disclosure of information on corporate plans to government departments. Part of this campaign involved the claim that bilateral or trilateral negotiations with government and unions would not be possible because of the complexity of decision-making in the modern corporation, with its multiproduct, multidivisional and multinational structures. On the other hand, as indicated by the analysis in this chapter, strategic decision-making of interest to both governments and unions is still actively controlled by the top management board of big business. Decentralisation of product planning, market tactics or research and development does not mean denial of control, from the top, in any successful corporation.

Hierarchy and Innovation

One of the more interesting implications of the analysis by Brankovic (1987) of the process of innovation in market economies has been his finding that the main obstacle to technical progress comes less from the workforce than from management itself. Summarising the findings of a ten-year investigation, Brankovic concludes:

> Resistance does not come from workers but from managers. The major reasons for such resistance include fear of the unknown; suspicion that automation and reduction of the number of workers under their control would lead to a loss of prestige and the esteem which they enjoy as leaders of companies with a large number of employees. Some observers feel that resistance is strongest among middle managers who are afraid of losing their jobs in a new set-up required by flexible automation.

As Brankovic argues, such attitudes by middle management register not only on top managers but also on shareholders. By contrast, his international research project found that workers in technically progressive companies were in general prepared to accept change where this resulted in higher income. Such an argument is pregnant with implications for the potential of innovation in any economy which overall can achieve innovation and productivity gains without loss of personal or social income, as analysed in more detail in *The Political Economy* (Holland, forthcoming).

It is perhaps unsurprising that Brankovic found that resistance to the introduction of new technology was least evident in the Japanese economy (and in particular the big business sector in Japan), where the combination of guaranteed lifetime employment for core workers with early retirement benefits avoided the confrontation of innovation versus employment typical of other market economies.

8.6   Summary

(1) The Berle and Means thesis on the managerial revolution claimed not only the decline of the owner-entrepreneur but also a divorce between ownership and control in the modern capitalist corporation.

(2) By implication the Berle and Means thesis suggested both a managerial revolution and the emergence of managerial capitalism in which access to control was open to talent rather than simply inheritance.

(3) Hilferding's Finance Capital thesis was more sophisticated than Berle and Means in showing the relation between banks and blocks of shareholders whose combination could both constrain and where necessary control the modern corporation.

(4) Until recently the Finance Capital thesis was unavailable in English translation, and influenced only those economists who could

command it in other languages. For some time it was also more relevant to the German and US economies (where banks and trusts held shares in individual companies on an extensive scale) than to other economies.

(5) The globalisation of financial markets in recent years has both modified and extended the application of the Hilferding Finance Capital thesis.

(6) Within individual economies such as the UK, the postwar rise of shareholdings by insurance companies and pension funds has given a handful of mesoeconomic finance companies control of half the shares in British industry.

(7) In continental European economies, private banks or public banks and state credit institutions are major shareholders in leading private companies. In Japan the close liaison between big business and big banking has been established since the late nineteenth century.

(8) Within both financial and non-financial companies the evolution of multifunctional, multidivisional and multinational structures has not essentially qualified the control of top management over the top companies in the world economy.

(9) Constraint on top management autonomy in the modern big business sector is increasingly exerted by institutional shareholders and lenders in the mesoeconomic sector.

(10) Trades unions have not yet matched their passive role as investors in big business through pension funds with a coherent strategy to exert control through shareholding on the modern capitalist corporation.

(11) Resistance to the introduction of new technologies comes more from middle-rank management afraid of losing its command prerogative than from other workers. Such resistance is less evident in those economies which have achieved a combination of high productivity and high employment, such as postwar Japan.

9 Power and Accountability

According to liberal market theory, welfare is best expressed by market choice, and state intervention should umpire fair play. By the same token, the state may give a helping hand to small and medium enterprise and restrain abuse of competition or a dominant market position. Aids and incentives should be indirect rather than direct, dealing with the general climate of competition rather than with individual firms. According to this theory, public enterprise has grown, should not grow further, and in most cases should be privatised. If companies are to be held to account for their activities it should be by consumers rather than public agencies.

9.1   Private and Public Interests

Theory and Practice

The divorce between such market theory and the realities of big business market power has now assumed dramatic proportions. Chapter 2 has shown that the claims made for market freedom by Milton Friedman and his school bear little relation to the reality of state intervention either in the United States, or in the European, Japanese or South East Asian economies. Chapter 3 has argued that the theory of imperfect competition still has relevance to product differentiation by big business within its own product range, but that perfect competition is virtually irrelevant to the modern market economy. There still is a microeconomic sector of small and medium firms, but the rise of the mesoeconomy – multimarket, multidivisional and multinational companies – has transformed conventional market theory. Unequal competition prevails in all markets, and consumer sovereignty is exerted as much by big buyers on big suppliers, as by individual consumers.

Market and Non-market

Market or 'exchange value' was never considered the be-all and end-all by classical economists. Adam Smith recognised that 'use value' or the usefulness of a commodity was not necessarily measured by whether it need be paid for on the market, or the price it could command. More recently Schumacher has reminded us that 'Society, or a group or an individual within society, may decide on an activity for *non-economic reasons* – social, aesthetic, moral or political' and that these activities may well be more important than any which are undertaken through the market itself. On these grounds he stresses that the judgement of market economics is 'an extremely *fragmentary* judgement; out of the larger number of aspects which in real life have to be seen and judged before a decision can be taken, economics supplies only one – whether a thing yields a money profit *to those who undertake it* or not' (Schumacher, 1974, p. 35).

Observing further that the profit calculus is necessarily narrow in relation to the wider issues affecting life and living, Schumacher also observes that cost and profit criteria 'exclude all "free goods", that is to say the entire God given environment, except for those parts of it which have been privately appropriated. This means that an activity can be economic although it plays hell with the environment, and that a competing activity, if at some costs it protects and preserves the environment, will be uneconomic' (ibid., pp. 35–6).

The Natural Environment

Market theory tries to deal with environmental and social costs through the analysis of economies and diseconomies. Thus, reflecting the argument analysed in Chapter 6, textbook theory allows that the unpaid-for external economies may accrue to beekeepers from the pollen in adjacent orchards which they do not own and for which they do not pay. Such theory, in a standard example, also allows for external diseconomies where people living near a polluting factory suffer social costs which can be measured in market terms – such as the cost of the health bills arising from infections or disabilities caused by the pollution.

But there are other social costs, for those directly or indirectly concerned. For instance, how does one measure the psychological loss to families from the premature deaths of workers infected by silicosis in mining or asbestosis in asbestos production? Moreover, the textbook concept of local pollution from factory emissions has been transformed into continental or global pollution. Thus emissions into the atmosphere of acid from high chimney stacks in Britain pollutes the environment of West Germany or Scandinavia, destroying areas of forest or vegetation thousands of miles away.

Permanent Pollution

Similarly, high-technology industries which have been applauded as symptoms of economic progress have, in some cases, produced environmental pollution to which no monetary compensation is readily applicable. Thus nuclear power generation at the Windscale/Sellafield plant in North West England has polluted the sea off virtually the whole of the British western and southern coasts. Waste materials dumped in corrosive casings either underground or in the sea risk polluting water and the natural environment for thousands of years.

More directly, modern industries such as motor vehicles and aircraft have brought mobility gains for those who can afford to use them, but imposed social costs on many who do not, especially those living in urban areas close to airports and major roadways. Smog afflicts some cities more than others, notably Los Angeles or Athens, where in the latter case the problem has become so intense in summer that the government has restricted road use by private vehicles to alternate days for alternate licence plate numbers. Emission controls on exhausts can reduce but not solve the problem of higher lead content in the blood of those adjacent to major road systems, with evidence of not only damaged health but also possibly, for children, retarded learning.

Economies and Diseconomies

While such examples from the natural environment have with reason attracted increased public attention and protest in recent years, other divergences between private profit and social costs have received less attention.

Standard economic theory on external diseconomies focuses in a micro framework on environmental pollution. But there is a wider framework of divergence between social or public policy priorities and private or corporate objectives which now entail major interest conflicts. Substantially, these conflicts reflect the changing structures of market power, and the significant macroeconomic impact of policies pursued by mesoeconomic enterprise.

Foreign Investment

Such new economies and new diseconomies cover the macroeconomic aggregates which are part of the main range of government economic policy. They include, for instance, foreign investment – whether portfolio or direct. By conventional logic, enterprise will decide whether to invest abroad in terms of remitted returns from foreign profits. Such remitted profits are registered in national accounts, and represent a nominal 'plus' on the balance of payments. But multinational capital does not invest abroad only to gain remitted profits in direct investment. It does so to extend or defend its global position relative to other multinational capital in foreign markets. It does not necessarily finance the bulk of its foreign investment from domestic capital in the parent company in the parent country, nor of necessity remit profits rather than re-invest them abroad.

De-Industrialisation

In principle, according to conventional theory, the process should be neutral rather than negative for the parent country. But decisions made by multinational companies to invest abroad frequently relate to lower investment or de-industrialisation in the parent country, as has been the case with the United Kingdom and to a considerable extent the older industrial regions of the United States through the 1970s and 1980s. Lower investment sets in train the negative circle of lower innovation, lower productivity and lower employment – all of which are crucial to government macroeconomic objectives.

According to market theory, the companies following such a strategy should not be able to do so indefinitely without penalties of loss of market share and profit. In the British and US cases, this certainly has been the case to some extent through Japanese penetration of 'home markets'. Yet some penetration increases visible imports without necessarily offsetting invisible earnings from portfolio investment abroad. It also further weakens longer-term competitive potential by throwing domestic producers into 'defensive' market strategies. Where foreign multinational companies choose direct investment rather than trade, whether or not through fear of protection, they can decrease 'spread' effects on domestic industry through leakage of purchases for components abroad, and thereby further diminish the feasibility of rebuilding an indigenous industrial base.

This is not to claim that the objectives of public policy and private profit always diverge. In many cases they clearly coincide. But the coincidence is no longer automatic, or susceptible to adjustment by government shifting the gears through changes in taxation, interest rates, exchange rates or conventional competition policy. Certainly, the new divergence is more pronounced and more problematic than any consonance allegedly occurring in the long run through a freer working of market forces.

Anti-Trust and Anti-Monopoly

Conventional anti-trust or anti-monopoly policies clearly depend for their effectiveness on conditions which have for some time been surpassed in the modern market economy.

So long as the model of perfect or imperfect competition implied equal costs and normal profits, it could be assumed by trust or monopoly busters that higher-than-average profits reflected an abuse of competition. But with the unequal costs from unequal competition in the national or international economy such assumptions are no longer secure.

For instance, early in the product cycle a company may 'profit cream' at a phenomenal rate. But by the time this has been drawn to the attention of the 'powers that be' by consumers, the firm may have dropped price to more normal profit levels. While probably acceptable to the authorities for a small-scale entrant to a new market anxious to maximise revenue early in the product cycle to finance and sustain its survival, such 'profit creaming' may be less acceptable from a multinational major on a range of products which simply thereby increase its self-financing and potential predation on smaller companies through takeover. The multi-product major nonetheless will be likely to escape the authorities while increasing its share of one or several markets.

Similarly, it is difficult for the competition or anti-trust authorities to establish without legal challenge that a low price sustained during inflation by a market leader amounts in practice to the double sanction of no-entry pricing or elimination pricing in an individual market. Perversely, while such pricing will tend to increase concentration or centralisation (through softening up competitors for takeover), its contribution to the government's anti-inflation policy could gain public accolades and the preference of the company's senior management to a representative position on a Monopolies or Anti Trust Commission. This is apart from the range of transfer- pricing practices including the under-invoicing of exports and over-invoicing of imports which are employed routinely by multinational companies in their trade with subsidiaries in different countries, and rarely challenged by those government departments still operating on textbook premises of equal costs and normal profit mark-ups.

9.2   Private and Public Strategies

In the private sector, it already is clear that there no longer is a standard market strategy for typical firms in typical industries. Similarly, no government concerned to countervail concentrated economic power in the public and social interest can any longer stand back from the market and umpire today's new game by yesterday's old rules.

Multiple Strategies

Especially, policy-makers need to be aware that the same company may be pursuing different strategies in different markets at the same time. Some of its activities may broadly accord with the conventions of normal profit and 'fair' competition, serving the consumer and increasing social welfare. Others, within the same company, may reap super-normal profits, abuse dominant positions, and impose costs both on the consumer and on governments which are seeking to fulfil strategic objectives for which they have a political mandate.

For instance, in terms of Figure 9.1, a multiproduct company may be maximising sales and revenue in one of its product lines while stabilising sales and revenue in another. A multi-sectoral company may be defensively hanging onto what it has in one market while offensively go-getting and maximising growth in another. Again, a private enterprise company may behave in a different manner in its private market operations from its public spending contracts.

FIG. 9.1   Multiple corporate strategies

Taking the public spending axis in Figure 9.1, a public enterprise may well operate under different constraints from a company in the private sector. Also, in Figure 9.1, the range of price tactics pursued by national or multinational, defensive or offensive, maximising or minimising firms will depend very much on where their specific activities are focused in the overall corporate policy framework, and how such tactics serve the strategic ends of the companies concerned.

Thus, a multi-sectoral company may pursue offensive takeover and elimination-pricing tactics, of the kind analysed in Chapter 5, in some of its divisional or area markets. It may be especially aggressive in the area of the military-industrial complex, with a strategy of 'forcing an entry' into new public markets.

Yet the same company may prove relatively defensive in other regional or national markets, pursuing policies of no-entry pricing, or normal profit mark-up, or seeking administered-price leadership in the manner of rule-of-thumb, focal-point or barometric pricing.

Similarly, a company with multi-market and multinational range in the mesoeconomic sector, may maintain good public relations in the civil industrial complex, conscious not only of public image but also the teeth of anti-trust action. Thus – if its management has talent to match its salary – it may consciously pursue policies of sales or revenue stabilisation in the civil industrial field, with a price restraint commended as laudable, while at the same time aggressively pursuing profit maximisation in the military-industrial market where deception, overcharging, collusion or sheer corruption are simply regarded as 'rules of the game'.

Variable Tactics

In choosing between administered price leadership, normal profit mark-up or capacity maximisation, the same mesoeconomic or multinational company will trade off various feasible price tactics against complementary regional, national or multinational strategies. The choice of pricing techniques will depend upon the global overview. For instance, capacity maximisation will be traded against exchange-rate changes, and the scope and limits of transfer pricing (analysed in *The Global Economy*, Holland, 1987).

Figure 9.1 outlines the range of options open today not only to different firms but to the same firm in different product markets in different countries. This is the reality of mesoeconomic and multinational enterprise versus the national microeconomic company of the competitive model. Instead of debates about 'the aim' of the firm we are now in a world in which it is routine that different strategies and tactics for different products markets will be pursued in different countries by the same company, according to the dictates of its own central profit interest.

Public Priorities

Private companies are not alone in seeking to trade off a range of objectives against feasible strategies and tactics. Governments, all the time, do the same. As shown in Figure 9.2, they may pursue an export offensive to maximise growth, while also adopting an import-defensive strategy to defend domestic employment. Their 'front door' attitude to foreign trade and foreign investment may well be matched by a 'back door' concern with national and regional development priorities.

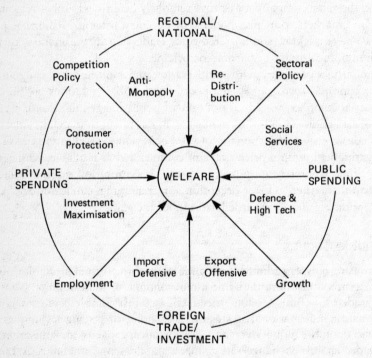

FIG. 9.2   Multiple public strategies

In contrast with profit maximisation for private companies, a main concern of governments may well be combining investment maximisation with consumer protection. But in a market framework, neither of these may be compatible with anti-monopoly or anti-trust policies, which thereby restrain the growth of private productivity from economies of scale.

Similarly, governments may seek to preserve welfare objectives wider than consumer choice alone, yet find themselves in a dilemma within the conventional market paradigm, since greater incentives to enterprise through reduced taxation thereby reduce the tax revenue available for public spending.

Society and Welfare

Some governments are more serious about welfare than others. But, as indicated in Figure 9.2, welfare in the broad sense is central to any government's public objectives. Those in office tend to defend their record in terms of the overall welfare of producers and consumers, those in work and out of work, rather than baldly backing the rich and strong, and sending the poor and the weak to the wall. In reality, of course, concepts of what welfare, for whom, why and how much vary as widely as the political spectrum. For Mrs Thatcher and President Reagan, specific welfare programmes have a low priority, or are being cut as a means of widening the gap between those in work and those without it, although they would deny that such cuts diminish overall national welfare.

The argument relates to the incentives seen to be necessary to gain efficiency in a market economy. One of the key features of market policies endorsed by some governments is projection of the interest of 'the firm' and 'the entrepreneur' through to the national economy. But a key contradiction for such policies now lies in the fact that there is no single standard, or 'representative', firm to which the paradigm of the market can be applied.

The Tax Burden

It was central to the Keynesian revolution that the economics of profit and loss crucial to firms was inappropriate when applied to national budgets. In a recession, firms in deficit risked going under. But governments with tax surpluses would reduce demand and further depress the economy. Similarly, Keynes stressed that expansion tends to generate more expansion, and cuts more cuts. But conflicts between private interests such as profit, and public welfare objectives such as full employment, have been served by the Friedmanite or monetarist counter-revolution in recent years.

Small firms or their representatives in trade associations rarely take account of the Keynesian argument that lower tax revenue and lower public spending in turn lowers demand for private enterprise. Similarly, some governments pursue market policies based on saving and 'self-reliance'. For Mrs Thatcher there are laudable 'Victorian' values and for President Reagan the principles of homespun, homestead America.

Likewise, small-scale microeconomic entrepreneurs see themselves as burdened with taxation. In their view, if only government would 'get off their backs' they could reinvest more profit, employ more workers, and pay higher wages. They assume that big government rather than big business is the main barrier to their own expansion.

Small Business

What small firms and their apologists rarely recognise is that even with no tax burden and no constraints from government legislation they have next to no chance of unlimited expansion in markets dominated by big business. As stressed in Chapters 4, 5 and 6, the hopes of any inherent restraint on the growth of big business through the market mechanism are analytically unfounded. Smaller firms have held onto markets where it does not pay big business to intervene due to insufficient demand to allow scale economies with minimally efficient plant.

As we have seen in Chapter 5, where there is evidence that small firms have created more new jobs, as in Birch's 1974–76 sample in the United States, less than a tenth of these have been in manufacturing and most have been in face-to-face customer services or 'satellite' supply to big business (Birch, 1979). Where concentration either has not increased or has decreased, as in sectors of US manufacturing, this has been the result either of technical progress and capital intensity displacing labour, or through more successful competition from big business abroad, especially from Japan.

Big Business

The big business sector is more sensitive to such issues precisely because it appreciates the real nature of unequal competition in modern capitalist markets. It knows that virtually no small company poses a threat to its survival, even if it may occasionally encroach on a single market or product division. It is aware that the real competition comes from its own league – national or multinational – in the mesoeconomic sector.

Big business also tends to be more sensitive to the real role played by public spending and social programmes in the welfare state economies. Many multinational companies appreciate that while they can exploit labour in Third World countries at a fraction of the cost of labour in developed countries – as we saw in Chapter 6 – they also need high public spending in the welfare states of the advanced capitalist countries to realise the sales and profits which they cannot achieve in Third World markets.

Not least, unlike the local Rotarian in small business, big business can readily appreciate that it needs high welfare spending in the advanced capitalist countries to educate its own personnel. General Motors, Ford, Unilever and Shell are very big business. But they do not want to be obliged to establish their own universities and business schools, rather than cream talent from a wider range of higher education institutes. In the same way, such companies can easily run in-house management training courses for staff once recruited. But there is no way in which they could supplant the state in secondary education for the millions of youngsters from whom a mere handful will become their executives and a small number their employees. In reality, for such reasons, as well as its benefit from public purchasing, big business by and large understands and accepts big government, even though it wants it on its own terms.

Regional and Urban Development

In addition, as indicated in Figure 9.2, governments may be concerned with the redistribution of resources towards less developed regions or urban areas. This may be attempted through a fiscal incentives policy. But in terms of the analysis of Chapter 6, with unequal competition between regional and multinational companies, it is clear that government is beating industry with carrots and attracting it with sticks. It is not that firms have profits so high that they can afford to ignore regional investment incentives and grants. Rather, precisely because profit is important, they cannot afford to accept assistance from governments for locating in problem regions when the gains on costs from going multinational so much exceed the incentive gains from going multiregional.

Likewise, the incentives offered in inner-city areas by so-called 'free enterprise zones' may abolish business rates or local taxation, eliminate planning controls or public enquiries and even suspend general legislation on employment protection. In the perception of some policy-makers, this should represent a sizeable gain to entrepreneurs, measurable in saved time, saved costs and increased profits. In the British case, before becoming Chancellor of the Exchequer, Conservative MP Sir Geoffrey Howe endorsed such an enterprise-zone approach on Friedmanite lines, arguing that 'independent countries like Hong Kong and Singapore have been entirely free to make themselves magnets for enterprise' (Sir Geoffrey Howe, 1978). Later, in government, the Conservatives scheduled several such zones around the United Kingdom.

But the incentive argument was by and large spurious. A reply to a parliamentary question put by this author in 1983 showed that rates (or local taxes) on business in Britain as a whole amounted to only one per cent of total industrial costs, rather than the crippling burden claimed by some companies (*Hansard*, 21 December 1983). Some small firms welcomed the new 'enterprise zone' legislation because it gave them freedom to ignore a range of environmental and social controls. But other small firms complained of discrimination since they could not bend or suspend the rules obtaining elsewhere. Most of the enterprise which moved to the zones was found to have shifted the location of existing business rather than created entirely new enterprise. Big business by and large maintained a discreet silence during the enterprise-zone debate, since such gains as were available in the scheduled zones were nothing in comparison with those which they had already achieved, for years, by going multinational.

9.3   National and International

Export Offensives

Conflict between the public and private interest – with different effects for different kinds of firm – can and does occur in the arena of foreign trade. For instance, as indicated by the different objectives of the private and public sectors in Figures 9.1 and 9.2, governments may commit themselves to a national 'export offensive' aiming at a minimum to generate sufficient export revenues to strengthen the balance of trade, and at a maximum to promote 'export led' growth.

But small firms typical of the micro sector may not respond to the 'lifting of the tax burden' or lowered exchange rates by which governments seized of the competitive model seek to restore some kind of balance-of-payments equilibrium. In practice they may be less concerned by domestic taxation than by their inability to mobilise any effective counter-offensive to domestic or foreign competition without recourse to state funding of the kind to which their competitors abroad have become accustomed over many years.

In effect, one of the biggest problems faced by small firms is not big government but big business. It is not the short-term burden of corporate taxation which inhibits market growth, so much as the dynamics of unequal competition between micro and meso enterprise on a global scale. For instance, in practice, one of the main barriers to an 'export offensive' by small national firms is the dominance of foreign markets by large multinational companies which could respond to such an offensive by dropping 'entry barriers' abroad or lowering 'elimination' prices on them in their home markets, on the lines already analysed in Chapter 6.

Alternatively, multinational big business may choose a defensive strategy in the domestic market of a mature economy – to prevent anti-trust or anti-monopoly action by governments, or to avoid destabilising the market share of other leading firms, thereby maximising existing investment capacity without undertaking investment in entirely new plant. The multinational may well pursue an offensive investment strategy, but abroad rather than at home, either substituting foreign production for domestic exports, or reducing the rate of growth of domestic exports.

Import Defences

Likewise, as shown in Figure 9.2, a government may also seek to pursue an 'import defensive' policy, for a range of reasons. One strategy may be protection through tariffs or through non-tariff barriers. Another reason may be on the basis that only a protected home market can ensure fuller plant utilisation and economies of scale in domestic production to breach the critical threshold which makes possible low unit costs for competitive exports. Alternatively, on a macroeconomic basis, the government may not seek to block import trade outright, rather than aim to restrain the rate of growth of imports.

While such a strategy may benefit domestic production and employment by reducing imports, new techniques open to multinational capital such as transfer pricing can seriously qualify its effects.

The techniques of transfer pricing are analysed in detail in *The Global Economy* (Holland, 1987). But their mechanisms are in essence simple, and relevant to the scope and limits of the market economy. They amount to overstating the input price from one subsidiary to another over and above a normal 'cost-plus' level. This can have three main effects in multinational trade: (1) overstating imports, (2) understating exports and profits, and (3) inflating the final price level. What amounts to an internal economy through either profit maximisation or tax minimisation for the multidivisional and multinational company, therefore registers significant external diseconomies for the national economy through (a) the escalation of the value of imports and the import bill, (b) tax avoidance and the reduction of tax revenue, and (c) inflation of the final price level over what would obtain with more competitive cost-plus pricing.

Transfer pricing is not necessarily a conspiracy against the public interest susceptible to easy monitoring through conventional competition, anti-trust or anti-monopoly policy. The analysis of the range of pricing techniques open to mesoeconomic business shows that the concept of a normal industry price and normal profit has been superceded by multiple prices and profits, at different phases of the product cycle, depending on strategies of no-entry, takeover or elimination pricing.

Nor are techniques such as transfer pricing necessarily efforts at tax evasion rather than tax avoidance. If one leading firm begins such practices, inflating input or import costs as a means of understating profit, and thus tax, others are bound to follow suit – or lose retained earnings and the self-financing necessary for survival in a further round of the competitive struggle.

'National Champions'

Reference has already been made to the rise of 'entirely new' sectors of activity, where electrical industry is supplemented by electronics, calculators by computers, or mere aviation by aerospace and avionics. Modern policy-makers in general are well aware of the significance of such change, and employ a range of compromises and devices to promote it in their national interest. Thus governments have widely used public spending, public purchasing, public enterprise, and grants and incentives to seek to promote sufficient scale economies for large national suppliers of modern goods and services.

But governments have twofold problems. First, they need to ensure that their 'national champions' (Vernon, 1974) can stay within reach of the expanding 'technology frontier' of new industries or services. Second, as illustrated in Chapter 6, they have had to promote private-sector inter-national joint ventures, or countervail the private sector by multinational public-enterprise joint ventures with mesoeconomic business abroad, in order to mobilise the research and development necessary to 'stay in the field' with the scale necessary to achieve the continually raised threshold of scale economies in production.

Neither response may be sufficient to preserve an autonomous national enterprise in a multinational economy.

Balanced and Unbalanced

In turn, the twin pressures for international joint ventures or combined multinational production raise fundamental questions for the viability of national industrial policies. They are relevant to the issue of balanced or unbalanced growth in both more and less developed economies. This concept was formulated initially in the context of under-development by theorists such as Ragnar Nurkse (Nurkse, 1958). Nurkse argued that what could be called a balanced intersectoral policy could promote self-reinforcing beneficial effects, as the inputs for industry A promoted purchases for industries B to n. Thus 'a wave of capital investments in a number of different industries' could stimulate self-generating growth or development.

In the development context, Nurkse was especially concerned about the promotion of such a 'supply side' broad wave in basic industries, thereby contesting the emphasis on 'demand side' specialisation in international trade in development economics. But his argument for an intersectoral supply-side economics is also relevant to the problems faced by governments in developed countries which are seeking to stay at or in reach of new technology frontiers. Reinforcing and promoting success in a single modern sector, dominated by one or a few 'national champions' may entail higher risk and lower returns than a broader based policy promoting research, development and production in a range of mutually reinforcing activities. For instance, staying only in aircraft production without a national aero-engine producer, or avionics without aerospace potential, will be a one-way path down a high technology cul-de-sac rather than a breakthrough to new technology pastures.

There is a further dualism in most developed and less developed countries between the public and private sectors. We have seen in Chapter 2 how federal, state and local government in the United States initially ventured beyond basic infrastructure or industry into public or state enterprise in manufacturing and banking. Such an action of the public sector has been paralleled this century in Europe, where frontiers between the public and private sectors are more open, and the sectoral structure of the economy more 'mixed' than in the United States today.

Nonetheless, the state has mainly intervened to subsidise agriculture, restructure traditional industry or salvage failing enterprise rather than venture into the higher risk capital areas of new technology. In the latter areas, it has only rarely combined public purchasing on the demand side with a 'balanced growth' of supply-side public enterprise (for instance within state-owned public telephone and telecommunication systems purchased from state-owned equipment suppliers). In Britain, it is reversing the process under the second Thatcher government, with the privatisation of telecommunications. In Western Europe, public enterprise typically represents a tenth or less of total output, and a twentieth of total employment in the national economy. (Only France and Italy show significantly higher shares.) The result is an unequally mixed economy, with the manufacturing or financial sectors of the economy overwhelmingly composed of private, mesoeconomic and multinational companies.

Workshops or Talkshops?

With multinational capital so dominant in sectors in different countries, how can national governments pursue a meaningful sector policy in one country? Some sectors in basic loss-making or advanced low-profit activities may be in public ownership, but the intermediate broad range of industry and finance will tend to be controlled by private companies owing no special allegiance to, or subject to no special leverage from, national governments. Tax incentives and subsidies bite little or not at all in wage-cost-sensitive sectors. As shown in Chapter 6, multinational companies have more incentive to go to intermediate newly-industrialised countries with markedly lower wages and major cost savings which outstrip even the payment of total investment costs by government subsidy in developed countries.

Indicative planning policies tend to be undermined or qualified by the multinational spread of the mesoeconomy within and between individual sectors. Such sectoral planning is well known in the European context from the examples of the French Modernisation Commissions and the British National Economic Development Council. Useful in principal in disaggregating national economic objectives for investment, output and productivity down to the level of sectoral targets, such committees risk relegation to 'talkshops' rather than 'workshops' if they have no direct or indirect leverage on the mesoeconomy of the multinationals which dominate the modern sectors of the economy. Their recommendations at best become binding for the public sector and voluntary for the private sector, with a resulting imbalance in overall policy.

Public Priorities

If market strategy is to prove a viable dimension of economic policy, it needs both to account for and gain increased accountability in the mesoeconomy. This implies both an intrasectoral and intersectoral dimension to economic policy. To account for the asymmetry and imbalance of markets, governments in the first instance need to be able to identify the *inter*sectoral dynamics of change, including:

- Which sectors are growing or declining, in relative or absolute terms for both output and employment, and for what reasons?
- In declining sectors, what is the social cost or benefit, national or international (e.g. for Third World countries) of speeding or arresting their decline?
- In growing sectors, which are expanding fastest or have the highest growth potential, and which are at, within range of or falling behind new technology frontiers?
- What is the intersectoral balance or imbalance between domestic supply and demand, and where are supply bottlenecks or underproduction leading to high import propensity?
- What is the scope for public policy, public purchasing or public enterprise in achieving a more effective balance in the sectoral structure of the economy?

Public Policies

But policy-makers also need information which is not immediately transparent from market performance. They therefore need to identify the *intra*sectoral dynamics of change, including:

- What share of individual markets is supplied by meso and micro-economic enterprise, broadly defining the meso sector by four- or five-firm concentration ratios, or those firms which account for the upper half of activity?
- Who are the market leaders in either price or profit, and how are they leading, by what strategy and with which effects?
- Who are the sector leaders, are they growing or declining in share and are they innovating closest to the feasible technical frontier for the sector?
- Which are the led, or 'satellite', firms within the sector, dependent for their output on other firms in the same or other sectors, and how vulnerable are they to subcontracting for individual mesoeconomic enterprise?
- Which are the laggard companies, and are they falling behind through internal inefficiency and failure to innovate, low growth in traditional markets, unequal competition with mesoeconomic leaders, or abuse by such leaders of a dominant market position?
- What is the relative national and multinational structure and the relative export and import profile of the meso and microeconomic enterprise within the sector?
- What are the main implications for public policy, public purchasing or public enterprise of prevailing and projected intrasectoral structure?

9.4 Accounting and Accountability

If public authorities and agencies are to gain accountability of market power in the modern capitalist economy, they need methods of accounting which are aligned with the reality of multisectoral and multinational enterprise. Conventional national accounting does not fit the bill, any more than it gives an adequate measurement of social welfare. Such limits in social accounting have given rise to various proposals for new means of accounting for welfare, taking environmental and other factors into account. These are considered, and also extended, in the context of welfare economics and the economics of distribution in *The Political Economy* (Holland, forthcoming). In the present context we focus on the sectoral structure of economic activity, and its implications for the micro, meso and macroeconomy.

National Accounting

Modern national accounting was profoundly influenced by Keynes, and in one sense measures what Keynes at the time thought important. This is not surprising granted the gathering impact in the last ten years of his life of *The General Theory* and his major influence on the institutions of the international economy which emerged (just before his death) at the end of the Second World War. Keynes's emphasis was on overall macroeconomic phenomena, on the circularity of national income and expenditure, and on both gross and net (or additional) economic aggregates.

In some respects, none of this was entirely new. Adam Smith, following William Petty and others, had stressed the distinction between gross and net — or in his terms, 'neat' — revenue. Marx had advanced on Smith by recognising the identity of income and product aggregates. But until 1940 there were no systematic evaluations of national income and expenditure. Professional economists in the previous twenty years had pioneered new principles of accounting, but it was only after the outbreak of the Second World War and the acceptance by government of the imperative of accounting adequately for war expenditure that Richard Stone and James Meade, under guidance and with encouragement from Keynes, were invited to draw up new estimates from which policy decisions might be derived (Stone and Meade, 1944).

Sectoral Accounting

Thus it was only during the Second World War that government resources were allocated to (1) estimates of national income and expenditure; (2) evaluation of both gross and net product figures (with the inclusion of depreciation and indirect taxes in the evaluation of national product and income); and (3) the drawing up of 'sector accounts' (apparently Stone's idea) whereby double-entry records were kept of income and expenditure in different sectors of the economy. Such sector accounts are now commonplace and standardised, even if they receive less attention from many of those teaching and studying national accounting than the interrelations of global economic aggregates. They are readily apparent by opening any volume of national income and expenditure published by any government.

Meade and Stone had originally suggested four sectoral categories, including (1) the private household account, representing largely personal income, consumption and saving; (2) the business enterprise account, including both distributed and undistributed profits and private capital formation; (3) the government account, representing collective consumption and investment, and its surplus or deficit; as well as (4) a 'rest of the world' account, showing transactions of the national and international economy. Most of this has been embodied in contemporary national accounting.

But there are limits to the present framework of national accounting. For one thing, while governments compile output and other data on the basis of information gained from firms, they do not publish them in a form which makes it possible to gain insight into changes in the structure of supply in the economy. This has been left to individual research and enquiry.

Inputs and Outputs

In principle, economics can cope with the measurement of inter-sectoral effects through input-output analysis. Pioneered by Nobel Prize winner Wassily Leontief (1951, 1966), input-output has offered pathbreaking potential to the analysis of sectors and structures in the modern market economy. Put simply, and as illustrated in Figure 9.3, all sectors of activity are represented twice, i.e. in both the horizontal (input) and vertical (output) columns of an inter-industry or inter-sectoral matrix. Thus automobiles purchase 10 units (e.g. 10 millions worth of output, whether measured in sterling, dollars or another currency) from the steel sector; 30 millions from mechanical engineering; 6 millions from the automobile sector itself as classified in national accounts (i.e. wheel rims, carburettors or whatever); 2 millions from the glass sector for windows, etc. This enables actual sales or outputs from any given sector to be traced in the purchases from or sales to

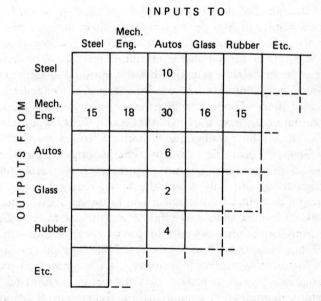

FIG. 9.3   A basic input-ouput table

328 · The Market Economy

other sectors throughout the economy. The major virtues of such an input-output approach include the degree to which in principle it can make transparent what otherwise would remain opaque transactions between sectors of the economy.

Scope and Limits

Leontief was one of the first to admit that input-output analysis has significant limitations.

First, there are the assumptions which have to be made on technical change and innovation. Any static 'picture' of the economy given in an input-output table needs to be dynamised over time if it is to be of practical use to policy-makers. Yet over time the coefficient or relation between different sectors changes, as technical progress and innovation mean that more is bought from some sectors, and less sold to others. The rise of entirely new industries or sectors of activity tends not to be separately accounted by government statisticians, reducing the extent to which input-output programmers can trace real change in the structure of the economy.

Second, there is the qualification of any national input-output table and its outcome over time through changes in imports or exports, or capital inflow and outflow. This may not be of crucial significane for the United States economy on the trade side, since foreign trade is a relatively small proportion of US national income – less than 10 per cent for most of the postwar period. But for other economies such as those of Europe, where foreign trade may constitute up to a third or more of national income, the impact of the international economy on the national input-output matrix can be decisive.

Third, there is the inadequate statistical basis of most input-output tables or matrices. This is not a limitation of the technique, but rather a reflection of the dominance of macroeconomic aggregates in most postwar statistics. Established internationally from the end of the Second World War under the influence of Keynes and his paradigm, such statistics tended to reflect what Keynes in his *General Theory* had thought to be important. Thus governments tend to publish monthly or quarterly figures on employment, output, prices or foreign trade, but only ten-yearly or five-yearly figures on the structure of output through an industrial census of the economy. Since few governments allocate more than a handful of statisticians to collate such industry or sector information, it can take three to four years before such data is available for input-output analysis. By the time it has been processed, and then projected forward for another four to five years, a decade may pass in which the change in technical coefficients between sectors is estimated from out-of-date data, with implausible relation to the real change in the economy.

Fourth – going beyond the Leontief framework – there is the micro-meso and national-multinational dimension of sectoral analysis. So far, national accounts have not accounted for the role of multinational big business in the economy. But in practice, strategic decisions taken in the boardroom of only a few mesoeconomic companies can transform the foreign trade or domestic production profile of one or several of the sector boxes of an input-output table. The lack of such an intra-sectoral dimension to economic structure can substantially vitiate the outcome projected from the best motivated and managed input-output table.

Fifth, for many years input-output calculations were handicapped by the laborious process of calculating the vast range of respective inputs and outputs between the individual sector 'boxes' in the matrix. Modern computers have transformed such laborious calculations in input-output analysis. Thus one of the most obvious technical constraints on input-output technique has been lifted by technology. In principle, this could massively reduce the time for the translation of inputs into outputs in the matrix of intersectoral tables. If governments would standardise the basic data for such tables, and allocate more resources to information processing, the previous delays between formulation and projection could be massively reduced.

However, such technical progress and the potential for allocating greater resources will still yield only partial gains for matrix analysis unless they are complemented by three new dimensions to input-output and accounting methodology.

A Micro-Meso Matrix

The first new dimension is introducing a consistent meso and microeconomic dimension to the intra and inter-sectoral information available for input-output programming. Such information could be systematised on the basis of introducing a standard breakdown of activity represented by the four or five leading firms in the sector or – in exceptional cases – for those firms over five in number accounting for half of sectoral activity. Microeconomic enterprise would broadly be represented by the remaining firms in the sector.

For instance, Figure 9.4 illustrates the inter-sectoral relations of five top firms in both engineering and automobiles. With a five-firm concentration ratio, C_r^5, of 85 per cent for both engineering and auto production in sectors which may include a dozen auto manufacturers and several hundred engineering companies, it is clear that the mesoeconomic giants marginalise microeconomic enterprise and dominate the macroeconomic outcome.

Current information on such mesoeconomic sector leaders would give policy-makers an insight into the internal dynamics of sectoral structure. *Advance* information would make it possible to transform the limitations of conventional input-output analysis by incorporating the changing co-

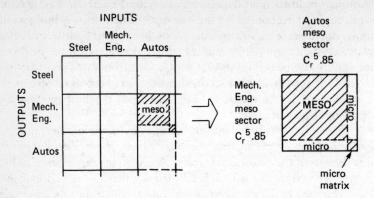

FIG. 9.4   Input-output: meso and micro dimensions

efficients from technical progress in the mesoeconomic sector which is so crucial to *ex ante* projections of the macroeconomic future by policy-makers.

It has already been established that many or most microeconomic firms are market adaptors and react to rather than actively initiate change. But mesoeconomic enterprise typically plans ahead to varying degrees which cover not only short- but also medium-term plans, with longer-term 'soft' planning or projections. Typically the medium-term plan coincides with the four- or five-year period in which policy-makers are projecting or planning macroeconomic aggregates such as productivity, output, employment, trade, investment and consumption.

A Meso-Macro Matrix

For governments, forecasting technical change and innovation over the medium term has hitherto been fraught with uncertainty. Forecasting over the longer term is plain hazardous. Even mesoeconomic enterprise cannot be sure of the market or supply conditions which will guarantee a precise level of investment, innovation, employment, productivity or exports over the medium term. But the corporate plans of individual mesoeconomic enterprise tend to be more certain – and frequently more committed – than the macroeconomic plans of governments.

By introducing the second new dimension of forward information from meso enterprise into a revised input-output matrix, policy-makers would be far better placed than before to incorporate *ex ante* the changed technical coefficients planned by leading companies into both sectoral and macro-economic projections. But this meso-macro information effect from firms to government can and should be two-way. With advance information from leading firms, the government's own statement of its planned intentions would be of more use to leading companies than the art of best guesstimate, intuition and hunch which sometimes is practised under the title of economic forecasting.

Such information has implications for the theory of expectations, whether such theory is Keynesian or monetarist in character. As shown in detail in *The Global Economy* (Holland, 1987), there are differences between Keynes' theory, the theory of many so-called Keynesians, and between both Keynesians and monetarists. Yet most reasoning on expectations is flawed on practical grounds. The past has to prove sufficiently stable for warranted predictions to be made into the future by the enterprise. A few months or even a few years stability may still not ensure an 'appropriate' micro reaction to such macro data, since the gestation period for forward investment is so long.

Forward Planning

Moreover, especially for big projects typical of the mesoeconomy, forward planning of research and development may take anything from two to five years, while investment itself may extend this period from five years to a decade. Added to this is the uncertainty for micro firms of the barriers to entry which may be raised by meso competitors, or the intra-sectoral takeover or elimination pricing which they may suffer irrespective of the trends in the macro or sector price level.

Meso-micro linkages traced through new imput-output programming could put public policy-makers in a position to be able to identify some of the main actual and potential relationships between what have to date been dual and unequal markets. If information were obligatory from the mesoeconomic companies which at present constitute less than one per cent of firms, but from half to most of sectoral transactions, it would not be necessary for government to gain similar information from micro enterprise to be able to gain a much improved picture of the actual and potential performance of the macroeconomy and its constituent sectors. Information from meso companies alone would make it feasible to trace the intersectoral and intrasectoral linkages of both meso and microeconomic enterprise, provided that the information from meso companies also covered their transactions with subsidiaries and their principal buyers and suppliers. Thus links with satellite firms, the implications for externalised economies or contracts, and the multiplier from either private or public spending contracts in the meso sector could be traced through such new forms of accounting.

Intra and Inter Sectoral

Leontief has demonstrated the use of input-output analysis for predicting changes in national income and expenditure following a change in one particular sector. He has also shown how to take into account and predict the consequence of technical change (see, e.g., Leontief, 1985).

When the meso sector is fused with Leontief's analysis it becomes possible to build a national income and expenditure analysis, predicting the consequences of changes in any sector (output or technology) which explicitly focus on the behaviour of giant corporations. The whole economy thereby becomes more transparent. Measuring the impact of the behaviour of the meso sector becomes easier and the targeting of policy more simple because the relation of the concentration of output in each sector and branch (including government) is made explicit. As a sub-system there is an input-output framework between the meso sector and the government, together with an additional sub-system for meso relations with public enterprise. It therefore becomes possible to create a framework of national income and expenditure accounts built on the meso and micro structure of individual sectors. For each sector in manufacturing its accounts would be similar to those in Figure 9.4. Aggregated for all sectors, these represent the complete system of national accounts emphasising the role of the meso sector in relation to government consumption and public enterprise.

Inter and Multinational

What can be achieved for the domestic structure of the economy through a mesoeconomic dimension to national accounting could also be achieved for the accounting for the main features of multinational companies. This obtains for both foreign trade statistics and the export and import columns of input-output tables. It is the third new dimension now possible for matrix analysis.

The argument from the analysis of sectors and structures in Chapter 7 make it plain that the trade and investment decisions taken by a handful of mesoeconomic companies can now register major effects on the macro performance of a national economy. For instance, devaluations have been forced on leading governments when their balance-of-payments deficit amounted to less than five per cent of total trade and even – in the case of the first devaluation of the franc under the Mitterrand government – when total gold and foreign-currency reserves exceeded the deficit itself. Smaller national firms comprising 15 to 25 per cent of visible export trade may seek to follow through such devaluation with lower export prices and higher export volume. But the two and a half dozen firms accounting for two-fifths of visible export trade in the UK may disinvest in the national economy, and reduce exports, or fail to respond through lower export prices and higher export volume.

Governments no longer have simple macro options on trade ensuring a uniform micro-sector response. To identify what is happening both in international trade, multinational investment and their effects on micro-economic firms, they need to align their information with the new structures of the mesoeconomy.

Multinational Accounting

As illustrated in Figure 9.5, such accounting could and should identify the share of foreign trade of multinational enterprise. In individual sectors this typically would involve less than half a dozen leading firms (in the given example, a five-firm concentration ratio or C_r^5). The data could be represented in additional columns in national accounts and the input-output matrix for exports, imports and the share in both of the multinational's subsidiary or intra-firm trade (IFT). Such information is already gathered and available, but published by governments and international agencies only in aggregate form.

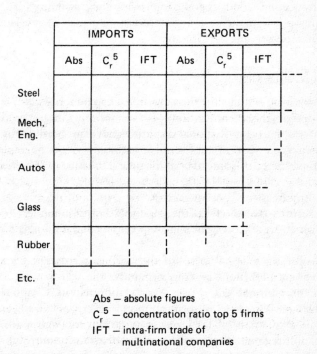

Abs — absolute figures
C_r^5 — concentration ratio top 5 firms
IFT — intra-firm trade of
multinational companies

FIG. 9.5   International trade: meso and multinational accounting

It has been central to the argument of this volume that mesoeconomic enterprise is now typically multiproduct and multisectoral as well as multinational. The new data therefore should match this multisectoral range and spread for individual mesoeconomic companies if policy-makers are to be in a position to trace the inter- and intra-sectoral effects of changes in the investment or trade decisions of leader firms. In a matrix or input-output context, this can place governments in a far more effective position to exert countervailing power to the multinationals' autonomy in either inward or outward investment decisions. In both forms of investment, providing the micro-linkages of meso enterprise are systematically traced in the new accounting framework, the positive or negative effects of inward or outward investment on 'satellite' buyers or suppliers can be more readily identified at short notice than the ad hoc once-off estimates made by government departments in either 'crisis' closures or efforts to bid for incoming foreign investment.

The argument for such a new and systematic mesoeconomic dimension to accounting is neither for nor against inward or outward investment per se. It is essentially a matter of gaining transparency on what is done, where, why and when by sector leaders, thereby improving the possibility for informed bargaining by policy-makers on private decisions which can register major effects on macroeconomic performance.

Inter and Multiregional

The same argument obtains for the new dimension now possible for matrix analysis through the identification of the multiregional operations of mesoeconomic enterprise. Regional disparities have not been diminished by the concern in recent years about overall or national levels of unemployment. In reality, as predicted by some of us at the time (Holland, 1975), the regional problems of the 1960s and 1970s have been overtaken by major regional crisis. This in part is the consequence of low growth or negative growth in traditional sectors. It also reflects the job displacement in modern industries in regions which were yesteryear's growth centres and are today's problem regions.

In the deepening regional crisis of the northeastern United States, the northern regions of Britain or southern Italy, the role played by meso-economic multinational enterprise – as elaborated in Chapter 6 – is multidimensional. The array of location incentive 'carrots' has been under-mined by the availability of far larger cost savings through multinational rather than multiregional location. The 'sticks' of location controls have been bent by government-condoned evasion, or broken by legislation, reducing their effect. Mesoeconomic enterprise has rationalised and closed many of its branch plants in the peripheral regions of developed countries. What Averitt (1968) has called 'centre firms' in 'new' industries such as electronics and computers now locate increasingly in high-income and high-skilled areas, and – in Europe – central areas, backwashing the regional periphery.

It has been acknowledged for decades in regional theory that governments misplace their hopes for area development by concentrating on a narrow range of industries. This has very evidently been the case with steel and shipbuilding, coal and coal mining, or shoes and clothing. It is now also evident in the US Great Lakes and the British Midlands, with over-concentration on the motor industry. But there is little chance of offsetting such regional decline unless leverage can be gained on the location decisions of the pacemakers in new industries and services. The basic reasons remain that many services are personal, demanding face-to-face contact with customers and thereby reflecting existing population distribution. Oil, mining, minerals and agriculture are by definition geologically or geograph-ically specific and immobile. Therefore, while services have some role to play through decentralisation of office employment, manufacturing remains a key regionally mobile activity with longer-term development potential for many problem regions.

Structural, Social and Spatial

The fuller relation of structural, social and spatial distribution in resource allocation is analysed in some detail in *The Political Economy*. But at a minimum, any public policy aiming to offset or reduce regional disparities must aim to relate structural change to spatial distribution. Similarly, a re-distribution strategy needs to be both inter- and intra-sectoral, as well as inter- and intra-regional.

Mesoeconomic enterprise dominates both the national and regional economy and is more able to manage multiregional ventures than micro-economic enterprise. Lacking managerial or locational cost constraints in multinational operations, meso enterprise can certainly manage multi-regional location, where net distance costs – certainly in developed countries – are negligible.

As with foreign investment and trade, however, the objective of diversified regional structure is best served by gaining adequate accounts and account-ability on the operations of mesoeconomic enterprise. This further 'spatial' dimension to national accounts – a regional input-output matrix – is not difficult in principle. Interregional input-output models have been devised for decades, *inter alia* by Hollis Chenery (1965). Regional data is already published by most developed countries, but this mainly regionalises con-ventional national accounts. Lacking the systematic component of the meso sector, they fail to account for the main actors in regional location or for the linkages with led or laggard firms in the micro sector which constitute so large a share of actual regional imbalance.

As illustrated in Figure 9.6, the components of the micro, meso and macro dimensions of economic activity can in principle be represented (and thus dynamised) through their translation (or collation) on a regional basis for the main areas of the modern economy. In countries such as Japan or Italy, which for decades have collated information on regional employment and value added by region, such a framework is readily feasible. In others, for example in Australia under the Labour government in the 1980s, it has recently been pioneered and prototyped. Certainly such a framework makes it possible to represent which firms are doing what and where within the national economy. This includes not only the broad category of more developed regions (MDR), intermediate regions (IMR) and less developed regions (LDR) but also thereby the relative inequality between town and country, and inner city and suburbs.

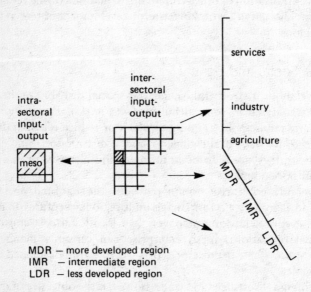

MDR — more developed region
IMR — intermediate region
LDR — less developed region

FIG. 9.6   Regionalised input-output analysis

If translated through from national accounting categories in such international organisations as the European Community, a new framework of this sort could introduce transparency to information on the spatial distribution of the structure of production and thereby enable policy-makers to adopt more appropriate policies for regional development.

9.5 Unequal Shares

The previous analysis should indicate that the pattern of what is done, where, by whom and for whom in the modern capitalist economy is complex rather than simple. The macro and micro categories of the conventional Keynesian or monetarist paradigms need to be supplemented by new dimensions for national and international accounting if we are to move towards a framework in which policy-makers can represent, let alone influence or change, what occurs in the modern market economy.

Such complexity does not mean that little can be explained or nothing done to improve our economic prospects. But it does imply that simple models and simplist solutions to economic problems need to be modified to take account of the rise of big business and its dominance of the national and international economy.

No such subtlety is allowed by Martin Weitzman in his recent recommendations for a share economy which would overcome both stagflation and unemployment in the modern market economy (Weitzman, 1984). Weitzman is a professional economist whose mastery of the art of the dismal science is not in question. Moreover, his concern about the current economic crisis is not disputed. As he argues, the market economies have long been racked by persistent unemployment. Unemployment imposes intolerable social and economic costs. In the 1930s more resources were lost through the slump than were generated by all the spending of the Second World War. Moreover, the casualties were not suffering for any cause. Their sacrifice was manifestly meaningless and unnecessary.

This was the issue to which Keynes addressed himself in his *General Theory* in 1936, and Weitzman claims that no one really doubts that the capitalist countries have turned a critical corner since the Keynesian revolution. On the other hand, he recognises that the high peak of the Keynesian revolution has passed, and that many Keynesians have lost confidence in the feasibility of achieving full employment. Not least, Weitzman claims, Keynes underestimated the possibility of stagnation and inflation (Weitzman, 1984, pp. 55–7).

So far so good, and many Keynesians would agree. But some Keynesians and many others would disagree about Weitzman's analysis of inflation in the global economy. For Weitzman, the cause of inflation is that 'capitalism has become a relatively more compassionate and softer-hearted system. Not only have [governments] opted to cast a fairly broad safety net for the unemployed in their midst, but the citizens of democratic mixed economies everywhere will not tolerate high unemployment rates.' In a one-line observation which may not persuade more than four million people unemployed in Britain, he observes that 'the re-election of Prime Minister Margaret Thatcher in 1983 is the kind of exception that proves the rule' (ibid., pp. 66–7).

So where did Keynes go wrong? Weitzman claims that 'like a great magician, Keynes removed the wage issue from centre stage and replaced it by a discretionary government policy to manage aggregate demand.' He adds that in the long course of history 'this disappearing act must increasingly come to be viewed as something of a dazzling digression from the main route to economic prosperity' (p. 54). That route, in his view, leads directly to his own analysis of the share economy which would 'vaccinate capitalism against stagflation' (ch. 9).

The General Motors Case

So how would the share economy work? Weitzman sees shareholding by workers as complementing the wage system. In itself, this is compatible with a range of options for shareholding such as the Swedish Investment Loans Fund principle by which trades unions would hold and manage the investment of shares on behalf of the workers in individual companies. But this is not what Weitzman has in mind. In his scheme, workers are not only offered shares in lieu of a proportion of their pay, but their 'compensation is tied to a formula that makes it vary inversely with the firm's level of employment.' Or, put more simply, in his own words: 'the essence of a share contract is that if workers are laid off or quit, the remaining employees are paid more, whereas if new workers are hired, all employees are paid less' (ibid., pp. 83–5).

Weitzman illustrates the case with a hypothetical contract between the United Automobile Workers Union and General Motors. Instead of each employee receiving a wage of $24 per hour, the UAW and GM agree that each employee will be paid a two-thirds share of GM's average revenue per worker. Thus, if GM hires an extra worker its revenue goes up by $24 per hour of labour, but its total labour cost increases by only $16 per hour. Weitzman therefore claims that under the new contract GM has an incentive to resist lay-offs and to expand production: 'the expansion ends when every qualified person in the economy seeking work has a job' (ibid., pp. 4–6).

Without impugning Weitzman's sincerity, his argument amounts to an amazing sleight of reasoning. For one thing, the costs to GM or any other company do not simply disappear because workers are paid shares rather than wages for a percentage of their earnings. Abstracting current labour costs from total corporate costs simply shifts the basis of compensation. Further, unless labour can earn as much from dividend income on shares as from forgone wages, how many workers will take up the scheme in the first place? Such a scheme would amount to income reduction pure and simple. Besides which, what happens to aggregate demand? With lower incomes, sales would fall, and profits decline as the fixed costs of enterprise were covered by less corporate income. Even unemploying more labour would not offset such increased costs, for which big business would tend to compensate by raising prices to protect its cash flow and profit rate.

Misapplication of Marginal Costs

Weitzman tries to answer the issue in terms of the theory of marginal costs, with the implication that the marginal profit for GM will be increased by employing additional workers at a lower wage cost. Marginal analysis has already been criticised extensively in chapter 3 of this volume. It is as relevant to the pricing and profits of the modern capitalist corporation as is astrology to astrophysics. As cited earlier, ATT sought for ten years to measure marginal costs and gave up the exercise because of the difficulty of identifying them.

As significantly, a key question is what role would be played by the new shareholding workers in the control of companies offering shares instead of wage income? In practice, Weitzman does not face the control question at all. He assumes that shares are accepted by workers, and also that this might occur within the top 500 corporations in the United States which command the heights of the American economy. Yet he provides no argument on the role which workers as shareholders might play in what is done by the corporation, why, where, when, for whom or by whom, despite the fact that in reality this range of decisions is precisely the frontier which those advocating industrial democracy or workers' control would seek as an advance for the rights of workers beyond the wage bargain.

Further, Weitzman makes no reference to the issue of preference or non-preference, or voting or non-voting shares, nor to the question whether workers could in principle achieve majority control of the top 500 corporations. Despite the fact that these corporate giants are multinationals composed of many subsidiary companies, he makes no allowance for the fact that overall control – including the decision whether to close subsidiaries or expand their operations – is exercised by top rather than local management, so that anything less than shareholding in the parent company would amount to paper equity rather than shared control. The lapse cannot be accidental. Weitzman is interested in offering workers shares rather than wage increases as a means of reducing labour costs and inflation rather than as a programme for extended social control by workers themselves.

Unions and Natural Rights

This is underlined by Weitzman's claim that the wage system of paying labour is outmoded, that the 'sacred cross we continue to bear is the wage standard,' and his claim that – through trades unionism – wages are at least ten per cent higher than they otherwise would be. He puts it more bluntly in claiming that 'the bargaining power of labour unions is not a natural right' (p. 109) and opposing the closed shop: 'in law and in custom, hiring new workers is a management prerogative, not a mandatory subject for bargaining. This is a doctrine the public can legitimately insist upon as a quid pro quo for the rights and privileges granted to labour unions.'

At this stage it is not hard to see why both Nigel Lawson and David Owen endorse Weitzman's share economy. Workers are invited to take shares in lieu of pay, to reduce their wages, and to leave to management the prerogative of deciding how their company is run. According to Weitzman, workers have no 'natural rights', but capitalists do.

With this *ingenue* digression into eighteenth-century natural law Weitzman as dazzlingly compares his own recommendations with 'share-cropping', i.e. the pernicious system of *métayage* abolished in France with the revolution of 1789 and by which sharecroppers gave half of their produce to the landlord instead of being paid money wages. Rushing in where others will not tread, Weitzman claims that 'wherever sharecropping is practised, the landowner never voluntarily turns away a willing worker'. Such neo-feudal fantasy did not prevent hyper-inflation in France before the fall of the Bourbons. Nor is it likely to attract many workers today.

Inflation Vaccination?

So what of Weitzman's equally sweeping claims that his shareholding formula will vaccinate contemporary capitalism against inflation?

In his example from General Motors, he argues that as the United Automobile Workers trade lower wages for shareholdings, 'GM automobile prices must come down because more Chevrolets can be sold only if their price is lowered relative to Fords, Toyotas and the rest' (p. 5). The assumption is both cavalier and counter-factual. Immediately after the first OPEC oil price increases in 1973, General Motors raised its prices substantially to compensate for the fall in its cash flow caused by reduced automobile sales in the United States. This classic stagflation reflected less the bargaining power of the UAW than the price-making power of General Motors as the dominant vehicles producer in the United States.

Moreover, a globalisation of Weitzman's argument shows its irrelevance to the world economy as a whole. While it may be attractive to some to assume that the global crisis of stagflation from the mid 1970s was due to wage demands, no evidence is available to demonstrate that postwar economic growth was ground to a halt by the spontaneous solidarity of international labour against global capital. It was OPEC, not the workers of the world uniting, which reduced GM's profits in the early 1970s. Further, wage demands alone are insignificant for the winners among the new world competition states. For instance, as demonstrated by Ohmae (1985), Japanese companies such as Toyota and Nissan have been able to penetrate world markets by a combination of high wages and high innovatory investment. The simple reason is that automation has increased productivity, and thus the share of labour costs, in total production. The direct labour cost in such Japanese companies is less than ten per cent of the total costs of manufacture.

National and Multinational

In the context of Weitzman's argument that trades unions have in general increased costs by ten per cent over their 'competitive' level, it is evident in the case of the Japanese motor manufacturers that such a ten per cent increase would add less than one per cent to their total costs. The crisis for traditional manufacturing in the United States or the United Kingdom lies less in undue wage demands than elsewhere. In both cases, the reasons reflect (i) the failure to invest in new products and innovation on a sufficient scale to reduce the competitive advantage of Japanese producers; and (ii) the disproportionate scale of US and UK foreign investment by American and British multinational companies, which has meant that their foreign production has been up to four times (for the US) and double (for the UK) the value of total visible exports in recent years. Thus US and UK firms have exported investment rather than goods, in contrast with Japan, which has exported high-quality, low-labour-content products, with devastating success.

Further, in contrast with Weitzman's simplism that stagflation is due to wage cost increases alone, deflation in the global economy has been the result of beggar-my-neighbour policies by leading governments, while inflation is a highly complex phenomenon irreducible to simple wage-cost causes. The reasons for such inflation since the early 1970s have included (i) the devaluation of the dollar in 1971, and its knock-on effects on other currencies; (ii) the OPEC oil price increases, especially in 1973 and 1979; (iii) the setting of prices by leading companies at a level which allows less efficient smaller companies to survive, to avoid the teeth of anti-trust or anti-monopoly legislation, rather than the marginal cost levels assumed by Weitzman's textbook premises; (iv) multinational companies' transfer pricing, which normally takes the form of over-invoicing the value of imports to developed countries from subsidiaries abroad, in order to reduce declared profits and tax liability; (v) the obligation on leading firms to meet fixed interest payments on bank and bond borrowing (especially Euromarket issues), which has increased since the early 1970s and thereby eclipsed share issues as a principal means of corporate finance; (vi) the stagflation achieved by dominant companies in national or global markets when they compensate for falling sales by raising prices.

9.6 Summary

(1) Conventional theory claims rationality for the market versus the irrationality of public intervention. But the calculus of private profit is narrow in relation to the social demand for housing, health, education, welfare or the environment.

(2) With price-making power, global big business no longer ensures that efficiency in production is translated through to consumer welfare. Neither marginal pricing nor the assumption of a standard cost plus average profit markup enable anti-trust or competition bodies to evaluate the competitive or uncompetitive nature of multinational big business.

(3) There is no longer a standard theory of the firm which can provide a benchmark for divergence between profit and welfare. Multi-product, multi-divisional and multinational enterprise pursue varying market strategies and price and profit tactics in markets in the same or different economies.

(4) Despite claims that big business can afford to be concerned with social issues (and allowing for the funding of charitable foundations), the heart of the soulful corporation still pumps on profit.

(5) The matrix of variable ends and means employed by big business is paralleled by a complex matrix for modern government. For instance, simple anti-trust or competition remedies such as price restraint may throw smaller firms into crisis if bigger business has lower costs. Public intervention to preserve a fabric of small and medium firms, or promote regional versus multinational location, have become imperative to assure a range of public welfare objectives.

(6) Tax incentives and rebates, or investment and employment grants, have only limited effects on big business when the gains from going multinational vastly outstrip the gains from staying in a given national economy. New forms of public, social and co-operative enterprise are needed to achieve public leverage on private big business, and to ensure that government can directly fulfil what indirect policies such as tax rebates and incentives cannot achieve.

(7) Structural policy in the above sense needs to complement the social and

spatial (regional-urban) policies of governments. Public-spending contracts are a key means of implementing conditions for public-sector leverage over private multinational enterprise.

(8) Effective accounting is a key to greater public accountability over the multinational big business sector. It is feasible, from the information which it already collates, for governments to introduce systematic representation of the share of the mesoeconomy into macroeconomic accounts.

(9) Such new accounting make it possible to overcome limits to conventional input-output analysis, and to dynamise a forward view of the macro outcome of the economy by tracing the current and projected behaviour of mesoeconomic enterprise. This accounting would enable identification of the convergence or divergence between the actual, expected and potential growth of the economy.

(10) A mesoeconomic dimension for national accounting becomes more effective if jointly pursued by several governments. The share of multinational companies in international trade should register not only concentration ratios but also the intra-firm trade of multinationals between subsidiaries in different countries.

(11) Mesoeconomic accounting can make a major contribution to regionalised input-output analysis, whether the region is defined in broad terms as more developed, less developed or intermediate, or identified as a metropolitan region and inner-city area.

(12) Proposals for a share economy are only meaningful if they involve extended economic democracy for workers over corporate decision-making. They are not meaningful if they simply allow a minority to privatise what hitherto were public assets; nor if they are offered as panaceas for the end of inflation or achievement of full employment irrespective of the global decision-making of multinational big business.

9.7 Postscript and Preview

Such wider issues concerning the nature of the modern macroeconomy, and the structural, social and spatial distribution of resources, will be examined in the next two volumes of this trilogy – The Global Economy (1987) and The Political Economy (Holland, forthcoming).

The argument of the second volume focuses on the manner in which the rise of mesoeconomic and multinational capital has profoundly qualified both the Keynesian and monetarist syntheses of the micro and macro economies. For Keynes, the reliance on a supply-side economics of microeconomic competition was understandable. As already shown in this volume, the supply side of the economy at the time when Keynes wrote his *General Theory* was composed of a large number of competing enterprises within individual national economies (nearly 140 such companies flourished in the 1930s in the UK automobile sector alone). The rise of the giant global company typical of the modern meso sector had not yet occurred.

Keynes might have been better served in his own micro-macro synthesis by looking to the continental economies and Marxist theorists in understanding the dynamics of unequal competition between big and small business. Kalecki, in his own time, certainly did so, incorporating key features of oligopoly theory into a macro dynamics which arguably was more seminal in its long-term implications for theory than the analysis of Keynes himself. But it took some time for Kalecki's own key arguments to be translated into English and for his anticipation of Keynes, within both a supply and demand context, to be recognised by Anglo-American economists (Kalecki, 1954).

Meanwhile, the combination of inflation with unemployment in the period following the first OPEC 'oil shock' of 1973 first perplexed and then paralysed most of those policy-makers who had declared themselves to be Keynesians. Neglecting the rise of multinational big business and its own contribution to inflation, Keynesians conceded the monetarist claim that inflation arose from too much money chasing too few goods, and in turn followed monetarist prescriptions for remedying economic crisis, such as cutting the money supply through the main expedient available – cuts in public spending.

Designed to remedy short-term balance-of-payments constraints by reducing imports to make way for the higher cost of oil imports, such spending cuts in turn reduced mutual export trade and aggravated global recession. Structural factors in the economic crisis of the 1970s and 1980s such as the end of the long-term reconstruction of the postwar market economies, or the role of rising public spending in sustaining postwar economic growth, were ignored. With this, in turn, the better-my-neighbour recovery of the postwar period gave way to a beggar-my-neighbour restriction of mutual imports and thus in turn mutual exports.

For further analysis of both the postwar recovery and the ensuing crisis the reader should turn to the second volume of this trilogy, *The Global Economy*.

Bibliography

AARONOVITCH, S. and SAWYER, M. C. (1975) *Big Business: Theoretical and Empirical Aspects of Concentration and Mergers in the United Kingdom*, Macmillan Press, London and New York.

ACKLEY, Gardner (1961) *Macroeconomic Theory*, Macmillan, New York.

ACOCELLA, Nicola (1975) *Imprese Multinationale e Investimenti Diretti*, Guiffre, Milan.

ANSOFF, H. I. (and others) (1972) *Twenty Years of Acquisition Behaviour in America*, Cassell, London.

AVERITT, R. T. (1968) *The Dual Economy: The Dynamics of American Industry*, Norton and Co., New York.

AYER, A. J. (1936) *Language, Truth and Logic*, Victor Gollancz, London.

BAIN, J. S. (1956) *Barriers to New Competition*, Harvard University Press, Cambridge, Mass.

BANNOCK, G. (1971) *The Juggernauts*, Weidenfeld and Nicolson, London.

BARAN, Paul A., with SWEEZY, Paul M. (1966) *Monopoly Capital*, Monthly Review Press, New York and Penguin Books, Harmondsworth (1968).

BARNET, Richard J. and MULLER, Ronald E. (1974) *Global Reach: The Power of the Multinational Corporations*, Simon and Schuster, New York.

BAUMOL, William J. (1959) *Business Behavior, Value and Growth*, Macmillan, New York (2nd edition 1967, Harcourt Brace, New York).

(1982) 'Contestable Markets: an Uprising in the Theory of Industrial Structure', *American Economic Review*, March.

with PANZAR, J. C. and WILLIG, R. D. (1982) *Contestable Markets and the Theory of Industrial Structure*, Harcourt Brace Jovanovich, San Diego.

BEGG, David, FISCHER, Stanley and DORNBUSCH, Rudiger (1984) *Economics*, McGraw-Hill (UK) Ltd, London.

BEIDA, K. (1970) *The Structure and Operation of the Japanese Economy*, John Wiley and Sons, Sydney and New York.

BELL, David (1985) 'How the Triad Forces the Pace', *Financial Times*, 21 June.

BERLE, Adolf A. and MEANS, Gardiner C. (1932) *The Modern Corporation and Private Property*, Macmillan, London. References are to 1968 edition, with new Preface by Berle.

BIRCH, David L. (1979) *The Job Generation Process*, MIT Press, Cambridge, Mass.

BODDY, Martin (1980) *The Building Societies*, Macmillan, London.

BORTKIEWICZ, L. Von (1952) 'Value and Price in the Marxian System', *International Economic Papers* (English translation of the second and third parts of a three-part article originally published in German in 1906 and 1907).

BOWLES, Samuel, GORDON, David M. and WEISSKOPF, Thomas (1983) *Beyond the Wasteland: A Democratic Alternative to Economic Decline*, Anchor Press/Doubleday, New York.

BRANDT, Willy and MANLEY, Michael (1985) *Global Challenge: From Crisis to Cooperation*, Pan Books, London.

BRANKOVIC, S. (1987) 'Flexible Factory Automation', Paper to the International Economy Conference, Cavtat, in *Socialism in the World* (ed. Milos Nikolic), Belgrade.

BROCARD, Lucien (1929–31) *Principes d'Economie Nationale et Internationale*, 3 vols, Sirey, Paris.

BRUCHEY, S. (1965) *The Roots of American Economic Growth*, Hutchinson, London.

BUKHARIN, Nicolai (1927) *Imperialism and World Economy*. Written in 1915, first published in 1927. References are to Merlin Press edition, London, 1972.

BYE, Maurice (1970) *Les Problèmes Economiques Européens*, Editions Cujas, Paris.

CALLENDER, Guy (1902) 'The Early Transportation and Banking Enterprises of the States', *Quarterly Journal of Economics*, vol. xvii.

CARNOY, Martin (1983) *A New Social Contract: The Economy and Government After Reagan*, Harper and Row, New York.

CASTLES, S. and KOSACK, G. (1973) *Immigrant Workers and Class Structure in Western Europe*, Oxford University Press.

CHAMBERLIN, Edward (1933) *The Theory of Monopolistic Competition*, Harvard University Press, Cambridge, Mass.

  (1952) 'Full Cost and Monopolistic Competition', *The Economic Journal*, June.

  (1954) (ed.) *Monopoly and Competition and Their Regulation*, Harvard University Press, Cambridge, Mass.

CHANDLER, Alfred D. (jnr.) (1962) *Strategy and Structure: Chapters in the History of the Industrial Enterprise*, MIT Press, Cambridge, Mass.

  (1982) 'M-Formed Industrial Groups', *European Economic Review*, September.

CHANNON, Derek F. (1973) *The Strategy and Structure of British Enterprise*, Macmillan, London.

CHENERY, H. B. (with CLARK, P. G.) (1965) *Interindustry Economics*, John Wiley and Sons, New York.

CLAIRMONTE, Frederick F. and CAVANAGH, John E. (1984) 'Transnational Corporations and Services: The Final Frontier', UNCTAD, *Trade and Development*, No. 5, Geneva.

CLARK, Colin (1940) *The Conditions of Economic Progress*, Macmillan, London.

CLARK, J. M. (1961) *Competition as a Dynamic Process*, Brookings Institution, Washington DC.

DAVIS, Lance E. and LEGLER, J. (1966) 'The Government in the US Economy 1815–1902', *The Journal of Economic History*, December.

DOWNIE (1958) *The Competitive Process*, Duckworth, London.

DOYLE, J. R. and GALLAGHER, C. C. (1986) 'Size Distribution, Potential for Growth, and Contribution to Job Generation of Firms in the UK 1982–84', Research Report No. 7, Newcastle University Department of Industrial Management.

DUNNING, John H. and PEARCE, Robert D. (1981) *The World's Largest Industrial Enterprises*, Gower Press, London.

EATWELL, J. L. (1971) 'Growth, Profitability and Size: The Empirical Evidence',

Appendix in R. Marris and A. Wood (eds), *The Corporate Economy*, Macmillan, London.

THE ECONOMIST INTELLIGENCE UNIT (1971) *The Growth and Spread of Multinational Corporations*, QER Special, No. 5.

EICHNER, Alfred S. (1976) *The Megacorp and Oligopoly*, Cambridge University Press.

ERGAS, H. (1984) 'Corporate Strategies in Transition', in A. Jacquemin (ed.), *European Industry: Public Policy and Corporate Strategy*, Oxford University Press.

FEIWEL, G. R. (1975) *The Intellectual Capital of Michael Kalecki*, University of Tennessee Press, Knoxville.

FELLNER, W. J. (1949) *Competition Among the Few*, Knopf, New York.

THE EDITORS OF *FORTUNE* (1970) *The Conglomerate Commotion*, The Viking Press, New York and Time Inc.

FOTHERGILL, Steven and GUDGIN, Graham (1979) *The Job Generation Process in Britain*, Centre for Environmental Studies, Research Series 32.

FRANKO, L. (1976) *The European Multinationals*, Harper and Row, New York.

FRIEDMAN, Milton (1962a and 1976) *Price Theory*, Aldine Publishing Company, Chicago.

(1962b) *Capitalism and Freedom*, Phoenix Books, University of Chicago Press.

and FRIEDMAN, Rose (1980) *Free to Choose*, Harcourt Brace Jovanovitch, New York and also Pelican Books and Secker & Warburg, London.

GALBRAITH, John Kenneth (1957) *American Capitalism: the Concept of Counter-vailing Power*, Hamish Hamilton, London. First published 1952.

(1967a) *The New Industrial State*, André Deutsch, London.

(1967b) *The Affluent Society*, André Deutsch, London. First published 1957.

(1974) *Economics and the Public Purpose*, André Deutsch, London.

GERSHUNY, J. and MILES, I. (1983) *The New Service Economy*, Frances Pinter, London.

GLC (1984) *London Financial Strategy*, internal paper.

GORDON, David M. (1983) *Beyond the Wasteland: A Democratic Alternative to Economic Decline*, Anchor Press/Doubleday, New York.

HALL, R. L. and HITCH, C. J. (1939) 'Price Theory and Business Behaviour', *Oxford Economic Papers*, May.

HARCOURT, G. C. (1977) (ed.) *The Microfoundations of Macroeconomics*, Macmillan, London.

HARROD, Roy F. (1952) *Economic Essays*, Macmillan, London.

HAYEK, F. von (1944) *The Road to Serfdom*, Routledge, London.

HILFERDING, Rudolf (1910) *Finance Capital: A Study of the Latest Development of Capitalism*, ed. Tom Bottomore, Routledge and Kegan Paul, London, 1981.

HOLLAND, Stuart (1972) (ed.) *The State as Entrepreneur*, Weidenfeld and Nicolson, London.

(1974) 'Mesoeconomics, New Public Enterprise and Economic Planning', *Annals of Public and Cooperative Economy*, Volume 4–5, April–June.

(1975) *The Socialist Challenge*, Quartet Books, London.

(1976a) *Capital versus the Regions*, Macmillan, London and St Martin's Press, New York.

(1976b) *The Regional Problem*, Macmillan, London and St Martin's Press, New York.

(1978) (ed.) *Beyond Capitalist Planning*, Basil Blackwell, Oxford.

(1980) *Uncommon Market*, Macmillan, London.

(1983) (ed.) *Out of Crisis*, Spokesman Books, Nottingham.

(1987) *The Global Economy* (vol. 2 of *Towards a New Political Economy*), Weidenfeld and Nicolson, London.

(forthcoming) *The Political Economy* (vol. 3 of *Towards a New Political Economy*), Weidenfeld and Nicolson, London.

and ANDERSON, Donald (1984) *Kissinger's Kingdom?*, Spokesman Books, Nottingham.

HOLMES, Peter (1978) *Industrial Pricing Behaviour and Devaluation*, Macmillan, London.

HOWE, Sir Geoffrey (1978) 'Enterprise Zones', in *The Right Angle*, Bow Group, London.

IMF (1985) *Foreign Private Investment in Developing Countries*, Washington, DC.

JACQUEMIN A. and LICHTBUER, M. (1973) 'Size, Structure, Stability and Performance of the Largest British and EEC Firms', *European Economic Review*, December.

JOHNSCHER, C. (1983) 'Information Resources and Economic Productivity', *Information, Economics and Policy*, vol. 1, no. 1, North Holland Publishing Co., Amsterdam.

JUMP, N. F. (1983) 'Competition and Cooperation in Consumer Durable Industries: An Apparent Paradox', *Barclays Review*, May.

KALDOR, Nicholas (1934) 'The Equilibrium of the Firm', *Economic Journal*, March.

(1982) *The Scourge of Monetarism*, Oxford University Press.

KALECKI, Michael (1954) *Theory of Economic Dynamics*, George Allen & Unwin, London.

KAPLAN, A. D. H., DIRLAN, J. B., LANZILLOTI, R. F. (1958) *Pricing in Big Business*, Brookings Institution, Washington DC.

KESTNER, Fritz (1912) *Der Organisationszwang* (The Comparative Organisation) Berlin.

KEYNES, John Maynard (1936) *The General Theory of Employment, Interest and Money*, Macmillan, London.

KINDLEBERGER, C. P. (1967) *Europe's Postwar Growth: the Role of Labor Supply*, Harvard University Press, Cambridge, Mass.

(1970) (ed.) *The International Corporation*, Harvard University Press, Cambridge, Mass.

KOLKO, Gabriel (1962) 'Max Weber on America: Theory and Evidence', *History and Theory*, 1, No. 2.

KONO, T. (1984) *Structure and Strategy of Japanese Enterprises*, Macmillan, London.

KUHN, (1962) *The Structure of Scientific Revolutions*, University of Chicago Press.

(1970) *Criticism of the Growth of Knowledge*, ed. Lakatof and Musgrave, Cambridge University Press.

KUMAR, Manmohan S. (1984) *Growth, Acquisition and Investment*, University of Cambridge, Department of Applied Economics, occasional paper 56, Cambridge University Press.

KUZNETS, Simon (1958) *Quantitative Aspects in the Economic Growth of Nations, in Economic Development and Cultural Change*, Heinemann, London.

(1966) *Modern Economic Growth*, Heinemann, London.

LAMFALUSSY, A. (1961) *Investment and Growth in Mature Economies*, Macmillan, London.

LEIJONHUFVUD, A. (1968) *On Keynesian Economics and the Economics of Keynes*, Oxford University Press, London and Toronto.

LENIN, V. I. (1917) *Imperialism, the Highest Stage of Capitalism*. References in this text are to Lenin, *Selected Works*, FLPH, Moscow, 1952.

LEON, Paolo (1967) *Structural Change and Growth in Capitalism*, Johns Hopkins University Press, Baltimore.

LEONTIEF, W. (1951) *The Structure of the American Economy 1919–1939*, Oxford University Press (2nd edition).

(1966) *Input-Output Economics*, Oxford University Press.

(1985) 'The Choice of Technology', *Scientific American*, June.

LEWIS, W. A. (1954) 'Economic Development with Unlimited Supplies of Labour', *The Manchester School*, May.

LICHTBUER, M. and JACQUEMIN, A. (1973) 'Size, Structure, Stability and Performance of the Largest British and EEC Firms', *European Economic Review*, December.

LIPSEY, Richard G. (1975) *An Introduction to Positive Economics*, 4th edition, Weidenfeld and Nicholson, London. Lipsey (1979) refers to the 5th edition, and Lipsey (1983) to the sixth edition.

LIST, Friedrich (1965) *The National System of Political Economy*, Longmans Green, London.

LOCKSLEY, Gareth (1981) 'A Study of the Evolution of Concentration in the Data Processing Industry', Commission of the European Communities, Brussels (mimeo).

(1983) 'Pricing Strategy of Car Manufacturers in the UK Compared with Some Other EEC Member States', Commission of the European Communities, Brussels (mimeo).

(1984) 'Big Business and the EEC', graduate thesis, University of Sussex.

LUEDDE-NEURATH, R. (1984) 'State Intervention and Foreign Direct Investment in South Korea', in *Developmental States in East Asia: Capitalist and Socialist*, Bulletin of the Institute of Development Studies, University of Sussex, April.

MACFIE, A. L. (1967) *The Individual in Society*, Allen & Unwin, London.

MALLOCH BROWN, Mark (1984) 'India's Growing Pains', in Development Report, *The Economist*, June.

MANDEL, Ernest (1975) *Late Capitalism*, New Left Books, London.

MARSHALL, Alfred (1890) *The Principles of Economics*, Macmillan, London. References in this text are to the 8th edition (1962).

MARRIS, Robin (1964) *The Economic Theory of 'Managerial Capitalism'*, Macmillan, London.

MARX, Karl (1887) *Capital*, vol 1. References in this text are to the English language translation from the 3rd German edition (ed. Friedrich Engels), published by the Foreign Languages Publishing House, Moscow, 1962.

MILIBAND, Ralph (1969) *The State in Capitalist Society*, Weidenfeld and Nicholson, London.

MILL, John Stuart (1873) *Autobiography*, ed. J. Stillinger, Clarendon Press, Oxford.
   (1848) *Principles of Political Economy*, ed. Donald Winch, Pelican, London.
   Essays on Economics and Society, ed. Donald Winch.

MINNS, Richard and THORNLEY, Jennifer (1978) *State Shareholding: the Role of Local and Regional Authorities*, Macmillan, London and New York.

THE MONOPOLIES AND MERGERS COMMISSION (1985) *The Dee Corporation PLC and Booker McConnel PLC*, HMSO, London.

MYRDAL, Gunnar (1953) *The Political Element in the Development of Economic Theory*, Routledge and Kegan Paul, London
   (1957) *Economic Theory and Underdeveloped Regions*, Duckworth, London.

NURKSE, Ragnar (1958) *The Conflict Between 'Balanced Growth' and International Specialisation, Lectures on Economic Development*, Istanbul.

OECD (1982) *Stimulating Innovation in Small and Medium Firms*, Paris.
   (1984) *Structures et Performances des Plus Grandes Entreprises Européenes*, Paris.

OHMAE, K. (1985) *Triad Power: the Coming Shape of Global Competition*, Macmillan, London and New York.

OWEN, Geoffrey (1973) 'Constraints on Corporate Growth', *The Financial Times*, 21 March.

PEARCE, Jenny (1982) *Under the Eagle: US Intervention in Central America and the Caribbean*, Latin America Bureau, London.

PENNANT-REA, Rupert, with COOK, Clive and BEGG, David (1985) *Economics: Ancient and Modern*, The Economist, London.

PENROSE, Edith (1963) *The Theory of Growth of the Firm*, Basil Blackwell, Oxford.

PERROUX, François (1964) *L'Economie du XXe Siècle*, Presses Universitaires de France, Paris.
   (1965) *Les Techniques Quantitatives de la Planification*, Presses Universitaires de France, Paris.

PETERS, H. R. (1981) *Grundlagen der Mesoekonomie und Strukturpolitik*, Haupt, Berne.
   (1983) 'La Theorie Meso-Economique', *Problèmes Economiques*, December.

POPPER, Karl (1934) *The Logic of Scientific Discovery*, Hutchinson, London.
   (1944) *The Poverty of Historicism*, Routledge and Kegan Paul, London.

PRAIS, S. J. (1976) *The Evolution of Giant Firms in Britain*, Cambridge University Press. New preface on developments between 1970–76 published in 1981.

PRESTON, Lee E. (1983) 'Mesoeconomics: Concepts, Analysis, Policy', paper presented at the AFEE annual meeting, San Francisco, December.

RADA, Juan F. (1984) 'Advanced Technologies and Development: Are Conventional Ideas About Comparative Advantage Obsolete?', in UNCTAD, *Trade and Development*, Geneva.

REDDAWAY, W. B. (1967) *The Effects of UK Direct Investment Overseas*, Cambridge University Press.

RICHARDSON, G. B. (1960) *Information and Investment*, Oxford University Press.

ROBERTSON, D. H. (1950) *Some Recent Writings on the Theory of Pricing*, Economic Commentaries.

ROBINSON, Joan (1933) *The Economics of Imperfect Competition*, Basil Blackwell, Oxford.

(1953) 'Imperfect Competition Revisited', *Economic Journal*, September.

(1954) 'The Impossibility of Competition', in Edward Chamberlin (ed.), *Monopoly and Competition and Their Regulation*, Harvard University Press, Cambridge, Mass.

(1971) *Economic Heresies*, Macmillan, London and Basic Books, New York.

ROBINSON, Romney (1961) Quarterly Journal, May.

ROSTOW, W. W. (1960) *The Stages of Economic Growth*, Cambridge University Press, London.

ROWTHORN, R. with HYMER, S. (1970) 'The Multinational Corporation: the Non-American Challenge', in C. P. Kindleberger (ed.), *The International Corporation*, Harvard University Press, Cambridge, Mass.

ROWTHORN, R. with HYMER, S. (1971) *International Big Business 1957–67*, Cambridge Department of Economics Occasional Paper no. 24, Cambridge University Press.

SAMPSON, Anthony (1973) *The Sovereign State of ITT*, Stein & Day and Fawcett Crest, New York.

(1975) *The Seven Sisters: Great Oil Companies and the World They Made*, Hodder and Stoughton, Kent.

SAMUELSON, Paul (1976) *Economics*, 10th edition, McGraw-Hill, New York.

SCHELLING, T. C. (1960) *The Strategy of Conflict*, Harvard University Press, Cambridge, Mass.

SCHERER, F. M. (1978) *Industrial Pricing: Theory and Evidence*, Rand McNally, Chicago.

SCHUMACHER, E. F. (1974) *Small is Beautiful*, Abacus edition, Sphere Books, London.

SCHUMPETER, J. A. (1934) *The Theory of Economic Development*, Harvard University Press, Cambridge, Mass.

SCIBBERRAS, Edmond (1977) *Multinational Electronics Companies and National Economic Policies*, JAI Press, Greenwich, Connecticut.

SCITOVSKY, Tibor (1952) *Welfare and Competition*, Allen & Unwin, London.

(1954) 'Two Concepts of External Economies', *Journal of Political Economy*, April.

SERVAN-SCHREIBER, Jean-Jacques (1969) *The American Challenge*, Penguin Books, Harmondsworth.

SHEARER, Derek and CARNOY, Martin (1980) *Economic Democracy: The Challenge of the 1980s*, M. E. Sharpe, Armonck, New York.

with RUMBERGER, Russell (1983) *A New Social Contract: the Economy and Government After Reagan*, Harper and Row, New York.

SHEPHERD, William G. (1979) *The Economics of Industrial Organisation*, Prentice-Hall International, London.

SHONFIELD, Andrew (1965) *Modern Capitalism*, RIIA and Oxford University Press, New York and London.

SKIDELSKY, Robert (1983) *John Maynard Keynes*, Macmillan, London.

SMITH, Adam (1776) *The Wealth of Nations*. References in this text to the 1983 edition, Methuen, London.

(1759) *The Theory of Moral Sentiments*, Henry Bohn, London.

SMITH, Richard Austin (1963 and 1966) *Corporations in Crisis*, Doubleday Anchor, New York.

SPRU (1982) *Innovation in Britain since 1945*, Science Policy Research Unit, University of Sussex.

SRAFFA, Piero (1926) 'The Laws of Return Under Competitive Conditions', *The Economic Journal*.

(1960) *Production of Commodities by Means of Commodities*, Cambridge University Press.

STEEDMAN, Ian (1977) *Marx After Sraffa*, New Left Books, London.

STIGLER, George (1956) *Trends in Employment in the Service Industries*, Princeton University Press, New Jersey.

STONE, Richard and MEADE, James (1944) *National Income and Expenditure*, Oxford University Press.

SWEEZY, Paul (1981) *Four Lectures on Marxism*, Monthly Review Press, New York and London.

SYLOS-LABINI, Paolo (1962 and 1969) *Oligopoly and Technical Progress*, Harvard University Press, Cambridge, Mass.

(1983) *Il Sottosviluppo e L'Economia Contemporanea*, Laterza, Rome.

TEN RAA, Thijs (1980) 'A Theory of Value and Industry Structure', doctoral dissertation, New York University.

TUGENDHAT, Christopher (1971) *The Multinationals*, Eyre and Spottiswoode, London.

UNITED NATIONS (1973) *Multinational Corporations in World Development*, New York.

VAN DUIJN, J. J. and LAMBOOY, J. G. (1983) *Technical Innovation and Regional Growth: A Meso-Economic Analysis*, University of Amsterdam, Research Memorandum No. 8207.

VEBLEN, Thorstein (1921) *The Engineers and the Price System*, in Max Lerner (ed.), Veblen edition, Viking Press, New York, 1948.

(1923) *Absentee Ownership and Business Enterprise in Recent Times*, in Max Lerner (ed.), op. cit.

VERNON, R. (1966) 'International Investment and International Trade in the Product Cycle', *Quarterly Journal of Economics*, vol. 80.

(1974) (ed.) *Big Business and the State*, Harvard University Press, Cambridge, Mass. and Macmillan, London.

VON NEUMANN WHITMAN, Marina (1967) *International and Interregional Payments Adjustment*, Princeton Studies in International Finance, no. 19.

WATSON, P. (1986) 'Wherefore art thou, Alfa Romeo?', *The Observer*, 26 October.

WEISSKOPF, Thomas (1983) *Beyond the Wasteland: A Democratic Alternative to Economic Decline*, Anchor Press/Doubleday, New York.

WEITZMAN, M. L. (1984) *The Share Economy*, Harvard University Press, Cambridge, Mass. and London.

WIJERS, C. J. (1982) 'Institutional Aspects of Industrial Policy', *Journal of Economic Issues*, XVI, June.

WILES, P. J. D. (1961) *Price, Cost and Output*, Basil Blackwell, Oxford.

WILSON, Harold (1980) *Committee to Review the Functioning of Financial Institutions*, Cmnd 7937, 2 vols, HMSO, London, June.

WITTGENSTEIN, Ludwig (1922) *Tractatus Logico-Philosophicus*, Routledge and Kegan Paul, London.

(1958) *Philosophical Investigations*, Basil Blackwell, Oxford.

WOODCOCK, C. (1986) 'Creating Jobs – But No More Than Twenty', *The Guardian*, 13 October.

ZINN, Karl-Georg (1978) 'The Social Market in Crisis', in Stuart Holland (ed.), *Beyond Capitalist Planning*, Basil Blackwell, Oxford.

Index

state intervention, 140
tariffs, 45

Jacquemin, A., 255
Japan
  corporate strategy, 209–11
  financial services, 270
  foreign investment, 225–6
  infant industries, 46–7
  labour, 47
  Ministry of International Trade and
    Industry (MITI), 48, 109, 139
  state intervention, 47–8
  tariffs, 45–6
  see also keiretsu; zaibatsu
Jastrow, 12
job creation, 141–3, 153
Johnscher, C., 260
joint-stock companies, 277–80, 304
joint ventures, 200, 201–4
Joseph, Sir Keith, 142, 253, 320

Kaldor, Nicholas, 59, 98
Kalecki, Michael, 87, 344
Kant, Immanuel, 31
Kaplan, A. D. H., 153
keiretsu, 81, 211
Keynes, John Maynard, 8, 100–1
  on aggregation, 26–7
  on mathematical economics, 23
kinks, 91–4
Kolko, Gabriel, 54
Kono, T., 113
Krupps, 299
Kuhn, O., 18
Kumar, Manmohan S., 157, 250
Kuznets, Simon, 258

labour, 299–307
  costs, 167, 220–1, 222, 302
  displacement by new technologies,
    139
  Japan, 47
Laker Airways, 206–7
Lambooy, J. G., 29
Lamfalussy, Alexander, 162
land tenure, 234
Lanzilloti, R. F., 153

Latin America, 35
law of large numbers, 24–5
Lawson, Nigel, 340
leasing, 160–1
Legler, J., 56
Leijonhufvud, A., 27–8, 100
Lenin
  on monopoly, 183–4, 186
Leon, Paolo, 25–6
Leontief, Wassily, 21–2, 327
less developed countries (LDCs), 217–
    18; *see also* Third World countries
  labour costs, 220–1, 222
Lichtbuer, M., 255
Lichtenberg, 12
Lipsey, Richard, 5, 118–20
  on law of large numbers, 24–5
  on perfect competition, 68–9, 79–80
List, Friedrich, 48–9
Litton, 213–14, 288
location
  multinational enterprise, 216–19
Locke, John, 1
Locksley, Gareth, 199, 257
loss leaders, 150, 151
Luedde-Neurath, Richard, 36
Luxemburg, Rosa, 1

macroeconomics, 2, 25
management, 110–14, 126–7
  multinational enterprise, 113–14
  owner-entrepreneur, 123, 136
  specialisation, 123
management control, 276, 278–80,
    286–8
managerial diseconomies, 109–10, 122
marginal costs, 70–3, 80–2, 95, 99, 339
marginal efficiency of capital, 23
market research, 99
market strategy, 149
market theory, 4, 15–16, 37
Marks and Spencer, 86
Marris, Robin, 60, 126–8
Marshall, Alfred, 2, 59, 65–6, 99,
    115–17, 193
Marshall's 'scissors', 62–5
Marx, Karl, 1, 326

(OECD), report on innovation, 143–4

Organisation of Petroleum Exporting Countries (OPEC), 75, 243–4

Owen, David, 340

Pan Am, 206–7
parent companies, 288–9
Pareto, W., 1
Pearce, Robert, D., 194
Pennant-Rea, Rupert, 21
Penrose, Edith, 122–4, 130, 164, 170
pension funds, 276, 292–5, 298, 304–5
  TUC report, 294, 295
  United States, 295
pensions, 52
perfect competition, 16, 38, 65–9, 72–3, 79
Perroux, François, 105, 190–1, 219
personnel, 153
Peters, H. R., 29
petroleum industry, 242–4
petroleum revenue tax, 244
Petty, William, 326
Philippines, 36
Philips corporation, 208
pollution, 310–11
portfolio investment, 224, 226
Prais, S. J., 246–51
Preston, Lee E., 30
price cartels, 178–9, 185–6
  oil, 243–4
price controls, 101, 247
price elasticity, 69
price-makers, 148–9
price restraint, 156
price-takers, 148–9
price umbrella, 140, 149, 164, 169–70
prices, 37
  EEC farm, 236
pricing, 96–7
  cost-plus, 94–102, 149, 153
  elimination, 163, 165–7, 171, 221
  focal-point, 149, 171, 178, 180
  laggard, 150
  no-entry, 165, 171, 221, 313, 315
  offensive, 166–7

standard, 149, 153–4
privatisation, 51, 53, 302–3
processes of production, 138–9
product cycle, 128–40, 227–30, 313
  barriers to expansion, 135–8
product differentiation, 83–91, 96, 150, 156
production, 40
  costs, 109
  process, 138–9
profit centres, 180
profit creaming, 313
profit maximisation, 150–3, 155
profits, 17
  mark-up, 95–6
protection, 48–9, 50, 321
  Germany, 46
  Japan, 45–6, 47
  United States, 54
Protestant ethic, 54
public enterprises, 54–5, 223
public spending, 51–3, 285–6, 344
pull-effect, 237
push-effect, 237

R. J. Reynolds Industries Inc., 262
Rada, Juan, 259–60, 261
rational expectations, 68
Reaganomics, 59, 141
Reddaway, W. B., 253
regional development, 319–20
regional incentives, 223
reinsurance, 273
research and development, 230, 331
retail industry, 262–7
Reuters Commodity Services, 261
revenue maximisation, 150–2
Ricardo, 1, 224
Richardson, G. B., 68, 96
risks, 106
Robertson, D. H., 22, 99
Robinson, Joan, 59, 83–4, 98, 147, 148
Robinson, Romney, 95, 98
robotics, 139
Rockefeller, John D., 180, 244–5
Rolls-Royce, 203
Roosevelt, F. D., 140